THE
QUALITATIVE
RESEARCHER'S
COMPANION

THE
QUALITATIVE
RESEARCHER'S
COMPANION

A. MICHAEL HUBERMAN
MATTHEW B. MILES

Sage Publications
International Educational and Professional Publisher
Thousand Oaks ■ London ■ New Delhi

For information:

Sage Publications, Inc.
2455 Teller Road
Thousand Oaks, California 91320
E-mail: order@sagepub.com

Sage Publications Ltd.
6 Bonhill Street
London EC2A 4PU
United Kingdom

Sage Publications India Pvt. Ltd.
M-32 Market
Greater Kailash I
New Delhi 110 048 India

Printed in the United States of America

Library of Congress Cataloging-in-Publication Data

The qualitative researcher's companion / A. Michael Huberman and Matthew B. Miles, editors.
    p. cm.
Includes bibliographical references and index.
  ISBN 0-7619-1190-1 (c) -- ISBN 0-7619-1191-X (p)
  1. Social sciences--Research. I. Huberman, A. M. II. Miles, Matthew B.
  H62 .Q3564 2002
  001.4´2--dc21

                                2001008003

02   03   04   05   10   9   8   7   6   5   4   3   2   1

Acquiring Editor:	Margaret H. Seawell
Editorial Assistant:	Alicia Carter
Production Editor:	Claudia A. Hoffman
Copy Editor:	Judy Selhorst
Indexer:	Molly Hall
Cover Designer:	Michelle Lee

Contents

Foreword

This book is the final product of the long and fruitful collaboration between A. Michael Huberman and Matthew B. Miles. It stems from the prodigious reading underlying all their research and writing, in particular their work on the original and revised volumes of their classic sourcebook, Qualitative Data Analysis (1984, 1994).

In their own research, Huberman and Miles firmly believed in making their processes explicit; they were convinced that all researchers profit from their colleagues' open discussion of the ways they do their work. In that spirit, this book provides an exemplary sampling of firsthand reports from the expanding field of qualitative data analysis in the period from the mid-1970s through the mid-1990s. Miles and Huberman's selection of articles is the result of an energetic dialogue—heated, zestful, and informed by their many years of working together.

Matt Miles died in October 1996. Michael Huberman continued the work, despite grave illness, until his death in January 2001. This book is a tribute to their dedication to their profession and to their long friendship.

—Betty Miles
March 2002

Introduction

The use of qualitative research in the social sciences has grown geometrically since the 1980s and continues to expand. In professional journals and at professional meetings, research reports take on a new variety of forms: case studies, ethnographies, narratives, discourse analysis, symbolic interaction studies, literary journalism, and all manner of hybrids.

Writing *about* qualitative research has also proliferated and, in many ways, ripened. In 1984, when we published the first edition of *Qualitative Data Analysis*, we were hard-pressed to find specified, usable methodological examples in and around the fields of education, psychology, and sociology. By the time of the second edition, in 1994, we were able to replace our own examples with dozens of new ones from these and cognate fields. Today, researchers can hardly keep up with their own expanding specialties, much less with useful, innovative work in related areas.

For some critics, qualitative research has been getting better and more inventive. Even such a demanding veteran as Van Maanen suggests, in *Tales of the Field* (1988), that ethnographers, especially those in the vanguard of the new ethnographic genres, are "learning to write better, less soothing, more faithful and ultimately more truthful accounts of their fellow humans than ever before." And Denzin (1994) sees methodological blossoming in the cross-fertilization of new epistemologies (pragmatism, postpositivism, poststructuralism) and new genres of critical discourse, such as semiotics and literary journalism.

But despite the increase in the sheer number and the widening range of qualitative research studies, there has been no parallel proliferation of studies of the actual *process* of doing qualitative research since we noted the lack of attention to it in 1984. Certainly there are more texts on how to do qualitative analysis and many more books and articles reporting on studies done. But the two seldom match up; all too often, the textbooks work with hypothetical cases or with fragments of empirical work, and the empirical reports are vague about how the analyses were actually done. And "methods" sections are sometimes no more than shopping lists of devices commonly cited in the literature for unearthing, condensing, corroborating, and interpreting data—a sort of buzzword methodology, with scant demonstration of the processes involved in analyzing particular sets of data.

Similarly, terms such as *patterns, leitmotiv, capturing* and *bracketing*, and core codes seem to appear almost magically in reports that have boiled down hundreds of pages of transcripts and field notes to a half dozen pages of meaningful findings, with little explanation of *how* this process was accomplished. In an experimental or survey study, such a report would be summarily dismissed. In many well-received qualitative studies, on the other hand, arguments made for the trustworthiness, validity, or usefulness of the findings are largely rhetorical or, at best, questionable. The same is true of studies that blend quantitative and qualitative information, where corroborations between the two data sets are often claimed but seldom spelled out.

This inattention to the process of doing qualitative research is not a trivial issue. It leads to reports that strain the credulity of the research community; leaves graduate students at a loss when they undertake empirical, mostly nonquantitative, work in the field; and blurs the distinctions between robust and fanciful methodologies, fogging the real import of the findings.

It is important to note that the problem cannot simply be dismissed as an inevitable result of epistemological wars between "critical" or "transcendental" realists and "postfoundationalists" or of struggles within the poststructural movement itself. Of course, researchers who espouse different methodologies will typically use different research methods. But *all* researchers need to be concerned with describing their procedures. When they spend more pages explaining why they will not deploy particular methods than on describing their own conceptual and analytic moves, they leave behind too few footprints to allow others to judge the utility of the work, and to profit from it.

Much current qualitative research ignores its own history, and, in some instances, the researchers seem pleased to do so. Yet we have well over 60 years of powerful, reliable, and transferable methods in social anthropology, social phenomenology, and linguistics—a trove of procedures for collecting, analyzing, verifying, and interpreting nonstatistical data that are seriously underused in contemporary qualitative analysis. Many of these methods have been progressively "debugged" and enriched over time. But too often, methodological bootstrapping in qualitative research leaves us with underutilization of well-honed methods, lowered credibility among peers in the research community, and neglect of promising methodologies in cognate fields.

Our wish to help researchers avoid such pitfalls and to suggest the wide range of useful methods available to them today led us to develop this book. A critical goal in our decades of work together has been to make the actual conduct of qualitative research transparent, to ourselves and to others. Reporting on our first collaborative research project in *Innovation Up Close* (Huberman & Miles, 1984), we tried to spell out our methodological procedures in ways that added verification and showed how we borrowed from and adapted others' work. In both the original edition and the (heavily) revised second edition of *Qualitative Data Analysis* (Miles & Huberman, 1984, 1994), we offered sourcebooks of methods for qualitative data analysis, suggesting and "walking through" a variety of approaches. And in *Computer Programs for Qualitative Data Analysis* (Weitzman & Miles, 1995) one of us and a colleague surveyed, assessed, and described in operational terms the most promising forms of software available for different kinds of qualitative inquiries.

Now, with this book of readings—selections from a quarter century in which the field expanded rapidly—we consider some of the significant theoretical and methodological issues in qualitative research, as seen through the eyes of researchers committed to continuous conceptualization and analysis. Our goal is to present a selection of what we judge to be among the strongest contributions of the period—contemporary classics from a variety of disciplines that will outlive their own decades. To this end, we reviewed more than a thousand candidate pieces in several fields of research. We looked for readings that address salient issues in qualitative inquiry. We looked for genuinely seminal pieces, among them those that challenge prior or contemporary orientations, including our own, and those that come to grips with nagging problems in qualitative research, such as sampling, researcher-informant interaction, condensation of information, tolerance of contradictions and paradoxes, and issues of generalizability.

Our final choices are broadly ecumenical, both philosophically and methodologically. They include reports that document the use of long-standing methods in social anthropology, linguistics, narratology, and social phenomenology, along with some that, without excessive polarization, illuminate underexamined assumptions. And they include some as-yet "undiscovered" classics—pieces our readers may have overlooked and reports from fields they may not follow.

Finally, our selections are, very simply, eminently readable. All of them are, in our view, the kinds of pieces readers will like to return to periodically for pleasure or enlightenment or to reset their compass coordinates. We hope these selections will serve to extend the field of qualitative research in usable and communicable ways as they make explicit the process—the adventure—of iterative conceptualization and analysis.

❖ REFERENCES

Denzin, N. K. (1994). The art and politics of interpretation. In N. K. Denzin & Y. S. Lincoln (Eds.), *Handbook of qualitative research* (pp. 500—515). Thousand Oaks, CA: Sage.

Huberman, A. M., & Miles, M. B. (1984). *Innovation up close: How school improvement works.* New York: Plenum.

Miles, M. B., & Huberman, A. M. (1984). *Qualitative data analysis: A sourcebook of new methods.* Beverly Hills, CA: Sage.

Miles, M. B., & Huberman, A. M. (1994). *Qualitative data analysis: An expanded sourcebook* (2nd ed.). Thousand Oaks, CA: Sage.

Van Maanen, J. (1988). *Tales of the field: On writing ethnography.* Chicago: University of Chicago Press.

Weitzman, E. A., & Miles, M. B. (1995). *Computer programs for qualitative data analysis: A software sourcebook.* Thousand Oaks, CA: Sage.

Part I

Theories and Analysis

In this first set of pieces, we look at issues surrounding the construction of concepts and theories. Conceptual frames are notoriously various, depending on their field of reference; unless they derive from large, formal theories, their genesis is often uncertain. Concepts may be the products of the researcher's personal or technical knowledge, prior experience, or even thought experiments. They may come at the outset of a study or progressively during it and may sometimes be irreconcilable. Typically, concepts are sets of classifications that vie for our attention because they are compelling, coherent, and elegant. They are maps for generating or revising a research design and, in the best case, for broadening our understanding of a situation.

The contributors whose works appear in Part I do not specifically confront the issue of conceptual validity. Realists contend that the phenomena we study are fundamentally "unknowable," but that we can make plausible sense of them through warranted analysis. Along with House (1991), we think that social phenomena not only exist in the mind but are externally derived from the regularities and determinisms that surround us. It is what Van Maanen refers to as "second-order concepts" that are difficult to organize and use to explain the facts we have assembled in the field. We can, however, assemble the components. Here, several authors evoke recurrent patterns as paths to stronger concepts; others draw attention to the power of description, interpretation, and explanation in accounting for and understanding individual and social surrounds.

In "Building Theories From Case Study Research," originally published in 1989, Eisenhardt provides a cogent rationale for building theory inductively from case study research and reviews the steps involved. Eisenhardt's chapter includes specific illustrations, incisive remarks on the progression from data collection to the identification of cross-case patterning, and a careful consideration of issues, applicability, and validation.

Maxwell breaks through arbitrary paradigm distinctions with his discussion in "Understanding and Validity in Qualitative Research," originally published in 1992. Seldom, we think, has anyone handled the ornery distinction between different types of validity—in this case, descriptive, interpretive, evaluative, and explanatory—with as much elegance and with clear illustrations. Maxwell borrows from different epistemological traditions to show their complementarity, by which he means not a simplistic integration, but a thoughtful recognition of which streams of analysis are useful in different types of studies.

Hammersley's "Ethnography and Realism," originally published in 1992, is often cited but less often read. It is a conversational review of ethnographic analysis and its relationship to theory building, which includes a balanced discussion of issues related to validity, a bit of commonsensical epistemology, and a well-argued case (i.e., we go along with it) for "subtle realism."

We like Gherardi and Turner's "Real Men Don't Collect Soft Data," originally published in 1987, only partly for its title. The segment of this article that is reproduced here presents an analysis of how and why qualitative research is critical to the understanding of individual perceptions and social interactions. Moreover, the authors suggest that the absence of qualitative analysis in certain crucial empirical studies leads to skewed findings. The monograph is humorous, insightful, and sometimes biting.[1] Gherardi and Turner illustrate their conception of several types of qualitative inquiry and suggest appropriate analyses for them.

We close Part I with a long-standing favorite, Van Maanen's 1979 article "The Fact of Fiction in Organizational Ethnography," a classic known mainly among social anthropologists and specialists in public administration. It is autobiographical and reflective, and laden with generous chunks of illustrative data (on police bookings). Van Maanen makes an important distinction between first- and second-order constructs. He shares the insights of a clear-eyed observer into sleight-of-hand analyses, hidden assumptions, outright biases and self-delusions, and questionable paths to verification. The piece is replete with the wisdom of experience; it helps to keep us honest and humble when we actually do fieldwork and pretend that we can capture rapidly the vocabularies and meanings of informants.

❖ NOTE

1. We get bitten here ourselves, but not, we feel, justifiably: we were straw-manned.

❖ REFERENCE

House, E. R. (1991). Realism in research. *Educational Researcher, 20*(6), 2–9.

1

Building Theories From Case Study Research

Kathleen M. Eisenhardt

Development of theory is a central activity in organizational research. Traditionally, authors have developed theory by combining observations from previous literature, common sense, and experience. However, the tie to actual data has often been tenuous (Perrow, 1986; Pfeffer, 1982). Yet, as Glaser and Strauss (1967) argue, it

AUTHOR'S NOTE: I appreciate the helpful comments of Paul Adler, Kenneth Bettenhausen, Constance Gersick, James Frederickson, James Jucker, Deborah Myerson, Dorothy Leonard-Barton, Robert Sutton, and the participants in the Stanford NIMH Colloquium. I also benefited from informal conversations with many participants at the National Science Foundation Conference on Longitudinal Research Methods in Organizations, Austin, 1988.

5

is the intimate connection with empirical reality that permits the development of a testable, relevant, and valid theory.

This paper describes building theories from case studies. Several aspects of this process are discussed in the literature. For example, Glaser and Strauss (1967) detailed a comparative method for developing grounded theory, Yin (1981, 1984) described the design of case study research, and Miles and Huberman (1984) codified a series of procedures for analyzing qualitative data. However, confusion surrounds the distinctions among qualitative data, inductive logic, and case study research. Also, there is a lack of clarity about the process of actually building theory from cases, especially regarding the central inductive process and the role of literature. Glaser and Strauss (1967) and more recently Strauss (1987) have outlined pieces of the process, but theirs is a prescribed formula, and new ideas have emerged from methodologists (e.g., Yin, 1984; Miles & Huberman, 1984) and researchers conducting this type of research (e.g., Gersick, 1988; Harris & Sutton, 1986; Eisenhardt & Bourgeois, 1988). Also, it appears that no one has explicitly examined when this theory-building approach is likely to be fruitful and what its strengths and weaknesses may be.

This paper attempts to make two contributions to the literature. The first is a road map for building theories from case study research. This road map synthesizes previous work on qualitative methods (e.g., Miles & Huberman, 1984), the design of case study research (e.g., Yin, 1981, 1984), and grounded theory building (e.g., Glaser & Strauss, 1967) and extends that work in areas such as a priori specification of constructs, triangulation of multiple investigators, within-case and cross-case analyses, and the role of existing literature. The result is a more nearly complete road map for executing this type of research than has existed in the past. This framework is summarized in Table 1.1.

The second contribution is positioning theory building from case studies into the larger context of social science research. For example, the paper explores strengths and weaknesses of theory building from case studies, situations in which it is an attractive research approach, and some guidelines for evaluating this type of research.

❖ BACKGROUND

Several pieces of the process of building theory from case study research have appeared in the literature. One is the work on grounded

Table 1.1 Process of Building Theory From Case Study Research

Step	Activity	Reason
Getting Started	Definition of research question	Focuses efforts
	Possibly a priori constructs	Provides better grounding of construct measures
	Neither theory nor hypotheses	Retains theoretical flexibility
Selecting Cases	Specified population	Constrains extraneous variation and sharpens external validity
	Theoretical, not random, sampling	Focuses efforts on theoretically useful cases—i.e., those that replicate or extend theory by filling conceptual categories
Crafting Instruments and Protocols	Multiple data collection methods	Strengthens grounding of theory by triangulation of evidence
	Qualitative and quantitative data combined	Synergistic view of evidence
	Multiple investigators	Fosters divergent perspectives and strengthens grounding
Entering the Field	Overlap data collection and analysis, including field notes	Speeds analyses and reveals helpful adjustments to data collection
	Flexible and opportunistic data collection methods	Allows investigators to take advantage of emergent themes and unique case features
Analyzing Data	Within-case analysis	Gains familiarity with data and preliminary theory generation
	Cross-case pattern search using divergent techniques	Forces investigators to look beyond initial impressions and see evidence through multiple lenses
Shaping Hypotheses	Iterative tabulation of evidence for each construct	Sharpens construct definition, validity, and measurability
	Replication, not sampling, logic across cases	Confirms, extends, and sharpens theory
	Search evidence for "why" behind relationships	Builds internal validity
Enfolding Literature	Comparison with conflicting literature	Builds internal validity, raises theoretical level, and sharpens construct definitions
	Comparison with similar literature	Sharpens generalizability, improves construct definition, and raises theoretical level
Reaching Closure	Theoretical saturation when possible	Ends process when marginal improvement becomes small

theory building by Glaser and Strauss (1967) and, more recently, Strauss (1987). These authors have detailed their comparative method for developing grounded theory. The method relies on continuous comparison of data and theory beginning with data collection. It emphasizes both the emergence of theoretical categories solely from evidence and an incremental approach to case selection and data gathering.

More recently, Yin (1981, 1984) has described the design of case study research. He has defined the case study as a research strategy, developed a typology of case study designs, and described the replication logic which is essential to multiple case analysis. His approach also stresses bringing the concerns of validity and reliability in experimental research design to the design of case study research.

Miles and Huberman (1984) have outlined specific techniques for analyzing qualitative data. Their ideas include a variety of devices such as tabular displays and graphs to manage and present qualitative data, without destroying the meaning of the data through intensive coding.

A number of active researchers also have undertaken their own variations and additions to the earlier methodological work (e.g., Gersick, 1988; Leonard-Barton, 1988; Harris & Sutton, 1986). Many of these authors acknowledge a debt to previous work, but they have also developed their own "homegrown" techniques for building theory from cases. For example, Sutton and Callahan (1987) pioneered a clever use of a resident devil's advocate, the Warwick group (Pettigrew, 1988) added triangulation of investigators, and my colleague and I (Bourgeois & Eisenhardt, 1988) developed cross-case analysis techniques.

Finally, the work of others such as Van Maanen (1988) on ethnography, Jick (1979) on triangulation of data types, and Mintzberg (1979) on direct research has provided additional pieces for a framework of building theory from case study research.

As a result, many pieces of the theory-building process are evident in the literature. Nevertheless, at the same time, there is substantial confusion about how to combine them, when to conduct this type of study, and how to evaluate it.

❖ THE CASE STUDY APPROACH

The case study is a research strategy which focuses on understanding the dynamics present within single settings. Examples of case study research include Selznick's (1949) description of TVA, Allison's (1971) study of the Cuban missile crisis, and Pettigrew's (1973) research on decision making at a British retailer. Case studies can involve either single or multiple cases, and numerous levels of analysis (Yin, 1984). For example, Harris and Sutton (1986) studied 8 dying organizations, Bettenhausen and Murnighan (1986) focused on the emergence of norms in 19 laboratory groups, and Leonard-Barton (1988) tracked the progress of 10 innovation projects. Moreover, case studies can employ an embedded design, that is, multiple levels of analysis within a single study (Yin, 1984). For example, the Warwick study of competitiveness and strategic change within major U.K. corporations is conducted at two levels of analysis: industry and firm (Pettigrew, 1988), and the Mintzberg and Waters (1982) study of Steinberg's grocery empire examines multiple strategic changes within a single firm.

Case studies typically combine data collection methods such as archives, interviews, questionnaires, and observations. The evidence may be qualitative (e.g., words), quantitative (e.g., numbers), or both. For example, Sutton and Callahan (1987) rely exclusively on qualitative data in their study of bankruptcy in Silicon Valley, Mintzberg and McHugh (1985) use qualitative data supplemented by frequency counts in their work on the National Film Board of Canada, and Eisenhardt and Bourgeois (1988) combine quantitative data from questionnaires with qualitative evidence from interviews and observations.

Finally, case studies can be used to accomplish various aims: to provide description (Kidder, 1982), test theory (Pinfield, 1986; Anderson, 1983), or generate theory (e.g., Gersick, 1988; Harris & Sutton, 1986). The interest here is in this last aim, theory generation from case study evidence. Table 1.2 summarizes some recent research using theory building from case studies.

❖ BUILDING THEORY FROM CASE STUDY RESEARCH

Getting Started

An initial definition of the research question, in at least broad terms, is important in building theory from case studies. Mintzberg (1979, p. 585) noted: "No matter how small our sample or what our interest, we have always tried to go into organizations with a well-defined

Table 1.2 Recent Examples of Inductive Case Study Research*

Study	Description of Cases	Research Problem	Data Sources	Investigators	Output
Burgelman (1983)	6 internal corporate ventures in 1 major corporation	Management of new ventures	Archives Interviews Some observation	Single investigator	Process model linking multiple organizational levels
Mintzberg & McHugh (1985)	1 National Film Board of Canada, 1939-1975, with 6 periods	Formulation of strategy in an adhocracy	Archives Some interviews	Research team	Strategy-making themes, "grassroots" model of strategy formation
Harris & Sutton (1986)	8 diverse organizations	Parting ceremonies during organizational death	Interviews Archives	Research team	Conceptual framework about the functions of parting ceremonies for displaced members
Eisenhardt & Bourgeois (1988)	8 microcomputer firms	Strategic decision making in high velocity environments	Interviews Questionnaires Archives Some observation	Research team Tandem interviews	Mid-range theory linking power, politics, and firm performance
Gersick (1988)	8 project groups with deadlines	Group development in project teams	Observation Some interviews	Single investigator	Punctuated equilibrium model of group development
Leonard-Barton (1988)	10 technical innovations	Internal technology transfer	Interviews Experiment Observation	Single investigator	Process model
Pettigrew (1988)	1 high performing & 1 low performing firm in each of 4 industries	Strategic change & competitiveness	Interviews Archives Some observation	Research teams	In progress

*Examples were chosen from recent organizational writings to provide illustrations of the possible range of theory building from case studies.

focus—to collect specific kinds of data systematically." The rationale for defining the research question is the same as it is in hypothesis-testing research. Without a research focus, it is easy to become overwhelmed by the volume of data. For example, Pettigrew and colleagues (1988) defined their research question in terms of strategic change and competitiveness within large British corporations, and Leonard-Barton (1988) focused on technical innovation of feasible technologies. Such definition of a research question within a broad topic permitted these investigators to specify the kind of organization to be approached, and, once there, the kind of data to be gathered.

A priori specification of constructs can also help to shape the initial design of theory-building research. Although this type of specification is not common in theory-building studies to date, it is valuable because it permits researchers to measure constructs more accurately. If these constructs prove important as the study progresses, then researchers have a firmer empirical grounding for the emergent theory. For example, in a study of strategic decision making in top management teams, Bourgeois and Eisenhardt (1988) identified several potentially important constructs (e.g., conflict, power) from the literature on decision making. These constructs were explicitly measured in the interview protocol and questionnaires. When several of these constructs did emerge as related to the decision process, there were strong, triangulated measures on which to ground the emergent theory.

Although early identification of the research question and possible constructs is helpful, it is equally important to recognize that both are tentative in this type of research. No construct is guaranteed a place in the resultant theory, no matter how well it is measured. Also, the research question may shift during the research. At the extreme, some researchers (e.g., Gersick, 1988; Bettenhausen & Murnighan, 1986) have converted theory-testing research into theory-building research by taking advantage of serendipitous findings. In these studies, the research focus emerged after the data collection had begun. As Bettenhausen and Murnighan (1986, p. 352) wrote: " . . . we observed the outcomes of an experiment on group decision making and coalition formation. Our observations of the groups indicated that the unique character of each of the groups seemed to overwhelm our other manipulations." These authors proceeded to switch their research focus to a theory-building study of group norms.

Finally and most importantly, theory-building research is begun as close as possible to the ideal of no theory under consideration and no hypotheses to test. Admittedly, it is impossible to achieve this ideal of a clean theoretical slate. Nonetheless, attempting to approach this ideal is important because preordained theoretical perspectives or propositions may bias and limit the findings. Thus, investigators should formulate a research problem and possibly specify some potentially important variables, with some reference to extant literature. However, they should avoid thinking about specific relationships between variables and theories as much as possible, especially at the outset of the process.

Selecting Cases

Selection of cases is an important aspect of building theory from case studies. As in hypothesis-testing research, the concept of a population is crucial, because the population defines the set of entities from which the research sample is to be drawn. Also, selection of an appropriate population controls extraneous variation and helps to define the limits for generalizing the findings.

The Warwick study of strategic change and competitiveness illustrates these ideas (Pettigrew, 1988). In this study, the researchers selected cases from a population of large British corporations in four market sectors. The selection of four specific markets allowed the researchers to control environmental variation, while the focus on large corporations constrained variation due to size differences among the firms. Thus, specification of this population reduced extraneous variation and clarified the domain of the findings as large corporations operating in specific types of environments.

However, the sampling of cases from the chosen population is unusual when building theory from case studies. Such research relies on theoretical sampling (i.e., cases are chosen for theoretical, not statistical, reasons; Glaser & Strauss, 1967). The cases may be chosen to replicate previous cases or extend emergent theory, or they may be chosen to fill theoretical categories and provide examples of polar types. While the cases may be chosen randomly, random selection is neither necessary nor even preferable. As Pettigrew (1988) noted, given the limited number of cases which can usually be studied, it makes sense to choose cases such as extreme situations and polar types in which the process of interest is "transparently observable." Thus, the goal of theoretical sampling is to choose cases which are likely to replicate or extend the emergent theory. In contrast, traditional, within-experiment hypothesis-testing studies rely on statistical sampling, in which researchers randomly select the sample from the population. In this type of study, the goal of the sampling process is to obtain accurate statistical evidence on the distributions of variables within the population.

Several studies illustrate theoretical sampling. Harris and Sutton (1986), for example, were interested in the parting ceremonies of dying organizations. In order to build a model applicable across organization types, these researchers purposefully selected diverse organizations from a population of dying organizations. They chose eight organizations, filling each of four categories: private, dependent; private, independent; public, dependent; and public, independent. The sample was not random, but reflected the selection of specific cases to extend the theory to a broad range of organizations. Multiple cases within each category allowed findings to be replicated within categories. Gersick (1988) followed a similar strategy of diverse sampling in order to enhance the generalizability of her model of group development. In the Warwick study (Pettigrew, 1988), the investigators also followed a deliberate, theoretical sampling plan. Within each of four markets, they chose polar types: one case of clearly successful firm performance and one unsuccessful case. This sampling plan was designed to build theories of success and failure. Finally, the Eisenhardt and Bourgeois (1988) study of the politics of strategic decision making illustrates theoretical sampling during the course of research. A theory linking the centralization of power to the use of politics in top management teams was built and then extended to consider the effects of changing team composition by adding two cases, in which the executive teams changed, to the first six, in which there was no change. This tactic allowed the initial framework to be extended to include dynamic effects of changing team composition.

Crafting Instruments and Protocols

Theory-building researchers typically combine multiple data collection methods. While interviews, observations, and archival sources are particularly common, inductive researchers are not confined to these choices. Some investigators employ only some of these data collection methods (e.g., Gersick, 1988, used only observations for the first half of her study), or they may add others (e.g., Bettenhausen & Murnighan, 1986, used quantitative laboratory data). The rationale is the same as in hypothesis-testing research. That is, the triangulation made possible by multiple data collection methods provides stronger substantiation of constructs and hypotheses.

Of special note is the combining of qualitative with quantitative evidence. Although the terms *qualitative* and *case study* are often used interchangeably (e.g., Yin, 1981), case study research can involve qualitative data only, quantitative only, or both (Yin, 1984). Moreover, the combination of data types can be highly synergistic. Quantitative evidence can indicate relationships which may not be salient to the researcher. It also can keep researchers from being carried away by vivid, but false, impressions in qualitative data, and it can bolster findings when it corroborates those findings from qualitative evidence. The qualitative data are useful for understanding the rationale or theory underlying relationships revealed in the quantitative data or may suggest directly theory which can then be strengthened by quantitative support (Jick, 1979). Mintzberg (1979) described this synergy as follows:

> For while systematic data create the foundation for our theories, it is the anecdotal data that enable us to do the building. Theory building seems to require rich description, the richness that comes from anecdote. We uncover all kinds of relationships in our hard data, but it is only through the use of this soft data that we are able to explain them. (p. 587)

Also, of special note is the use of multiple investigators. Multiple investigators have two key advantages. First, they enhance the creative potential of the study. Team members often have complementary insights which add to the richness of the data, and their different perspectives increase the likelihood of capitalizing on any novel insights which may be in the data. Second, the convergence of observations from multiple investigators enhances confidence in the findings. Convergent perceptions add to the empirical grounding of the hypotheses, while conflicting perceptions keep the group from premature closure. Thus, the use of more investigators builds confidence in the findings and increases the likelihood of surprising findings.

One strategy for employing multiple investigators is to make the visits to case study sites in teams (e.g., Pettigrew, 1988). This allows the case to be viewed from the different perspectives of multiple observers. A variation on this tactic is to give individuals on the team unique roles, which increases the chances that investigators will view case evidence in divergent ways. For example, interviews can be conducted by two person teams, with one researcher handling the interview questions, while the other records notes and observations (e.g., Eisenhardt & Bourgeois, 1988). The interviewer has the perspective of personal interaction with the informant, while the notetaker retains a different, more distant view. Another tactic is to create multiple research teams, with teams being assigned to cover some case sites, but not others (e.g., Pettigrew, 1988). The rationale behind this tactic is that investigators who have not met the informants and have not become immersed in case details may bring a very different and possibly more objective eye to the evidence. An extreme form of this tactic is to keep some member or members of the research team out of the field altogether by exclusively assigning to them the role of resident devil's advocate (e.g., Sutton & Callahan, 1987).

Entering the Field

A striking feature of research to build theory from case studies is the frequent overlap of data analysis with data collection. For example, Glaser and Strauss (1967) argue for joint collection, coding, and analysis of data. While many researchers do not achieve this degree of overlap, most maintain some overlap.

Field notes, a running commentary to oneself and/or research team, are an important means of accomplishing this overlap. As described by Van Maanen (1988), field notes are an ongoing stream-of-consciousness commentary about what is happening in the research, involving both observation and analysis—preferably separated from one another.

One key to useful field notes is to write down whatever impressions occur, that is, to react rather than to sift out what may seem important, because it is often difficult to know what will and will not be useful in the future. A second key to successful field notes is to push thinking in these notes by asking questions such as "What am I learning?" and "How does this case differ from the last?" For example, Burgelman (1983) kept extensive idea booklets to record his ongoing thoughts in a study of internal corporate venturing. These ideas can be cross-case comparisons, hunches about relationships, anecdotes, and informal observations. Team meetings, in which investigators share their thoughts and emergent ideas, are also useful devices for overlapping data collection and analysis.

Overlapping data analysis with data collection not only gives the researcher a head start in analysis but, more importantly, allows researchers to take advantage of flexible data collection. Indeed, a key feature of theory-building case research is the freedom to make adjustments during the data collection process. These adjustments can be the addition of cases to probe particular themes which emerge. Gersick (1988), for example, added several cases to her original set of student teams in order to more closely observe transition point behaviors among project teams. These transition point behaviors had unexpectedly proved interesting, and Gersick added cases in order to focus more closely on the transition period.

Additional adjustments can be made to data collection instruments, such as the addition of questions to an interview protocol or questions to a questionnaire (e.g., Harris & Sutton, 1986). These adjustments allow the researcher to probe emergent themes or to take advantage of special opportunities which may be present in a given situation. In other situations adjustments can include the addition of data sources in selected cases. For example, Sutton and Callahan (1987) added observational evidence for one case when the opportunity to attend creditors' meetings arose, and Burgelman (1983) added interviews with individuals whose importance became clear during data collection. Leonard-Barton (1988) went even further by adding several experiments to probe her emergent theory in a study of the implementation of technical innovations.

These alterations create an important question: Is it legitimate to alter and even add data collection methods during a study? For theory-building research, the answer is "yes," because investigators are trying to understand each case individually and in as much depth as is feasible. The goal is not to produce summary statistics about a set of observations. Thus, if a new data collection opportunity arises or if a new line of thinking emerges during the research, it makes sense to take advantage by altering data collection, if such an alteration is likely to better ground the theory or to provide new theoretical insight. This flexibility is not a license to be unsystematic. Rather, this flexibility is controlled opportunism in which researchers take advantage of the uniqueness of a specific case and the emergence of new themes to improve resultant theory.

Analyzing Within-Case Data

Analyzing data is the heart of building theory from case studies, but it is both the most difficult and the least codified part of the process. Since published studies generally describe research sites and data collection methods, but give little space to discussion of analysis, a huge chasm often separates data from conclusions. As Miles and Huberman (1984, p. 16) wrote: "One cannot ordinarily follow how a researcher got from 3600 pages of field notes to the final conclusions, sprinkled with vivid quotes though they may be." However, several key features of analysis can be identified.

One key step is within-case analysis. The importance of within-case analysis is driven by one of the realities of case study research: a staggering volume of data. As Pettigrew (1988) described, there is an ever-present danger of "death by data asphyxiation." For example, Mintzberg and McHugh (1985) examined over 2500 movies in their study of strategy making at the National Film Board of Canada—and that was only part of their evidence. The volume of data is all the more daunting because the research problem is often open-ended. Within-case analysis can help investigators cope with this deluge of data.

Within-case analysis typically involves detailed case study write-ups for each site. These write-ups are often simply pure descriptions, but they are central to the generation of insight (Gersick, 1988; Pettigrew, 1988) because they help researchers to cope early in the analysis process with the often enormous volume of data. However, there is no standard format for such analysis. Quinn (1980) developed teaching cases for each of the firms in his study of strategic decision making in six major corporations as a prelude to his theoretical work. Mintzberg and McHugh (1985) compiled a 383-page case history of the National Film Board of Canada. These authors coupled narrative description with extensive use of longitudinal graphs tracking revenue, film sponsorship, staffing, film subjects, and so on. Gersick (1988) prepared transcripts of team meetings. Leonard-Barton (1988) used tabular displays and graphs of information about each case. Abbott (1988) suggested using sequence analysis to organize longitudinal data. In fact, there are probably as many approaches as researchers. However, the overall idea is to become intimately familiar with each case as a stand-alone entity. This process allows the unique patterns of each case to emerge before investigators push to generalize patterns across cases. In addition, it gives investigators a rich familiarity with each case which, in turn, accelerates cross-case comparison.

Searching for Cross-Case Patterns

Coupled with within-case analysis is cross-case search for patterns. The tactics here are driven by the reality that people are notoriously poor processors of information. They leap to conclusions based on limited data (Kahneman & Tversky, 1973), they are overly influenced by the vividness (Nisbett & Ross, 1980) or by more elite respondents (Miles & Huberman, 1984), they ignore basic statistical properties (Kahneman & Tversky, 1973), or they sometimes inadvertently drop disconfirming evidence (Nisbett & Ross, 1980). The danger is that investigators reach premature and even false conclusions as a result of these information-processing biases. Thus, the key to good cross-case comparison is counteracting these tendencies by looking at the data in many divergent ways.

One tactic is to select categories or dimensions, and then to look for within-group similarities coupled with intergroup differences. Dimensions can be suggested by the research problem or by existing literature, or the researcher can simply choose some dimensions. For example, in a study of strategic decision making, Bourgeois and Eisenhardt (1988) sifted cases into various categories including founder-run vs. professional management, high vs. low performance, first vs. second generation product, and large vs. small size. Some categories such as size and product generation revealed no clear patterns, but others such as performance led to important patterns of within-group similarity and across-group differences. An extension of this tactic is to use a 2 × 2 or other cell design to compare several categories at once, or to move to a continuous measurement scale which permits graphing.

A second tactic is to select pairs of cases and then to list the similarities and differences between each pair. This tactic forces researchers to look for the subtle similarities and differences between cases. The juxtaposition of seemingly similar cases by a researcher looking for differences can break simplistic frames. In the same way, the search for similarity in a seemingly different pair also can lead to more sophisticated understanding. The result of these forced comparisons can be new categories and concepts which the investigators did not anticipate. For example, Eisenhardt and Bourgeois (1988) found that CEO power differences dominated initial impressions across firms. However, this paired comparison process led the researchers to see that the speed of the decision process was equally important (Eisenhardt, in press). Finally, an extension of this tactic is to group cases into threes or fours for comparison.

A third strategy is to divide the data by data source. For example, one researcher combs observational data, while another reviews interviews, and still another works with questionnaire evidence. This tactic was used in the separation of the analyses of qualitative and quantitative data in a study of strategic decision making (Bourgeois & Eisenhardt, 1988; Eisenhardt & Bourgeois, 1988). This tactic exploits the unique insights possible from different types of data collection. When a pattern from one data source is corroborated by the evidence from another, the finding is stronger and better grounded. When evidence conflicts, the researcher can sometimes reconcile the evidence through deeper probing of the meaning of the differences. At other times, this conflict exposes a spurious or random pattern, or biased thinking in the analysis. A variation of this tactic is to split the data into groups of cases, focusing on one group of cases initially, while later focusing on the remaining cases. Gersick (1988) used this tactic in separating the analyses of the student group cases from her other cases.

Overall, the idea behind these cross-case searching tactics is to force investigators to go beyond initial impressions, especially through the use of structured and diverse lenses on the data. These tactics improve the likelihood of accurate and reliable theory, that is, a theory with a close fit with the data. Also, cross-case searching tactics enhance the probability that the investigators will capture the novel findings which may exist in the data.

Shaping Hypotheses

From the within-site analysis plus various cross-site tactics and overall impressions, tentative themes, concepts, and possibly even relationships between variables begin to emerge. The next step of this highly iterative process is to compare systematically the emergent frame with the evidence from each case in order to assess how well or poorly it fits with case data. The central idea is that researchers constantly compare theory and data—iterating toward a theory which closely fits the data. A close fit is important to building good theory because it takes advantage of the new insights possible from the data and yields an empirically valid theory.

One step in shaping hypotheses is the sharpening of constructs. This is a two-part process involving (1) refining the definition of the construct and (2) building evidence which measures the construct in each case. This occurs through constant comparison between data and constructs so that accumulating evidence from diverse sources converges on a single, well-defined construct. For example, in their study of stigma management in bankruptcy, Sutton and Callahan (1987) developed constructs which described the reaction of customers and other parties to the declaration of bankruptcy by the focal firms. The iterative process involved data from multiple sources: initial semistructured telephone conversations; interviews with key informants including the firm's president, other executives, a major creditor, and a lawyer; U.S. Bankruptcy Court records; observation of a creditors' meeting; and secondary source material including newspaper and magazine articles and firm correspondence. The authors iterated between constructs and these data. They eventually developed definitions and measures for several constructs: disengagement, bargaining for a more favorable exchange relationship, denigration via rumor, and reduction in the quality of participation.

This process is similar to developing a single construct measure from multiple indicators in hypothesis-testing research. That is, researchers use multiple sources of evidence to build construct measures, which define the construct and distinguish it from other constructs. In effect, the researcher is attempting to establish construct validity. The difference is that the construct, its definition, and measurement often emerge from the analysis process itself, rather than being specified a priori. A second difference is that no technique like factor analysis is available to collapse multiple indicators into a single construct measure. The reasons are that the indicators may vary across cases (i.e., not all cases may have all measures), and qualitative evidence (which is common in theory-building research) is difficult to collapse. Thus, many researchers rely on tables which summarize and tabulate the evidence underlying the construct (Miles & Huberman, 1984;

Sutton & Callahan, 1987). For example, Table 1.3 is a tabular display of the evidence grounding the CEO power construct used by Eisenhardt and Bourgeois (1988), which included qualitative personality descriptions, quantitative scores from questionnaires, and quotation examples. The reasons for defining and building evidence for a construct apply in theory-building research just as they do in traditional, hypothesis-testing work. That is, careful construction of construct definitions and evidence produces the sharply defined, measurable constructs which are necessary for strong theory.

A second step in shaping hypotheses is verifying that the emergent relationships between constructs fit with the evidence in each case. Sometimes a relationship is confirmed by the case evidence, while other times it is revised, disconfirmed, or thrown out for insufficient evidence. This verification process is similar to that in traditional hypothesis testing research. The key difference is that each hypothesis is examined for each case, not for the aggregate cases. Thus, the underlying logic is replication, that is, the logic of treating a series of cases as a series of experiments with each case serving to confirm or disconfirm the hypotheses (Yin, 1984). Each case is analogous to an experiment, and multiple cases are analogous to multiple experiments. This contrasts with the sampling logic of traditional, within-experiment, hypothesis-testing research in which the aggregate relationships across the data points are tested using summary statistics such as F values (Yin, 1984).

In replication logic, cases which confirm emergent relationships enhance confidence in the validity of the relationships. Cases which disconfirm the relationships often can provide an opportunity to refine and extend the theory. For example, in the study of the politics of strategic decision making, Eisenhardt and Bourgeois (1988) found a case which did not fit with the proposition that political coalitions have stable memberships. Further examination of this disconfirming case indicated that the executive team in this case had been newly formed at the time of the study. This observation plus replication in another case led to a refinement in the emergent theory to indicate that increasing stabilization of coalitions occurs over time.

At this point, the qualitative data are particularly useful for understanding why or why not emergent relationships hold. When a relationship is supported, the qualitative data often provide a good understanding of the dynamics underlying the relationship, that is, the

(Text Continues on Page 24)

Table 1.3   Example of Tabulated Evidence for a Power Centralization Construct*

Firm	CEO Decision Description	CEO Power Score	CEO Power Distance[a]	CEO Dominated Functions	Story Decision Style[b]	Examples[c]
First	Strong Volatile Dogmatic	9.6	3.5	Mkt, R&D, Ops, Fin	Authoritarian	Geoff [Chairman] is THE decision maker. He runs the whole show. (VP, Marketing)
Alpha	Impatient Parental Tunes You Out	9.6	3.8	Mkt, R&D, Ops, Fin	Authoritarian	Thou shalt not hire w/o Presidential approval. Thou shalt not promote w/o Presidential approval. Thou shalt not explore new markets w/o Presidential approval. (VP, Operations)
Cowboy	Strong Power Boss Master Strategist	9.1	3.1	Mkt, R&D, Fin	Authoritarian Consensus	The tone of meetings would change depending upon whether he was in the room. If he'd leave the room, discussion would spread out, go off the wall. It got back on focus when he came back. (Director of Marketing)
Neutron	Organized Analytic	9.1	2.3	Mkt, Ops, Fin	Authoritarian	If there is a decision to make, I will make it (President)
Omicron	Easygoing Easy to Work With	8.4	1.2	Fin	Consensus	Bill [prior CEO] was a suppressor of ideas. Jim is more open. (VP, Mfg.)

(Continued)

Tabel 1.3 *(Continued)*

Firm	CEO Decision Description	CEO Power Score	CEO Power Distance[a]	CEO Dominated Functions	Story Decision Style[b]	Examples[c]
Promise	People-Oriented Pragmatic	8.9	1.3	Ops, Fin	Consensus	[My philosophy is] to make quick decisions involving as many people as possible. (President)
Forefront	Aggressive Team Player	8.3	1.2	None	Consensus	Art depends on picking good people and letting them operate. (VP, Sales)
Zap	Consensus-Style People-Oriented	7.5	0.3	Fin	Consultative	It's very open. We're successful most of the time in building consensus. (VP, Engineering)

a. Difference between CEO power score and score of next most powerful executive.
b. Authoritarian—Decisions made either by CEO alone or in consultation with only one person.
   Consultative—Decisions made by CEO in consultation with either most of or all of the team.
   Consensus—Decisions made by entire team in a group format.
c. Individual in parentheses is the source of the quotation.
*Taken from Eisenhardt & Bourgeois, 1988.

"why" of what is happening. This is crucial to the establishment of internal validity. Just as in hypothesis-testing research an apparent relationship may simply be a spurious correlation or may reflect the impact of some third variable on each of the other two. Therefore, it is important to discover the underlying theoretical reasons for why the relationship exists. This helps to establish the internal validity of the findings. For example, in her study of project groups, Gersick (1988) identified a midpoint transition in the lives of most project groups. She then used extensive qualitative data to understand the cognitive and motivational reasons why such abrupt and precisely timed transitions occur.

Overall, shaping hypotheses in theory-building research involves measuring constructs and verifying relationships. These processes are similar to traditional hypothesis-testing research. However, these processes are more judgmental in theory-building research because researchers cannot apply statistical tests such as an F statistic. The research team must judge the strength and consistency of relationships within and across cases and also fully display the evidence and procedures when the findings are published, so that readers may apply their own standards.

Enfolding Literature

An essential feature of theory building is comparison of the emergent concepts, theory, or hypotheses with the extant literature. This involves asking what is this similar to, what does it contradict, and why. A key to this process is to consider a broad range of literature.

Examining literature which conflicts with the emergent theory is important for two reasons. First, if researchers ignore conflicting findings, then confidence in the findings is reduced. For example, readers may assume that the results are incorrect (a challenge to internal validity), or if correct, are idiosyncratic to the specific cases of the study (a challenge to generalizability). Second and perhaps more importantly, conflicting literature represents an opportunity. The juxtaposition of conflicting results forces researchers into a more creative, framebreaking mode of thinking than they might otherwise be able to achieve. The result can be deeper insight into both the emergent theory *and* the conflicting literature, as well as sharpening of the limits to generalizability of the focal research. For example, in their study of strategy making at the National Film Board of Canada, Mintzberg and McHugh (1985) noted conflicts between their findings for this highly creative organization and prior results at Volkswagenwerk and other sites. In the earlier studies, they observed differences in the patterns of strategic change whereby periods of convergence were long and periods of divergence were short and very abrupt. In contrast, the National Film Board exhibited a pattern of regular cycles of convergence and divergence, coupled with a long-term trend toward greater diversity. This and other conflicts allowed these researchers to establish the unique features of strategy making in an "adhocracy" in relief against "machine bureaucracies" and "entrepreneurial firms." The result was a sharper theory of strategy formation in all three types of organizations. Similarly, in a study of politics, Eisenhardt and Bourgeois (1988) contrasted the finding that centralized power leads to politics with the previous finding that *decentralized* power creates politics. These conflicting findings forced the probing of both the evidence and conflicting research to discover the underlying reasons for the conflict. An underlying similarity in the apparently dissimilar situations was found. That is, both power extremes create a climate of frustration, which leads to an emphasis on self-interest and ultimately politics. In these extreme situations, the "structure of the game" becomes an interpersonal competition among the executives. In contrast, the research showed that an intermediate power distribution fosters a sense of personal efficacy among executives and ultimately collaboration, not politics, for the good of the entire group. This reconciliation integrated the conflicting findings into a single theoretical perspective, and raised the theoretical level and generalizability of the results.

Literature discussing similar findings is important as well because it ties together underlying similarities in phenomena normally not associated with each other. The result is often a theory with stronger internal validity, wider generalizability, and higher conceptual level. For example, in her study of technological innovation in a major computer corporation, Leonard-Barton (1988) related her findings on the mutual adaptation of technology and the host organization to similar findings in the education literature. In so doing, Leonard-Barton strengthened the confidence that her findings were valid and generalizable because others had similar findings in a very different context. Also, the tie to mutual adaptation processes in the education setting sharpened and enriched the conceptual level of the study.

Similarly, Gersick (1988) linked the sharp midpoint transition in project group development to the more general punctuated equilibrium phenomenon, to the literature on the adult midlife transition, and to strategic transitions within organizations. This linkage with a variety of literature in other contexts raises the readers' confidence that Gersick had observed a valid phenomenon within her small number of project teams. It also allowed her to elevate the conceptual level of her findings to the more fundamental level of punctuated equilibrium, and strengthen their likely generalizability to other project teams. Finally, Burgelman (1983) strengthened the theoretical scope and validity of his work by tying his results on the process of new venture development in a large corporation to the selection arguments of population ecology. The result again was a higher conceptual level for his findings and enhanced confidence in their validity.

Overall, tying the emergent theory to existing literature enhances the internal validity, generalizability, and theoretical level of theory building from case study research. While linking results to the literature is important in most research, it is particularly crucial in theory-building research because the findings often rest on a very limited number of cases. In this situation, any further corroboration of internal validity or generalizability is an important improvement.

Reaching Closure

Two issues are important in reaching closure: when to stop adding cases, and when to stop iterating between theory and data. In the first, ideally, researchers should stop adding cases when theoretical saturation is reached. (Theoretical saturation is simply the point at which incremental learning is minimal because the researchers are observing phenomena seen before; Glaser & Strauss, 1967.) This idea is quite similar to ending the revision of a manuscript when the incremental improvement in its quality is minimal. In practice, theoretical saturation often combines with pragmatic considerations such as time and money to dictate when case collection ends. In fact, it is not uncommon for researchers to plan the number of cases in advance. For example, the Warwick group planned their study of strategic change and competitiveness in British firms to include eight firms (Pettigrew, 1988). This kind of planning may be necessary because of the availability of resources and because time constraints force researchers to develop cases in parallel. Finally, while there is no ideal number of cases, a number between 4 and 10 cases usually works well. With fewer than 4 cases, it is often difficult to generate theory with much complexity, and its empirical grounding is likely to be unconvincing, unless the case has several mini-cases within it, as did the Mintzberg and McHugh study of the National Film Board of Canada. With more than 10 cases, it quickly becomes difficult to cope with the complexity and volume of the data.

In the second closure issue, when to stop iterating between theory and data, again, saturation is the key idea. That is, the iteration process stops when the incremental improvement to theory is minimal. The final product of building theory from case studies may be concepts (e.g., the Mintzberg & Waters, 1982, deliberate and emergent strategies), a conceptual framework (e.g., Harris & Sutton's, 1986, framework of bankruptcy), or propositions or possibly mid-range theory (e.g., Eisenhardt & Bourgeois's, 1988, mid-range theory of politics in high velocity environments). On the downside, the final product may be disappointing. The research may simply replicate prior theory, or there may be no clear patterns within the data. The steps for building theory from case studies are summarized in Table 1.1.

❖ COMPARISON WITH OTHER LITERATURE

The process described here has similarities with the work of others. For example, I have drawn upon the ideas of theoretical sampling, theoretical saturation, and overlapped coding, data collection, and analysis from Glaser and Strauss (1967). Also, the notions of case study design, replication logic, and concern for internal validity have been incorporated from Yin (1984). The tools of tabular display of evidence from Miles and Huberman (1984) were particularly helpful in the discussion of building evidence for constructs.

However, the process described here has important differences from previous work. First, it is focused on theory building from cases. In contrast, with the exception of Glaser and Strauss (1967), previous work was centered on other topics such as qualitative data analysis (e.g., Miles, 1979; Miles & Huberman, 1984; Kirk & Miller, 1986), case study design (Yin, 1981, 1984; McClintock et al., 1979), and ethnography (Van Maanen, 1988). To a large extent, Glaser and Strauss (1967) focused on defending building theory from cases, rather than on how actually to do it. Thus, while these previous writings provide pieces of the process, they do not provide (nor do they intend to provide) a framework for theory building from cases as developed here.

Second, the process described here contributes new ideas. For example, the process includes a priori specification of constructs, population specification, flexible instrumentation, multiple investigators, cross-case analysis tactics, and several uses of literature. Their inclusion plus their illustration using examples from research studies and comparison with traditional, hypothesis-testing research synthesizes, extends, and adds depth to existing views of theory-building research.

Third, particularly in comparison with Strauss (1987) and Van Maanen (1988), the process described here adopts a positivist view of research. That is, the process is directed toward the development of testable hypotheses and theory which are generalizable across settings. In contrast, authors like Strauss and Van Maanen are more concerned that a rich, complex description of the specific cases under study evolve and they appear less concerned with development of generalizable theory.

❖ DISCUSSION

The process of building theory from case study research is a strikingly iterative one. While an investigator may focus on one part of the process at a time, the process itself involves constant iteration backward and forward between steps. For example, an investigator may move from cross-case comparison, back to redefinition of the research question, and out to the field to gather evidence on an additional case. Also, the process is alive with tension between divergence into new ways of understanding the data and convergence onto a single theoretical framework. For example, the process involves the use of multiple investigators and multiple data collection methods as well as a variety of cross-case searching tactics. Each of these tactics involves viewing evidence from diverse perspectives. However, the process also involves converging on construct definitions, measures, and a framework for structuring the findings. Finally, the process described here is intimately tied with empirical evidence.

Strengths of Theory Building From Cases

One strength of theory building from cases is its likelihood of generating novel theory. Creative insight often arises from the juxtaposition of contradictory or paradoxical evidence (Cameron & Quinn, 1988). As Bartunek (1988) argued, the process of reconciling these contradictions forces individuals to reframe perceptions into a new gestalt. Building theory from case studies centers directly on this kind of juxtaposition. That is, attempts to reconcile evidence across cases, types of data, and different investigators, and between cases and literature increase the likelihood of creative reframing into a new theoretical vision. Although a myth surrounding theory building from case studies is that the process is limited by investigators' preconceptions, in fact, just the opposite is true. This constant juxtaposition of conflicting realities tends to "unfreeze" thinking, and so the process has the potential to generate theory with less researcher bias than theory built from incremental studies or armchair, axiomatic deduction.

A second strength is that the emergent theory is likely to be testable with constructs that can be readily measured and hypotheses that can be proven false. Measurable constructs are likely because they have already been measured during the theory-building process. The resulting hypotheses are likely to be verifiable for the same reason. That is, they have already undergone repeated verification during the theory-building process. In contrast, theory which is generated apart from direct evidence may have testability problems. For example, population ecology researchers borrowed the niche concept from biology. This construct has proven difficult to operationalize for many organizational researchers, other than its originators. One reason may be its obscure definition, which hampers measurability: ". . . that area in constraint space (the space whose dimensions are levels of resources, etc.) in which the population outcompetes all other local populations" (Hannan & Freeman, 1977, p. 947). One might ask: How do you measure an area in constraint space?

A third strength is that the resultant theory is likely to be empirically valid. The likelihood of valid theory is high because the theory-building process is so intimately tied with evidence that it is very likely that the resultant theory will be consistent with empirical observation. In well-executed theory-building research, investigators answer to the data from the beginning of the research. This closeness can lead to an intimate sense of things—"how they feel, smell, seem" (Mintzberg, 1979). This intimate interaction with actual evidence often produces theory which closely mirrors reality.

Weaknesses of Theory Building From Cases

However, some characteristics that lead to strengths in theory building from case studies also lead to weaknesses. For example, the intensive use of empirical evidence can yield theory which is overly complex. A hallmark of good theory is parsimony, but given the typically staggering volume of rich data, there is a temptation to build theory which tries to capture everything. The result can be theory which is very rich in detail, but lacks the simplicity of overall perspective. Theorists working from case data can lose their sense of proportion as they confront vivid, voluminous data. Since they lack quantitative gauges such as regression results or observations across multiple studies, they may be unable to assess which are the most important relationships and which are simply idiosyncratic to a particular case.

Another weakness is that building theory from cases may result in narrow and idiosyncratic theory. Case study theory building is a bottom-up approach such that the specifics of data produce the generalizations of theory. The risks are that the theory describes a very idiosyncratic phenomenon or that the theorist is unable to raise the level of generality of the theory. Indeed, many of the grounded case studies mentioned earlier resulted in modest theories. For example, Gersick (1988) developed a model of group development for teams with project deadlines, Eisenhardt and Bourgeois (1988) developed a mid-range theory of politics in high velocity environments, and Burgelman (1983) proposed a model of new product ventures in large corporations. Such theories are likely to be testable, novel, and empirically valid, but they do lack the sweep of theories like resource dependence, population ecology, and transaction cost. They are essentially theories about specific phenomena. To their credit, many of these theorists tie into broader theoretical issues such as adaptation, punctuated equilibrium, and bounded rationality, but ultimately they are not theories about organization in any grand sense. Perhaps "grand" theory requires multiple studies—an accumulation of both theory-building and theory-testing empirical studies.

Applicability

When is it appropriate to conduct theory-building case study research? In normal science, theory is developed through incremental empirical testing and extension (Kuhn, 1970). Thus, the theory-building process relies on past literature and empirical observation or experience as well as on the insight of the theorist to build incrementally more powerful theories. However, there are times when little is known about a phenomenon, current perspectives seem inadequate because they have little empirical substantiation, or they conflict with each other or common sense. Or, sometimes, serendipitous findings in a theory-testing study suggest the need for a new perspective. In these situations, theory building from case study research is particularly appropriate because theory building from case studies does not rely on previous literature or prior empirical evidence. Also, the conflict inherent in the process is likely to generate the kind of novel theory which is desirable when extant theory seems inadequate. For example, Van de Ven and Poole (in press) have argued that such an approach is especially useful for studying the new area of longitudinal change processes. In sum, building theory from case study research is most appropriate in the early stages of research on a topic or to provide freshness in perspective to an already researched topic.

Evaluation

How should theory-building research using case studies be evaluated? To begin, there is no generally accepted set of guidelines for the assessment of this type of research. However, several criteria seem appropriate. Assessment turns on whether the concepts, framework, or propositions that emerge from the process are "good theory." After all, the point of the process is to develop or at least begin to develop theory. Pfeffer (1982) suggested that good theory is parsimonious, testable, and logically coherent, and these criteria seem appropriate here. Thus, a strong theory-building study yields good theory (that is, parsimonious, testable, and logically coherent theory) which emerges at the end, not beginning, of the study.

Second, the assessment of theory-building research also depends upon empirical issues: strength of method and the evidence grounding the theory. Have the investigators followed a careful analytical procedure? Does the evidence support the theory? Have the investigators ruled out rival explanations? Just as in other empirical research, investigators should provide information on the sample, data collection procedures, and analysis. Also, they should display enough evidence for each construct to allow readers to make their own assessment of the fit with theory. While there are no concise measures such as correlation coefficients or F values, nonetheless thorough reporting of information should give confidence that the theory is valid. Overall, as in hypothesis testing, a strong theory-building study has a good, although not necessarily perfect, fit with the data.

Finally, strong theory-building research should result in new insights. Theory building which simply replicates past theory is, at best, a modest contribution. Replication is appropriate in theory-testing research, but in theory-building research, the goal is new theory. Thus, a strong theory-building study presents new, perhaps framebreaking, insights.

❖ CONCLUSIONS

The purpose of this article is to describe the process of theory building from case studies. The process, outlined in Table 1.1, has features which range from selection of the research question to issues in reaching closure. Several conclusions emerge.

Theory developed from case study research is likely to have important strengths like novelty, testability, and empirical validity, which arise from the intimate linkage with empirical evidence. Second, given the strengths of this theory-building approach and its independence from prior literature or past empirical observation, it is particularly well-suited to new research areas or research areas for which existing theory seems inadequate. This type of work is highly complementary to incremental theory building from normal science research. The former is useful in early stages of research on a topic or when a fresh perspective is needed, while the latter is useful in later stages of knowledge. Finally, several guidelines for assessing the quality of theory building from case studies have been suggested. Strong studies are those which present interesting or framebreaking theories which meet the tests of good theory or concept development (e.g., parsimony, testability, logical coherence) and are grounded in convincing evidence.

Most empirical studies lead from theory to data. Yet, the accumulation of knowledge involves a continual cycling between theory and data. Perhaps this article will stimulate some researchers to complete the cycle by conducting research that goes in the less common direction from data to theory, and equally important, perhaps it will help others become informed consumers of the results.

❖ REFERENCES

Abbott, A. (1988, September) *Workshop on sequence methods*. National Science Foundation Conference on Longitudinal Research Methods in Organizations, Austin.

Allison, G. (1971) *Essence of decision*. Boston: Little, Brown.

Anderson, P. (1983) Decision making by objection and the Cuban missile crisis. *Administrative Science Quarterly, 28*, 201–222.

Bartunek, J. (1988) The dynamics of personal and organizational reframing. In R. Quinn & K. Cameron (Eds.), *Paradox and transformation: Towards a theory of change in organization and management* (pp. 137–162). Cambridge, MA: Ballinger.

Bettenhausen, K., & Murnighan, J. K. (1986) The emergence of norms in competitive decision-making groups. *Administrative Science Quarterly, 30*, 350–372.

Bourgeois, L., & Eisenhardt, K. (1988) Strategic decision processes in high velocity environments: Four cases in the microcomputer industry. *Management Science, 34*, 816–835.

Burgelman, R. (1983) A process model of internal corporate venturing in a major diversified firm. *Administrative Science Quarterly, 28*, 223–244.

Cameron, K., & Quinn, R. (1988) Organizational paradox and transformation. In R. Quinn & K. Cameron (Eds.), *Paradox and transformation: Towards a theory of change in organization and management* (pp. 1–81). Cambridge, MA: Ballinger.

Eisenhardt, K. (in press) Making fast strategic decisions in high velocity environments. *Academy of Management Journal*.

Eisenhardt, K., & Bourgeois, L. J. (1988) Politics of strategic decision making in high velocity environments: Toward a mid-range theory. *Academy of Management Journal, 31*, 737–770.

Gersick, C. (1988) Time and transition in work teams: Toward a new model of group development. *Academy of Management Journal, 31*, 9–41.

Glaser, B., & Strauss, A. (1967) *The discovery of grounded theory: Strategies of qualitative research*. London: Wiedenfeld and Nicholson.

Hannan, M., & Freeman, J. (1977) The population ecology of organizations. *American Journal of Sociology, 82*, 929–964.

Harris, S., & Sutton, R. (1986) Functions of parting ceremonies in dying organizations. *Academy of Management Journal, 29,* 5–30.

Jick, T. (1979) Mixing qualitative and quantitative methods: Triangulation in action. *Administrative Science Quarterly, 24,* 602–611.

Kahneman, D., & Tversky, A. (1973) On the psychology of prediction. *Psychological Review, 80,* 237–251.

Kidder, T. (1982) *Soul of a new machine.* New York: Avon.

Kimberly, J. (1988) A review of Walter R. Nord and Sharon Tucker: Implementing routine and radical innovations. *Administrative Science Quarterly, 33,* 314–316.

Kirk, J., & Miller, M. (1986) *Reliability and validity in qualitative research.* Beverly Hills, CA: Sage.

Kuhn, T. (1970) *The structure of scientific revolutions* (2nd ed.). Chicago: University of Chicago Press.

Leonard-Barton, D. (1988) *Synergistic design for case studies: Longitudinal single-site and replicated multiple-site.* Paper presented at the National Science Foundation Conference on Longitudinal Research Methods in Organizations, Austin.

McClintock, C., Brannon, D., & Maynard-Moody, S. (1979) Applying the logic of sample surveys to qualitative case studies: The case cluster method. *Administrative Science Quarterly, 24,* 612–629.

Miles, M. B. (1979) Qualitative data as an attractive nuisance: The problem of analysis. *Administrative Science Quarterly, 24,* 590–601.

Miles, M. B., & Huberman, A. M. (1984) *Qualitative data analysis: A sourcebook of new methods.* Beverly Hills, CA: Sage.

Mintzberg, H. (1979) An emerging strategy of "direct" research. *Administrative Science Quarterly, 24,* 580–589.

Mintzberg, H., & McHugh, A. (1985) Strategy formation in an adhocracy. *Administrative Science Quarterly, 30,* 160–197.

Mintzberg, H., & Waters, J. (1982) Tracking strategy in an entrepreneurial firm. *Academy of Management Journal, 25,* 465–499.

Nisbett, R., & Ross, L. (1980) *Human inference: Strategies and shortcomings of social judgment.* Englewood Cliffs, NJ: Prentice Hall.

Perrow, C. (1986) *Complex organizations* (3rd ed.). New York: Random House.

Pettigrew, A. (1973) *The politics of organizational decision making.* London: Tavistock.

Pettigrew, A. (1988) *Longitudinal field research on change: Theory and practice.* Paper presented at the National Science Foundation Conference on Longitudinal Research Methods in Organizations, Austin.

Pfeffer, J. (1982) *Organizations and organization theory.* Marshfield, MA: Pitman.

Pinfield, L. (1986) A field evaluation of perspectives on organizational decision making. *Administrative Science Quarterly, 31,* 365–388.

Quinn, J. B. (1980) *Strategies for change.* Homewood, IL: Dow-Jones Irwin.

Selznick, P. (1949) *TVA and the grass roots.* Berkeley, CA: University of California Press.

Strauss, A. (1987) *Qualitative analysis for social scientists.* Cambridge, England: Cambridge University Press.

Sutton, R., & Callahan, A. (1987) The stigma of bankruptcy: Spoiled organizational image and its management. *Academy of Management Journal, 30,* 405–436.

Van de Ven, A., & Poole, M. S. (in press) Methods to develop a grounded theory of innovation processes in the Minnesota Innovation Research Program. *Organization Science*, 1.

Van Maanen, J. (1988) *Tales of the field: On writing ethnography.* Chicago: University of Chicago Press.

Yin, R. (1981) The case study crisis: Some answers. *Administrative Science Quarterly*, 26, 58–65.

Yin, R. (1984) *Case study research.* Beverly Hills, CA: Sage.

2

Understanding and Validity
in Qualitative Research

Joseph A. Maxwell

> Within the last few years, the issue of validity in qualitative research has come to the fore. (Kvale, 1989, p. 7)

> All field work done by a single field-worker invites the question, Why should we believe it? (Bosk, 1979, p. 193)

Validity has long been a key issue in debates over the legitimacy of qualitative research; if qualitative studies cannot consistently produce valid results, then policies, programs, or predictions based on these studies cannot be relied on. Proponents of quantitative and experimental approaches have frequently criticized the absence of "standard" means of assuring validity, such as quantitative measurement, explicit controls for various validity threats, and the formal testing of prior hypotheses. Their critique has been bolstered by the fact that existing

Reprinted from Joseph A. Maxwell, "Understanding and Validity in Qualitative Research," *Harvard Educational Review*, 62:3 (Fall 1992), pp. 279–300. Copyright © 1992 by the President and Fellows of Harvard College. All rights reserved.

categories of validity (for example, concurrent validity, predictive validity, convergent validity, criterion-related validity, internal/external validity) are based on positivist assumptions that underlie quantitative and experimental research designs (Salner, 1989). Qualitative researchers have generally responded either by denying the relevance of the quantitative or scientific paradigm for what they do (for example, Guba & Lincoln, 1989), or by arguing that qualitative research has its own procedures for attaining validity that are simply different from those of quantitative approaches (for example, Kirk & Miller, 1986).

However, explicit attention to *how* qualitative researchers conceptualize validity issues in their research has been slow to develop. Phillips (1987) and Kvale (1989) have argued that the concept is legitimate and useful in qualitative research; Goetz and LeCompte (1984), Kirk and Miller (1986), and Erickson (1989) have proposed various definitions of validity and of different types of validity. Eisenhart and Howe (1992) also accept the legitimacy of the concept, but argue for a unitary conception of validity rather than a typology; they see research studies as arguments and propose various standards for valid arguments in educational research. In contrast, Guba and Lincoln (1989) view validity as a positivist notion and propose to substitute for this the concept of "authenticity" in qualitative research. Finally, Wolcott (1990a) is skeptical that validity or any analogous concept is legitimate or useful in qualitative inquiry.

Mishler (1990) has recently argued that, while the concept of validity is applicable to what he calls "inquiry-guided" research, the attempt to extend the dominant experimental/quantitative model of validity to such research is misguided, since the dominant model's categories of validity are themselves fundamentally flawed. He asserts that the demonstration by Campbell and Stanley (1963), and later by Cook and Campbell (1979), "that validity assessments are not assured by following procedures but depend on investigators' judgments" has proved "to be a death blow for the typology approach" (Mishler, 1990, p. 418), and argues that for this reason, issues of meaning and interpretation have become central. Mishler proposes a model of validity that relies on exemplars of scientific practice, rather than on abstract rules or categories, as the grounds for validating the trustworthiness of observations, interpretations, and generalizations.[1]

I agree with many of Mishler's arguments and conclusions, in particular with his emphasis on the importance of exemplars (see Maxwell, 1990b; Pitman & Maxwell, 1992). However, I think that his report of the demise of validity typologies is greatly exaggerated. His argument is directed mainly at typologies based on the procedures used for determining validity, which certainly comprise the majority of such typologies. Phillips states what seems to be a consensus: "In general it must be recognized that there are *no* procedures that will regularly (or always) yield either sound data or true conclusions" (1987, p. 21). Brinberg and McGrath make the same point: "Validity is not a commodity that can be purchased with techniques. . . . Rather, validity is like integrity, character, and quality, to be assessed relative to purposes and circumstances" (1985, p. 13).

But defining types of validity in terms of procedures, an approach generally labeled instrumentalist or positivist, is not the only approach available. The most prevalent alternative is a realist conception of validity that sees the validity of an account as inherent, not in the procedures used to produce and validate it, but in its relationship to those things that it is intended to be an account *of* (Hammersley, 1992; House, 1991; Maxwell, 1990a,b; Norris, 1983). This article is not a response to or critique of Mishler's approach, but an alternative, complementary view: it presents a realist typology of the kinds of validity that I see as relevant to qualitative research.[2]

In adopting a realist approach to validity, I am in basic agreement with the main point of Wolcott's critique—that is, that *understanding* is a more fundamental concept for qualitative research than validity (1990a, p. 146). I see the types of validity that I present here as derivative from the kinds of understanding gained from qualitative inquiry; my typology of validity categories is also a typology of the kinds of understanding at which qualitative research aims (see Runciman, 1983).

However, in explicating the concept of validity in qualitative research, I want to avoid applying or adapting the typologies developed for experimental and quantitative research, for reasons quite separate from Mishler's disapproval of procedure-based typologies. These typologies cannot be applied directly to qualitative research without distorting what qualitative researchers actually do in addressing validity issues, and tautologically confirming quantitative researchers' critiques.

An illustration of this is Campbell and Stanley's (1963) attack on what they disparagingly refer to as the "one-shot case study." They argue that this design is "well-nigh unethical" on the grounds that a single observation of one group, following an intervention, with no control groups or prior measures, provides no way of discriminating among numerous possible alternative explanations for the outcome, explanations that any valid design must be able to rule out. From an experimentalist's perspective, this argument is perfectly logical, but it completely ignores the ways that qualitative researchers actually rule out validity threats to their conclusions. Campbell later recognized the fallacy in his earlier critique and retracted it, stating that "the intensive ... case study has a discipline and a capacity to reject theories which are neglected in my caricature of the method" (1975, p. 184).

This situation, I believe, is similar to one in the history of the study of kinship terminologies in anthropology. Early investigators of kinship often assumed an equivalent conceptual structure between English and the language of the society they were studying (indeed, they often took the English terms to refer to real, natural categories), and simply sought the equivalents for the English kinship terms in the language being investigated. The major contribution of Lewis Henry Morgan (1871) to the study of kinship, and the basis for nearly all subsequent work on kinship terminology, was the recognition that societies have different classification systems for relatives, systems that can differ markedly from those of our own society and that cannot be represented adequately by a simple translation or correlation of their terminology with that of the English language (Trautmann, 1987, p. 57).

This article is thus intended to be a Morgan-like reformulation of the categorization of validity in qualitative research—an account from "the native's point of view" (Geertz, 1974) of the way qualitative researchers think about and deal with validity in their actual practice. Any account of validity in qualitative research, in order to be productive, should begin with an understanding of how qualitative researchers actually think about validity. I am not assuming that qualitative methods for assessing validity are infallible, but a critique of these methods is beyond the scope of this paper. However, if my account of the categories in which validity is conceived is valid, it obviously has implications for the latter task.

In developing these categories, I will work not only with qualitative researchers' explicit statements about validity—their "espoused theory" (Argyris & Schoen, 1974), or "reconstructed logic" (Kaplan, 1964)—but also with the ideas about validity that seem to me to be implicit in what they actually do—their "theory-in-use" (Argyris & Schoen, 1974) or "logic-in-use" (Kaplan, 1964). I am here following Einstein's advice that

> if you want to find out anything from the theoretical physicists about
> the methods they use, I advise you to stick closely to one principle:
> Don't listen to their words, fix your attention on their deeds. (cited by
> Manicas, 1987, p. 242)

In this, however, I have the additional advantage that I am myself a qualitative researcher and can draw on my own practice and my understanding of that practice, in the same way that a linguist is able to draw on his or her own "intuitions" about his or her native language in constructing an analysis of that language. (I am not claiming infallibility for such intuitions, but simply acknowledging them as a source of data.)

I do not think that qualitative and quantitative approaches to validity are incompatible. I see important similarities between the two, and think that the analysis I present here has implications for the concept of validity in quantitative and experimental research. I am, however, arguing that a fruitful comparison of the two approaches depends on a prior understanding of each of the approaches in its own terms.

❖ THE NATURE OF VALIDITY IN QUALITATIVE RESEARCH

All qualitative researchers agree that not all possible accounts of some individual, situation, phenomenon, activity, text, institution, or program are equally useful, credible, or legitimate. Furthermore, the ways in which researchers make these discriminations do not pertain entirely to the internal coherence, elegance, or plausibility of the account itself, but often refer to the relationship between the account and something external to it—that is, the phenomena that the account is *about*. Validity, in a broad sense, pertains to this relationship between an account and something outside of that account, whether this something is construed as objective reality, the constructions of actors, or a variety of other possible interpretations.

However, I am not assuming that there is only one correct, "objective" account—what Putnam (1990) refers to as the "God's eye view"— of this realm outside of the account itself. As observers and interpreters of the world, we are inextricably part of it; we cannot step outside our own experience to obtain some observer-independent account of what we experience. Thus, it is always possible for there to be different, equally valid accounts from different perspectives.[3]

My approach, therefore, does not depend on a correspondence theory of truth, at least not in the usual sense of a mirroring or isomorphism between account and reality, a sense that has been criticized by Rorty (1979). My analysis employs a critical realism (Bhaskar, 1989; Campbell, 1988; Hammersley, 1992; Manicas, 1987; Putnam, 1990) that assumes that we can have no direct knowledge of the objects of our accounts and thus no independent entity to which to compare these accounts (see Maxwell, 1990a,b). The applicability of the concept of validity presented here does not depend on the existence of some absolute truth or reality to which an account can be compared, but only on the fact that there exist ways of assessing accounts that do not depend entirely on features of the account itself, but in some way relate to those things that the account claims to be about.[4] This concept specifically differs from positivism and instrumentalism in that it does not take these tests to be critical for validity, but only as fallible means for generating evidence about the relationship between the account and its object (see Cook & Campbell, 1979).

An important point about this approach to validity is that it refers primarily to accounts, not to data or methods. This is consistent with the point made previously that validity is relative to purposes and circumstances. Hammersley and Atkinson (1983, p. 191) state that "data in themselves cannot be valid or invalid; what is at issue are the inferences drawn from them." And a classic work on survey research, after critiquing one study, asks, "May one, therefore, conclude that the Gluecks's measurements of these variables are invalid? In order to answer this question, it is necessary to ask what the Gluecks wish to learn from their data" (Hirschi & Selvin, 1967, p. 195).

It is possible to construe data as a kind of account—a description at a very low level of inference and abstraction. In this sense, it is sometimes legitimate to speak of the validity of data, but this use is derived from the primary meaning of validity as a property of accounts. In contrast, a method by itself is neither valid nor invalid; methods can produce valid data or accounts in some circumstances and invalid ones in others. Validity is not an inherent property of a particular method, but pertains to the data, accounts, or conclusions reached by using that method in a particular context for a particular purpose. To speak of the validity of a method is simply a shorthand way of referring to the validity of the data or accounts derived from that method.

I agree with Mishler that validity is always relative to, and dependent on, some community of inquirers on whose perspective the account is based. Validity is relative in this sense because understanding is relative; as argued above, it is not possible for an account to be independent of any particular perspective. It is always possible to challenge an account from outside that community and perspective, but such a challenge amounts to expanding the community that is concerned with the account and may change the nature of the validity issues in ways to be discussed below.

However, the grounding of all accounts in some particular community and perspective does not entail that all accounts are incommensurable in the sense of not being comparable. Bernstein (1983) argues in detail that the incommensurability thesis has been widely misinterpreted in this way, and that the rejection of objectivism does not require the adoption of extreme relativism in this sense. "What is sound in the incommensurability thesis has *nothing to do* with relativism, or at least that form of relativism which wants to claim that there can be no rational comparison among the plurality of theories" (Bernstein, 1983, p. 92; emphasis in the original). He quotes Winch, one of the authors most often cited in support of incommensurability:

> We should not lose sight of the fact that the idea that men's ideas and beliefs must be checkable by reference to something independent—some reality—is an important one. To abandon it is to plunge straight into a Protagorean relativism, with all the paradoxes that involves. (Winch, 1958, p. 11, cited in Bernstein, 1983, p. 98)

Bernstein claims that incommensurability, properly understood, is not a rejection of comparability, nor an abandonment of any attempt to assess the validity of accounts, but instead offers a way to compare or assess accounts that goes beyond the sterile opposition between objectivism and relativism (see also Bernstein, 1991, pp. 57–78).

I argued above that validity pertains to the kinds of understanding that accounts can embody. I see five broad categories of understanding that are relevant to qualitative research, and five corresponding types of validity that concern qualitative researchers. I will refer to these categories, respectively, as descriptive validity, interpretive validity, theoretical validity, generalizability, and evaluative validity.

The typology presented here has been influenced by others' work, particularly Cook and Campbell (1979), Kirk and Miller (1986), and

Erickson (1989). However, my primary debt is to the detailed analysis by Runciman (1983) of the types of understanding involved in social theory (though I depart significantly from his definitions of these), and to the discussion of description, interpretation, and explanation by Kaplan (1964). I believe that the distinctions made by Runciman, Kaplan, and others are simply explicit codifications and elaborations of a widespread commonsense conceptual structure, and that this structure is implicit in the work of many qualitative researchers. My account of validity is an attempt, in part, to explicate this implicit theory-in-use. Specific connections between my categories and those of these authors cited will be discussed below.

Because my analysis of validity is based on this taken-for-granted structure, the distinctions I propose may seem unoriginal or even old-fashioned, and lacking in philosophical sophistication. But philosophical sophistication is of value only when it engages with our ordinary ways of seeing and thinking. Although in this article I draw on a number of philosophical concepts and arguments, my primary purpose is not to advance the philosophical understanding of qualitative research, but to explicate how qualitative researchers think about validity. For this reason, I have not attempted to provide a detailed philosophical justification for the positions I have taken (for some of these justifications, see Bernstein, 1983, 1991; Bohman, 1991; Lakoff, 1987; Manicas, 1987; Putnam, 1990), nor to cite all of the relevant philosophical literature. Clearly, my assumptions and arguments are open to philosophical critique. However, as I argue for accounts in general, the validity of the account I provide here should be evaluated not simply on its internal logic and coherence, but also on its relationship to what qualitative researchers actually do in their research.

In addition, I am not arguing that the categories I define are clearly and explicitly demarcated or that every instance of a validity concern falls neatly into one and only one category. The entire approach to categorization that depends on precise and uniform criteria for determining category boundaries and assigning membership has been undermined by recent research (Lakoff, 1987), and it has become increasingly apparent that ambiguity and fuzzy boundaries are the rule rather than the exception in categorization. I will discuss specific instances of such fuzziness below; here I want to emphasize that I do not accept such cases as evidence *per se* for the inadequacy of the typology. Instances that do not fit my categories *may*, of course, challenge the validity of these categories, but they do so as a result of their implications, not simply because they cannot be assigned unambiguously to a single category.

❖ DESCRIPTIVE VALIDITY

The first concern of most qualitative researchers is with the factual accuracy of their account—that is, that they are not making up or distorting the things they saw and heard. If you report that an informant made a particular statement in an interview, is this correct? Did he or she really make that statement, or did you mis-hear, mis-transcribe, or mis-remember his or her words? Did a particular student in a classroom throw an eraser on a specific occasion? These matters of descriptive accuracy are emphasized by almost every introductory qualitative methods textbook in its discussion of the recording of field notes and interviews.

All of the subsequent validity categories I will discuss are dependent on this primary aspect of validity. As Geertz puts it, "behavior must be attended to, and with some exactness, because it is through the flow of behavior—or, more precisely, social action—that cultural forms find articulation" (1973, p. 17). Wolcott, similarly, states that "description is the foundation upon which qualitative research is built" (1990b, p. 27) and that "whenever I engage in fieldwork, I try to record as accurately as possible, and in precisely their words, what I judge to be important of what people do and say" (Wolcott, 1990a, p. 128).

I will refer to this first type of validity as descriptive validity; it corresponds, to some extent, to the category of understanding that Runciman (1983) calls "reportage" or "primary understanding." Insofar as this category pertains to humans, it refers to what Kaplan (1964, p. 358) calls "acts" rather than "actions"—activities seen as physical and behavioral events rather than in terms of the meanings that these have for the actor or others involved in the activity.

The above quotes refer mainly to what I will call primary descriptive validity: the descriptive validity of what the researcher reports having seen or heard (or touched, smelled, and so on). There is also the issue of what I will call secondary descriptive validity: the validity of accounts of things that could in principle be observed, but that were inferred from other data—for example, things that happened in the classroom when the researcher was not present. (This secondary description is also included in Runciman's concept of "reportage.") Secondary descriptive validity can pertain to accounts for which the inference is highly complex and problematic: for example, the claim that the person known as William Shakespeare actually wrote Hamlet, or that a particular stone object was used as a cutting tool by a member of an early human population. These issues concern descriptive validity because they pertain to physical and behavioral events that are, in principle, observable.

There are several characteristics of these sorts of descriptive concerns that I want to emphasize. First, they all refer to specific events and situations. No issue of generalizability or representativeness is involved. Second, they are all matters on which, in principle, intersubjective agreement could easily be achieved, given the appropriate data. For example, a tape recording of adequate quality could be used to determine if the informant made a particular statement during the interview, a videotape could be used to decide if the student threw the eraser, and so on.

Put another way, the *terms* of the description (for example, "throw" in the example above) are not problematic for the community involved in the discussion of the event; their meaning—how they ought to be applied to events and actions—is not in dispute, only the accuracy of the application. This situation is quite different, for example, from the case of an account claiming that a student *assaulted* another student. In this case, it is possible that no amount of videotape or other data could resolve disagreements about the applicability of the term "assault" to the action that took place. This latter dispute is not about descriptive validity, but about the interpretive, theoretical, and/or evaluative validity of the account.

Descriptive validity is by no means independent of theory; all observation and description are based on theory, even if this theory is implicit or common sense. However, descriptive validity is free from *disagreement* about the theory in question. This assertion does not mean that there cannot be disagreement about the descriptive validity of an account, only that such disagreement could in principle be resolved by the appropriate data. Of course, the theory could be *made* problematic by one of the participants in the discussion—for example, by challenging the applicability of "throwing" to what the student did with the eraser. However, this challenge would change the nature of the validity questions involved and make them no longer an issue of descriptive validity for participants in that discussion.

In framing descriptive validity in this way, I am not seeking to revive the positivist view that all disagreements in science ought to be resolvable in principle by means of the appropriate evidence. In my opinion, this view has been convincingly criticized by Kuhn (1970), Rorty (1979), Bernstein (1983), and others. Instead, I am attempting to incorporate into my typology one of Kuhn's fundamental insights: that in normal practice, many scientific disagreements *are* resolved in this way, and that incommensurability becomes crucial mainly in times of scientific crisis. Descriptive understanding pertains, by definition, to matters for which we have a framework for resolving such disagreements, a framework provided in large part by taken-for-granted ideas about time, space, physical objects, behavior, and our perception of these. Raising questions about the definition or applicability of these categories changes the type of validity at issue from descriptive to theoretical, in particular to that aspect of theoretical validity generally known as construct validity.

Descriptive validity can refer to issues of omission as well as of commission; no account can include everything, and "accuracy is a criterion relative to the purposes for which it is sought" (Runciman, 1983, p. 97). For example, a verbatim interview transcript might be descriptively invalid in omitting features of the informant's speech, such as stress and pitch, that are essential to the understanding of the interview. The omission of things that participants in the discussion feel are significant to the account (for the purposes at issue) threatens the descriptive validity of that account.

Descriptive validity can also pertain to statistically descriptive aspects of accounts. A claim that a certain phenomenon was frequent, typical, or rare in a specific situation at the time it was observed—for example, that few students raised their hands in response to the teacher's question—is also subject to threats to descriptive validity. This is an issue for which Becker (1970) has advocated the use of what he calls "quasi-statistics"—simple counts of things to support claims that are implicitly quantitative. What makes this a matter of descriptive validity is that it does not involve statistical *inference* to some larger universe than the phenomenon directly studied, but only the numerical description of the specific object of study. This is different from what Cook and Campbell (1979) call "statistical conclusion validity," which refers to the validity of inferences from the data to some population. I treat the latter issue below, as one type of generalizability.

Reliability, in my view, refers not to an aspect of validity or to a separate issue from validity, but to a particular type of threat to validity. If different observers or methods produce descriptively different data or accounts of the same events or situations, this puts into question the descriptive validity (and other types of validity as well) of the accounts. This problem could be resolved either by modification of the accounts, so that different observers come to agree on their descriptive accuracy, or by ascertaining that the differences were due to differences in the perspective and purposes of the observers and were both descriptively valid, given those perspectives and purposes.

❖ INTERPRETIVE VALIDITY

However, qualitative researchers are not concerned solely, or even primarily, with providing a valid description of the physical objects, events, and behaviors in the settings they study; they are also concerned with what these objects, events, and behaviors *mean* to the people engaged in and with them. In this use of the term meaning, I include intention, cognition, affect, belief, evaluation, and anything else that could be encompassed by what is broadly termed the "participants' perspective," as well as communicative meaning in a narrower sense. This construction is inherently ideational or mental, rather than physical, and the nature of the understanding, validity, and threats to validity that pertain to it are significantly different from those involved in descriptive validity.

I will call this sort of understanding interpretive, and the type of validity associated with it interpretive validity, following Erickson (1989).[5] The term "interpretive" is appropriate primarily because this aspect of understanding is most central to interpretive research, which seeks to comprehend phenomena not on the basis of the researcher's perspective and categories, but from those of the participants in the situations studied—that is, from an "emic" rather than an "etic" perspective (Bohman, 1991; Headland, Pike, & Harris, 1990). In contrast to descriptive validity, which could apply equally well to quantitative and qualitative research, interpretive validity has no real counterpart in quantitative-experimental validity typologies.

Thus, while the terms involved in descriptive validity can be either etic or emic, interpretive validity necessarily pertains to aspects of an account for which the terms are emic. This is because, while accounts of physical and behavioral phenomena can be constructed from a variety of perspectives, accounts of meaning must be based initially on the conceptual framework of the people whose meaning is in question. These terms are often derived to a substantial extent from the participants' own language. The terms are also necessarily, to use Geertz's phrase (1974), "experience-near"—based on the immediate concepts employed by participants (for example, "love"), rather than on theoretical abstractions (for example, "object cathexis").

Like descriptive validity, then, interpretive validity, while not atheoretical, refers to aspects of accounts for which the terms of the account are not themselves problematic. Interpretive accounts are grounded in the language of the people studied and rely as much as possible on their own words and concepts.[6] The issue, again, is not the appropriateness of these concepts for the account, but their accuracy as applied to the perspective of the individuals included in the account. For example, was the teacher, in yelling at the student for throwing the eraser, really "mad" at the student, or just trying to "get control" of the class? While the relevant consensus about the categories used in description rests in the research community, the relevant consensus for the terms used in interpretation rests to a substantial extent in the community studied.

Unlike descriptive validity, however, for interpretive validity there is no in-principle access to data that would unequivocally address threats to validity. Interpretive validity is inherently a matter of inference from the words and actions of participants in the situations studied. The development of accounts of these participants' meanings is usually based to a large extent on the participants' own accounts, but it is essential not to treat these latter accounts as incorrigible; participants may be unaware of their own feelings or views, may recall these inaccurately, and may consciously or unconsciously distort or conceal their views. Accounts of participants' meanings are never a matter of direct access, but are always *constructed* by the researcher(s) on the basis of participants' accounts and other evidence.[7]

The realist approach to validity that I am adopting here has been held by some interpretive researchers to be incompatible with a concern for interpretive understanding. For example, Lincoln has argued that "critical realism's assumption that there is a singular reality 'out there' ... ignores the issue of whether that reality is recognized or rejected by those who may be disadvantaged by that construction" (1990, p. 510).

This critique misses the point that the meanings and constructions of actors are part of the reality that an account must be tested against in order to be interpretively as well as descriptively valid. Social theorists generally agree that any valid account or explanation of a social situation must respect the perspectives of the actors in that situation, although it need not be centered on that perspective (Bohman, 1991; Harre, 1978; Menzel, 1978). My inclusion of interpretive validity in this typology is a recognition of this consensus: that a key part of the realm external to an account is the perspective of those actors whom the account is about (see House, 1991).

Interpretive validity does not apply only to the conscious concepts of participants; it can also pertain to the unconscious intentions, beliefs, concepts, and values of these participants, and to what Argyris and Schoen (1974) call "theory-in-use," as opposed to "espoused theory." However, this aspect of interpretive validity also raises another category of understanding and validity, which, following Kirk and Miller (1986), I will call "theoretical validity."

❖ THEORETICAL VALIDITY

The two previous types of understanding have a number of similarities. First, they depend on a consensus within the relevant community about how to apply the concepts and terms used in the account; any disagreements refer to their accuracy, not their meaning. Second, and closely connected to the first, the concepts and terms employed are "experience-near," in Geertz's sense (1974).

There are two major differences between theoretical understanding and the two types discussed previously. The first is the degree of abstraction of the account in question from the immediate physical and mental phenomena studied. The reason for calling this sort of understanding theoretical is that it goes beyond concrete description and interpretation and explicitly addresses the theoretical constructions that the researcher brings to, or develops during, the study.

This theory can refer to either physical events or mental constructions. It can also incorporate participants' concepts and theories, but its purpose goes beyond simply describing these participants' perspectives. This distinction comprises the second major difference between the theoretical validity of an account and the descriptive or interpretive validity of the same account: theoretical understanding refers to an account's function as an *explanation*, as well as a description or interpretation, of the phenomena.

Theoretical validity thus refers to an account's validity as a *theory* of some phenomenon. Any theory has two components: the concepts or categories that the theory employs, and the relationships that are thought to exist among these concepts. Corresponding to these two aspects of a theory are two aspects of theoretical validity: the validity of the concepts themselves as they are applied to the phenomena, and the validity of the postulated relationships among the concepts. The first refers to the validity of the blocks from which the researcher builds a model, as these are applied to the setting or phenomenon being studied; the second refers to the validity of the way the blocks are put together, as a theory of this setting or phenomenon.

For example, one could label the student's throwing of the eraser as an act of resistance, and connect this act to the repressive behavior or values of the teacher, the social structure of the school, and class relationships in U.S. society. The identification of the throwing as "resistance" constitutes the application of a theoretical construct to the descriptive and interpretive understanding of the action; the connection of this to other aspects of the participants, the school, or the community constitutes the postulation of theoretical relationships among these constructs.

The first of these aspects of theoretical validity closely matches what is generally known as construct validity, and is primarily what Kirk and Miller (1986) mean by theoretical validity. The second aspect includes, but is not limited to, what is commonly called internal or causal validity (Cook & Campbell, 1979); it corresponds to what Runciman calls "explanation" and in part to what Erickson calls "critical validity."[8] This second aspect is not limited to causal validity because theories or models can be developed for other things besides causal explanation—for example, for semantic relationships, narrative structure, and so on—that nevertheless go beyond description and interpretation. Theories can, and usually do, incorporate both descriptive and interpretive understanding, but in combining these they necessarily transcend either of them.

What counts as theoretical validity, rather than descriptive or interpretive validity, depends on whether there is consensus within the community concerned with the research about the terms used to characterize the phenomena. Issues of descriptive and interpretive validity focus on the accuracy of the application of these terms (Did the student really throw the eraser? Was the teacher really angry?) rather than their appropriateness (Does what the student did count as resistance?). Theoretical validity, in contrast, is concerned with problems that do not disappear with agreement on the "facts" of the situation; the issue is the legitimacy of the application of a given concept or theory to established facts, or indeed whether any agreement can be reached about what the facts are.

The distinction between descriptive or interpretive and theoretical validity is not an absolute, because (contrary to the assumptions of positivism) objective "sense data" that are independent of the researcher's perspective, purposes, and theoretical framework do not exist. My distinction between the two types is not based on any such assumption, but on the presence or absence of agreement within the community of inquirers about the descriptive or interpretive terms used. Any challenge to the meaning of the terms, or the appropriateness of their application to a given phenomenon, shifts the validity issue from descriptive or interpretive to theoretical.

These three types of understanding and validity are the ones most directly involved in assessing a qualitative account as it pertains to the actual situation on which the account is based. There are, however, two additional categories of validity issues that I want to raise. The first of these deals with the generalizability of an account, or what is often labeled external validity; the second pertains to the evaluative validity of an account.

❖ GENERALIZABILITY

Generalizability refers to the extent to which one can extend the account of a particular situation or population to other persons, times, or settings than those directly studied. This issue plays a different role in qualitative research than it does in quantitative and experimental research, because qualitative studies are usually not designed to allow systematic generalizations to some wider population. Generalization in qualitative research usually takes place through the development of a theory that not only makes sense of the particular persons or situations studied, but also shows how the same process, in different situations, can lead to different results (Becker, 1990, p. 240). Generalizability is normally based on the assumption that this theory may be useful in making sense of similar persons or situations, rather than on an explicit sampling process and the drawing of conclusions about a specified population through statistical inference (Yin, 1984).

This is not to argue that issues of sampling, representativeness, and generalizability are unimportant in qualitative research. They are crucial whenever one wants to draw inferences from the actual persons, events, or activities observed to other persons, events, or situations, or to these at other times than when the observation was done. (The particular problems of interviewing will be dealt with below.) Qualitative research almost always involves some of this sort of inference because it is impossible to observe everything, even in one small setting. The sort of sampling done in qualitative research is usually "purposeful" (Patton, 1990) or "theoretical" (Strauss, 1987) sampling, rather than random sampling or some other method of attaining statistical representativeness. The goal of the former types of sampling is twofold: to make sure one has adequately understood the variation in the phenomena of interest in the setting, and to test developing ideas about that setting by selecting phenomena that are crucial to the validity of those ideas.

In qualitative research, there are two aspects of generalizability: generalizing within the community, group, or institution studied to persons, events, and settings that were not directly observed or interviewed; and generalizing to other communities, groups, or institutions. I will refer to the former as internal generalizability, and to the latter as external generalizability. The distinction is analogous to Cook and Campbell's (1979) distinction in quasi-experimental research between statistical conclusion validity and external validity. This distinction is not clear-cut or absolute in qualitative research. A researcher studying a school, for example, can rarely visit every classroom, or even gain information about these classrooms by other means, and the issue of whether to consider the generalizability of the account for those unstudied classrooms internal or external is moot. However, it is important to be aware of the extent to which the times and places observed may differ from those that were not observed, either because of sampling or because of the effect of the observation itself.[9]

Internal generalizability in this sense is far more important for most qualitative researchers than is external generalizability because qualitative researchers rarely make explicit claims about the external generalizability of their accounts. Indeed, the value of a qualitative study may depend on its lack of external generalizability in a statistical sense; it may provide an account of a setting or population that is illuminating as an extreme case or "ideal type." Freidson, discussing his qualitative study of a medical group practice, notes that

> there is more to truth or validity than statistical representativeness. … In this study I am less concerned with describing the range of variation than I am with describing in the detail what survey questionnaire methods do not permit to be described—the assumptions, behavior, and attitudes of a very special set of physicians. They are interesting *because* they were special. (1975, pp. 272–273)

He argues that his study makes an important contribution to theory and policy precisely because this was a group for whom social controls on practice should have been most likely to be effective. The failure of such controls in this case not only elucidates a social process that is likely to exist in other groups, but also provides a more persuasive argument for the unworkability of such controls than would a study of a "representative" group.

Interviewing poses some special problems for internal generalizability because the researcher usually is in the presence of the person interviewed only briefly, and must necessarily draw inferences from what happened during that brief period to the rest of the informant's life, including his or her actions and perspectives. An account based on interviews may be descriptively, interpretively, and theoretically valid as an account of the person's actions and perspective in that interview, but may miss other aspects of the person's perspectives that were not expressed in the interview, and can easily lead to false inferences about his or her actions outside the interview situation. Thus, internal generalizability is a crucial issue in interpreting interviews, as is widely recognized, for example, by Dean and Whyte (1958) and Dexter (1970).[10] The interview is a social situation and inherently involves a relationship between the interviewer and the informant. Understanding the nature of that situation and relationship, how it affects what goes on in the interview, and how the informant's actions and views could differ in other situations is crucial to the validity of accounts based on interviews (Briggs, 1986; Mishler, 1986).

❖ EVALUATIVE VALIDITY

Beyond all of the validity issues discussed above are validity questions about such statements as, "The student was wrong to throw the eraser at the teacher," or, "The teacher was illegitimately failing to recognize minority students' perspectives." This aspect of validity differs from the types discussed previously in that it involves the application of an evaluative framework to the objects of study, rather than a descriptive, interpretive, or explanatory one. It corresponds to Runciman's "evaluation" as a category of understanding (1983), and is an important component of what Erickson (1989) terms "critical validity."

I have little to say about evaluative validity that has not been said more cogently by others. In raising it here, my purpose is twofold: to acknowledge evaluative validity as a legitimate category of understanding and validity in qualitative research, and to suggest how it relates to the other types of validity discussed. Like external generalizability, evaluative validity is not as central to qualitative research as are descriptive, interpretive, and theoretical validity: many researchers make no claim to evaluate the things they study. Furthermore, issues of evaluative understanding and evaluative validity in qualitative research do not seem to me to be intrinsically different from those in any other approach to research; debates about whether the student's throwing of the eraser was legitimate or justified do not depend on the methods used to ascertain that this happened or to decide what interpretive or theoretical sense to make of it, although they do depend on the particular description, interpretation, or theory one constructs. To raise questions about the evaluative framework implicit in an account, however, as many critical theorists do, *creates* issues of an account's evaluative validity, and no account is immune to such questions.

❖ IMPLICATIONS

I have presented a model of the types of validity that I believe are relevant to, and often implicit in, qualitative research. I have approached this task from a realist perspective, and have argued that this realist approach, which bases validity on the kinds of understanding we have of the phenomena we study, is more consistent and productive than prevailing positivist typologies based on research procedures. A realist view of validity both avoids the philosophical and practical difficulties associated with positivist approaches and seems to me to better represent what qualitative researchers actually do in assessing the validity of their accounts.

However, having presented this typology, I must add that validity categories are of much less direct use in qualitative research than they are (or are assumed to be) in quantitative and experimental research. In the latter, threats to validity are addressed in an anonymous, generic fashion by prior design features (such as randomization and controls) that can deal with both anticipated and unanticipated threats to validity. In qualitative research, however, such prior elimination of threats is less possible, both because qualitative research is more inductive and because it focuses primarily on understanding particulars rather than generalizing to universals (Erickson, 1986). Qualitative researchers deal primarily with specific threats to the validity of particular features of their accounts, and they generally address such threats by seeking evidence that would allow them to be ruled out. In doing this, they are using a logic similar to that of quasi-experimental researchers such as Cook and Campbell (1979).

This strategy of addressing particular threats to validity, or alternative hypotheses, *after* a tentative account has been developed, rather than by attempting to eliminate such threats through prior features of the research design, is in fact more fundamental to scientific method than is the latter approach (Campbell, 1988; Platt, 1964). This method is accepted by qualitative researchers from a wide range of philosophical positions (for example, Eisner, 1991; Hammersley & Atkinson, 1983; Miles & Huberman, 1984; Patton, 1990). Its application to causal inference has been labeled the "modus operandi" approach by Scriven (1974), but the method has received little formal development in the qualitative research literature, although it is implicit in many substantive qualitative studies.

Thus, researchers cannot use the typology presented here to eliminate, directly and mechanically, particular threats to the validity of their accounts. Qualitative researchers already have many methods for addressing validity threats, and, although there are ways that the state of the art could be improved (see Eisenhart & Howe, 1992; Miles & Huberman, 1984; Wolcott, 1990a), that is not my main goal here. Instead, I am trying to clarify the validity concepts that many qualitative researchers are using—explicitly or implicitly—in their work, to tie these concepts into a systematic model, and to reduce the discrepancy between qualitative researchers' "logic-in-use" and their "reconstructed logic" (Kaplan 1964, pp. 3–11)—a discrepancy that I think has caused both substantial misunderstanding of qualitative research and some shortcomings in its validation practices. I see this typology as being useful both as a checklist of the *kinds* of threats to validity that one needs to consider and as a framework for thinking about the nature of these threats and the possible ways that specific threats might be addressed.

I do not see the typological framework presented in this article as antithetical to the exemplar-based approach that Mishler has advocated. In fact, one of my main assumptions is that category-based and context-based approaches to qualitative research in general, and to validity in particular, are both legitimate, and that these are compatible and complementary, rather than competing, alternatives (Maxwell & Miller, n.d.). The ways in which these two approaches could be used in combination is a topic beyond the scope of this article, but I hope that the analysis I have presented is helpful in facilitating this rapprochement.

❖ NOTES

1. The difference between approaches to validity based on exemplars and those based on typologies can be seen as one example of the distinction between syntagmatic (contextualizing or contiguity-based) and paradigmatic (categorizing or similarity-based) strategies (Bruner, 1986; Jakobson, 1956; Maxwell & Miller, n.d.). It is understandable that Mishler prefers a syntagmatic model for validity, since his overall orientation to research is primarily syntagmatic rather than paradigmatic in its emphasis on contextual and narrative analysis rather than categorization and comparison (Mishler, 1986). My approach, in contrast, emphasizes the complementarity of syntagmatic and paradigmatic strategies.

2. The instrumentalist approach to validity is simply one instance of the positivist or logical empiricist program of substituting logical constructions, based on research operations and the sense data that they generate, for inferred (that is, theoretical) entities (see Hunt, 1991; Manicas, 1987, p. 271; Phillips, 1990). As Norris (1983) points out, most approaches to construct validation have combined positivist and realist assumptions without recognizing the problems that this inconsistency creates. One influential validity typology that

is predominantly (and explicitly) realist is that of Cook and Campbell (1979), but even this has some residual positivist features (Maxwell, 1990a).

3. For a more general critique of objectivist views, see Bernstein (1983), Bohman (1991), Hammersley and Atkinson (1983), and Lakoff (1987).

4. To apply the distinction introduced previously, between paradigmatic (similarity-based) and syntagmatic (contiguity-based) relationships, I am conceptualizing the relationship between an account and its object as based not on similarity or resemblance (the traditional correspondence theory), but on contiguity—on the implications and consequences of adopting and acting on a particular account. This approach obviously resembles "pragmatist" approaches in philosophy (Kaplan, 1964, pp. 42–46; Rorty, 1979), and is analogous to Helmholtz's (1971) view of experience as a sign rather than an image or reflection of the world (Manicas, 1987, pp. 176ff.); however, a discussion of these connections is beyond the scope of this article. I have attempted to explore some of the implications of such a "non-reflectionist" (McKinley, 1971) view elsewhere (Maxwell, 1979, 1986).

5. As Eisner (1991, p. 35) notes, the term "interpretive" has two meanings in qualitative research. One is the meaning I am adopting here; the other refers to studies that attempt to explain, as well as describe, the things that they study. The latter use is similar to that of Merriam (1988, pp. 27–28) and Patton (1990, p. 423), who use "descriptive" for studies that do not attempt to develop or apply explicit theory and reserve "interpretive" for studies that generate theory or interpret the data from some theoretical perspective. This second use of "interpretive" corresponds to the type of understanding that I term "theoretical." Kaplan's distinction between "semantic explanation," or interpretation, and "scientific explanation" is similar in some ways to my distinction between interpretation and theory, but my use of "theory" includes semantic as well as explicitly explanatory theories.

My use of "interpretation" corresponds, confusingly, to what Runciman (1983) calls "description." The latter term may be related to Geertz's (1973) phrase "thick description," which has been widely employed in discussions of interpretive research. Thick description, for Geertz, is *meaningful* description—that is, the description embedded in the cultural framework of the actors; the term does not refer to the richness or detail of the account. This point is often misunderstood, in part because Geertz uses the phrase precisely to avoid making the distinction between descriptive and interpretive understanding that I have drawn here: between physical/behavioral description, on the one hand, and inference to meaning as a mental phenomenon on the other. Thus, "thick description" pertains to interpretive as well as to descriptive understanding, as I have defined these terms.

It is ironic that Geertz adopted this term, and its associated philosophical argument, as a characterization of interpretive research, because Gilbert Ryle, who coined the term in his work *The Concept of Mind* (1949), used it as part of an explicit attempt to eliminate mental concepts (what he referred to as "the ghost in the machine") from philosophy and to replace them with dispositional statements referring to an individual's propensity to behave in particular ways. This approach, which came to be known as "logical behaviorism," was a classically positivist strategy of replacing theoretical entities with logical constructions based on observables. (As noted above, this strategy was the Achilles' heel of positivism.)

This positivist view that mental constructs are theoretical abstractions that ultimately *refer to* behavior and behavioral dispositions is quite different from the realist position I take here, that such mental constructs refer to unobservable but real entities whose existence is *inferred* from observations of behavior (see Manicas, 1987).

Within the category of interpretive understanding, it is possible to make a distinction, similar to that between primary and secondary descriptive understanding, between the *communicative* meaning of speech or actions (which is nonetheless always meaning for some actor or interpreter) and the actor's subjective intentions, beliefs, values, and perspective (see Gellner, 1962; Hannerz, 1992, pp. 3–4; Keesing, 1987, pp. 174–175; Ricoeur, 1981). Both of these types of understanding are ultimately based on inferences from the descriptive evidence, but the validity of inferences to the actor's subjective states depends on the validity of the researcher's account of the meaning of the actor's words and actions. My own alternative to Geertz's attempt to get meaning out of the "secret grotto in the skull" and into the public world rests on this distinction between meaning as a property of discourse, on the one hand, and the actor's subjective states, on the other.

6. In providing a valid account of individuals who lack such an accessible language, such as preverbal children, interpretive validity merges with the following category, theoretical validity.

7. I cannot deal systematically here with one challenge to this approach embodied in the poststructuralist slogan that "there is nothing outside the text." I agree with Manicas that this view represents not just a repudiation of realist conceptions of validity, but "an epistemological nihilism in which truth is an illusion" (1987, p. 269). I would also argue that, ironically, this approach exemplifies the same goal of eliminating inferred entities that characterized positivism and is vulnerable to the same critiques that led to positivism's demise.

I want to emphasize that my distinction between descriptive and interpretive validity is not between the "real world" and actors' constructions of that world. First, both descriptive and interpretive understanding pertain to the researcher's *accounts* of the world—that is, to accounts of its physical/behavioral and mental aspects or components, respectively. Both types of accounts are the researcher's constructions. Second, the physical and mental components refer to entities that are equally real, rather than one being a reflection of the other. (For a more detailed analysis of the relationship between the mental and physical frameworks, see Maxwell, 1986.)

8. Runciman, however, places explanation *before* interpretation (his "description") in his typology of kinds of understanding, and argues more generally that "there is no special problem of explanation in the human sciences, but only a special problem of description" (1983, p. 1). This is my main disagreement with Runciman's account of the different types of understanding involved in social theory. In attempting to justify his claim that explanation can be based solely on reportage, without requiring what he calls descriptive understanding (what I call "interpretation"), Runciman is forced to include a substantial amount of interpretation in reportage, such as inferences from behavior to the mental states of actors. This view, that valid explanations of behavior can generally be formulated prior to, and independently of, an adequate understanding of the perspective of the actors, has been criticized by Bohman (1991), MacIntyre (1967), and Menzel (1978).

My distinction between interpretation and explanation is quite different from that of Ricoeur (1981), who contrasts the explanation of a text in terms of its internal structure (an approach based on linguistics rather than the natural sciences) with its interpretation in terms of its connection to the world outside of the text (including the reader). I cannot deal here with this alternative, nor with the complex and much-debated issue of what constitutes an explanation (see Bohman, 1991; Kitcher & Salmon, 1989; Salmon, 1984). This current debate over explanation is one of the reasons I have chosen to call this type of understanding "theoretical" rather than "explanatory."

9. The difference between secondary descriptive validity and internal generalizability deserves clarification, because the two seem superficially similar. Both refer to the extension of one's account to things that were not directly observed but that remain within the setting or group studied. The difference between the two is based on the kind of relationship postulated between the immediate data or account and the claim whose validity is in question. In internal (as well as external) generalizability, the claim is that those things not directly observed are *similar* to those described in the account; that the account can be *generalized* to some wider context. For secondary descriptive validity, the issue is not similarity, but the validity of the chain of *inference* from one's primary data to things that were not directly observed—for example, whether one can infer, from an eraser on the floor, a chalk mark on the wall above it, and a student's sullen silence about what had happened when the researcher briefly left the room, that an eraser was thrown. There is no assumption that the primary data resemble or generalize to the secondary conclusion in any way, only that the inferential connection between the two is valid. In addition, internal (and external) generalizability can pertain to interpretive, theoretical, or evaluative conclusions, as well as descriptive ones.

10. I have indicated earlier my disagreement with the approach that deals with this problem by denying it—that is, by treating the interview (or even the interview transcript) as a "text" and asserting that it is illegitimate to attempt to make inferences to some "real" actor.

❖ REFERENCES

Argyris, C., & Schoen, D. A. (1974). *Theory in practice: Increasing professional effectiveness*. San Francisco: Jossey-Bass.

Becker, H. S. (1970). Problems of inference and proof in participant observation. In H. S. Becker (Ed.), *Sociological work: Method and substance* (pp. 25–38). New Brunswick, NJ: Transaction Books.

Becker, H. S. (1990). Generalizing from case studies. In E. W. Eisner & A. Peshkin (Eds.), *Qualitative research in education: The continuing debate* (pp. 233–242). New York: Teachers College Press.

Bernstein, R. J. (1983). *Beyond objectivism and relativism*. Philadelphia: University of Pennsylvania Press.

Bernstein, R. J. (1991). *The new constellation: The ethical-political horizons of modernity/post-modernity*. Cambridge, MA: MIT Press.

Bhaskar, R. (1989). *Reclaiming reality*. London: Verso.

Bohman, J. (1991). *New philosophy of social science*. Cambridge, MA: MIT Press.

Bosk, C. (1979). *Forgive and remember: Managing medical failure.* Chicago: University of Chicago Press.

Briggs, C. (1986). *Learning how to ask: A sociolinguistic appraisal of the role of the interview in social science research.* Cambridge, Eng.: Cambridge University Press.

Brinberg, D., & McGrath, J. E. (1985). *Validity and the research process.* Beverly Hills, CA: Sage.

Bruner, J. (1986). Two modes of thought. In J. Bruner (Ed.), *Actual minds, possible worlds* (pp. 11–43). Cambridge, MA: Harvard University Press.

Campbell, D. T. (1975). "Degrees of freedom" and the case study. *Comparative Political Studies, 8*(2), 178–193. (Reprinted in Campbell, 1988)

Campbell, D. T. (1988). *Methodology and epistemology for social science: Selected papers.* Chicago: University of Chicago Press.

Campbell, D. T., & Stanley, J. C. (1963). Experimental and quasi-experimental designs for research on teaching. In N. L. Gage (Ed.), *Handbook of research on teaching* (pp. 171–246). Chicago: Rand McNally.

Cook, T. D., & Campbell, D. T. (1979). *Quasi-experimentation: Design and analysis issues for field settings.* Boston: Houghton Mifflin.

Dean, J., & Whyte, W. F. (1958). How do you know if the informant is telling the truth? *Human Organization, 17*(2), 34–38. (Reprinted in L. A. Dexter, 1970, pp. 119–131)

Dexter, L. A. (1970). *Elite and specialized interviewing.* Evanston, IL: Northwestern University Press.

Eisenhart, M., & Howe, K. (1992). Validity in educational research In M. D. LeCompte, W. L. Millroy, & J. Preissle (Eds.), *The handbook of qualitative research in education* (pp. 643–680). San Diego: Academic Press.

Eisner, E. W. (1991). *The enlightened eye: Qualitative inquiry and the enhancement of educational practice.* New York: Macmillan.

Erickson, F. (1986). Qualitative methods in research on teaching. In M. C. Wittrock (Ed.), *Handbook of research on teaching* (3rd ed.). New York: Macmillan.

Erickson, F. (1989, March). *The meaning of validity in qualitative research.* Unpublished paper presented at the annual meeting of the American Educational Research Association, San Francisco.

Freidson, E. (1975). *Doctoring together: A study of professional social control.* Chicago: University of Chicago Press.

Geertz, C. (1973). Thick description: Toward an interpretive theory of culture. In C. Geertz, *The interpretation of cultures* (pp. 3–30). New York: Basic Books.

Geertz, C. (1974). "From the native's point of view": On the nature of anthropological understanding. *Bulletin of the American Academy of Arts and Sciences, 28*(1), 26–45. (Reprinted in K.H. Basso & H.A. Selby (Eds.) (1976), *Meaning in anthropology,* pp. 221–237. Albuquerque: University of New Mexico Press)

Gellner, E. (1962). Concepts and society. *Transactions of the Fifth World Congress of Sociology. Vol. 1* (pp. 153–183). Louvain, Belg.: International Sociological Association. (Reprinted in B. R. Wilson, Ed., 1970, *Rationality,* pp. 18–49. London: Harper & Row)

Goetz, J. P., & LeCompte, M. D. (1984). *Ethnography and qualitative design in educational research.* San Diego: Academic Press.

Guba, E. G., & Lincoln, Y. S. (1989). *Fourth generation evaluation.* Newbury Park, CA: Sage.

Hammersley, M. (1992). *What's wrong with ethnography?* London: Routledge.

Hammersley, M., & Atkinson, P. (1983). *Ethnography: Principles in practice.* London: Tavistock.

Hannerz, U. (1992). *Cultural complexity: Studies in the social organization of meaning.* New York: Columbia University Press.

Harre, R. (1978). Accounts, actions, and meanings—The practice of participatory psychology. In M. Brenner, P. Marsh, & M. Brenner (Eds.), *The social contexts of method.* New York: St. Martin's Press.

Headland, T. N., Pike, K. L., & Harris, M. (Eds.). (1990). *Emics and etics: The insider/outsider debate.* Newbury Park, CA: Sage.

Helmholtz, H. (1971). *Selected writings* (R. Kahn, Ed.). Middletown, CT: Wesleyan University Press.

Hirschi, T., & Selvin, H. C. (1967). *Principles of survey analysis.* New York: Free Press.

House, E. (1991). Realism in research. *Educational Researcher, 20*(6), 2–9.

Hunt, S. D. (1991). Positivism and paradigm dominance in consumer research: Toward critical pluralism and rapprochement. *Journal of Consumer Research, 18,* 32–44.

Jakobson, R. (1956). Two aspects of language and two types of aphasic disturbance. In R. Jakobson & M. Halle (Eds.), *Fundamentals of language* (pp. 55–82). The Hague: Mouton. (Reprinted in R. Jakobson, 1987, *Language in literature.* Cambridge, MA: Harvard University Press)

Kaplan, A. (1964). *The conduct of inquiry.* San Francisco: Chandler.

Keesing, R. (1987). Anthropology as interpretive quest. *Current Anthropology, 28,* 161–176.

Kirk, J., & Miller, M. L. (1986). *Reliability and validity in qualitative research.* Beverly Hills, CA: Sage.

Kitcher, P., & Salmon, W. C. (Eds.). (1989). *Scientific explanation.* Minneapolis: University of Minnesota Press.

Kuhn, T. S. (1970). *The structure of scientific revolutions* (2nd ed.). Chicago: University of Chicago Press.

Kvale, S. (1989). Introduction. In S. Kvale (Ed.), *Issues of validity in qualitative research.* Lund, Sweden: Studentlitteratur.

Lakoff, G. (1987). *Women, fire, and dangerous things: What categories reveal about the mind.* Chicago: University of Chicago Press.

Lincoln, Y. S. (1990). Campbell's retrospective and a constructivist's perspective. *Harvard Educational Review, 60,* 501–540.

MacIntyre, A. (1967). The idea of a social science. *Aristotelian Society Supplement, 41,* 93–114.

Manicas, P. T. (1987). *A history and philosophy of the social sciences.* Oxford, Eng.: Blackwell.

Maxwell, J. A. (1979). The evolution of Plains Indian kin terminologies: A nonreflectionist account. *Plains Anthropologist, 23*(79), 13–29.

Maxwell, J. A. (1986). *The conceptualization of kinship in an Inuit community: A cultural account.* Unpublished doctoral dissertation, University of Chicago.

Maxwell, J. A. (1990a). Up from positivism. *Harvard Educational Review, 60,* 497–501.

Maxwell, J. A. (1990b). Response to "Campbell's retrospective and a constructivist's perspective." *Harvard Educational Review, 60,* 504–508.

Maxwell, J. A., & Miller, B. A. (n.d.). *Two aspects of thought and two components of qualitative data analysis.* Unpublished manuscript.

McKinley, R. (1971). A critique of the reflectionist theory of kinship terminology: The Crow/Omaha case. *Man, 6,* 228–247.

Menzel, H. (1978). Meaning: Who needs it? In M. Brenner, P. Marsh, & M. Brenner (Eds.), *The social contexts of method* (pp. 140–171). New York: St. Martin's Press.

Merriam, S. (1988). *Case study research in education: A qualitative approach.* San Francisco: Jossey-Bass.

Miles, M. B., & Huberman, A. M. (1984). *Qualitative data analysis: A sourcebook of new methods.* Beverly Hills, CA: Sage.

Mishler, E. G. (1986). *Research interviewing: Context and narrative.* Cambridge, MA: Harvard University Press.

Mishler, E. G. (1990). Validation in inquiry-guided research: The role of exemplars in narrative studies. *Harvard Educational Review, 60,* 415–442.

Morgan, L. H. (1871). Systems of consanguinity and affinity of the human family. *Smithsonian Contributions to Knowledge. Vol. 17.* Washington, DC: Smithsonian Institution.

Norris, S. P. (1983). The inconsistencies at the foundation of construct validation theory. In E. R. House (Ed.), *Philosophy of evaluation* (pp. 53–74). San Francisco: Jossey-Bass.

Patton, M. Q. (1990). *Qualitative evaluation and research methods* (2nd ed.). Newbury Park, CA: Sage.

Phillips, D. C. (1987). Validity in qualitative research: Why the worry about warrant will not wane. *Education and Urban Society, 20,* 9–24.

Phillips, D. C. (1990). Positivistic science: Myths and realities. In E. G. Guba (Ed.), *The paradigm dialog* (pp. 31–45). Newbury Park, CA: Sage.

Pitman, M. A., & Maxwell, J. A. (1992). Qualitative approaches to evaluation. In M. D. LeCompte, W. L. Millroy, & J. Preissle (Eds.), *The handbook of qualitative research in education* (pp. 729–770). San Diego: Academic Press.

Platt, J. R. (1964). Strong inference. *Science, 146,* 347–353.

Putnam, H. (1990). Realism with a human face. In H. Putnam, *Realism with a human face* (pp. 3–29). Cambridge, MA: Harvard University Press.

Ricoeur, P. (1981). *Hermeneutics and the human sciences* (J. B. Thompson, Ed. and Trans.). Cambridge, Eng.: Cambridge University Press.

Rorty, R. (1979). *Philosophy and the mirror of nature.* Princeton, NJ: Princeton University Press.

Runciman, W. G. (1983). *A treatise on social theory. Vol. 1. The methodology of social theory.* Cambridge, Eng.: Cambridge University Press.

Ryle, G. (1949). *The concept of mind.* London: Hutchinson.

Salmon, W. C. (1984). *Scientific explanation and the causal structure of the world.* Princeton, NJ: Princeton University Press.

Salner, M. (1989). Validity in human science research. In S. Kvale (Ed.), *Issues of validity in qualitative research* (pp. 47–71). Lund, Sweden: Studentlitteratur.

Scriven, M. (1974). Maximizing the power of causal investigations: The modus operandi method. In W. J. Popham (Ed.), *Evaluation in education—Current applications* (pp. 68–84). Berkeley, CA: McCutchan. (Reprinted in G. V. Glass, Ed., 1976, *Evaluation Studies Review Annual, 1,* pp. 101–118. Beverly Hills, CA: Sage)

Strauss, A. (1987). *Qualitative analysis for social scientists.* Cambridge, Eng.: Cambridge University Press.

Trautmann, T. R. (1987). *Lewis Henry Morgan and the invention of kinship.* Berkeley: University of California Press.

Winch, P. (1958). *The idea of a social science and its relation to philosophy.* London: Routledge & Kegan Paul.

Wolcott, H. F. (1990a). On seeking—and rejecting—validity in qualitative research. In E. W. Eisner & A. Peshkin (Eds.), *Qualitative inquiry in education: The continuing debate* (pp. 121–152). New York: Teachers College Press.

Wolcott, H. F. (1990b). *Writing up qualitative research.* Newbury Park, CA: Sage.

Yin, R. K. (1984). *Case study research: Design and methods.* Beverly Hills, CA: Sage.

3

Ethnography and Realism

Martyn Hammersley

In this chapter I want to discuss some of the philosophical underpinnings of ethnographic research. For some ethnographers such a discussion may seem irrelevant at best. There is a strong anti-philosophical strand in ethnographic thinking that places value on the practice and products of research and has little patience with or interest in discussions *about* research.[1] I have some sympathy with this. Philosophical discussion and debate can easily become a distraction; a swapping of one set of problems for another, probably even less tractable, set. Certainly, I do not believe that philosophy is foundational, in the sense that the problems in that realm can or should be resolved before we engage in social research. Indeed, in my view empirical research, accompanied by reflection on its practice and products, has much to contribute to philosophy. But there is no escape from philosophical assumptions for researchers. Whether we like it or not, and whether we are aware of them or not, we cannot avoid such assumptions.

Reprinted from Martyn Hammersley, "Ethnography and Realism," in *What's Wrong With Ethnography?* (pp. 43–56). London: Routledge. Copyright 1992 by Taylor & Francis Books Ltd. Reprinted by permission.

And, sometimes, the assumptions that we make lead us into error. I believe that this is the case with some of the epistemological ideas current amongst ethnographers. These ideas are my concern in this chapter.

At the centre of these problems is the doctrine of realism, by which I mean the idea that there is a reality independent of the researcher whose nature can be known, and that the aim of research is to produce accounts that correspond to that reality. There can be little doubt about the widespread acceptance of this view. It is a philosophical doctrine on which much ethnography is founded. One of the most common rationales for the adoption of an ethnographic approach is that by entering into close and relatively long-term contact with people in their everyday lives we can come to understand their beliefs and behaviour more accurately, in a way that would not be possible by means of any other approach. This was the reason for the shift within social and cultural anthropology in the late nineteenth and early twentieth centuries from relying on the reports of travellers and missionaries to first-hand fieldwork by anthropologists themselves. Similarly, within sociology, the same idea motivated Robert Park's advocacy of case-study research in Chicago in the 1920s. One of the most developed versions of the argument is to be found in the methodological writings of the Chicago sociologist Herbert Blumer. He criticises experimental and survey research for failing to grasp the distinctive nature of human social life, and the key feature of the naturalistic research strategy that he recommends is 'getting close' to naturally occurring social phenomena. The metaphors he uses to describe this approach—notably, 'lifting the veils' and 'digging deeper'—illustrate the realist assumptions that underlie his views (Hammersley 1989: 127–8). In much the same way, David Matza advocates 'naturalism', arguing that its core is a commitment to capture the nature of social phenomena in their own terms. And today this idea is found in explicit form in many introductions to ethnographic method (Lofland 1972; Schatzman and Strauss 1973; Hammersley and Atkinson 1983). From this point of view the goal of ethnographic research is to discover and represent faithfully the true nature of social phenomena. And the superiority of ethnography is based precisely on the grounds that it is able to get closer to social reality than other methods.

Despite this commitment to realism, however, there is an important strand in ethnography that pushes in a contrary direction. Central to the way in which ethnographers think about human social action is the idea that people *construct* the social world, both through their interpretations of it and through the actions based on those interpretations. Again, Blumer is an influential figure here; though the same idea can be found in many other sources.[2] Blumer argues at one point that even people in geographical proximity to one another may live in different 'social worlds' (Blumer 1969: 11). Furthermore, the implication seems to be that these worlds are incommensurable, so that one cannot be treated as superior to another (and certainly not in the sense of being a truer representation of reality because these worlds *constitute* reality for the people concerned). This same idea has long been central to social and cultural anthropology, with its attempts to understand alien belief systems 'from inside', rather than judging them from a Western, scientific point of view.[3]

This constructivism is quite compatible with realism so long as it is not applied to ethnographic research itself. It can be taken simply to require ethnographers to seek to understand (rather than judge) other people's beliefs, and to document the multiple perspectives to be found within and between societies. But we must ask: why should ethnographers be treated in a different way to others? To do so implies that they are outside of society, and this is surely unacceptable. Yet, once we treat ethnographic research as itself a social activity and seek to apply the constructivist approach to it, the question of the epistemological status of ethnographic findings is immediately raised. What may seem to follow is that in their work ethnographers create a social world (or worlds), rather than merely representing some independent reality (more or less accurately). And, it may be concluded, this world is no more nor less true than others; for instance than the perceptions and interpretations of the people studied. In this way, ethnographic constructivism seems to result in a relativism that is in conflict with ethnography's commitment to realism.

Faced with this apparent contradiction within ethnography, there are two obvious candidate solutions: to apply either realism or relativism consistently across the board, to both ethnographic method and to the social life that is studied. As I shall try to show, however, neither of these strategies is satisfactory.

If we apply ethnographic realism to our understanding of the people studied as well as to the research process, this implies an approach that is at odds with what is characteristic of ethnography. It means interpreting people's beliefs as the product *either* of contact with reality *or* of cultural bias. This abandons what is in my view one of the most valuable features of ethnography: its commitment to seeking to *understand* the perspectives of others, rather than simply judging them as true or false. It also involves the adoption of an asymmetrical approach to explaining beliefs, so that we appeal to different explanatory factors, depending on whether we take the beliefs to be valid or invalid. Those that are true are explained as products of the impact of reality, while those that are false are explained as the result of causal (probably cultural) factors producing error. There are good reasons to avoid this approach. One is that it is implausible, since it is clear that true conclusions can be reached on the basis of false premises; and even vice versa if there are implicit assumptions that are false. And, given that we can have no direct contact with reality, beliefs can never be a simple product of such contact. Cultural assumptions and social interests are always involved in perception and cognition, and they may mislead us or they may lead us towards the truth (or more likely they may do both at the same time, in different respects). Given this, in my view there should be no difference between the mode of explanation we employ to deal with what we take to be true beliefs (or rational actions) and those we believe to be false (or irrational). Another reason why the asymmetrical approach is counterproductive is that we can never know for sure whether beliefs are true or false. Hence, we can never be certain which of the two explanatory schemes ought to be applied in any particular case. As a result, what we treat as a sound explanation at one point in time may later need to be abandoned in favour of a different explanation, not because we have found out anything new about the production or functioning of the belief itself, but simply because our assessment of its validity has changed.[4]

The alternative strategy for solving the conflict between realism and relativism within ethnography is to apply relativism to the research process. This has been more popular among ethnographers than the first strategy, especially in recent times. And this reflects, in part, the influence of a variety of trends in philosophical ideas. In the 1960s and 1970s the impact of phenomenology often encouraged relativism.[5] What was taken from Husserl and other phenomenologists was primarily the idea that our understanding of the world is constructed on the basis of assumptions, those assumptions being interpreted not as universal givens (in the manner of Husserl), but as culturally relative. Particularly influential here was Schutz's discussion of multiple realities; an idea derived from William James rather than from Husserl. While Schutz specified these as the worlds of everyday life, dreams, science and religion, his discussion has sometimes been interpreted as predicating multiple realities constituted by different cultures; and indeed this is compatible with some of what he says, and certainly with James's treatment of the idea (Schutz and Luckmann 1974: 22–3; Berger and Luckmann 1966).

Similar relativistic conclusions have been drawn from the later Wittgenstein's view that our language sets the limits of our world, and his discussions of forms of life and language games. Particularly influential here was Winch's application of these ideas to the understanding of other cultures. Winch argues that we can understand the beliefs and actions of people in a society very different from our own, for example those surrounding Zande magic, only by seeing them in the context of the cultural rules characteristic of that society. Furthermore, he claims that we cannot judge those beliefs without presupposing our own mode of thinking, the validity of whose assumptions and criteria can no more be established independently of our culture than can those of the Azande (Winch 1958 and 1964). In a rather similar manner to Schutz, Winch treats science and religion as different cultural worlds.

Both these philosophical traditions had an impact on ethnography during the 1960s and 1970s. Often, their influence was diffuse, blending with constructivist and relativist thinking generated within it. In the case of ethnographers influenced by ethnomethodology, though, their impact was more focused; and it led to distinctive forms of ethnographic work.[6]

Running alongside these developments, and having a similar effect, was the emergence of revisionist ideas in the philosophy of science. Up until the early 1950s there was a substantial consensus among Anglo-American philosophers of science that the distinguishing feature of science was that the knowledge it produced was based on observation and logic. However, at that time, this 'received view' came under increasing criticism, to the point where there was wide recognition that it could not be sustained (Suppe 1974). A variety of alternative views were developed, though none has formed a new consensus. Much the most influential product of this debate was Thomas Kuhn's book *The Structure of Scientific Revolutions* (Kuhn 1962). Kuhn argued that we cannot see the history of science as the cumulative development of more accurate and precise knowledge about the physical world.

Rather, what we find in each field is a sequence of periods in which research is dominated by a particular paradigm, consisting of assumptions about the phenomena investigated and how they are to be studied and understood, these being embodied in investigations treated by scientists as exemplary. These periods of paradigmatic consensus are punctuated by what Kuhn calls 'scientific revolutions', in which one paradigm is gradually abandoned and a new one takes its place. Kuhn argues that the replacement of one paradigm by another is not, and cannot be, based entirely on a rational appraisal of each paradigm in terms of the evidence for and against it. This is because what counts as evidence, and its significance, are determined by the paradigms themselves; so that scientists operating in terms of different paradigms effectively see the world in different ways. There has been much debate about whether Kuhn's views are relativist, and Kuhn has sought to clarify this matter himself (Kuhn 1970, appendix). However, there is no doubt that his views have been interpreted in relativistic terms by many social scientists, including ethnographers.

These developments in the philosophy of science also stimulated changes within Anglo-American philosophy more generally, and in recent years there has been intense debate over realism. Here anti-realists have drawn both on resources present within the Anglo-American tradition, such as the early phenomenalism of the logical positivists and the later work of Quine, as well as on Dewey's pragmatism and continental European ideas (especially hermeneutics and post-structuralism). This anti-realist renaissance has also recently begun to have an impact on ethnography.[7]

The consequence of all these influences has been to encourage the application of a constructivist perspective to the research process itself; and thereby to undercut the realist rationale for ethnography, with its associated claim to objective description. Instead, it has been concluded by some ethnographers, often more informally than formally, that their accounts are simply one version of the world amongst others. This view is becoming increasingly popular, for example with ethnography being presented as a research paradigm that is incommensurable with others (Smith and Heshusius 1986; Smith 1989), or ethnographic accounts being treated as *creating* cultural realities through the rhetorical devices they employ (Clifford and Marcus 1986; Tyler 1985). Here, any vestige of ethnography as representation of an independent reality is abandoned. Thus, Tyler (1986: 138) suggests that 'no object of any kind precedes and constrains the ethnography. It creates its own objects in its unfolding and the reader supplies the rest'. Without the ethnographer there is 'only a disconnected array of chance happenings'. This has led some to argue for ethnographic texts to be multi-vocal or dialogical, with the voice of the ethnographer playing only an equal, or perhaps even a subordinate, role to those of the people studied. Yet others have stressed the necessarily rhetorical character of ethnographic accounts and have advocated modernist and post-modernist textual experiments.[8]

In my view, however, applying relativism to ethnographic method is no less problematic than extending the realism assumed in much ethnographic methodology to our understanding of social life. The problems of relativism are well known. Central is the old question of what status we are to give to the claim that all knowledge is culturally relative. If it is true, then it applies to itself; and therefore it is only true relative to a particular culture or framework, and may be false from the perspective of other cultures or frameworks. Moreover, how are we to identify cultures or paradigms in a way that does not result in their proliferation, with people perhaps drawing cultural boundaries simply to protect the validity of their beliefs? In fact, any claims about the nature and boundaries of particular cultures would themselves presumably have to be treated as relative. This leaves us abandoned in circularity (Hammersley 1991b).

Over and above the self-refuting character of relativism it is also worth pointing out its practical implications for ethnography. If it is true that what ethnographers produce is simply one version of the world, true (at best) only in its own terms, what value can it have? And there is no reason to suppose that ethnographers produce just one version of the world. Given that they differ among themselves in cultural assumptions, we must surely conclude that their accounts are to be viewed as creating multiple, incommensurable worlds on the basis of the same or similar research experience. In the words of one of the advocates of anti-realism, we may have to conclude that 'there are as many realities as there are persons' (Smith 1984: 386). If this is so, what is the point in spawning yet more versions of 'reality', especially given the relative costs of ethnography compared with, say, armchair reflection? And why should some 'realities' be published and discussed at the expense of others? Of course, in place of the claim to provide true representations of the world we might appeal to the idea that our accounts, while not true, are useful in some way; for example, in providing instructive ideas or even entertainment. But do not etiquette books, books counselling how to make friends and influence people, political tracts, novels, plays, films, as well as newspaper articles and television programmes fulfil these functions? What need is there for ethnography given all this? The practical implications of relativism for ethnography are worth reflection.

It seems to me, then, that we can resolve the ambivalence towards realism that is built into ethnography neither by extending ethnographic realism to our theorising about human social life, nor by applying relativism to ethnographic method. In what direction does a solution lie, then? The first step, I think, is to recognise that the realism often built into ethnographic methodology is of a relatively naïve or crude kind. Effectively, it assumes not only that the phenomena we study are independent of us, but that we can have direct contact with them, contact which provides knowledge whose validity is certain.[9] In practice, most ethnographers probably assume a weaker version than this: that the closer we can get to reality the more likely it is that our conclusions will be true. But the implication is the same: that if we could only get rid of the barriers lying between us and reality, most obviously our cultural preconceptions, we would be able to see reality itself. Once these barriers have been overcome, once the veil has been lifted, once we have dug below the surface impressions, reality itself will be revealed. Such a view is clearly indefensible. It assumes that there is some foundation of direct knowledge to which we can get access. But what form could that foundation take? All perception and observation are assumption-laden. And even if there were such a foundation, there is no means by which we could logically induce knowledge from our observations in such a fashion that its validity would be guaranteed.

The next step in the argument is to recognise that relativism is not the only alternative to naïve realism. There is a great danger of backing ourselves into a corner by deploying a dichotomy which obscures the wide range of epistemological positions available. We can maintain belief in the existence of phenomena independent of our claims about them, and in their knowability, without assuming that we can have unmediated contact with them and therefore that we can know with certainty whether our knowledge of them is valid or invalid. The most promising strategy for resolving the problem, in my view, then, is to adopt a more subtle form of realism. Let me summarise the key elements of such a view.

1. The definition of 'knowledge' as beliefs whose validity is known with certainty is misconceived. On this definition there can be no knowledge, since we can never be absolutely sure about the validity of any claims; we could always be wrong. In my view, we should instead define knowledge as beliefs about whose validity we are reasonably confident. While we can never be absolutely certain about the validity of any knowledge claim, and while we may sometimes be faced with a choice between contradictory claims that are equally uncertain in validity, often we *can* be reasonably confident about the relative chances of validity of competing claims. Assessment of claims must be based on judgements about plausibility and credibility: on the compatibility of the claim, or the evidence for it, with the assumptions about the world that we currently take to be beyond reasonable doubt; and/or on the likelihood of error, given the conditions in which the claim was made.

2. There are phenomena independent of our claims about them which those claims may represent more or less accurately. And true knowledge is true by virtue of the fact that it corresponds to the phenomena it is intended to represent (though, as I indicated, we can never be *certain* that any knowledge claim is true). This assumption is clearly an essential element of any realism. However, we must consider the issue of what the term 'independence' means in this basic tenet of realism. This is complex. In one sense we are all part of reality and from that point of view cannot be independent of it. The same is true of any knowledge claims we make. However, what I mean by 'independence' here is simply that our making of a claim does not itself change relevant aspects of reality in such a way as to make the claim true (or false). And it seems to me that most social science accounts are neither self-fulfilling nor self-refuting. While some predictions may become self-fulfilling, even here the relationship is not entirely determinate. Whether a prediction is fulfilled as a result of its being made public always depends on other conditions: on whether it is believed and on whether other factors intervene, for example. And I suspect that most social research findings have (at best, or worst)

only an extremely weak influence on what they predict or describe. Other powerful factors are always involved. In this sense, then, for the most part reality is independent of the claims that social researchers make about it.

3. The aim of social research is to represent reality, but this is not to say that its function is to *reproduce* it (that is, to represent it 'in its own terms'). Rather, representation must always be from some point of view which makes some features of the phenomena represented relevant and others irrelevant. Thus, there can be multiple, non-contradictory and valid descriptions and explanations of the same phenomenon.[10]

This subtle realism retains from naïve realism the idea that research investigates independent, knowable phenomena. But it breaks with it in denying that we have direct access to those phenomena, in accepting that we must always rely on cultural assumptions, and in denying that our aim is to reproduce social phenomena in some way that is uniquely appropriate to them. Obversely, subtle realism shares with scepticism and relativism a recognition that all knowledge is based on assumptions and purposes and is a human construction, but it rejects these positions' abandonment of the regulative idea of independent and knowable phenomena. Perhaps most important of all, subtle realism is distinct from both naïve realism and relativism in its rejection of the notion that knowledge must be defined as beliefs whose validity is known with certainty.[11]

What are the implications of subtle realism for the way we think about and practise ethnography? For one thing, subtle realism requires us to be rather more vigilant regarding the dangers of error than naïve realism would lead us to be. We must accept that we necessarily rely on cultural assumptions, and that these can lead us astray, just as easily as leading us in the right direction. Certainly, we cannot legitimately claim that simply because we were 'there' we 'know'. Yet this is the fundamental rhetorical strategy employed by ethnographers, as Geertz points out:

> The ability of anthropologists to get us to take what they say seriously has less to do with either a factual look or an air of conceptual elegance than it has with their capacity to convince us that what they say is a result of their having actually penetrated (or, if you prefer,

been penetrated by) another form of life, of having, one way or another, truly 'been there'. And that, persuading us that this offstage miracle has occurred, is where the writing comes in. (Geertz 1988: 4–5)

Nor can we rely on the fact that because participants are 'there' that *they* 'know', as do those who define credibility in terms of respondent validation (Guba and Lincoln 1982). What we have here are rhetorical appeals to naïve realism, and they are not sustainable because of the weakness of that philosophical position. However, the fact that the observer was there and/or that participants believe the account to be true are important sorts of *evidence* for the validity of an account. As researchers, we must develop the ways in which we monitor our assumptions and the inferences we make on the basis of them, and investigate those we judge not to be beyond reasonable doubt. This is not suggesting something that is new or novel. Ethnographers have become increasingly concerned with ways of checking their conclusions. Subtle realism simply encourages greater concern with this.[12] However, it runs counter to the implications of relativism, which undercut the rationale for such checks by denying that there is any reality to be known and implying that this rationale is based on arbitrary philosophical or political assumptions; assumptions which might, with equal warrant, be replaced by others, such as those generating fictional accounts.

What is implied by subtle realism is not, then, a complete transformation of ethnographic practice. We must still view people's beliefs and actions as constructions, and this includes their accounts of the world *and* those of researchers. At the same time, though, we should not assume that people's accounts are necessarily 'true' or 'rational' in their own terms. Whether we should be concerned with the truth or falsity of any account depends on how we plan to use it. There are two sorts of interest we can have in accounts, implying different requirements. First, we may treat them as social phenomena that we are seeking to understand and explain, or as indicators of cultural perspectives held by the people producing them. Here we must ignore our judgements about their validity or rationality, since this is not relevant to the task of understanding them. Indeed, the ethnographer should suspend any of her/his own beliefs that conflict with those being described and explained; otherwise there is a danger of misunderstanding. As I argued earlier, the question of the truth or falsity of an account carries no implications for how it should be explained. On the other hand, we may use accounts as a source of information about the phenomena to which they refer. They may, for example, provide us with information about events that we could not ourselves witness (for example that happened in the past or in settings to which we do not have access). Or they may allow us to check our own or others' observations through triangulation. Here we *must* be concerned with the truth or otherwise of the accounts, and we must judge this as best we can, both in terms of the likelihood of error of various kinds and according to how the information relates to our other knowledge. We can, of course, apply both these approaches to the same account; indeed, understanding an account may well help us in assessing its validity. However, it is very important to maintain the distinction between these two ways of analysing informants' accounts. Only if we do so can we retain the valuable ethnographic approach of seeking to understand and explain people's behaviour and beliefs independently of their supposed rationality or truth, while not lapsing into relativism.[13]

There is one area where subtle realism does imply something of a break with conventional ethnographic practice founded on naïve realism. This arises from its abandonment of the ideal of reproduction in favour of selective representation. Given that what is produced is, at best, only one of many possible valid accounts of the phenomena studied, it is a requirement that ethnographers make explicit the relevances on which their accounts are based. This is not always done.

❖ CONCLUSION

In this chapter I have addressed what seems to me to be one of the central ambiguities in ethnography: between a commitment to a methodology based on naïve realism and a theoretical approach founded on constructivism that is often taken to imply relativism. I looked at each of the two most obvious solutions to this problem: the adoption of a consistent (naïve) realism or a consistent relativism. However, I concluded that neither of these offered an adequate solution. The first involves unacceptable assumptions about the asymmetry of explanations of true and false beliefs and of actions based upon them. The second leads to all those problems that usually follow from the adoption of a relativist epistemology, notably internal inconsistency. I argued that satisfactory resolution of this problem requires us to recognise that we are not faced with a stark choice between naïve realism and relativism, that there are more subtle forms of realism that avoid the problems of these two positions. I outlined what seem to me to be the main components of such a subtle realism, and sketched some of its implications for the principles and practice of ethnographic method.

❖ NOTES

1. Something of this attitude is to be detected, for example, in Geertz's attack on 'anti-relativism' (Geertz 1984).

2. Blumer draws this idea from pragmatism; but it can also be found in one or another form in nineteenth-century historicism and in the eighteenth century in the writings of Vico and Herder (Berlin 1976).

3. For useful discussions of this idea in anthropology, see Jarvie (1964 and 1983), Winch (1964), Tennekes (1971) and Herskovits (1972). See also Geertz (1984).

4. For an application of this argument to social scientists' use of the concept of ideology, see Hammersley (1981).

5. This is ironic since the origins of phenomenology lie in Husserl's attempt to ground knowledge in fundamental essences that are constitutive of human experience and therefore of the world, an enterprise resolutely opposed to scepticism and relativism: see Kolakowski (1975) and Bell (1990).

6. See, for example, Sudnow (1967) and Wieder (1974). For a useful general discussion of ethnomethodology in this respect, see Atkinson (1988).

7. Bernstein (1983) provides a useful overview of recent anti-realist trends. An example of the impact of these ideas on ethnography is the recent work of Denzin which seems to combine them in a relatively indiscriminate fashion (see, for example, Denzin 1989 and 1990). The differences and inconsistencies among the views I have outlined are at least as important as the similarities. And, as I have indicated, many of them are by no means unambiguously relativistic, even though that is often how they have been interpreted.

8. See the discussion of anthropological examples of 'experimental' ethnographic writing in Marcus and Fischer (1986). In sociology, Krieger (1983) provides an example of a text in which the voice of the researcher is suppressed in favour of those of the people studied.

9. It is also worth noting that to think of the phenomena studied as consisting of a reality independent of the ethnographer is misleading. We can treat them as independent of the researcher while recognising that both are part of the same reality.

10. Here I am adopting the neo-Kantian idea that reality is infinitely extensive and intensive (Rickert 1986). However, I do not believe that reality is structureless. In constructing our relevances we must take account of what we know and can discover about that structure if we are to get the information we need to serve our purposes (that is, in part at least, we must *discover* what is relevant).

11. Relativists' attitude to this definition is often ambivalent. On the one hand, they adopt it in arguing against realism, claiming that because there can be no knowledge of reality in this strong sense there is no sense in which we can reasonably claim to understand phenomena that are independent of us. In more constructive mode, however, relativists define knowledge in terms of what is taken to be certain within a particular culture or paradigm. While my conception of knowledge shares something with this latter view, it differs from it in treating agreement as an indicator not as a definition of validity; and like all indicators it is subject to error.

12. For a more extended account of the assessment of ethnographic claims, see Hammersley (1991a).

13. Once again, this is not to recommend something that is entirely novel. Ethnographers have long employed both these forms of analysis, though they do not always distinguish between them sufficiently clearly. Something like this distinction is to be found in McCall and Simmons (1969: 4). The sort of subtle realism I have outlined clarifies the basis, and underlines the need, for this distinction.

❖ REFERENCES

Atkinson, P. (1988) 'Ethnomethodology: a critical review', *Annual Review of Sociology*, 14, pp. 441–65.

Bell, D. (1990) *Husserl*. London: Routledge.

Berger, P. and Luckmann, T. (1966) *The Social Construction of Reality*. Harmondsworth: Penguin.

Berlin, I. (1976) *Vico and Herder*. London: Hogarth.

Bernstein, R. (1983) *Beyond Objectivism and Relativism*. Philadelphia: University of Pennsylvania Press.

Blumer, H. (1969) 'The methodological position of Symbolic Interactionism', in H. Blumer *Symbolic Interactionism*. Englewood Cliffs, N.J.: Prentice Hall.

Clifford, J. and Marcus, G. (eds.) (1986) *Writing Culture: the poetics and politics of ethnography*. Berkeley: University of California Press.

Denzin, N. K. (1989) *Interpretive Interactionism*. Newbury Park: Sage.

———. (1990) 'The spaces of postmodernism: reading Plummer on Blumer', *Symbolic Interaction*, 13, 2, pp. 145–54.

Geertz, C. (1984) 'Anti anti-relativism', *American Anthropologist*, 86, pp. 263–78.

———. (1988) *Works and Lives: the anthropologist as author*. Stanford: Stanford University Press.

Guba, E. G. and Lincoln, Y. S. (1982) 'Epistemological and methodological bases of naturalistic inquiry', *Educational Communication and Technology Journal*, 30, 4, pp. 233–52.

Hammersley, M. (1981) 'Ideology in the staffroom? A critique of false consciousness', in L. Barton and S. Walker (eds.) *Schools, Teachers and Teaching*. Lewes: Falmer.

———. (1989) *The Dilemma of Qualitative Method: Herbert Blumer and the Chicago tradition*. London: Routledge.

———. (1991a) *Reading Ethnographic Research*. London: Longman.

———. (1991b) 'Some reflections on ethnography and validity', forthcoming in *International Journal of Qualitative Studies in Education*.

Hammersley, M. and Atkinson, P. (1983) *Ethnography: principles in practice*. London: Tavistock.

Herskovits, M. (1972) *Cultural Relativism*. New York: Random House.

Jarvie, I. C. (1964) *The Revolution in Anthropology*. London: Routledge and Kegan Paul.

———. (1983) *Rationality and Relativism*. London: Routledge and Kegan Paul.

Kolakowski, L. (1975) *Husserl and the Search for Certitude*. New Haven: Yale University Press.

Krieger, S. (1983) *The Mirror Dance: identity in a women's community*. Philadelphia: Temple University Press.

Kuhn, T. S. (1962) *The Structure of Scientific Revolutions*. Chicago: University of Chicago Press (2nd edn 1970).

Lofland, J. (1972) *Analyzing Social Settings*. Belmont, CA: Wadsworth. (2nd edn, Lofland and Lofland 1984).

Marcus, G. and Fischer, M. (1986) *Anthropology as Cultural Critique*. Chicago: University of Chicago Press.

McCall, G. and Simmons, J. L. (1969) *Issues in Participant Observation*. Reading, Mass.: Addison-Wesley.

Rickert, H. (1986) *The Limits of Concept Formation in Natural Science*. Cambridge: Cambridge University Press. (First published in German in 1902.)

Schatzman, L. and Strauss, A. (1973) *Field Research: strategies for a natural sociology*. Englewood Cliffs, N.J.: Prentice Hall.

Schutz, A. and Luckmann, T. (1974) *The Structures of the Life-World*. London: Heinemann.

Smith, J. K. (1984) 'The problem of criteria for judging interpretive inquiry', *Educational Evaluation and Policy Analysis*, 6, 4, pp. 379–91.

———. (1989) *The Nature of Social and Educational Inquiry: empiricism versus interpretation*. Norwood, N.J.: Ablex.

Smith, J. K. and Heshusius, L. (1986) 'Closing down the conversation: the end of the quantitative-qualitative debate among educational inquirers', *Educational Researcher*, 15, 1, pp. 4–12.

Sudnow, D. (1967) *Passing On: the social organization of dying*. Englewood Cliffs, N.J.: Prentice Hall.

Suppe, F. (ed.) (1974) *The Structure of Scientific Theories*. Chicago: University of Chicago Press.

Tennekes, J. (1971) *Anthropology, Relativism and Method*. Assen: Van Gorcum.

Tyler, S. A. (1985) 'Ethnography, intertextuality, and the end of description', *American Journal of Semiotics*, 3, 4, pp. 83–98.

———. (1986) 'Post-modern ethnography: from document of the occult to occult document', in J. Clifford and G. Marcus (eds.) *Writing Culture: the poetics and politics of ethnography*. Berkeley: University of California Press.

Wieder, D. L. (1974) *Language and Social Reality: the case of telling the convict code*. The Hague: Mouton.

Winch, P. (1958) *The Idea of a Social Science and Its Relation to Philosophy*. London: Routledge and Kegan Paul.

———. (1964) 'Understanding a primitive society', *American Philosophical Quarterly*, 1, pp. 307–24.

4

Real Men Don't Collect Soft Data

Silvia Gherardi and Barry Turner

> Assumptions ultimately mean choice, and the exploration of assumptions involves the exploration of choice. (Morgan, 1983: 382)

A common usage in discussion of social science links quantitative styles of inquiry and data collection with a 'hard' view of the world, and qualitative approaches with a 'soft' view. As with many

AUTHORS' NOTE: *Real Men Don't Collect Soft Data* is a booklet that presents some reflections that emerged during the research project "Qualitative Methods for Organizational Analysis." This project was carried out jointly by both the Dipartimento di Politica Sociale of the University of Trento and the Organizational Research Unit of the Department of Sociology, University of Exeter, U.K. A seminar on qualitative methods was held at the University of Trento in September 1986, where Barry Turner presented "The Cognitive Processes Associated With the Generation of Grounded Theory." Silvia Gherardi received an honorary research fellowship from the University of Exeter for the academic years 1985–86 and 1986–87 to develop studies and applications of grounded theory in organizational studies. The Universities of Exeter and Trento and the Consiglio Nazionale delle Ricerce supported the project financially.

Excerpted from Silvia Gherardi and Barry Turner, *Real Men Don't Collect Soft Data* (Booklet 13, Dipartimento di Politica Sociale of the University of Trento). Reprinted by permission of Silvia Gherardi.

unexamined language patterns, these distinctions serve to convey tacit attitudes about the topic under discussion: the connotations of these terms are such as to suggest that 'hard' social science is masculine and to be respected, whilst 'soft' social science is feminine and of a lower order of activity. The message conveyed in these tacit usages is that quantitative work is courageous, hard biting, hard work.

Collecting hard data means making hard decisions, taking no non-sense, hardening one's heart to weaklings, building on a hard core of material, using hard words to press on to hard-won results which often carry with them promises of hard cash for future research and career prospects. By contrast, soft data are weak, unstable, impressible, squashy and sensual. The softies, weaklings, or ninnies who carry it out have too much of a soft spot for counter-argument for them to be taken seriously; they reveal the soft underbelly of the social science enterprise, are likely to soft-soap those who listen to them. They are too softhearted, pitying and maybe even foolish to be taken seriously so that it is only right that they should be employed on soft money.

These contrasts are sufficiently firmly established for journal editors to refuse to accept the phrase 'hard qualitative data' on the grounds that it would be "confusing to readers", and they deserve discussion because the current usage serves to bias assessments of current new directions in social science research. They are used as code words for a cluster of issues relating not only to the *style of inquiry*, to the *style of questions asked* and the *style of answers* sought, but also to the association of quantitative investigations with major institutionalised patterns of research, and the consequent access to machinery, to research aides and to control over concentrations of resources. The 'hard', macho image is also likely to be associated with the distancing of senior researchers from 'subjects' on 'objects' of inquiry; with the reduction of threats to the self by the use of anxiety-reducing research rituals of execution and research presentation; and with a reduced willingness to tolerate ambiguity in procedures and findings (Silverman, 1985).

The recent growth of interest in qualitative research makes it impor-tant to challenge these clusters of assumptions which get smuggled into discussion of research—and also of research funding—and to question the extent to which such views can automatically be held to be correct. A parallel argument has recently been advanced in the field of manage-ment theory, where Basoux (1987) has noted that management was originally formulated as a rational-deductive task to be tackled by men:

> The good manager is aggressive competitive, firm, just. He is not
> feminine; he is not soft or yielding or dependent or intuitive in the
> womanly sense. The very expression of emotion is viewed as a
> feminine weakness that would interfere with effective business
> processes. (McGregor, 1967: 23)

But with the recognition of the central importance of cultural issues in
management (Peters and Waterman, 1982) and the need to cope with
incursions into the West from Japanese firms, management virtues are
now seen to include consensus, involvement, patience, compromise
and moderation. The new view promotes a modified role model of the
manager as "intuitive, nurturing and accessible—a job description
which women are well-placed to fulfil" (Basoux, 1987).

In the complex world of contemporary social science, similar shifts
are taking place, and the issues to be confronted are too subtle and too
important to be handled by means of a crude and over-simplified
dichotomy, especially when this presumed opposition is accompanied
by properties derived from sexist stereotypes. In the remainder of this
paper, we wish to explore some of the complexities of the current
changes which are being handled within social science research, and to
relate them especially to the developing trends of investigations within
the field of organisational sociology.

❖ THE PROCESS OF RESEARCH

The bureaucratisation of scientific research proceeds on the assumption that the task of research is one which is amenable to the same kind
of hierarchical division of labour as are tasks in manufacturing industry or in official administration. This view of research is reinforced by
much of the abstract and elaborate edifice of 'research methodology'
which the social sciences have generated (Willer & Willer, 1974;
Zetterberg, 1954; Hage, 1972), and which has generated its own
momentum and its own autonomy as an area of abstract learning. But
there is an obscurity about how the detailed and rule-bound practices
advocated for the definition of concepts and for the construction of
theory relate to the actual process of ongoing research. Such writings,
while pursuing theoretical and logical rigour, produce systems of
abstraction with normative undertones—this is how research should
be done—whilst retaining a problematic relationship to the processes

which they claim to explicate. In a similar manner, as we shall see, attempts to absorb the new emphasis upon qualitative research into existing orthodoxies of research methodology produce an illusory clarity, for they do not look closely enough at the research process.

As always, we find that social reality confounds our simple armchair theorising: it is more messy, more convoluted and more surprising than we thought it would be. Fortunately this realisation, prompted by the growth in the sociology of natural science, has now given us some accounts of how research is pursued in fact, rather than in research methodology. Hammond's pioneering collection *Sociologists at Work* (1964) has been supplemented by other accounts (Bell & Newby, 1984; Bryman, 1988).

There is, then, another opposition, between the structures advocated by the methodologists and the 'theorologists' on the one hand, and the accounts of research as it is done, and theory generation as it occurs, which have been produced by Hammond and his successors. To resolve this opposition, we need to look for an emerging middle ground which presents guides to research procedure and theory generation which accord more with the nature of research practice. And, when we look for this middle ground, we find also that we must tackle issues which blur the simple qualitative/quantitative, hard/soft contrasts with which we began.

We are helped in our task by the way in which investigations into the sociology and the philosophy of natural science have shown it not to be the gleaming aseptic edifice promoted in developments after World War II, but to be a human enterprise, fraught with all of the personal, emotional and political difficulties displayed by any human undertaking. Natural science is, as Ravetz (1971) has demonstrated, a craft process: judgement, craft skills and intuitive knowledge are deployed by natural scientists in the assessment of the satisfactory operation of equipment; in descriptive and other scientific reporting skills: in the intuitive adoption of appropriate preliminary theories about a given context; in judgements about the appropriate use and the appropriate fit of mathematical models; in evaluations of the reliability of data collected, making the transition from collected data to usable information; in the elaboration of argument (Feyerabend, 1975); in the appropriate use of pre-existing information gathered by other researchers; in the development of tools and techniques and in the acquisition of skills in using them; in the avoidance of pitfalls characteristic of the field of inquiry; and, throughout, in the style of research pursued:

> The investigation of a scientific problem is creative work, in which personal choices as well as personal judgements are involved at every stage up to the last. . . . Even though [the scientist] is concerned with properties of the external world the work he [*sic*] produces will be characterised by a certain style unique to himself. . . . There is no conflict between a highly individual style in the investigation of problems and the production of results which meet the socially imposed criteria of adequacy for the field. (Ravetz, 1971: Ch 2)

It is clear that all of the craft elements which Ravetz identifies with the procedures of natural science, and which account for the distinctive development of 'schools' of natural science associated with 'master-pupil' pedigrees stretching over centuries (Pledge, 1939) will be evident within even the most quantitative of social sciences. Judgements about equipment, procedures, abstracting and typifying activities, theorising, modelling and so on pervade any quantitative social science investigation. Baldamus (1976) has drawn attention to the way in which fundamental approaches to theorising and abstraction are embedded in such commonplace social science activities as cross-classification and the construction of two-by-two tables, and has pointed out the manner in which the practical procedures of survey research are saturated with theoretical and value-judgements. Survey research is almost entirely conceived of as a rule-bound methodology, but its operations depend upon the tacit knowledge, developed by researchers in the process of use, which underpins the process of cross-classification, of elaboration analysis, the handling of variables in a statistical manner and so on (Rosenberg, 1968). Without such implicit theoretical techniques, the rules of survey research would enable us to build, as Ravetz phrases it, a plane which would not fly.

And, again, the structures of the research handbooks have to be reconciled with accounts of how research is actually carried out. Lower's (1977) analysis of the accounts in Hammond demonstrate that, with one exception, the projects embarked upon by these distinguished researchers all reached a point of disruption where the original plan, the original project, the original rationale for the research suffered a breakdown, precipitating a crisis and requiring activities of what Lower calls theoretical 'patchworking' or theoretical 'bricolage' in order to repair the breakdown and to present an appearance of coherence in the work. Of course, if research is recognised to be a journey into the unknown rather than a task which can be fully specified and planned in advance, then such breakdowns look less surprising, and we can look (Lower suggests) at the patchworking as the injection of a creative element into the process.

All of the above is intended merely to make the point that the process of research, even natural science research, is one which involves the use of judgement, craft skills and what Polanyi (1959) calls tacit knowledge, that it frequently does not follow a preordained path and that the intelligence needed to pursue research is not wholly rational-deductive. Witkin (1971) has argued that all creative developments, in the field of both arts and science, involve the use not only of cognitive intelligence but also an affective intelligence, an 'intelligence of feeling': the objective which a scientist pursues is likely to have sensuous properties, and to be affectively or emotionally charged. The personal manner in which this objective is symbolised will direct the process of interaction between the investigator and the particular medium or context which is being investigated. Such a process is not a completely random one, or one without rules, but the rules will relate to the particular combination of [objective] and [investigatory context]. The rules will not be a universally applicable array, but will be context specific, and generated in the process of interaction between investigator and investigatory field, as part of the process of the exercise of the cognitive *and* the affective intelligence. As the American physicist Bridgeman commented, 'science is doing your damndest to understand with no holds barred'.

The rules of scientific investigation to which we have been referring are not those common to research methodology, nor are they the rules for the socially approved presentation of research findings to the scholarly community. They are the rules generated in interaction to guide further investigation in a manner likely to be scientifically fruitful. As the rules of a painting by numbers kit relate to artistic creation, so do sets of research procedures relate to successful scientific investigation.

Let us turn our attention, then, to the related question of number and counting. We would not wish to take up the obscurantist position sometimes encountered among qualitative researchers, that qualitative researchers are not permitted to count. If we are to understand the natural or the social world 'with no holds barred' then we need to deploy whatever appropriate means come to hand. As we suggested at the start, such simple oppositions as 'numbers *versus* no numbers' are inadequate for discussing and understanding the full complexity of the research process. We need, instead, to look a little more closely at what is meant by number and how number might be appropriately deployed in different research contexts.

But number is a metaphor. In counting and quantification, number is employed to draw similarities. Mathematics provides us with accounts of systems of logical operations and interconnections. In the use of mathematics we place sections of the world which we are interested in alongside portions of mathematical reasoning and assert that the two bear some resemblance to each other. This process is as true for the juxtaposition of a row of sheep and the numbers 'one, two, three' as it is for the explorations of parallels between the behaviour of a national economy and the properties of a complex econometric model. We should, therefore, be clear about which of the metaphorical properties of number we wish to use to assist our understanding of the social and organisational world. Is the case to be made that there are no relevant properties? That mathematical counting and related operations cannot possibly help us because we are interested in processes and properties which are inherently uncountable? Or, in a related position, one suggested by William Blake in his famous picture of a god-like figure leaning down from the heavens with a pair of callipers, do we wish to make the case that the process of measurement, of quantification in itself is damaging to the stature, to the quality and to the dignity of humankind? Or are the relevant distinctions not between "counting" and "not counting," but between "counting to one" (unity) and "counting to more than one," or between "counting to one, two and three" and "counting many" (as in several language forms).

Again, to resolve such questions in a research context, we need to think clearly about what we are intending to do when we are suggesting that properties of the systems and activities we are interested in are usefully close to the properties of abstract number systems. When the parallels are close ones, properly constituted, we are able to assist our enquiries because transformations which can be carried out powerfully and with great facility through manipulations of numbers tell us about properties of the social world, but in order to use these we need to ensure that the operations which we apply to our numbers are appropriate ones. The weakest kind of numbering is simply using numbers to identify and label phenomena (as in Mark I, Mark II, etc. James I, James II). These numbers identify unambiguously, but we can do nothing useful if we try operations such as 'James I + James II =' or still less if we ask questions about the square root of James II. At the opposite extreme, we have numbers which reflect all of the properties of natural numbers, so that we can add, subtract, multiply, divide and so on with impunity, confident that the operations carried out on the numbers also mean something for our data. Coleman's *Introduction to Mathematical Sociology* (1965), particularly in the earlier chapters, provides an excellent discussion of these issues. It is important to spend time on these topics because of the peculiar standing of numbers in our civilisation. On the one hand we are mesmerised by numbers, even when they are pseudo-numbers, those who deal with them frequently no less than those who are thrown into a panic by them. On the other hand, the general standard of teaching about mathematical issues is so poor that few people understand fully the nature of the properties of the numbers and number systems which they are advocating or excoriating.

A new and useful notation has recently been developed to draw attention to properties of numbers which are frequently ignored. Funtowicz and Ravetz (1986), alarmed by the misuse of numbers in debates about nuclear safety levels, constructed the NUSAP notation which, though intended for application to natural science and engineering in the first instance, can also helpfully clarify thought in the social science area. The essence of their system is simple: that a single number standing alone is misleading. To evaluate its meaning, we need an additional four pieces of information. Funtowicz and Ravetz express this as N:U:S:A:P—Number: Units: Spread: Assessment: Pedigree. When presenting others with a number to try to elucidate a portion of our research, we will mislead them if we allow this *number* to stand alone. Our audience will need to know the *units* of our measurement, and some measure of the *spread* or distribution around the point specified. And then perhaps even more importantly they need to know where the number has come from, its *pedigree*—is it based upon an exhaustive and detailed measurement process covering every possible variable which might influence the outcome, or upon a snap judgement from someone over the telephone? Associated with the pedigree, the audience would be assisted by an *assessment* of the standing of this number in the eyes of those well placed to make a judgement. Do those in the field think that this is a sensible guess, or a shoddy estimate, is it the best possible attempt at measurement, or a figure over which commentators disagree?

In qualitative analyses, there are no reasons why numbers should not be appropriately deployed. Suttles's use of small tables showing how many gang fights took place in a given period of time in a Chicago slum, or how many members of one ethnic group visited a shop owned by a member of another ethnic group in an afternoon (Suttles, 1978) help to inform us about his territory and add an element to a study otherwise based upon qualitative data gathered through participant observation. When Suttles specifies five fights in a month, we know that he is counting in units of one, that the number could rise above or fall below that in the preceding or following months, that he got the figure by talking to people around the neighbourhood, and that the trust that we can place in the figure is about the same as the trust which we can place upon Suttles's general account, as a competent but human individual observer spending some time in the vicinity. This kind of background information is needed, these kinds of judgements are made, tacitly or explicitly whenever *any* number is presented in a research context.

When is it difficult or inappropriate to count at all? Here it seems to be useful to introduce a distinction between standardised and non-standardised data. To count, the items or the features to be counted need to be available in a standardised form. And, since the world is rarely standardised in itself, we need to have strong rules to declare certain variations in the data as 'error' which can be safely disregarded; when we are happy to do this, we generate data which can be usefully tallied up, in conditions where we judge that anything that is not standard can be safely ignored. By contrast, when we are reluctant to specify units, or when we are reluctant to declare the variety in quality between units to be unimportant, or to disregard it, we find ourselves dealing with non-standardised data. We have weak rules for classifying portions of the data as 'error' and we have to find ways to cope with the resulting variations in our analysis which do not make use of the analogous properties of number systems.

To these distinctions we need to add others concerned with broader and deeper philosophical and epistemological issues: with whether our organisational research is to be concerned with prediction, with the generation of theory, with the acquisition of interpretative meanings, or with the informing of political action. Reason and Rowan (1981) offer a distinction, in discussing new approaches to organisational research, between those who are seeking theory as prediction and those who want theory as pattern. Broadly this distinction coincides with that between positivistic inquiry and what Lincoln and Guba (1985) somewhat controversially call 'naturalistic' inquiry. The distinction here is not merely between the uses of theory but also between the different canons which may appropriately be applied to the judgement of the research. Lincoln and Guba (1985) suggest that, whereas positivistic inquiries are judged according to their rigour, naturalistic inquiries should be assessed on the basis of trustworthiness and authenticity. Rigour conventionally looks at the truth value of propositions, at their validity or generalisability, at their reliability and at their objectivity. Research which fails to meet these criteria is confounded, atypical, unstable or biased. By contrast, they suggest that appropriate criteria for assessing naturalistic research, appropriate criteria of trustworthiness would be that the research should be credible, its findings should be transferable, dependable and confirmable, and they suggest techniques for the improvement of all of these qualities of 'naturalistic' research.[1]

A further distinction in research which can usefully be added to our considerations is that made by Glaser and Strauss (1967) between research which is concerned with *verification* and research which is concerned with *discovery*. In the former type, theory serves as a framework to guide verification. In the latter, theory is the 'jottings in the margins of ongoing research', a kind of research in which order is not very immediately attained, a messy, puzzling and intriguing kind of research in which the conclusions are not known before the investigations are carried out. This does not mean that the researcher is unprepared for investigation—"fortune favours the prepared mind". A domain of inquiry needs to be identified, and much preparation can be carried out by becoming familiar with the empirical and theoretical literature concerned with the given domain, several different literatures possibly being relevant to different facets of the research domain.

Against this background, empirical research can commence, with a sharpened perception and an array of questions, uncertainties and doubts. In 'discovery oriented' research, the extent to which the researcher acts as the research instrument is likely to be maximised. An openness of mind requires a faithful attention to the sensations offered in the field situation, but at the same time the essentially active part played by the investigator may be symbolised by the use of the term 'capta' rather than data (Miles and Huberman, 1984) to stress the extent to which information is captured from rather than given by the social setting. Non-standardised information, 'capta' acquired as a result of close attention to a portion of the social world relevant to the research domain will provide the fidelity, trustworthiness and authenticity which Lincoln and Guba have advocated, giving such data an author- ity which is difficult to overturn in relation to the context in which it was gathered, but which then poses immediately the question of the extent to which the findings are transferable to other contexts.

❖ THEORY GENERATION FROM QUALITATIVE DATA

We are labouring these basic points about painstaking fieldwork because they seem to us to be essential preparation for the work of theory generation in qualitative research.

Good fieldwork can be helped by guides currently available to researchers which explore the problems of data gathering, access and so on (Burgess, 1982, 1984) and which alert us to the importance of being appropriately prepared and equipped, of being suitably attentive and sensitive, of assessing the quality of our observations (Turner, 1988) and of being able to negotiate entry to the domain of inquiry. A more difficult process however, and one which is little discussed, is that which follows on the acquisition of a full set of field notes or inter- view transcripts—the process of typification and categorisation of the data in the initial steps of analysis.

We have learned enough over the past century about cognition and understanding and about the nature of social reality to realise that good research is not simply a matter of reportage, of listing events and encounters to show where we have been. The account of 'reality' which is being sought in the research process is a little different from that which might be offered in a chatty essay or in a short article for a colour supplement. What is wanted is not a social 'shopping list' which records what has been noticed, but an account of a series of interactions with the social world in a form which plausibly alerts us to the possi- bility of a new order not previously seen—a theoretical account.

This theoretical account of reality has to be one in which we, again, are active contributors. We are active in attending to various facets of the encounters which we experience, we are active in the early stages of analysis when we divide up our experiences into fragments, dimensions, characteristics and features which we make noteworthy and we are active in the new syntheses which we start to make as we structure our own past experiences and future expectations. As a young writer, V. S. Naipaul spent much time searching for real 'writer's material' and worrying because he could not find it. He did not, as he later realised, see the richness of the material which surrounded him all the time when he had arrived in his boarding house in post-war London, and only now, thirty years on, is he finding himself able actively to re-evaluate and reinterpret his experiences at that time, seeing or creating their meaning (Naipaul, 1987). The ordinary encounters which a new researcher is involved with in the field may not look very exciting. He or she may well need reassuring that they are real 'sociologist's material' and further, may need to be convinced that they are accessible in some way to theoretical interpretation.

Of course, as we are structuring our own expectations, we are also trying to structure the expectations of others. To perceive, we typify: there is no alternative. Without structure, perception is chaotic and any account of the world must typify. One of the most difficult tasks in qualitative social science research is deciding just what kind or level of typification is useful in the appraising of field notes and interview transcripts in order to allow the material to release its sociological messages (Martin & Turner, 1987; Strauss, 1987; Turner, 1988).

In the approach known as 'grounded theory' (Glaser & Strauss, 1967; Turner 1981) a crucial but little discussed stage involves precisely this matter of the appropriate level of typification which will serve to articulate a theoretical understanding of a given set of non-standardised data. Both Glaser (1978) and Strauss (1987) recognise this difficulty and suggest that this step can best be learned by example, in research meetings or in collaborative research workshops. This is good advice, and it is even possible to make use of such sessions to train engineering researchers concerned with analysing non-standardised data collected about engineering practice (Turner, 1987).

But what is happening in such encounters? What tacit research skills are being passed on? One such skill is the ability to judge what level of generality it is helpful to work with (Strauss, 1987) and another is the reassurance that the researcher has to *contribute* some elements to the data in order to generate a meaningful or an insightful pattern of typification. Only by coming to feel comfortable about 'putting meaning in' can the researcher structure the situation, initially for him- or herself and subsequently for the readers of the research account.

A parallel can perhaps be drawn with the painter's contribution to the process of Chinese *hseih-i* watercolour painting. Although in this style, the paintings of plants, animals and landscapes may be based upon many detailed studies and sketches from nature, these form no more than a preparatory stage in the work. The final painting is made from memory, in the studio:

> We would search in vain for the concrete scenery of Huang's pictures. Instead we would recognise how he unravelled the core of that immense confusion of natural miracles and caprices to create a dignified yet simple landscape core which does not confuse our vision. Huang created a picture of the Yellow Mountains in their sensual and spiritual character out of thousands of views and thousands of experiences. (Hejzlar, 1987: 52)

Or, again, in relation to Wang Ch'ing-Fang's studies of fish:

> His pictures of the ink carps and small fishes, or golden aquarium fishes in bright red were made with an understanding of the creatures' rhythm of movement and the resistance of the invisible element, water. Boldness and elegance of expression are the result of Wang's immense patience as an observer.[2] (Hejzlar, 1987: 57)

The ideal type, as Weber recognised, bears a similar relationship to a particular set of empirical data as these paintings do to the nature sketches which preceded them. In making sense of our experience we need to produce from a set of qualitative data a theoretical account which summarises our understanding of possible regularities associated with the set. These regularities will have the potential of unifying not only the empirical data which we have already dissected, but also other material which we have not yet seen. Without this potential neither science nor human life would be possible.

The theory will not list our experiences, but will offer an arrangement of elements of those experiences which we find useful and which might be useful to others. We are engaged in the generation of theory not primarily as a predictor of variables, but as a pattern which we will recognise when it recurs (Reason & Rowan, 1981). If the theoretical pattern is sufficiently recognisable, useful and sensitively constructed, and if our segment of the world is not too unrepresentative of aspects of that pattern, it may turn out to be recognisable, appealing and useful to others as well.

❖ RESEARCH COMMUNICATION OVER THEORY

One of the benefits from trying to make more explicit the processes of qualitative research is to make formerly hidden procedures and practices which have had to be discovered and rediscovered with varying degrees of success by each generation of researchers more accessible and open to discussion and improvement. We are concerned with universal processes of data transformation and the explicit discussion of them is likely to allow for collective improvements to be effected in the manner in which they are tackled.

In consequence of the explicitness, it is possible for communication about the intermediate stages of qualitative analysis to take place, between research principal and research assistants, between research collaborators, between research students and supervisors. Communication may occur by several means: through making explicit the 'low-level theoretical labels' which are generated in the early stages of data analysis as initial coding categories are invented; through discussion of the definitions of the most important and central of these concepts; through theoretical memoranda generated alongside the processes of detailed data analysis; through the use of sections of a research journal if one is being kept by the researchers in question; through communication of those occasional moments of high energy creative synthesis which is one of the rare delights of research and which Glaser has called the 'drugless trip' (1978). It is assumed in each of these possible strands of communication about research that writing is a research skill. We wish to urge a clear separation between writing as a means of organising and presenting final results to an audience and writing as a research skill. The goal of writing every day not only helps to avoid writing blocks, but gives regular practice to the qualitative researcher in externalising thoughts about the issues and evidence of the research in hand. Regular writing for oneself avoids the anxiety associated with having to write a paper for a seminar or a journal. Also, it demonstrates practically that writing is a skill which can be acquired and improved by practice.

Writing externalises thought and in doing so makes it less personal, more durable and more specific. Even without external intervention, writers are likely to learn from feedback from their own externalised thoughts, and this process can be augmented by comments from colleagues, critics and helpers who are able to read the written output (Barzun & Graaf, 1977: part III; Strunk & White, 1979; Mullins, 1977; Elbow, 1981). We all know people with rooms full of research material which they have never been able to publish because they have never been able to write about it. The researcher who makes a habit of writing regularly will find it easier to prepare drafts, discussion papers and outlines to be analysed in discussion session, and will find fewer problems in making the transition from the use of writing as a research skill to the use of writing for the presentation of accounts of research to a professional audience.

❖ LINKS WITH EXISTING THEORY

In the nature of the process outlined above the final theoretical stage will involve the building of bridges between the analysis of the field observations and theoretical aspects of existing studies. One would expect that some of these links will reflect the themes explored in initial literature searches, as the analysis picks up, amplifies, questions or modifies previous theoretical views. However, linked with the element of discovery which we have discussed above, we would also expect to be making use of other, more unexpected sets of theoretical writing.

We can trace several sequences in the preceding accounts of the pursuit of soft data. Given that one of the defining characteristics of such research is its stress upon interpretation and upon negotiation, Agar (1986) suggests, following Gadamer, a sequence of interpretations as follows: Encounter; leading to surprise and breakdown; then to resolution and finally to the production of a coherent account.

As Lower's inquiries have suggested, following breakdown the qualitative investigator has also, however, to strive to achieve some degree of coherence, or to move towards some mode of operation which does not in practice cause too much personal distress, between his/her relationships with the observed, and his/her relationships with the scientific community. Ways of seeking coherence may include the following:

♦ searching for observed actions to locate typical motives, typical ends, typical means in typical situations so that they can be placed in a frame or plan for communication *back* to those observed or *onward* to the scientific community (Goffman, 1975; Burke, 1969)

♦ searching for inferences derived from the observations for onward transmission to the scientific community, and in doing so, recognising that there may be a need to use varied forms of logic—logic which is 'fuzzy', or 'plausible', or statements which are only acceptable if they are hedged: "not exactly . . .", or "sort of . . ."

♦ searching for ways of accommodating to the difficulties provoked by competing accounts which are offered—Castaneda's works pose these difficulties nicely (Castaneda, 1973)

Transformation may be seen as an aspect of context, the elements which comprise a context and the relationship between the elements (information, objects, actions, symbols, identities). A context is a framework of memory, a set of related elements which gives sense to elements brought into relationship with it.

Transformation, then, is a process, although not all processes are transformations. We may change elements or relationships within a context, or we may shift the same element to another context without transformation (Bateson, 1972).

However, merging of contexts frequently generates inconsistency and thus transformation. Transformation requires some shift in the interdependency between context and content.

Transformation may occur when ambiguity or uncertainty appears—there is a strain to consistency in our handling of data, and in resolving inconsistencies at certain levels we may produce transformation. Position and dominance are important in these processes, as are aesthetics and play, and some symbols have transformation inherent within them.

In transforming data we are likely to cluster them or to link them by chronological sequence, or by spatial contiguity, or more generally, by the characteristics of the data gathering operations. In re-sorting and writing up, we rearrange according to criteria of interest, fitness for argument, relevance to certain issues or topics or propositions. In a sense, too, the transforming operation is a problem-solving operation, where the starting point poses questions or problems and the task is to answer those questions or to solve the problems. This parallel makes all of the problem-solving literature potentially relevant to these processes; it also throws into importance the difference between information in a channel of communication and information in a channel of observation. Related to this is the distinction between research in a context of verification and research in a context of discovery. Inquiries designed to solve a given problem, to *verify*, can be regarded as treating information as if in a channel of communication. The data located can be assessed according to how far they fill in the gaps in a known puzzle.

Each additional piece automatically has the property of reducing uncertainty, and learning, knowledge acquisition is synonymous with information acquisition. (Turner, 1977)

By contrast, however, inquiries designed to solve an unstated or an ambiguously stated problem, to *discover*, have to treat information as if in a channel of observation. The data located have to be assessed for relevance according to criteria of relevance generated by the observer. While a provisional puzzle may be delineated, and progress made towards solving it, the observer will also monitor this progress and may use judgement to jettison this goal and substitute another, particularly after *surprising* information has been acquired. This mode of progress is consistent with all of those accounts of puzzle-solving which require a reframing or a respecifying of the problem-assumption built into the original problem, transforming or understanding of it.

It is very helpful in this context to recall the observations by the natural scientist Hans Selye about the manner in which he saw natural science ideas and theories coming into existence:

> The human brain is so constructed that it refuses to handle thoughts unless they can be wrapped up more or less neatly in individual IDEA-PACKAGES. It is astonishing how much confusion has been caused by the failure to understand the following three simple facts:
>
> (a) Thoughts, like fluids, can be adequately handled (isolated, measured, mixed, sold) only when put up in individual containers.
>
> (b) The thought packages contain previous experiences; only the selection within the wrapping can be new. We have no thoughts of things whose likeness we have never perceived before.
>
> (c) The thought-packages, the idea units, are very loosely bound together and their contents are not homogeneous. (Selye, 1964:268)

As Selye says, we put into packages those things which we have seen before, but rearranged, and metaphor may be thought of as a way of rearranging them. We see that this part of the world is like another entirely different part of the world, and we use this vision as a guide to our reordering. How can we formalise this? Choose a metaphor. Then rearrange incoming data to resemble the metaphor. That of course is absurdly over-simple, but how must we complicate it to make it more realistic? We would want to bear in mind the complex, pervasive, connotative symbolic qualities of metaphor rather than looking upon them solely as an information processing device. Miles and Huberman refer to metaphor, but they seem to have a very impoverished idea of what metaphor is or does, and not to realise that virtually all language and thought is metaphoric.

❖ NOTES

1. Note that this usage is intended to refer to studies of social phenomena in their 'natural' settings, but it should be distinguished clearly from the long established philosophical use of the term 'naturalism', a position close to positivism and far removed from naturalistic inquiry.

2. We are indebted to Nedira Yakir for the information that Gauguin, too, commented that the only things worth painting are those which are remembered.

❖ REFERENCES

Agar M., 1986, *Speaking of Ethnography*, Qualitative Method Series, 2, Beverly Hills, CA: Sage.

Baldamus W., 1976, *Inference and Substance in Sociology*, London: Martin Robertson.

Barzun J. & Graff H. F., 1977, *The Modern Researcher*, 3rd ed., New York: Harcourt Brace Jovanovich.

Basoux J., 1987, 'Women's contribution and the new vogue', *Times Higher Educational Supp.*

Bateson G., 1972, *Steps to an Ecology of Mind*, San Francisco: Chandler.

Bell C. & Newby R., 1984, *Researching: Politics, Problems, Practice*, London: Routledge.

Bryman A., ed., 1988, *Doing Research in Organisations*, London: Routledge and Kegan Paul.

Burgess R.G., ed., 1982, *Field Research*, London: Allen and Unwin.

Burgess R. G., 1984, *In the Field*, London: Allen and Unwin.

Burke K., 1969, *A Grammar of Motives*, Berkeley: University of California Press.

Castaneda C., 1973, *Journey to Ixtlan: the lessons of Don Juan*, London: Bodley Head.

Coleman J. S., 1965, *Introduction to Mathematical Sociology*, New York: Basic Books.

Elbow P., 1981, *Writing With Power*, New York: Oxford Univ. Press.

Feyerabend P., 1975, *Against Method: outline of an anarchistic theory of knowledge*, London: N.L.B.

Funtowicz S. O. & Ravetz J. R., 1986, 'Policy-related research: a notational scheme for the expression of quantitative technical information', *J. Operational Research Soc.*, 37 (3), 243–247.

Glaser B., 1978, *Theoretical Sensitivity: advances in the methodology of grounded theory*, Mill Valley, CA: Sociology Press.

Glaser B. & Strauss A., 1967, *The Discovery of Grounded Theory*, New York: Aldine.

Goffman E., 1975, *Frame Analysis*, Harmondsworth: Penguin Book.

Hage J., 1972, *Techniques and Problems of Theory Construction in Sociology*, New York: Wiley.

Hammond P., ed. 1964, *Sociologists at Work*, New York: Basic Books.

Hejzlar J., 1987, *Chinese Watercolours*, London: Galley Press.

Lincoln Y. S. & Guba E. G., 1985, *Naturalistic Inquiry*, Beverly Hills, CA: Sage.

Lower A., 1977, 'Facts and frameworks: aspects of the research process', Unpublished MA thesis, University of Birmingham.

McGregor D., 1967, *The Professional Manager*, New York: McGraw-Hill.

Martin P. & Turner B. A., 1987, 'Grounded theory and organisational research', *J. Applied Behavioral Science*, 22 (2), 141–157.

Miles M. B. & Huberman A. M., 1984, *Qualitative Data Analysis: a sourcebook of new methods*, Beverly Hills, CA: Sage.

Morgan G., 1983, *Beyond Method*, Beverly Hills, CA: Sage.

Mullins C. J., 1977, *A Guide to Writing and Publishing in the Social and Behavioural Sciences*, New York: Wiley.

Naipaul V. S., 1987, 'The enigma of arrival', *New Yorker*, 11 (Aug.) 26–62.

Peters T. & Waterman R., 1982, *In Search of Excellence*, New York: Harper & Row.

Pledge H.T., 1939, *Science Since 1500*, London: H.M.S.O.

Polanyi M., 1959, *Personal Knowledge: towards a post-critical philosophy*, London: Routledge and Kegan Paul.

Ravetz J. R., 1971, *Scientific Knowledge and Its Social Problems*, Oxford: Clarendon Press.

Reason P. & Rowan J., 1981, *Human Inquiry: a sourcebook of new paradigm research*, Chichester: Wiley.

Rosenberg M., 1968, *The Logic of Survey Analysis*, New York: Basic Books.

Selye H., 1964, *From Dream to Discovery: on being a scientist*, New York: McGraw-Hill.

Silverman D., 1985, *Qualitative Methodology and Sociology*, Aldershot: Gower.

Strauss A., 1987, *Qualitative Analysis for Social Scientists*, Cambridge: C.U.P.

Strunk W. & White E. B., 1979, *The Elements of Style*, 3rd ed., New York: Collier Macmillan.

Suttles G. D., 1978, *The Social Order of the Slum: ethnicity and territory in the inner city*, Chicago: Univ. of Chicago Press.

Turner B. A., 1977, 'Research note: a comment on the nature of information in channels of observation', *Cybermetica* XX (1), 39–42.

Turner B. A., 1981, 'Some practical aspects of qualitative data analysis: one way of organising some of the cognitive processes associated with the generation of grounded theory', *Quality and Quantity*, 15, 225–247.

Turner B. A., 1987, 'Grounded theory and knowledge elicitation', Seminar presented at the Department of Civil Engineering, Bristol University, November, 1987.

Turner B. A., 1988, 'Connoisseurship in the study of organisational culture', in A. Bryman, ed., *Doing Research in Organizations*. London: Routledge and Kegan Paul..

Willer D. E. & Willer J., 1973, *Pseudo-empiricism: a critique of a pseudo-science*, Englewood Cliffs, N.J.: Prentice Hall.

Witkin R. W., 1971, *The Intelligence of Feeling*, London: Heinemann.

Zetterberg H., 1954, *On Theory and Verification in Sociology*, Stockholm: Almqvist & Wisksell.

5

The Fact of Fiction
in Organizational Ethnography

John Van Maanen

"The temptation to form premature theories upon insufficient data," remarked Sherlock Holmes to Inspector MacDonald in *The Valley of Fear* (Baring-Gould, 1967), "is the bane of our profession." The same could be said of those of us conducting social research in organizations since, following the customary and respected practices of the day, we tend also to theorize well in advance of our facts, thus allowing for the possibility that the facts that emerge from our studies are twisted to fit a given theory. Yet, it is still the case that provisional hypotheses, tentative speculations, commonsensical hunches, and other tenderly held presuppositions about the world often represent the best we can do when attempting to see, grasp, and perhaps decode empirical phenomena. Faced with routine uncertainty and doubt, the most we can

Reprinted from John Van Maanen, "The Fact of Fiction in Organizational Ethnography," *Administrative Science Quarterly*, 24, December 1979, 539–550. © 1979 by Cornell University. Reprinted by permission.

do with or without the scientific method is to wait for time and fuller knowledge to explode whatever theoretical constructions we have built.

From this perspective, the amount of time an investigator spends constructing a theory by actively seeking the facts is a variable and one that presumably should be related to the quality of the theory that emerges from the field of study. The Sherlockian prescription as applied to organizational research is therefore simple, sequential, and reflexive: less theory, better facts; more facts, better theory.

Methodologically, organizational researchers schooled in an ethnographic tradition take this prescription rather seriously. In essence, ethnographers believe that separating the facts from the fictions, the extraordinary from the common, and the general from the specific is best accomplished by lengthy, continuous, firsthand involvement in the organizational setting under study. Although capable of generating massive amounts of data, the strategy is risky nevertheless. Ethnographic research is guided as much from drift as design and is perhaps the source of far more failures than successes. Assuming an ethnographic stance is by no means a guarantee that one will collect accurate and theoretically useful data no matter how long one remains in the field. Much of this operational difficulty lies in the rather widespread confusion that surrounds the various kinds of empirical information generated by an ethnographic study as well as the confusion that surrounds the theoretical uses to which such information can be put. My objective in this paper is to reduce some of this confusion tying empirical discovery and conceptual development in ethnographic work to the specific experiences of the researcher.

❖ BACKGROUND

The ethnographic approach is that of anthropology, and, to a more limited extent, sociology, under the stiff but precise tag, participant observation.[1] As practiced, this approach allows a fieldworker to use the culture of the setting (the socially acquired and shared knowledge available to the participants or members of the setting) to account for the observed patterns of human activity. In organizational studies, the patterns of interest are typically the various forms in which people manage to do things together in observable and repeated ways. Procedurally, the ethnographic method is described by Conklin

(1968: 172) as involving "a long period of intimate study and residence in a well-defined community employing a wide range of observational techniques including prolonged face-to-face contact with members of local groups, direct participation in some of the group's activities, and a greater emphasis on intensive work with informants than on the use of documentary or survey data."

My own work has attempted to be true to this procedural decree and over the past decade I have been involved in several projects of which ethnographic fieldwork was the principal data-gathering method.[2] Analytically, the aim of these studies has been to uncover and explicate the ways in which people in particular work settings come to understand, account for, take action, and otherwise manage their day-to-day situation. Specifically, much of my work has taken place in police agencies and has addressed such matters as recruit socialization (Van Maanen, 1973, 1975), police careers (Van Maanen and Schein, 1976; Van Maanen, 1978a), the street behavior of patrolmen (Van Maanen, 1974), and police labeling practices (Van Maanen, 1978b).

In the sections that follow, I discuss certain aspects of the information I have managed to collect, categorize, and publicly report as a result of my police studies. First, a fundamental distinction is made between an informant's first-order conception of what is going on in the setting and the researcher's second-order conceptions of what is going on. Second, working with first-order concepts, the differences between presentational and operational data are described. In this section, I argue that maintaining the separation between these two types of first-order data is the key analytic task faced by the ethnographer in the field. Third, the various ways in which an ethnographer can be misled in the research setting as to what constitutes operational data are denoted. If undetected, such deceptions allow for the distinct possibility that fictions will be reported as facts (and facts as fictions). Fourth, the analysis is brought to a close by observing that ethnographers merge the empirical and analytic aspects of research work and by so doing create an elusive and ever-expanding procedural mandate.

❖ FIRST-ORDER AND SECOND-ORDER CONCEPTS

Put simply, first-order concepts are the "facts" of an ethnographic investigation and the second-order concepts are the "theories" an analyst uses to organize and explain these facts. The facts come in varying forms however. At one level, certain descriptive properties of the studied scene serve as facts, for example, the number of arrests made by the vice squad or the particular rules enforced by a certain patrol sergeant. Of course, such facts do not speak for themselves and the fieldworker must therefore deal with another level of first-order fact, namely: the situationally, historically, and biographically mediated interpretations used by members of the organization to account for a given descriptive property. Thus, the arrest pattern may be seen by some as the result of an administrative attempt to "crack down" on prostitution. The sergeant's activities might be rendered sensible to certain members of the organization by assigning the sergeant to an indigenous character type known to the police as "brown-nosers" (those aggressively ambitious supervisors who struggle to make rank by zealously enforcing departmental rules and regulations). Both the descriptive properties of the studied scene and the member interpretations of what stands behind these properties are first-order concepts. At the empirical level, then, both behavior and member depictions of such behavior must be viewed within the framework of the observed.

Second-order concepts are those notions used by the fieldworker to explain the patterning of the first-order data. Descriptively, many second-order concepts are simply statements about relationships between certain properties observed to covary in the setting and may occasionally converge with first-order interpretations. Arrest patterns, for example, may be seen by the ethnographer and the police administrator alike as sensitive to the organizational policies regarding pay for overtime and court time. On the other hand, second-order concepts are perhaps most interesting when they do not converge for it is here that the fieldworker may have something novel to say. Typically, the more theoretically engaging second-order concepts represent what could be called "interpretations of interpretations."

Consider everyday police talk. Here the ethnographer is often handling first-order conceptions that reveal an informant's formulation of social structure (i.e., the informant's version of an ordered set of social relationships). If a patrolman claims, for example, "I don't want nothing to do with Horton, he's a fucking call jumper,"[3] that patrolman is displaying his sense of social structure. Implicit in the statement are at least three second-order conceptions bearing upon: (1) the role relations existing among patrolmen; (2) the competitive structure of policing; and (3) the centrality of a patrolman's assigned territory or "turf" to the practice of policing. To the ethnographer, these matters are seen as deeply embedded in the commonsensical though unarticulated understandings carried by virtually all members of the police culture. They represent what Cicourel (1967) calls "background expectancies" and as such they must always be inferred by the fieldworker since such assumptions are regarded as fully unproblematic by members of the studied organization. To draw out such second-order concepts is perhaps the most difficult yet most interesting goal of the ethnographic enterprise.

It should be clear however that when first formulated such second-order conceptions are relevant primarily to the culture of the researcher, not the researched. Consciously selected strategies must then be employed by the ethnographer to build such concepts. The strategy most commonly employed by a fieldworker is to explicitly examine the linguistic categories used by informants in the setting to describe various aspects of their routine and problematic situations. To continue my illustration, initially the label call jumper first suggested to me a class of phenomena apparently important to the police but one with which I was unfamiliar. Thus, having generated the category, I attempted to distinguish between the category as *seen* and the category as *heard*. Only by observing the phenomena firsthand and questioning the police about the actions they had just taken (or not taken) was I able to corroborate and elaborate upon what my informants were telling me. This is simply to say that my second-order conceptions of the first-order class of events known to policemen as "call jumping" rested upon both my talking to the police and observing the contextual contingencies upon which the use of the label was based. On the other hand, the understanding of this class of events carried by my informants rested on their continuing socialization in the natural setting and the sense of normality that results from such a process (Van Maanen, 1977). Thus, the meaning of "call jumping" to an informant was self-evident and in no need of explanation while to me its meaning was almost totally obscured by my (initial) ignorance of police work.[4]

Given that one aim of ethnography in organizational settings is to derive second-order concepts, it is obvious that such concepts are dependent upon the faith the fieldworker can sustain in the first-order concepts uncovered in the setting. In brief, most first-order concepts can be typed as being primarily presentational or operational. A central task then is to correctly type first-order concepts for if they are mistyped, many second-order concepts developed by the ethnographer are likely to be rather thin, hollow, and perhaps altogether faulty.

❖ PRESENTATIONAL AND OPERATIONAL DATA

Field data represent primarily the ethnographer's recording of first-order concepts as they arise from the observed talk and action of participants in the studied scene. This information is of two generic but distinct types. First, there are the "operational data" which document the running stream of spontaneous conversations and activities engaged in and observed by the ethnographer while in the field. These data surface in known and describable contexts and pertain to the everyday problematics of informants going about their affairs. Second, there are the "presentational data" which concern those appearances that informants strive to maintain (or enhance) in the eyes of the field-worker, outsiders and strangers in general, work colleagues, close and intimate associates, and, to varying degrees, themselves. Data in this category are often ideological, normative, and abstract, dealing far more with a manufactured image of idealized doing than with the routinized practical activities actually engaged in by members of the studied organization. In short, operational data deal with observed activity (behavior per se) and presentational data deal with the appearances put forth by informants as these activities are talked about and otherwise symbolically projected within the research setting.

The line separating these two strains of data is not always distinct. Verbal depictions are invariably recorded along with the concrete activities observed to be taking place. What the researcher is told cannot always be observed or assessed with any confidence as to its accuracy. Even when dealing with directly observable behavior, it is sometimes quite difficult for an observer to grasp its contextual meaning to those whose behavior is being described. Often one only sees (and, hence, understands) what is happening after having been first told what to look for. A wink, a blink, or nod is not merely a fleck of behavior to be described without ambiguity but is rather a potential sign that must be read as to what is signified.

These bothersome facts suggest rather pointedly that separating operational and presentational data is an *analytic* accomplishment that must be attended to continually by a fieldworker. If the researcher somehow loses sight of this distinction there is the possibility that the presentational data will literally swamp the operational data, thus masking the difference between fact and fiction in the findings generated from ethnographic study. Fieldwork, despite the best intentions of the researcher, almost always boils down to a series of endless conversations intersected by a few major events and a host of less formidable ones. The information as recorded by the fieldworker is then primarily talk based not only because this is what occupies the vast majority of the ethnographer's time but also because, as noted above, understanding the concrete activities taking place in the field is grounded largely upon what members have to say about what such activities mean to them. Moreover, because the ethnographer focuses on both behavior and the symbolic worlds within which such behavior is located, the meaning and significance of the events of interest to one's informants cannot be known merely by analyzing the number of times such events are observed to take place.

To hear patrolmen talk of "street justice," for instance, might lead a listener to believe that its application occupies a fair amount of work time in police organizations.[5] Attempting to find out about "street justice" by talking to my informants, I collected information cast in ideal terms. At times, when asked to explain or describe what the phrase meant, a patrolman would respond by giving a recent example but on the basis of the example alone I was unable to assess whether the case cited was imaginary or real, exceptional or ordinary, unusual practice or standard. In order to separate the presentational from operational, I had to not only check the various features of the talk against other stories I had heard (and would later solicit), but, most important, I had to see the implementation of "street justice" firsthand and compare my direct observations with the accounts provided to me by others. In other words, if "street justice" was to be set in operational terms, it was imperative that I observe at least a few of its occasions. Yet no sample could be used. Indeed, in a year and a half of fieldwork, I have seen what my informants would unhesitatingly call "street justice" on only four or five occasions. The relative availability of operational data will of course vary by topic, by site, by informant, by time spent in the field, and so forth. But it is nonetheless true of fieldwork that when it comes to the events one's informants regard as significant, one must often lean far more on what one hears than on what one sees.[6]

Given this unavoidable aspect of fieldwork, the ethnographer always runs the risk of mistaking presentational for operational data. Worthy of further note in this regard is the nasty fact that the fieldworker may find it difficult to generalize (to develop second-order concepts) from specific practices (operational data) without merely parroting back the normative abstractions (presentational data) used by members of the studied group to both describe and account for their behavior. Events bearing on an individual's behavior are often quite literally hidden from view. For both the fieldworker and the informant, particular events take on significance and meaning insofar as at least one cultural interpretation exists for what is taking place. From this standpoint, ethnography (and everyday life) is as much "believing is seeing" as it is "seeing is believing." Inference and trust are central matters here and therefore evaluating the believability of what one hears and sees is critical in the analytic task of separating the operational from the presentational data.

❖ LIES, IGNORANCE, AND (TAKEN-FOR-GRANTED) ASSUMPTIONS

Do informants speak the truth as they know it to the fieldworker? Does a particular *in situ* activity have the characteristics ascribed to it by the fieldworker? These issues (and more) must be addressed by the researcher and, in some way, handled by typing the information obtained as true or false from the informant's perspective, as operational or presentational from the fieldworker's perspective, or as ambiguous and uncertain from one or both perspectives. This is not to say, however, that lies, deceptions, evasions, conjectures, and so on are categorically disregarded by the ethnographer. To the contrary, false and misleading information is exceedingly valuable to the fieldworker when it is recognized as false. Given this methodological premise, it is important to examine the ways ethnographic data, primarily talk-based data, can mislead the fieldworker.

First, the researcher can be misled because informants want it that way. People lie, evade, and otherwise deceive the fieldworker in numerous and inventive ways. I have often been purposely led astray by patrolmen in my police studies. Consider the recurring statements I heard from many officers attesting to the "fact" that they felt under no pressure whatsoever to make certain kinds of arrests when on patrol.

It was of some importance apparently to these patrolmen that they be seen as autonomous, independent actors in the police drama for they took great care to present themselves in such a manner. But their actions often belied their words for, on many occasions, I sat with these same officers in their prowl cars outside dimly lit taverns simply waiting for the first unsteady (and unlucky) patron to drive away. In this fashion, any number of drunk driving arrests could be enacted with dispatch and assured "quality." More to the point, however, on such occasions, these not-so-cunning arrests were said by the men to be necessary for "getting the drunk-hunting sergeant off our backs for a while."

A central postulate of the ethnographic method is that people lie about the things that matter most to them. Penetrating fronts, a phrase used with powerful effect by Douglas (1976), then becomes one of the more important goals of the competent fieldworker. If the ethnographer can uncover the lie, much is revealed about what is deemed crucial by the individual, group, or organization. Evasion too enters the calculus of deception for it is unfortunately true that most informants are only as good as the questions put to them. For example, after having become rather close to a particular informant over the course of a year, I learned from an ex-partner of his that he had twice been suspended from the department for alleged misconduct (brutality) on the street. When I later asked my friend why he had never bothered to mention this aspect of his police career to date, he remarked with a wry but embarrassed smile, "You never asked."[7]

Three kinds of discrediting information are most often shielded by the conscious deception. "Hidden failings" represent one category and deal with a particular informant's own private and personal flaws, disreputable interests, or shameful errors. Disclosures of this type are relatively rare in fieldwork for such information surfaces only when the researcher inadvertently stumbles over it or creates a very special relationship with a given informant. Another category is represented by certain "rotten apple" disclosures which refer to those perceived character defects, flagrant individual mistakes, or taboo-violating local activities thought to be associated with a specified other in the organization. Materials of this sort are again notoriously difficult for an ethnographer to come by since most informants are quite aware of the rather deep interpersonal rule that suggests the protection of one's own self is based in large measure on the protection of the selves of others. In police circles at least, peer protection at the street level is almost a point of honor though fleeting glimpses are sometimes provided of others by certain members of the organization (notably the most marginal and least occupationally committed members). The last category concerns those disclosures of "collective secrets." Information in this domain typically deals with certain widely known, but controversial practices engaged in by members within certain social segments of the organization. Once, after having been uncharacteristically but unmistakably waved from a dispatched "investigate open door" assignment by another patrol unit, my partner for the evening remarked: "those fucking mopes in Charlie Three, ripping the goddamn place off [a department store warehouse] and on my call yet." Information in this domain is relatively easy to come by—though not always easy to check—since such practices are often deeply resented (or strongly supported) by others and many people in the setting are only too eager to express their disdain (or approval).[8]

The second way a researcher can be misled in ethnography is when one's informants are themselves misled and wrong about matters of their concern. To wit, several informed observers of the police are woefully ignorant (yet still assertive) of the laws they are charged with enforcing (e.g., Banton, 1964; Black, 1971; Manning, 1977). Of methodological interest is the notion that randomness per se is of relatively little value to an ethnographer when assessing the believability of the data produced. A fundamental principle of fieldwork is that the researcher's account of the studied scene should be built on the information provided by the most knowledgeable (and candid) members of that scene. For example, several police recruits were convinced that the "policeman's discount" on retail goods in many downtown shops was a thing of the past. However, others in the department told me the opposite. To check these contradictory statements, I occasionally "buzzed a clerk" (displayed my police badge) when paying for certain goods in certain downtown stores and was rewarded with information as to who was more knowledgeable among my informants.

There is a general point underlying this cautionary tale. Not all informants are good informants since the information they possess— regardless of their willingness to part with it—is hardly equivalent. In the police world (as perhaps in all organizational worlds), those persons who strictly adhere to most departmental rules and regulations are unusual and are considered by many others on the scene to be culturally incompetent in the local setting. Patrolmen who always read an accused suspect their rights upon an arrest or patrolmen who answered every call dispatched to their unit were considered by most of their colleagues to be stupid. What is proper may not be either popular or rational to all members of an organization and informants will differ greatly along these lines. The distribution of knowledge about what is going on in any organization is an important part of the sociology of that organization and the fieldworker must take care to establish the limits of an informant's expertise.

The third way an ethnographer can be misled is because informants are sometimes totally unaware of certain aspects underlying many of their own activities. Like fish who are presumably unaware of the water in which they swim, there are things associated with police work that all policemen take more or less for granted and therefore have a difficult time articulating. All the patrolmen I studied, for example, talked of their "duck ponds" where it was felt they could write as many moving traffic citations as they so chose. Such duck ponds would be described, for example, as those busy but poorly marked intersections in the city where illegal turns were frequent or those unobtrusive side streets located just beyond certain hills where motorists would speed by. What was never mentioned when talking about these territories was, however, the crucial fact that pedestrian traffic was by and large virtually absent from the most popular duck ponds. Yet, this fact alone was what was common to duck ponds across the city since a working policeman had no desire to be pestered or otherwise bothered by the passing pedestrian who, if not seeking aid or direction, might accuse the officer of loafing on the job, being unnecessarily sneaky in the performance of the job, or acting as mere automaton in meeting what to the citizen might be seen as an obnoxious ticket quota. At any rate, by simply relying on the stated rationale supplied by patrol officers for choosing their duck ponds, I would have been easily misled and missed this rather taken-for-granted but critical aspect of police work.

Another class of "things everybody knows" (but are not typically aware of) are discovered in what Goffman (1971) refers to as "negatively eventful occasions." What is meant by this phrase is simply that the obviousness of certain features in a social scene comes about only when something else in that scene has been removed, goes awry, or is in some way altered. As Emerson (1970) so pointedly demonstrates, the notion of normality can only be described in reference to what is considered deviant. For instance, to answer a "barking dog" call when first dispatched was an occasion worthy of note to my informants since such calls were typically ignored by most patrol units (though routinely cleared as "unable to locate"). The example of "call jumping" is also good in this regard since the label itself arises from a breach in the taken-for-granted and usually unproblematic assumptions that surround police activity. In the interplay between theory and data as both are generated in the field, it is the empirical exception that often displays the analytic rule.

The potential the taken-for-granted features of an organization have for misdirection in fieldwork goes, however, far beyond what an informant may or may not say or do. The ethnographer's own taken-for-granted understandings of the social world under scrutiny are also tied closely to the nature and quality of the data produced. Take, for example, my surprise and initial puzzlement at the positive reactions a number of police officers expressed regarding the stiff, formal, thoroughly bureaucratic treatment they received from certain court officials, hospital personnel, and ranking officers—all of whom represented people with whom my informants had frequent dealings. As a middle-class academician, such treatment seemed improper and hence noteworthy to me since it violated my own sense of propriety about the "correct tone" for interpersonal conduct among people quite familiar with one another. Eventually, however, I came to realize that the police grow comfortable with this sort of orderly and highly predictable treatment from certain types of people and not only expect it but are sometimes confused, dismayed, and perhaps angered when this formal treatment is not forthcoming.

Another illustration is useful in this regard for it suggests an important constitutive base underlying the ethnographic enterprise. Consider here the fact that I was initially jolted by the visceral disdain most patrolmen expressed toward those citizens who, for some reason or other, required aid in settling a family dispute. At first, I regarded such vociferous distaste to occupational concerns: that such calls were considered open-ended and messy, that they were thought to be quite dangerous, that they interfered with what most police took to be their "realwork" of crime control and crook catching, that the typical "family beef" involved people whom the police regarded as beneath them both socially and economically, and so forth. But the matter went deeper because after exploring the various contextual contingencies upon which patrolmen expressed their most vehement reactions, it became apparent that they were reacting not to the call per se but were reacting to the specific kind of persons they encountered on such calls whom they saw in very personal terms as quite different from themselves since these people were obviously unable to control their own households. At an unstated level, it was a moral matter to them. Because the police believe that they would never require public assistance in attending to family matters, those that did request aid were viewed as craven, stupid, repugnant, or, in the idiom of the police, "the dumb fucks of the world." In this case, I was blinded by my own perceptual screen and did not see that persons who regarded themselves as very independent, self-reliant, and decisive would, naturally enough, find others who appeared to require outside help in what were thought to be private and usually trivial matters to be persons unworthy of human respect.

In sum, misdirection in fieldwork arises from several sources not the least of which is the ethnographer's own lack of sensitivity for the discrepant observation and lack of appreciation for the tacit bases of one's own understanding of the social world. The vast amount of what is unremarkable to me about police organizations is therefore underrepresented no doubt in my writings. The same bias informs all ethnographic work in that it is by and large the differences from one's own world (and unexpected similarities) that find their way into one's field notes. Without overlooking the lies and the areas of informant ignorance, it is clear that knowledge based on incongruity is as central to fieldwork as it is to any other area of scientific endeavor.

❖ THE ETHNOGRAPHIC ILLUSION

I have tried in this paper to detail what I consider to be the crucial analytic distinctions to be drawn when assessing the kind of data one must deal with in ethnographic studies. First, I noted the necessity of separating first- and second-order concepts, a separation based primarily on whose point of view is being reported, the informant's or the researcher's. Second, I suggested that the various bits of recorded information generated by the ethnographer as to the features of the studied organization must be typed as presentational or operational, a distinction resting in large part upon the ethnographer's ability to both see and understand what is occurring within the informants' framework. Third, I noted that the ethnographer must continually assess the believability of the talk-based information harvested over the course of a study, an evaluation dependent upon the fieldworker's interest, skill, and good fortune in uncovering lies, areas of ignorance, and the various taken-for-granted features of the studied organization. These tasks represent the essence of sound fieldwork and lie at the heart of any faithful description of a studied organization.

Accomplishing such tasks involves continual and careful attention to the details of one's adventures in the field. From this perspective, then, analysis and verification in ethnography is something one brings forth with them from the field, not something which can be attended to later, after the data are collected. When making sense of field data, one cannot simply accumulate information without regard to what each bit of information represents in terms of its possible contextual meanings. Moreover, such an analytic assessment can be accomplished only in the field where one has the opportunity to check out certain bits of information across informants and across situations. It is true of course that much of what one learns at the time is not fully understood and may in fact be reinterpreted and seen later in new ways. The theories developed by ethnographers in the field have an alterable and fluid character to them. Since ethnographic theories are tested, retested, and tested again in the field, they tend to be rather resistant to high-level abstractions. Even at the end of a long study, the theories proclaimed by ethnographers are likely to be only tentatively asserted, full of reservation and qualifying detail. But, if this is the typical version of a given social world that arises from those who study it most closely, it is also an argument for paying stricter attention in all forms of social research to the distinctions of the sort made in this paper regarding the kinds of data one collects.

This normative discussion raises a final concern because it suggests that the expressed aim of ethnography, "to depict," in Goodenough's (1964: 14) terms, "the system for perceiving, believing, evaluating and acting," is a shockingly broad and preposterous one. Culture is itself an interpretation and therefore most of the facts one goes into the field to discover are themselves already known about and interpreted in a particular light by the people one talks to in the setting. The results of ethnographic study are thus mediated several times over—first, by the fieldworker's own standards of relevance as to what is and what is not worthy of observation; second, by the historically situated questions that are put to the people in the setting; third, by the self-reflection demanded of an informant; and fourth, by the intentional and unintentional ways the produced data are misleading. Though most ethnographers are well aware of this irreducible dilemma, they still maintain the stance that if they spend some more time in the field to dig a little deeper and probe a little further, certain crucial facts will be revealed which will tie up loose ends and provide closure to a study in danger of infinite expansion. Ultimately, this is an illusion although, I hasten to add, it is an altogether necessary one. "The world," according again to Sherlock Holmes, "is full of obvious things which nobody by any chance will ever see."

❖ NOTES

1. Ethnographic research is of course more than a single method and can be distinguished from participant observation on several grounds one of which is that of its broader aim, the analytic description of a culture. This paper conveniently glosses over many of the fine points of methodological nuance and regards any social study as at least partially ethnographic if it allows a researcher to become immersed in the everyday life of the observed. In essence, the use of such techniques in organizational studies literally forces the researcher to come to grips with the essential ethnographic question of what it is to be rather than to see a member of the organization.

2. Though the main thrust of this paper is upon the kind of social information generated by ethnographic study, I have elsewhere considered other methodological aspects of my field experiences: the process of securing access and building a research role (Van Maanen, 1978c); the use of informants in fieldwork (Van Maanen, forthcoming); the process of collecting, recording, and reporting ethnographic data (Van Maanen, 1978d); and the moral and ethical implications of doing ethnographic work (Van Maanen, 1979). While much of this work can be viewed as proselytizing on my part, some of it is not for I agree with Becker (1970: 3) that methodology in the social sciences is far too important to be left to the methodologists.

3. "Call jumping" refers to those occasions where a patrol unit other than the unit taking the dispatched call arrives on the scene first and "handles" the call. Such behavior is relatively rare in police agencies and is considered, both officially and unofficially, improper though, under some conditions, call jumping may be considered a favor and be welcomed by the unit whose call was jumped. But that is another story.

4. This is an important distinction to make because, in the final analysis, fieldworkers can never fully apprehend the world of their informants in its "natural" form. Even though ethnographers may sense the situated meanings various informants attach to the objects of their concern, such meanings will remain largely exhibits of how informants think rather than the "true" meanings such objects have to informants. While I tried to listen, to see, to talk, to feel, and to get into every odd cultural corner I could, it would still be absurd

to suggest that I understand the police world as my informants do. A fieldworker is not interested solely in what things are for themselves as are the people studied, but rather the fieldworker is interested specifically in what things "stand for" to the people observed. Bittner's (1973) discussion on the ethnographer's "specimen knowledge" and the native's "innate knowledge" is revealing in this regard.

5. "Street justice" was a tactic employed by the patrolmen I observed (Van Maanen, 1974: 116–120) to rectify what they believed to be a situation badly in need of rearranging. Practically, "street justice" represented a "thumping" or "beating" administered, under certain conditions, on the street, though not quite in public. Typically, street justice was reserved for those who brazenly challenged an officer's definition of who was in charge of an interaction.

6. The importance of observing key episodes and how one decodes what is earned from their observation are covered nicely by Manning (forthcoming). The notion of "event sampling" is somewhat related to these issues as is discussed under various labels in Glaser and Strauss (1967), Lofland (1976), and Douglas (1976).

7. It is worth noting that there is often a good deal of symbolic violence involved in fieldwork since people are, to a degree, coaxed, persuaded, pushed, pressured, and sometimes almost blackmailed into providing information to the researcher that they might otherwise prefer to shield. Simply because the ethnographer is there may create problems for people. And, despite the preachings of modern moralists, many people feel that it is the unexamined life that is worth leading, not the examined. Ultimately, it is the researcher's own sense of morality that will determine how such symbolic violence will be used in the field. There are then limits, individually drawn, that will restrict the degree to which the believability of field data will be checked out. Failure to push another on delicate matters or voluntarily withdrawing from a scene embarrassing to another are good examples in this regard.

8. This segmentation of interests raises a related point for it is the very existence of such social division in organizations that makes fieldwork so valuable within them. It seems almost universally true that the secrets of one group are revealed most readily by members of another group. Were this not true, ethnographers would always be left to construct their field reports out of appearances, cliches, pieties, and conventional wisdom. Aside from the obvious race and rank divisions among the police, other social cleavages were important to my work. For example, lines of discord could be seen between the young and old, men and women, patrol officers and detectives, professionally oriented and traditionally oriented officers, and even patrolmen working different sectors and shifts were occasionally openly contemptuous of one another. These major and minor feuds and factions provide vital sources of information for the watchful but prudent fieldworker.

❖ REFERENCES

Banton, Michael. 1964. The Policeman in the Community. New York: Anchor.
Baring-Gould, William S., ed. 1967. The Annotated Sherlock Holmes, 2 Vols. New York: Clarkson N. Potter.

Becker, Howard S. 1970. Sociological Work. New Brunswick, NJ: Transaction Books.

Bittner, Egon. 1973. "Objectivity and realism in sociology." In George Psathas (ed.), Phenomenological Sociology: 108-125. New York: Wiley.

Black, Donald J. 1971. "The social organization of arrest." Stanford Law Review, 23: 1087–1111.

Cicourel, Aaron V. 1967. The Social Organization of Juvenile Justice. New York: Wiley.

Conklin, H. 1968. "Ethnography." In D. L. Sills (ed.), International Encyclopedia of the Social Sciences, 5: 115–208. New York: Free Press.

Douglas, Jack. 1976. Investigative Social Research. Beverly Hills, CA: Sage.

Emerson, Joan. 1970. "Nothing unusual is happening." In Thomas Shibutani (ed.), Human Nature and Collective Behavior: 208–222. New Brunswick, NJ: Transaction Books.

Glaser, Barney G., and Anselm Strauss. 1967. The Discovery of Grounded Theory. Chicago: Aldine.

Goffman, Erving. 1971. Relations in Public. New York: Harper & Row.

Goodenough, Ward H. 1964. "Introduction." In Ward H. Goodenough (ed.), Explorations in Cultural Anthropology: 3–21. New York: McGraw-Hill.

Lofland, John. 1976. Doing Social Life. New York: Wiley

Manning, Peter K. 1977. Police Work. Cambridge, MA: MIT Press.

———. forthcoming. "Making sense of field data." In Thomas J. Cottle and Robert Weiss (eds.), The Narrative Voice. New York: Basic.

Van Maanen, John. 1973. "Observations on the making of policemen." Human Organizations, 32: 407–418.

———. 1974. "Working the street." In Herbert Jacob (ed.), The Potential for the Reform of Criminal Justice, 3: 83–130. Beverly Hills, CA: Sage.

———. 1975. "Police socialization." Administrative Science Quarterly, 20: 207–228.

———. 1977. "Experiencing organization." In John Van Maanen (ed.), Organizational Careers: Some New Perspectives: 15–45. New York: Wiley.

———. 1978a. "People processing." Organizational Dynamics, 7: 18–36.

———. 1978b. "The asshole." In Peter K. Manning and John Van Maanen (eds.), Policing: A View from the Streets: 221–238. Santa Monica, CA: Goodyear.

———. 1978c. "Watching the watchers." In Peter K. Manning and John Van Maanen (eds.), Policing: A View from the Streets: 309–349. Santa Monica, CA: Goodyear.

———. 1978d. "Notes on the production of ethnographic data." In Robin Luckham (ed.), Anthropological Methods in the Study of Legal Systems: 112–157. Stockholm: Scandinavian Institute for African Studies.

———. 1979. "The moral fix." In Robert N. Smith (ed.), Social Science Methods,—Qualitative Social Research: 61–74. New York: Irvington.

———. forthcoming. "The informant game." Urban Life.

Van Maanen, John, and Edgar H. Schein. 1976. "Career development." In J. Richard Hackman and J. Lloyd Suttle (eds.), Improving Life at Work: 30–95. Santa Monica, CA: Goodyear.

Part II

Methodological Perspectives

The pieces in Part II address methodological issues from different perspectives. All are reflective, accompanied by concrete illustrations from different sectors of qualitative inquiry. Some are reviews of evolving genres of qualitative research. Others propose alternative ways of doing such qualitative work as achieving generalizability from small samples, analyzing cases in conjunction with the study of variables, and determining criteria for assessing the usefulness of study findings while avoiding sources of bias. The researchers whose work we include here like to get specific—to think about the details of things.

In "Intuitive Data Processing as a Potential Source of Bias in Naturalistic Evaluations," which was first published in 1981, Sadler provides a rapid but fairly thorough review of the most likely—and often the most pernicious—biases that can creep in when a lone researcher collects, sifts, and interprets information in the course of an empirical study. Sadler sees the one-person research machine as a potential fool, beset with self-delusions of which he or she may only gradually become aware—often as the study moves toward completion. The list of possible biases and companion illustrations comes largely from the increasingly influential field of cognitive social psychology.

Since 1971, John Lofland has charted a steady course among the sailors, trawlers, and buccaneers who have succeeded him. Here, more than two decades later, he lays out in "Analytic Ethnography: Features, Failings, and Futures" (originally published in 1995) the constituent features of a coherent analytic ethnography, warning his public that the more abstract and philosophical features undergird the concrete and operational ones. He also proposes that the features or practices that emerge early on are the ones he and his colleagues will approach with the most energy. Generally, Lofland is at home among experiments, surveys, and historical comparisons, but he is equally comfortable with the evolution of social domains and with what he calls "the striving to formulate empirically falsifiable and generically attuned answers to those questions." The effort, he tells us later on, is to lift the situation under study out of its historically specific details and bring it to broader audiences. In so doing, Lofland tells us, emotional matters are matters of consequence, just as is a deep familiarity with the setting. For Lofland, such a constellation may well hold together over time, except for the gradual dominance of "emergent analysis," a cousin to methods of "grounded theory" about which he has had many pungent and prickly things to say.

With "Increasing the Generalizability of Qualitative Research," originally published in 1990, Schofield clarifies an issue that has too often been muddied, dubiously transposed from experimental studies, or made technically infeasible by the typically small samples that characterize qualitative research. Here, Schofield provides an accessible, usable approach to case sampling and generalizability for graduate students and working researchers alike.

We have a special fondness for Lincoln and Guba's 1990 article "Judging the Quality of Case Study Reports." These authors have written a good deal about alternative paradigms but less often on their methodological preferences for specific empirical studies, particularly on their criteria for achieving "credibility." They do so here, succinctly, making careful distinctions that inform both analyses and interpretations of qualitative studies.

Writers in the proliferating field of narratives take various stances, from the anthropological and linguistic to the literary and postmodern. In these excerpts from her 1993 monograph *Narrative Analysis*, Riessman deals with the "representation of experience," with "practical models" for analyzing narrative materials, and with "doing narrative analysis." The pragmatic yet multilevel nature of the report is exemplary. Using carefully chosen transcriptions from real-life stories, Riessman covers a range of issues: the choice of interviewing techniques, the delicate elaboration of transcripts ("crunching"), the framing of sequences and recapitulations, and, more generally, the testing, clarifying, and deepening of understandings that lead to validation.

6

Intuitive Data Processing as a
Potential Source of Bias
in Naturalistic Evaluations

D. Royce Sadler

Whatever its other strengths, the mind is apt to make errors of judgment and inference. To most of us, this statement comes as no surprise. As one might expect, there has been a long history of attempts to identify and understand the nature and extent of these tendencies. Francis Bacon in the 17th century, for example, rebelled against the influence of Aristotelian thinking and the methods of acquiring knowledge (especially about the physical universe) current in his own day. In particular, he warned against a number of sources of distortion which he called *Idols*. Those associated with sensory

Reprinted from D. Royce Sadler, "Intuitive Data Processing as a Potential Source of Bias in Naturalistic Evaluations," *Educational Evaluation and Policy Analysis*, 3(4), 25–31. Copyright 1981 by the American Educational Research Association. Reprinted by permission of the publisher.

perception and intuitive methods of analysis he called the "Idols of the Tribe," since he believed them to be "inherent in human nature, and the very tribe or race of man" (Bacon 41).

Recent research in human perception and cognition has given substance and specificity to many of Bacon's concerns. In addition, there has been growing interest in the implications of this type of research in various social settings, in particular, to courtroom testimony (Yarmey, 1979) and to decision making in business (Wright, 1980).

Because bias threatens an evaluation, it is not surprising that there is considerable literature on the topic. It is possible to group various forms of bias under three broad headings. First, there are *ethical compromises*, actions for which the evaluator is personally culpable. Second are what may be called *value inertias*, unwanted distorting influences which reflect the evaluator's background experience. The first part of this paper is a brief survey of these two categories, mainly to indicate the scope of each and so distinguish them from the third category, *cognitive limitations* in dealing with data.

The major purpose of the paper is to elaborate the third category. This takes the form of a survey of faulty intuitions which have been identified in empirical research. Only those aspects which appear to have direct relevance to evaluation (in particular, naturalistic evaluation) are included. This is not to suggest that current naturalistic approaches to research and evaluation are undisciplined and merely impressionistic. They are not, of course. But such a catalog of commonly found intuitive biases is justified even if it is not accompanied by concrete proposals as to how each may be eliminated or reduced. To be sure, the presentation may appear to be somewhat negative (after all, it is a list of defects) but if it helps sensitize naturalistic inquirers to potential problem areas, its contribution will be positive.

❖ ETHICAL COMPROMISES AND VALUE INERTIAS

Potential sources of bias in the first category include (1) conflict of interest between the evaluator (or the agency) and the program evaluation itself (Scriven, 1976); (2) reactivity between the providers of information on the one hand and the evaluator as consumer of information on the other, because of the purposeful, goal-oriented activity of both parties (Cochran, 1978); and (3) sloppiness in the way the evaluation is carried out (shallowness, prejudice, capriciousness, and the intrusion of unsubstantiated opinion). Page (1979) refers to evaluations with some or all of these characteristics as self-serving, flexible, politicized, and compliant.

Taken together, ethical compromises are associated with one of the two meanings of the term "subjectivity" distinguished by Scriven (1972). The second has to do with values, preferences, and personal meaning; in this sense, subjectivity is, as Scriven (1967) and Krathwohl (1980) argue, a natural and necessary element of evaluation, which calls for no apology.

Some biases can be traced to a particular evaluator's background knowledge, prior experience, emotional makeup, or world view. Although these may affect what data are collected and how they are interpreted, they are not so much sinister and morally reprehensible as simply natural characteristics of a person *as a person*, hence the label *value inertias*.

Scriven (1973), for example, warned against the possible biasing effect of knowing a program's objectives. This knowledge may cause an evaluator to attend to goals as they are stated to the virtual exclusion of important side effects. Or an evaluator's attention may be captured by an incident known to have had great significance in another context (perhaps in a previous evaluation, or in the evaluator's own experience). A different evaluator may miss it altogether.

There is a sense in which knowledge and values are inseparable. Consciousness acts selectively on a great mass of stimuli, sorting out "what is and what is not worth noticing, what is important and valuable and what is insignificant or valueless" (Najder, 1975, p. 5). Granted that we all have different sensory thresholds, it is clear that there remain many idiosyncratic dispositions and presuppositions linked with our backgrounds of values.

To reduce the impact of ethical compromises and value inertias, a number of strategies have been developed or suggested. These include new methodologies (e.g., Wolf, 1975, on adversary proceedings), improved training of evaluators, periodic checks on the independence of evaluators, choosing an evaluator with a proven track record, requiring evaluators to disclose their interests (Scriven, 1976), the externalization of value positions (Hammond & Adelman, 1976), and openness in providing a rationale for subjective judgments

(Goodrich, 1978). Elimination of the biases mentioned so far, by whatever methods can be devised, is a necessary *but not sufficient* condition for an unbiased inquiry. It is necessary as well to identify and deal with biases due to the limitations of our information-processing capacity.

❖ NATURALISTIC APPROACHES TO EVALUATION

Among the developments in evaluation methodology over the past decade has been a growing interest in *in situ*, naturalistic approaches and a reduced emphasis on quantification, controlled experiments, and multivariate analyses. However, naturalistic modes of inquiry are susceptible to a hazard not normally a problem when researching in the positivist tradition. It is this: naturalistic inquirers typically do most of their data reduction and analysis using a marvelously designed piece of apparatus, the brain. No device or system so far devised, irrespective of size or complexity, can match its ability to extract information from noisy environments. But, of course, any inferences drawn from data can be only as good as native cognitive mechanisms allow.

Studies over the past 40 years into the processes of human decision making, clinical judgment, and problem solving have shown that the human mind as information processor frequently draws incorrect inferences about the nature of the world and that there are certain recurring patterns. Fortunately, our natural tolerance for ambiguity, together with our adaptive ability, allow us in everyday living to recover from the consequences of a partially incorrect judgment (unless it is a devastating one), to revise an opinion, or to salvage some pieces. Initially vague conceptions need to be clarified only to the extent that makes the next step possible.

The situation is more serious when it is the evaluator who stands between the program and the audience, and when policy decisions that may affect the lives of many people may depend on the outcome of an evaluation. The audience must of necessity reconstruct a conception of what the program is, how it operates, and what its effects are, by drawing upon what the evaluator as intermediary is able to convey. Direct access of the audience to the program for verification purposes is frequently inappropriate or impossible.

❖ INFORMATION PROCESSING LIMITATIONS

Incorrect inferences are broadly due to our inherent incapacity to deal effectively with large masses of information at once, our intuitive ignorance of notions of natural variability (randomness and probability), and our tendency to seek meaning in or impose meaning upon the world around us.

Man's performance as intuitive data processor (hereafter IDP) is certainly impressive, but it is still somewhat fallible. There is considerable consistent evidence of misperception, misaggregation, and defective inference, leading to suboptimal assessments. These biases appear to be in some fundamental way linked to our natural processes of cognition, though this is not to suggest that all of the weaknesses occur all of the time, or that any is invariant over persons, tasks, and contexts. Many of them are of lesser importance in positivistic evaluations because of the methods of analysis. Naturalistic inquirers, on the other hand, pursue their tasks sensitively and sequentially. It is these same characteristics that make the naturalistic inquirers more vulnerable.

The listing of IDP biases which follows draws from the review of Shulman and Elstein (1975) together with more recent material. Only one or two references are given for each item, and depending on how the headings are construed, there may be some overlap and interdependence among the items. Some of the research evidence comes from laboratory experiments (in particular those of Tversky & Kahneman, 1974) and some from investigations of actual clinical judgments. There appears to be no empirical evidence indicating the importance of IDP biases relative to those in the other two categories, nor is it clear how often they occur in naturalistic evaluations. It should be noted that some of the data-analytic techniques described in the literature on ethnography and naturalistic research methods implicitly recognize these cognitive limitations.

1. Data Overload

In his classic paper, Miller (1956) showed that an informational bottleneck exists which places severe limitations on the amount of data able to be received, processed, and remembered by the human mind. By reorganizing the way the information is structured, the limits can be stretched but there remain upper limits to capacity.

This is especially important when evaluators not only describe or portray (something which can be done serially), but make inferences as to cause and effect, or valuations as to the worth of a program's means and ends (processes which involve aggregation). Summers, Taliaferro, and Fletcher (1970) showed that in making judgments where there were many aspects to be considered simultaneously, evaluators actually used less information than they thought. When some information which judges *said* they were using was experimentally varied over wide limits while other information remained fixed, there was no change in the judgment.

2. First Impression

Poulton (1968) found that for physical stimuli judges effectively calibrated themselves on the first few stimuli received, and that this early baseline was persistent. Wason (1968) found the same for informational stimuli. The *order* in which information was received turned out to be important.

Tversky and Kahneman (1974) called the phenomenon "anchoring," and noted that estimates of simple quantities such as proportions tended to "creep" upwards or downwards from an initial starting point, and resisted adequate revision in the face of evidence. This effect is possibly more noticeable when an original estimate is provided by someone the evaluator regards as likely to be knowledgeable, for example, a program administrator or participant. But an evaluator's own first impression might be just as enduring.

3. Availability of Information

The impact of information for both evaluator and audience depends on whether it is easy to retrieve instances, to search for examples, or to understand reasons (Tversky & Kahneman, 1974). For example, if the researcher comes to a certain understanding of events (perhaps formulating a tentative hypothesis), but finds it difficult to find concrete supporting examples (even if they exist) or suitable analogies, that understanding is less likely to find its way into a report. Even if it does, a reader may judge the plausibility of a hypothesis by the ease with which instances can be recalled or imagined and these in turn depend on the reader's previous experience. Even the manner in which information is displayed (numerical, graphical, anecdotal) is important. Hawkins, Roffman, and Osborne (1978) found that decision makers often obtained their important evaluative information by word of mouth and personal contacts and tended to rely on this even when comprehensive evaluative information became available.

4. Positive and Negative Instances

When tentative hypotheses are held during the gathering of data, evidence is unconsciously selected in such a way that it tends to confirm the hypothesis. In other words, what is noticed, or what counts as a fact, depends in part on what is to be verified (Feyerabend, 1978). Wason (1968) found that people tended to ignore information which conflicted with an already held hypothesis, and that even intelligent individuals adhered to their own hypotheses with remarkable tenacity when they could produce confirming evidence for them.

It is not that people try to "save face" by deliberately ignoring disconfirming instances; the negative instances are simply not perceived at all, apparently because that aspect of the cognitive detection apparatus is not switched on. (The converse, of course, also applies: if one consciously looks for disconfirming evidence, the positive instances may go undetected.)

A related phenomenon sometimes occurs in analyzing taped conversations between researcher and informant. Some word with a certain folk meaning is discovered after listening to maybe an hour of tape; replay of the first hour of recording may show that the term was in fact being used all along, but simply escaped notice.

5. Internal Consistency, Redundancy, and Novelty of Information

Two sets of data about a particular phenomenon, from different but equally credible sources, might tell stories that are conflicting and unbalanced (that is, one is more extreme than the other). Wyer (1970) found a tendency to discount the importance of the less extreme data, leading to a more extreme evaluation overall. Novelty (which is, of course, a relative term because of the differing backgrounds of evaluators) tended to be impressive. Redundancy, on the other hand, reduced the likelihood of an extreme assessment. Thus, an aspect which appears novel at first may eventually be perceived as unimportant merely because there is enough redundancy to change the way an evaluator looks at it.

In passing, it is worth noting that balanced conflicting information does not "cancel out" and leave one with no knowledge at all. To be aware of ambiguity is not the same as being entirely ignorant.

6. Uneven Reliability of Information

Unreliability in the data is often ignored—people treat data from a poor source as though they have almost the same diagnostic power as reliable data (Kahneman & Tversky, 1973). More recently, Beach et al. (1978) found that people discounted information when the sources were discovered to be less credible than first thought, but that revision of an early hypothesis occurred by successive smaller amounts as the sources were found, one by one, to be fallible. Even when all sources were finally discredited, there appeared to be a residue of evidence for the hypothesis.

7. Missing Information

Slovic and MacPhillamy (1974) found that judges, in comparing two different phenomena, attached more importance to dimensions where commensurability was easy. In evaluations, the availability of a base-line (perhaps from previous evaluations) may result in a stronger emphasis on a particular dimension even when direct comparison of two programs is not the aim.

In a complementary study, Yates, Jagacinski, and Faber (1978) found that judges tended to devalue a dimension not fully described, but that some "filled in" the missing information in unpredictable ways: some assumed it to be at a desirable level, some at an "average" level, and some at an undesirable level. Their experiments also showed that one's evaluation is affected not only by what is considered "important" in the abstract but by what is actually attended to at the time of analysis.

Further, Johansson and Brehmer (1979) found that subjects who were told that certain key information necessary to successfully complete a predictive task was missing proceeded as though that condition made no difference.

8. Revision of a Tentative Hypothesis, Evaluation, or Diagnosis

When new information is received, revision tends to be either conservative (that is, not enough notice is taken of the new information) or excessive (overadjustment). There is clear evidence for conservatism in single-stage inference (Edwards, 1968; Peterson & Beach, 1967). On the other hand, when an inference is based not on raw data but on a previous inference drawn from data (multistage, or cascaded inference) there is less conservatism, and sometimes overcompensation (Youssef, 1973; Youssef & Peterson, 1973) but the reason is obscure. It appears that only the most salient of the information from the first stage is utilized in the second stage, the rest being ignored (Gettys et al., 1973a, 1973b). Under certain circumstances this may result in a better diagnosis, but through a partly invalid chain of inferences.

9. Base-Rate Proportion

By base-rate is meant the underlying proportion of a population which falls into a particular category (e.g., an ethnic group). Difficulties arise when the inquirer receives *both* base-rate and (say) clinical data. When base-rate information alone is available the impression of proportion or incidence is, as one would expect, simply the base-rate. However, when data which do not contribute at all to a knowledge of incidence are available, the base-rate information may be suppressed or even ignored in favor of a simplistic expectation: "no" information may be interpreted as a 50–50 proportion (Tversky & Kahneman, 1974). On the other hand, if the evaluator finds clinical information relevant, it tends to take precedence over base-rate information in forming an impression of incidence (Carroll & Siegler, 1977), even if the clinical data apply only to a very small number of exceptional cases. Of course, a single exceptional case (such as the misuse of funds) may be critically important for policy decisions but is not relevant in making an assessment of relative frequency.

Insensitivity to base-rate frequency is a persistent characteristic of intuitive data processing (Kahneman & Tversky, 1973; Peterson & Beach, 1967). Only under special conditions (such as a small number of cases with complete enumeration) does it seem that people can intuitively combine base-rate with other information.

10. Sampling Considerations

For a given base-rate, the proportions observed in small samples vary to a more marked degree than in large samples. Even experienced users of statistics intuitively expect less variation than probability theory would suggest. Tversky and Kahneman (1971) investigated this tendency by asking people to estimate the likelihood of replicating an initial result, other things being equal. They found that judgments were made in terms of how *representative* the sample or case seemed to be of the population, and so neglected to take adequate account of natural variability. Their research also showed that people expected a local result to hold true for a population, and for global characteristics to be evident in a sample, provided that the sample was thought to be representative of the population.

Bar-Hillel (1979) showed that in judging the accuracy of information obtained from a sample, people are less sensitive to the absolute size of the sample than to the ratio of sample size to population.

11. Confidence in Judgment

Once an assessment is made, people have been shown to have an almost unshakable confidence in the correctness of their decisions, even in the face of considerable, relevant, contrary evidence (Einhorn & Hogarth, 1978; Oskamp, 1965; Tversky & Kahneman, 1974).

12. Co-occurrences and Correlation

Observed co-occurrences are frequently interpreted as evidence of a strong correlation. Smedslund (1963) described it this way: "Normal adults with no training in statistics do not have a cognitive structure isomorphic with the concept of correlation. Their strategies and inferences typically reveal a particularistic, nonstatistical approach, or an exclusive dependence on ++ [double positive] instances" (p. 172). Chapman and Chapman (1969) provided corroborative evidence in a study of the use of illusory correlations among diagnosticians. It may sometimes be necessary, Einhorn (1970) suggested, to unlearn preconceived correlations between certain cues and start again.

It is possible that the type of preferential detection mentioned earlier in item 4 is responsible in the case of co-occurrences as well.

13. Consistency in Judgment

Repeated evaluations of the same data configurations are frequently different (Goldberg, 1970; Meehl, 1954). In particular, (1) if A is preferred to B, and B to C, then we should expect A to be preferred to C (the transitivity condition), and (2) if A is preferred to B at one time, it should, other things being equal, be preferred at a later time. Tversky (1969) demonstrated that, under experimental conditions involving uncertainty, consistent and predictable intransitivities occurred. Thurstone (1927) and Guilford (1928) actually based a theory of scaling on this phenomenon.

❖ CONCLUSION

This article began by classifying potential sources of bias into (1) ethical compromises, or distortions due to the possibility of payoffs and penalties, (2) background experience, the idiosyncratic trappings an evaluator brings to the task, and (3) limitations in human information-processing abilities. Thirteen specifics from the literature on intuitive thinking and judgmental processes were described under the third category. These specifics covered how people intuitively deal with such characteristics of the information as quantity, order, and availability (items 1–3), with mixed information (items 4–8), with revision of tentative inferences (items 9–10), and with variability in the data (items 11–13).

The purpose of the paper has been to draw the attention of naturalistic evaluators to some common failings, in the belief that better understanding of the ways data are intuitively processed will lead to better evaluations. The listing can serve as a checklist in the business of reducing, integrating, and drawing inferences from field data.

❖ REFERENCES

Bacon, F. *Novum organum,* 1620, Book I, Aphorisms 41, 45–52.
Bar-Hillel, M. The role of sample size in sample evaluation. *Organizational Behavior and Human Performance,* 1979, *24,* 245–257.
Beach, L. R., et al. Information relevance, content, and source credibility in the revision of opinions. *Organizational Behavior and Human Performance,* 1978, *21,* 1–16.

Carroll, J. S., & Siegler, R. S. Strategies for the use of base-rate information. *Organizational Behavior and Human Performance*, 1977, *19*, 392–402.

Chapman, L. J., & Chapman, J. P. Illusory correlation as an obstacle to the use of valid psychodiagnostic signs. *Journal of Abnormal Psychology*, 1969, *74*, 271–280.

Cochran, N. Grandma Moses and the "corruption" of data. *Evaluation Quarterly*, 1978, *2*, 363–373.

Edwards, W. Conservatism in human information processing. In B. Kleinmuntz (Ed.), *Formal representation of human judgment*. New York: Wiley, 1968.

Einhorn, H. J. The use of nonlinear, noncompensatory models in decision making. *Psychological Bulletin*, 1970, *73*, 221–230.

Einhorn, H. J., & Hogarth, R. M. Confidence in judgment: Persistence of the illusion of validity. *Psychological Review*, 1978, *85*, 395–416.

Feyerabend, P. K. *Against method*. London: Verso, 1978.

Gettys, C. F., Kelly, C., & Peterson, C. R. The best guess hypothesis in multistage inference. *Organizational Behavior and Human Performance*, 1973, *10*, 364–373. (a)

Gettys, C., et al. Multiple-stage probabilistic information processing. *Organizational Behavior and Human Performance*, 1973, *10*, 374–387. (b)

Goldberg, L. R. Man versus model of man: A rationale, plus some evidence, for a method of improving on clinical inferences. *Psychological Bulletin*, 1970, *73*, 422–432.

Goodrich, T. J. Strategies for dealing with the issue of subjectivity in evaluation. *Evaluation Quarterly*, 1978, *2*, 631–645.

Guilford, J. P. The method of paired comparisons as a psychometric method. *Psychological Review*, 1928, *35*, 494–506.

Hammond, K. R., & Adelman, L. Science, values, and human judgment. *Science*, 1976, *194*, 389–396.

Hawkins, J. D., Roffman, R. A., & Osborne, P. Decision makers' judgments: The influence of role, evaluative criteria, and information access. *Evaluation Quarterly*, 1978, *2*, 435–453.

Johansson, R., & Brehmer, B. Influences from incomplete information—A note. *Organizational Behavior and Human Performance*, 1979, *24*, 141–145.

Kahneman, D., & Tversky, A. On the psychology of prediction. *Psychological Review*, 1973, *80*, 237–251.

Krathwohl, D. R. The myth of value-free evaluation. *Educational Evaluation and Policy Analysis*, 1980, *2*, 37–45.

Meehl, P. E. *Clinical versus statistical prediction*. Minneapolis: University of Minnesota Press, 1954.

Miller, G. A. The magical number seven, plus or minus two: Some limits on our capacity for processing information. *Psychological Review*, 1956, *63*, 81–97.

Najder, Z. *Values and evaluations*. Oxford: Clarendon Press, 1975.

Oskamp, S. Overconfidence in case-study judgments. *Journal of Consulting Psychology*, 1965, *29*, 261–265.

Page, E. B. More objective! *Educational Evaluation and Policy Analysis*, 1979, *1*, 45–46.

Peterson, C. R., & Beach, L. R. Man as an intuitive statistician. *Psychological Bulletin*, 1967, *68*, 29–46.

Poulton, E. C. The new psychophysics: Six models for magnitude estimation. *Psychological Bulletin*, 1968, *69*, 1–19.

Scriven, M. The methodology of evaluation. In R. W. Tyler, R. M. Gagné, & M. Scriven (Eds.), *Perspectives of curriculum evaluation* (AERA Monograph Series on Curriculum Evaluation, No. 1). Chicago: Rand McNally, 1967.

Scriven, M. Objectivity and subjectivity in educational research. In L. G. Thomas (Ed.), *Philosophical redirection of educational research* (71st Yearbook Part I). Chicago: National Society for the Study of Education, University of Chicago Press, 1972.

Scriven, M. Goal-free evaluation. In E. R. House (Ed.), *School evaluation: The politics and process.* Berkeley, Calif.: McCutchan, 1973.

Scriven, M. Evaluation bias and its control. In G. V. Glass (Ed.), *Evaluation studies review annual* (Vol. 1). Beverly Hills, Calif.: Sage, 1976.

Shulman, L. S., & Elstein, A. S. Studies of problem solving, judgment, and decision making: Implications for educational research. *Review of Research in Education,* 1975, *3,* 3–42.

Slovic, P., & MacPhillamy, D. Dimensional commensurability and cue utilization in comparative judgment. *Organizational Behavior and Human Performance,* 1974, *11,* 172–194.

Smedslund, J. The concept of correlation in adults. *Scandinavian Journal of Psychology,* 1963, *4,* 165–173.

Summers, D. A., Taliaferro, J. D., & Fletcher, D. J. Subjective vs objective description of judgment policy. *Psychonomic Science,* 1970, *18,* 249–250.

Thurstone, L. L. A law of comparative judgment. *Psychological Review,* 1927, *34,* 273–286.

Tversky, A. Intransitivity of preferences. *Psychological Review,* 1969, *76,* 31–48.

Tversky, A., & Kahneman, D. Belief in the law of small numbers. *Psychological Bulletin,* 1971, *76,* 105–110.

Tversky, A., & Kahneman, D. Judgment under uncertainty: Heuristics and biases. *Science,* 1974, *185,* 1,124–1,131.

Wason, P. C. On the failure to eliminate hypotheses: A second look. In P. C. Wason & P. N. Johnson-Laird (Eds.), *Thinking and reasoning.* Baltimore: Penguin Books, 1968.

Wolf, R. L. Trial by jury: A new evaluation method. *Phi Delta Kappan,* 1975, *57,* 185–187.

Wright, W. F. Cognitive information processing biases: Implications for producers and users of financial information. *Decision Sciences,* 1980, *11,* 284–298.

Wyer, R. S., Jr. Information redundancy, inconsistency, and novelty and their role in impression formation. *Journal of Experimental Social Psychology,* 1970, *6,* 111–127.

Yarmey, A. D. *The psychology of eyewitness testimony.* New York: The Free Press, 1979.

Yates, J. F., Jagacinski, C. M., & Faber, M. D. Evaluation of partially described multiattribute options. *Organizational Behavior and Human Performance,* 1978, *21,* 240–251.

Youssef, Z. I. The effects of cascaded inference on the subjective value of information. *Organizational Behavior and Human Performance,* 1973, *10,* 359–363.

Youssef, Z. I., & Peterson, C. R. Intuitive cascaded inferences. *Organizational Behavior and Human Performance,* 1973, *10,* 349–358.

7

Analytic Ethnography

Features, Failings, and Futures

John Lofland

I want, in this article, to describe the distinctive strategy of social research sometimes labeled *analytic ethnography*, to assess its successes and failures as a research strategy, and to guess about aspects of its future.[1] I use the term "analytic ethnography" to refer to research processes and products in which, to a greater or lesser degree, an investigator (a) attempts to provide generic propositional answers to questions about social life and organization; (b) strives to pursue such an attempt in a spirit of unfettered or naturalistic inquiry; (c) utilizes data based on deep familiarity with a social setting or situation that is gained by personal participation or an approximation of it; (d) develops the generic propositional analysis over the course of doing the research; (e) strives to present data and analyses that are true; (f) seeks

Reprinted from John Lofland, "Analytic Ethnography: Features, Failings, and Futures," *Journal of Contemporary Ethnography*, 24(1), 30–67. Copyright 1995 by Sage Publications, Inc.

to provide data and/or analyses that are new; and (g) presents an analysis that is developed in the senses of being conceptually elaborated, descriptively detailed, and concept-data interpenetrated.

Some people familiar with analytic ethnography might be inclined to criticize what I do here on the grounds that I am not saying anything new, that all the features I describe have been much discussed and are well-known, both individually and as the package called analytic ethnography. I have two responses to this concern. First, it is true that all seven of the elements I treat have been discussed in the literature (albeit to different degrees and at varying levels of sophistication). It is not accurate, however, to say that the seven have already been assembled into an articulate profile that is asserted to be a distinctive strategy of research. Instead, the elements remain at the level of separate tracks along which people work without much reference to the overall profile of which each is a part. Second, based on a careful reading of Denzin and Lincoln's weighty *Handbook of Qualitative Research* (1994), I think there are good reasons to think that these seven are *not* very well-known among a great many people who lay claim to be heard on these matters—much less known as components that together form analytic ethnography. Disciplinary isolation and philosophical preferences are among the reasons for this ignorance, but it also results in part from analytic ethnography's lack of sledgehammer clarity. One consequence is that proponents of other types of qualitative or ethnographic research strategies differentiate themselves from yet other forms that exist largely in their minds rather than in reality; that is, they distinguish themselves from straw persons. If such researchers want to shoot at forms of qualitative work they do not like, they should at least be able to aim at genres that are actually "out there" and that have definite forms, rather than rail against mythical and/or at least exceedingly abstract assemblages. One of my aims here is to construct such a clear target in the hope of moving the conversation to more specific and detailed levels.

❖ CONTEXTS

I will explain each of these seven features—or, more accurately, tendencies—in the main section of this article, but before doing so, I want to set their aggregation—analytic ethnography—in historical and contemporary contexts. I hope these discussions will serve empirically to ground the more abstract considerations that follow. They will provide background for my subsequent discussions of analytic ethnography's successes, failures, and futures.

Contemporary

In addition, we need to understand the contemporary context to answer the question: Why should I care to know anything about analytic ethnography—features, failures, or whatever? The answer is that the upsurge of ethnographic projects and especially of writing about ethnographic projects over the 1980s and early 1990s has created a complex and confusing intellectual landscape in which there may be as many forms or conceptions of ethnography as there are ethnographers and commentators on it.[2] Although perhaps not *that* complicated, it is nevertheless true that divergent conceptions of ethnography abound. Even the broadest amalgamations and simplifications of this abundance identify at least four major approaches, as in Martyn Hammersley's (1992) distinctions among theoretical, critical, policy, and practitioner ethnography. Hammersley's categorization of approaches is, though, not widely accepted, just as others are not, and one derivative feature of the new ethnographic scene is disagreement over what is the most accurate analysis of this landscape.[3]

There are at least three ways to proceed in this knotty situation. The first is to compare and contrast various proposed orderings, seeking to find their common and divergent elements. From this, the analyst derives a third level, an ordering of the orderings. A second way is to start *de novo* and, in grounded theory fashion, see what one can find. We add yet another ordering to the existing stockpile of them. A third strategy is to begin to make sense of the larger scene by first focusing in some detail on a single approach to ethnography, one that the analyst is relatively certain is a coherent approach, and attempt to articulate the profile of features it exhibits. This is obviously the most modest of the three approaches in that it concentrates on an in-depth depiction of a single genre, postponing the larger task of overall portrayal of the scene itself. It has the virtue, though, of trying very hard to decipher at least one approach fully and precisely. If such intense work is then done on each and every approach, this would presumably result in a de facto depiction of the landscape of conceptions of ethnography. (This is one rationale of the "case study" approach in social research.)

In this spirit and to this end, I want here to use this third approach as an interim effort in the larger task of clarifying approaches to ethnography. My goal is to draw as accurate a picture as I can of analytic ethnography, reflect on some of its strengths and weaknesses, and attempt to look a little way into the future.

Historical

As in many other efforts to fix beginnings, it is difficult to declare definitively when research with analytic ethnography's collective tendencies or features "first" crystallized as a distinct genre. I tentatively trace its formation to members of the immediate post-World War II graduate sociology cohort at the University of Chicago. Pointing to outstanding early examples of it, I speak, specifically, of empirical analyses such as by Howard S. Becker on marijuana use and Fred Davis on taxicab drivers and children with polio.[4] Becker and Davis were, though, only two people in a large cohort of 1950s Chicago sociology doctorates who did similar work, all heavily influenced by Everett Hughes and Herbert Blumer, neither of whom themselves produced such work (or much empirical work at all), but who advocated a view of social science consistent with it. (Anselm Strauss and Alfred Lindesmith were simultaneously forerunners of and participants in this crystallizing milieu, providing both early models and ongoing exemplification.)

My conception of analytic ethnography was shaped at Berkeley in the early 1960s, in study with Herbert Blumer and Erving Goffman. I was among a large number of young scholars so influenced over the course of that decade and later. Like Blumer and Hughes earlier, Blumer and Goffman did little, if any, analytic ethnography themselves, but they nevertheless clearly communicated their preferences in works they pointed to as exemplary and in their responses to papers that graduate students wrote for them.

By the late 1960s and early 1970s, empirical work exhibiting features of analytic ethnography was also issuing from students trained at other graduate centers that featured Blumer-Hughes influenced sociologists trained at Chicago. Northwestern and Brandeis Universities and the San Francisco and San Diego campuses of the University of California were among the most productive of these other centers.

In the 1960s and 1970s, practitioners of analytic ethnography, as well as of related ethnographic strategies of research, tended to view themselves as an embattled minority railing against mainstream quantitative excesses and "positivism." There was, in particular, a belief that mainline journals were not appropriately sympathetic to ethnographic reports in general or analytically ethnographic reports in particular. This sense of embattlement prompted the formation of several new, ethnographically sympathetic journals.[5] For the particular research strategy of analytic ethnography, this was the journal initially titled *Urban Life and Culture*, first issued in April 1972.

The editorial policy of this journal was not informed by the exact term "analytic ethnography," but the conception was nevertheless clear in stressing "*close-up* and detailed, qualitative depiction of social life" that simultaneously "strives to be *analytic*—to search out patterns and regularities in the context of close-up depiction" (Lofland 1972, 3, emphasis in original). As a matter of historical context, it should be understood that at the time of conceiving and naming this journal the term ethnography was not yet widely used in social science outside of anthropology and without narrowly anthropological meanings. Thus, as its inventor and organizer, I had initially named the journal *Urban Ethnography*, a focus that combined analytic "ethnography" with a Chicagoesque enchantment with the "inner life and texture of the diverse social enclaves and personal circumstances of urban societies" (policy statement, *Urban Life and Culture*, April 1972, 2). Sara (SA) and George (GE) McCune, who formed SAGE Publications and were the journal's prospective publishers, checked this title with several librarian consultants only to find that the word "ethnography" was often taken to mean "ethnology" and thereby to evoke images of primitive peoples in distant lands. Some librarians also construed the title as about ethnic studies. Acceding to their concerns that *Urban Ethnography* would mislead acquisition librarians and restrict library subscriptions, I changed the name to *Urban Life and Culture*. It is testimony to the shifting meaning of words that slightly more than a decade later most people were comfortable with changing the name to what the journal should have been called in the first place; namely, the *Journal of Contemporary Ethnography* (Adler and Adler 1987, 4–6).

From the start to the present, the *Journal of Contemporary Ethnography* has been the flagship of research exhibiting features of analytic ethnography. Despite five distinct editorial regimes spread over almost a quarter of a century, continuity has been quite remarkable. By my reckoning, the overwhelming majority of articles published there have been decent to excellent examples of analytic ethnography.[6]

Some people might agree that I speak here of a distinctive genre but still have misgivings about the exact name I give it. I am sympathetic with such misgivings, because first, no simple, one- or two-word designation of anything can be entirely accurate, if only because any brief caption creates distortion by omission. Labels should nevertheless be simple. Other candidate names with this same simplicity problem include analytic description, naturalistic ethnography, and theoretical ethnography.

Second, I think a good case can be made for these alternatives or yet other possibilities. Aside from analytic ethnography's relatively greater precision, longevity of use is a major reason for my preferring it. The term with the meanings I give it dates from at least 1971, when it was used to caption a commercial series of ethnographic monographs, specifically, "The Wadsworth Series in Analytic Ethnography" (Lofland 1971, ii). The term "analytic description" perhaps has been used more commonly, however, and it is a working synonym for analytic ethnography. Apparently coined by McCall and Simmons (1969, 3), the terms "analytic description" and "attendant imagery" appear widely in analytic ethnographies and discussions of analytic ethnography (e.g., Lofland 1972; Athens 1984a, 1984b; Lofland and Lofland 1984; Charmaz 1983; Hammersley 1992, 12–22). Unfortunately, the word "description" is much too general to be used in designating a strategy of research; otherwise, I would employ it. Moreover, the two features of generic propositions and deep familiarity are integral to early meanings of the term "ethnography" that commend its use in preference to other labels.[7]

❖ FEATURES

Analytic ethnography is a composite of seven tendencies, practices, or features, but most if not all of these seven are not distinctive to it as a genre. Thus analytic ethnographers have no exclusive claim to striving for "unfettered inquiry," achieving "deep familiarity," or most of the other matters I will describe. Other nonethnographic forms of social research also and quite properly exhibit one or more of them, as do other approaches to ethnographic research. The distinctiveness of analytic ethnography resides instead in combining these seven tendencies into a pattern that has set it off from other research in general and other ethnographic research in particular.

This fact has more than merely logical or expositional import. It means that analytic ethnography is a subset of a large number of other sets of research approaches and shares much with other approaches even while differing from them. To isolate it is therefore not entirely to set it off from a wide variety of other research genres.

Two underlying dimensions inform the order in which I discuss these seven tendencies. First, the more abstract and philosophical features precede, in a general way, more concrete and operational ones. Second, features or practices that emerge or become centrally problematic earlier in an inquiry are discussed before those that begin or become problematic later in the research process.[8] Moreover, in the imagery of logical sets, each new feature constricts the size of the set until we finally get down to the subset that is analytic ethnography.

The seven items I often term "features" are, more carefully considered, actually variables; that is, they are seven dimensions of reality in terms of which instances can be ordered as displaying "more" or "less" of each. For simplicity's sake, I often speak of these dimensions as dichotomies rather than as the continuous variables they in fact are. Said differently, my picture of analytic ethnography is an ideal typical depiction of a logic and a direction, rather than a nuanced drawing of different degrees to which myriad instances of specific research reports vary in the extent to which they display each of the seven variables.[9]

1. Generic Propositions

Most fundamentally, work of an analytically ethnographic bent has been and remains to this day one variety of mainstream or even positivistic strategies of social research, sharing much with the strategies of experiments, surveys, and historical comparisons. Among these shared features is the framing of one's task as the asking of basic questions about the domain of human social life and organization combined with striving to formulate empirically falsifiable and generically attuned answers to those questions.

The main questions asked in analytically ethnographically inclined research have been—and are—very much the same as the questions asked by most other social researchers and by people in every viable society about almost everything. Put most simply (and therefore lacking in elaboration and qualification), these questions are:

1. *Type?* What is it? What are its defining features and its varieties?

2. *Frequency?* How often does it occur?

3. *Magnitude?* What is its size, strength, or intensity?

4. *Structure?* What is its detailed organization?

5. *Process?* How does it operate?

6. *Cause?* How does it come to be?

7. *Consequence?* What does it affect?

8. *Agency?* How do people strategize in or toward it?[10]

Questions obviously imply answers and, in tandem, social research generates—stated in the immaculately abstract—eight basic forms of them, which are:

1. *Type(s):* X exists (or, X-1, X-2, X-3, ... X-n exist).

2. *Frequencies:* X occurs with Y frequency in places 1, 2, 3 ... n over Z periods of time.

3. *Magnitudes:* X is of Y size, strength, or intensity.

4. *Structures:* X is structured in terms of 1, 2, 3 ... n.

5. *Processes:* X exhibits a process with the phases or cycles of 1, 2, 3 ... n.

6. *Causes:* X is caused by factors 1, 2, 3 ... n.

7. *Consequences:* X has consequences 1, 2, 3 ... n.

8. *Agency:* In X, people use strategies and tactics 1, 2, 3 ... n.[11]

We may think of answers to these questions as propositions, as one or another of eight kinds of assertions about whatever aspect of the social life or organization is under study. In social research (as in other enterprises) the idea of a propositional answer to a question has been given many linguistic renderings that should also be indicated lest my formulation seem exotic or eccentric. Other words and phrasings that have the same meaning or a meaning that is broader or narrower than developing a propositional answer to a question include stating a hypothesis; developing a thesis; formulating a concept; making an assertion; devising a theory; putting forth an idea; propounding a broad, unifying theme; fashioning an explanation; addressing a problem; identifying a story line; telling a story; constructing a general principle; and providing a general interpretation.

The eight questions differ in the degree to which they, in a positivist perspective, immediately call for quantitative versus qualitative data to answer them. The questions of frequency, magnitude, causes, and consequences (numbers 2, 3, 6, and 7) require, if one is a positivist, quantitative data. On the other hand, the questions of type, structure, process, and agency (numbers 1, 4, 5, and 8) are more immediately amenable to treatment with qualitative data. As qualitatively inclined social researchers, analytic ethnographers have therefore tended to ask and answer the latter more than the former set of questions.

Propositional answers to questions vary in terms of the concreteness or abstractness of the concepts in which they are cast. Toward the concrete end of this variation, answers (and the questions) are conceived in narrowly local terms, that is, in the historically particular terms used by the people studied or terms that are otherwise well-known and commonsensical in some localized milieu of discourse. Toward the other end of this dimension, many social researchers seek to conceive their answers as more abstract generic propositions rather than as historically particular information. By "historically particular" I mean primarily reporting the chronological activities observed in a situation or setting, and organizing the report temporally. Generic framing, in contrast, seeks to specify abstract propositions of which the historical particulars are instances. Max Heirich's two published analyses of social movement activity on the Berkeley campus of the University of California in 1964–65 provide quintessential examples of the contrast between historically particular and generic framing or abstraction. Knowing that different audiences are attuned to different kinds of accounts, Heirich's publisher asked him to publish two books on exactly the same events. One is titled *The Beginning: Berkeley, 1964* (1970). It runs 317 pages and is divided into sixteen chapters that only report the sheer history of the events involved. The second—the generically framed book that is an outstanding analytic ethnography—contains the same historical account, but it is also much longer, 502 pages divided into twenty-one chapters. It is longer and more complicated because it employs generic concepts that propositionally structure the data. Appropriately, it bears a title signaling the presence of that generic propositional analysis, which is *The Spiral of Conflict: Demonstrations at Berkeley 1964–1965* (1971).

In the coding and memoing process of the emergent analysis that I discuss below as the fourth feature of analytic ethnography, the analyst asks, "Of what more abstract and social analytic category are these data an instance?"[12] The goal is to translate the specific materials under study into instances of widely relevant and basic social types, processes, or whatever. In this upward categorization, generic propositional framing strives to find fundamental human themes and concerns in obscure and sometimes seemingly trivial social doings. The effort is to lift the situation under study out of its historically specific details and to place it among the array of matters of interest to broad audiences. In one sense, generic framing in social research—including analytic ethnography—is an effort to see the universe in a grain of sand.[13]

Unfettered Inquiry

Taking generic propositions as a prime goal is, of course, a quite considerable constraint. Adopting or rejecting it as a goal is also a major issue in terms of which all social researchers are divided, not simply researchers of ethnographic inclinations. For those who adopt it, the range of possibilities for empirical inquiry is nevertheless still vast and unspecific. Within having accepted this goal and constraint, there is still the basic question of why and to what end one attempts to develop generic propositions, that is, to study human society (Goffman 1983, 17).

A serious answer to this question forces one, of course, back to fundamental existential, religious, or perhaps even cosmic perspectives. What, indeed, is the point? People are drawn into social research from diverse backgrounds and philosophical and religious traditions. We should therefore not be surprised to find this social and philosophical diversity applied to the "why and to what end?" of social research. The upshot is a set of sharply different and conflicting answers to the question of "why and to what end?"

Holding aside a general consideration of how these answers differ and why, let me here suggest that the *tendency* among many of the analytic ethnographically inclined is in the direction of a spirit of unfettered or naturalistic inquiry. Of course, the clarity and extremeness with which this purpose is enunciated (or is even in a researcher's consciousness) differ. Some very few are quite radical, cosmically resolute, and austere in their view of "why and to what end?" Their version of unfettered inquiry is simply "because it is there," the view embraced by Erving Goffman (1983), who acknowledges his own extremeness:

"Louis Wirth, whose courses I took, would have found that answer a disgrace. He had a different one, and since his time his answer has become the standard one" (p. 17).

In his radicalness, Goffman is able, though, clearly to depict what it means to study society "naturalistically"; that is, in "a spirit of unfettered ... inquiry":

> I believe that human life is ours to study naturalistically, *sub specie aeternitatis*. From the perspective of the physical and biological sciences, human social life is only a small irregular scab on the face of nature, not particularly amenable to deep systematic analysis. And so it is. But it's ours. With a few exceptions, only students in our century have managed to hold it steadily in view in this way, without piety or the necessity to treat traditional issues. Only in modern times have university students been systematically trained to examine all levels of social life meticulously. I'm not one to think that so far our claims can be based on magnificent accomplishment. Indeed, I've heard it said that we should be glad to trade what we've so far produced for a few really good conceptual distinctions and a cold beer. But there's nothing in the world we should trade for what we do have: the bent to sustain in regard to all elements of social life a spirit of unfettered, unsponsored inquiry and the wisdom not to look elsewhere but ourselves and our discipline for this mandate. That is our inheritance and that so far is what we have to bequeath. (Goffman 1983, 17)

The Latin phrase *sub specie aeternitatis* that Goffman uses above means, in one definition: "in its essential or universal form or nature" (Gove 1971, 2279). *Oxford English Dictionary* writers translate and define the phrase as "'under the aspect of eternity,' i.e., viewed in relation to the eternal: in a universal perspective." Examples of its use given in this *OED* entry include: "Art enables us somehow to see things *sub specie aeternitatis*" and "The nature of any fact is not fully known unless we know it in all its relations to the system of the universe, or, in Spinoza's phrase, *sub specie aeternitatis*" (Burchfield 1987, 1197).

In this radical version of unfettered inquiry—of a naturalistic mind-set—human society is viewed from a great distance, in the largest terms, and over a very long time. The researcher stands very, very far back, adopting a cosmic or existential vision of humanity and its organization, attempting to strip away all fettering human assumptions or "pieties." This is a distance, I might note, that is more commonly encountered among theologians and kindred con-templators of human existence than among social scientists, although it is clearly also seen among them—and among many analytic ethnographers.[14]

Most versions of the spirit of unfettered inquiry do not seem to be as radical as that of Goffman and his sympathizers. Some distance is advocated and practiced, but the distance is not as austere and cosmic. Instead, it takes the milder form of using a long time frame in which to conceive social science, a wide social frame, and a dispassionate emotional frame.

1. In temporal terms, research is viewed as a complex activity of successive and unending revisions carried out over the long term. This is, of course, the classic view of liberal science, one that Hammersley (1990, 1992) has recently reasserted and forcefully reargued for analytic ethnography. This view of time and unending revision contrasts, certainly, with "why and to what end?" answers in which inquiry is conceived and valued as a strategy or tactic in battle skirmishes with a proximate enemy, as a service to people in power, as an isolated virtuoso or prima donna performance, or as some other such short-term endeavor.

2. Socially, research is thought of as a disciplined form of human inquiry and knowing that is addressed to larger and longer-term human concerns and values. Even though the proximate audience for and evaluators of research must be other social scientists, the larger audiences are all humans who care about whatever is the topic of study (cf. again, Hammersley 1990, chap. 5; Hammersley 1992). In this view, social science, including analytic ethnography, parallels other science. The proximate audience of cancer research, for example, is competent, evaluating cancer researchers, but the larger audience is everyone and anyone who cares about cancer. In contrast, the "why and to what end?" narrower answer can be that of service to particular social groupings whose purposes one seeks to advance.[15]

3. Emotionally, researchers may care very much about their research and the issues it raises, but, consonant with a long and large temporal and social view, a spirit of unfettered inquiry counsels a dispassionate and disinterested attitude (disinterested here meaning judicious rather than indifferent). Advocates of the contrasting view—of deep and abiding emotional engagement—of course

characterize this dispassion as emotionally distanced and uncaring. Such emotions, however, can be distinguished from an emotional attitude of judiciousness and calm concern, with patient and careful examination and continual reexamination of all data and concepts. This also contrasts with views of research—including ethnography—that counsel emotional partisanship and deep personal commitment to one or another political or equivalent grouping in human society.[16]

One wider way in which to think of this contrast between unfettered and fettered inquiry is as a specialized instance of the very broad and long-standing conflict among intellectuals as a social grouping over the degree to which they can have or should have a voice that is independent of other social groupings. Is it possible or desirable for intellectuals to seek an independent empirical-analytic posture that has social and intellectual value and integrity that is not the same as or reducible to any other grouping? Stated yet more broadly, how exactly are intellectuals to relate to their societies? Are they the servants of the powerful, of the oppressed, of themselves, of whom?

Within social research in general and ethnography in particular what we find, therefore, is a specialized version of this central and perennial struggle among intellectuals in the modern world. Pertinent here is that analytic ethnographers have tended, with varying degrees of radicalness and explicitness, to come down on the side of independence, of unfettered inquiry as both possible and desirable, even if it is unattainable in any absolute and permanent sense.

There might be some tendency to construe the pursuit of unfettered inquiry as a pleading for "value-free" social science. Lest this be erroneously surmised, let me suggest why the spirit of unfettered inquiry is not an argument for value-free research. As a first matter, the quest for unfettered inquiry is itself a value—albeit a precarious one. It is, moreover, a value that is embedded in the broad modern philosophical outlook commonly labeled humanism that analytic ethnographers are also likely to espouse (Kurtz 1983, 1992). This outlook is, to state the obvious, the dominant, pragmatic philosophy prevailing in the public arenas of all economically advanced democracies and it is the underpinning of organized scientific endeavor, an endeavor appropriately labeled "liberal science" (Rauch 1993). Within these outlooks, a central proposition is that because truth is elusive and error is legion, there is no final word. Unfettered research is the order of every day and its key guideline is "Do not block the way of inquiry," the well-known declaration of Charles Sanders Peirce that Jonathan Rauch features as the frontispiece epigram of his spirited and incisive explanation and defense of liberal science (Rauch 1993, vii).

3. Deep Familiarity

The quest for generic propositions and spirit of unfettered inquiry are obviously not unique to analytic ethnography. Their presence therefore tells us little about it as a research strategy, save to set it off from several varieties of both ethnographic and nonethnographic descriptively oriented fettered inquiry.[17]

It is only with the third feature or tendency that we begin radically to restrict the set of relevant concerns and enterprises. In a spirit of unfettered inquiry, the researcher of an analytically ethnographic bent positions her- or himself as someone subject to—a witness to—a social situation or setting. Erving Goffman captures this well in his posthumously published lecture remarks on participant observation, which is a technique of

> getting data . . . by subjecting yourself, your own body and your own personality, and your own social situation to the set of contingencies that play upon a set of individuals, so that you can physically and ecologically penetrate their circle of response to their social situation, or their work situation, or their ethnic situation, or whatever. So that you are close to them while they are responding to what life does to them. I feel that the way this is done is not, of course, just to listen to what they talk about, but to pick up on their minor grunts and groans as they respond to their situation. When you do that . . ., the standard technique is to try to subject yourself . . . to their life circumstances . . . and you try to accept all of the desirable and undesirable things that are a feature of their life. That "tunes your body up" and with your "tuned up" body . . . you are in a position to note their gestural, visual, bodily response to what is going on around them and you're empathetic enough—because you have been taking the same crap they've been taking—to sense what it is that they're responding to. To me, that's the core of observation.. . . You're artificially forcing yourself to be tuned into something that you then pick up as a *witness—not as an interviewer, not as a listener, but as a witness* to how they react to what gets done to and around them.. . . It's *deep familiarity* that is the rationale—that plus getting material on a tissue of events—that gives the justification and the warrant for such an apparently "loose" thing as fieldwork. (Goffman 1989, 125–26, 130, emphasis added)

Other writers have referred to this immersion as "intimate familiarity," and they have elaborated reasons why researchers need to get so physically, socially, and emotionally close to whatever people are under study. As is well-known, this reasoning centerpieces the idea of face-to-face contact as the foundation of entering the experience of others (e.g., Blumer 1969, chap. 1; Schutz 1967; Lofland 1971, 2–4; Altheide and Johnson 1994, 487–89). In the absence of this, one is prone simply to substitute preformed stereotypes or "typifications" for personal, empirical encounters with a situation or setting and the discipline that this involves.

Achieving and maintaining the prolonged physical proximity thought necessary in order to develop deep familiarity has been, of course, a delicate and often arduous task for researchers. Quite properly, therefore, an enormous literature of reporting on, and analysis of, it has arisen. As a literature of practical advice, it is commonly organized into the three categories of establishing a relation with a situation or setting, maintaining that relation, and observing and recording empirical materials.[18]

This insistence on deep familiarity is sometimes construed as coincident with—as requiring—rejection of the "positivist paradigm" of social research (see, for example, a large portion of the chapters in Denzin and Lincoln 1994). For many analytic ethnographers, however, this has not been the case. Deep familiarity has been advocated instead as simply a good, positivist practice of data collection. If one wants the best data, then deep familiarity is how one gets them.

4. Emergent Analysis

The analytically ethnographic research strategy departs sharply from more conventional social science in its view of the role of preformed hypotheses in social research. In the conventional view, investigators frame a hypothesis to be tested, collect data pertinent to the hypothesis, and evaluate the degree to which the data do or do not support it.

Analytic ethnographers have tended not to question the appropriateness of this conventional process in the investigation of a great many questions, situations, and settings. They have claimed, though, that this is an overly narrow, even constricting, and ultimately self-defeating view of how to develop knowledge. In addition to such hypothesis-testing or theory-driven inquiries, there must be open-ended, exploratory, inductive, and case studies.

This view and its procedures have been most thoroughly rationalized and elaborated in what is called "grounded theory" (Glaser and Strauss 1967). It is important to understand, however, that grounded theory is a broad approach to theorizing with data of many sorts and is not confined to its association with analytic ethnography. Even though a large portion of analytic ethnographers are, at least in spirit, grounded theorists, a great many grounded theorists are not at all analytic ethnographers. Indeed, some grounded theorists carefully distance themselves from analytic ethnography and sometimes seem to go out of their way to avoid reference to analytic ethnography in the quest to develop a pure, abstract methodology of grounded theory.[19]

The central process of grounded theory—of emergent analysis—is, nevertheless, an integral element of analytic ethnography. Its main features are the gradual accumulation of data through witnessing observation and the slow inductive analysis of these data. Even though much has been written on the mechanical aspects of doing this, the process has also rested on the sensitivities and intuition of the researcher. As such, emergent analysis has been—historically—also very much a creative act. Referring to the open-ended and inductive features of emergent analysis as "making it all come together," Paul Atkinson has thus reflected that

> making it all come together . . . is one of the most difficult things of all.. . . Quite apart from actually achieving it, it is hard to inject the right mix of (a) *faith* that it can and will be achieved; (b) recognition that it has to be *worked* at, and isn't based on romantic inspiration; (c) that it isn't like the solution to a puzzle or math problem, but has to be *created*; (d) that you can't pack *everything* into one version, and that any one project could yield several different ways of bringing it together. (Atkinson, quoted in Strauss 1987, 214, emphasis in original)

For the analytic ethnographer, the two most basic activities used to work at emergent analysis are coding data as they accumulate and writing memos on those codes, two processes that have generated a rather extensive instructional literature (Charmaz 1983; Strauss and Corbin 1990; Huberman and Miles 1994; Lofland and Lofland 1995, chap. 9).[20]

5. True Content

As a main tendency, I think we can say that analytic ethnographers have wanted their data and analyses to be true in the traditional (i.e., "positivist") senses of (a) correctly representing the empirical facts of a situation or setting and (b) constructing analyses that accurately amalgamate the welter of empirical details into one or another kind of proposition. The first is factual trueness and the second is analytic trueness in the sense of consistency between analysis and facts. This distinction is necessary, of course, because it is possible to have one without the other, and procedures of striving for each are somewhat different. Such views of "truth" thus tend to locate analytic ethnography among what are now called the "realists," the supposedly naive view that there is a (small t) truth to which we can have some reasonable degree of access. Or, when informed by social or reality constructionist perspectives, realism is qualified as "subtle" (Hammersley 1992, 52), "transcendental" (Huberman and Miles 1994, 429), or "analytic" (Altheide and Johnson 1994, 489).

The procedures used to strive for factual trueness have been an amalgam of techniques and safeguards drawn partly from quantitative research procedures and partly from historical and legal research traditions that focus on constructing accurate space-time specific descriptions. Regarding the former, the concern has been to exercise caution in estimating frequencies and magnitudes and in making assertions of causes and consequences (questions and answers number 2, 3, 6, and 7, above) (see, e.g., Lofland and Lofland 1984, 100–5). Regarding the latter, historical/legal cautions and criteria relating to avoiding and correcting for error and bias in space-time specific observations have sometimes been put forth and used (e.g., Lofland and Lofland 1984, 50–52). Work along either of these lines has not been extensive, though.[21]

Assessing analytic trueness has been accorded much more attention than assessing factual trueness. Tending to eschew the narrow, positivist conceptions of "reliability" and "validity," attention has turned, instead, to criteria of a personal testimony character in the absence of any more direct and clear way to assess trueness. By "personal testimony" criteria I mean reporting practices that analytic ethnographers have tended to adopt as elements of their reports and that inform the reports. Roger Sanjek has classified these personal testimony practices into three categories and made them proscriptive rather than simply descriptive in dubbing them "canons of ethnographic validity." He opines, correctly I think, that readers look for these three "canons" or reporting practices, and they use them in assessing the degree to which the facts are consistent with the analysis offered of them. Appreciating that readers look for these three kinds of reports, writers quite reasonably attempt to provide them—and previously to have engaged in the activities that make it possible to write these elements of reports.

Sanjek gives these three practices the fancy names of "theoretical candor," "the ethnographer's path," and "fieldnote evidence." Theoretical candor refers to providing a chronological, intellectual, and personal account of how the analysis evolved. In any analysis, only some from among a vast number of available facts are actually reported, and this reporting is structured by the scheme the ethnographer has devised. Therefore, "candid exposition of when and why" such schemes were developed is appropriately reported and, moreover, such reporting "enhances ethnographic validity" (Sanjek 1990, 396). Such accounts have not been all that common in analytic ethnographies, although they are certainly not unknown.

The practice of theoretical candor provides researchers' views of the sources of their analysis. An account of the ethnographer's path, in contrast, reports with whom researchers interacted, in what sequence, and how. In Sanjek's language this is a "description of the path connecting the ethnographer and informants" (Sanjek 1990, 400). In this spirit, analytic ethnographers have, with some but not universal frequency, provided such accounts. Conventions for constructing them have become increasingly clear (e.g., Lofland and Lofland 1984, 147–49). Even so, exactly what should be in them and how intimate they should be is still largely undetermined, although David Altheide and John Johnson have begun to chart the possibilities and requirements in some detail (Altheide and Johnson 1991, 1992, 1994; Johnson and Altheide 1990, 1993).

Sanjek's "canon" of field note evidence involves reporting (a) procedures of assembling and processing data and (b) practices of presenting data in the report. Regarding procedures, analytically ethnographic researchers often describe how they recorded data and worked with it, as well as processes of developing analysis (cf. Huberman and Miles 1994, 439–40). Sufficient amounts of the empirical materials themselves are presented, an aspect that overlaps with the feature of "developed treatment" that I will discuss in a moment.

These three kinds of discussions and practices have not, of course, absolutely ensured that researchers' reports have been analytically true, or that readers have assessed them as such. They have, though (analytic ethnographers claim), provided a mind-set with which to approach the data and their conceptualization, and that serves to heighten researchers' concerns with analytic trueness. Fully executed and reported, these practices at least move the researcher well along the road to analytic trueness (cf. Altheide and Johnson 1994).

The theme running through these three practices is that of exercising and exhibiting methodological concern and caution in treating data throughout the research and the development of its reports. Indeed, in addition to the three practices just enumerated, at every appropriate place in the report, in the ethic of the analytic ethnographer, researchers acknowledge and call attention to possible difficulties and shortcomings in both the data and the analysis (Johnson and Altheide 1993).

6. New Content

The more general stances of unfettered inquiry combined with deep familiarity that analytic ethnography brings to social research have implications for its view of "newness." By newness I mean the conventional concern not to waste resources in either (a) researching empirical facts that have already been reliably and amply reported or (b) reiterating analyses that are already well developed and widely known.[22]

Although analytic ethnographers often seem sympathetic with concerns that research provide new facts and new analysis, their commitments to unfettered inquiry and deep familiarity appear also to give them a good deal of faith in the possibility that even already well-researched facts and much-discussed analyses can yield newness when approached in the spirit of unfettered inquiry and with deep familiarity. Thus, in being oriented to direct relations with situations or settings, it is likely that even well-researched previous instances are not exactly the same as the one that might now be studied, if only in the passage of time or in a change of geographic location. These or other such differences then become points of newness that are thought worthy of exploration.

Well-known ideas, concepts, propositions, or whatever are likewise subject to revision in the face of deep familiarity with any new data at hand. All actual analyses are, of necessity, built on some limited range of empirical materials. The consequence is that any newer set of empirical materials scrutinized through the lens of existing analysis is very likely to discover neglected lines of conceptualization and even data that are inconsistent with existing analysis. These and other avenues of thought are then legitimate forms of newness.

In this spirit of unfettered inquiry and of faith in deep familiarity, analytic ethnographers have also been unusually open to inquiries whose only, at least initial, claim to attention has been that they would be the first report on a situation or setting that has only recently emerged or is emerging. In view of the fact that the vast churnings of the (post?) modern world throw up ever new situations and settings, the perspective of analytic ethnography provides an early reconnaissance apparatus because of its openness to newness of this more mundane but vital kind. It is analytic ethnographers, rather than more conventional researchers, who have been ready, sometimes on very short notice, to go running off to exotic or dangerous locales to scrutinize new turns of the world.[23]

At the conceptual level, analytic ethnography's emphasis on emergent analysis obviously, by its logic, places a premium on new generic propositions. Indeed, this stress becomes, for some, something of a fetish, and it spawns numerous discussions of how to find new ideas in one's data. These discussions are often framed (misleadingly, I think) as the problem of how to write up ethnography (e.g., Becker 1986; Wolcott 1990).

In the early 1990s there were increasing indications that newness in analytic ethnography had begun to take a more normal science turn in which researchers firmly situated themselves in an existing conceptual literature and undertook a new conceptual elaboration that derived from a literature, while at the same time also using the data as the vehicle of that elaboration. Hunt and Benford's (1994) analysis of "identity talk in the peace and justice movement" is a striking early 1990s example of this. Solidly rooted in theoretical discussions of "identity" as an ongoing achievement rather than a static "thing"—as something that people do rather than merely be—they provide an analytically ethnographic explication of, in detail, how this worked in one setting. This analysis was not the creative leap implied by notions of "new generic propositions," nor was it intended to be. What they did, however, was clearly quite new in being an empirical elaboration of what were simply abstract musings before their research. In the language of conventional research, this was a solid and significant advance and showed a clear line of development, features that have been quite rare in analytic ethnographies historically.

7. Developed Treatment

In ordinary scientific inquiry, if two people independently research and publish reports that are substantially identical and do so at the same time, the report that is the more thoroughly developed in empirical and conceptual ways is considered more important and elicits a higher degree of interest. The classic case of this in science is the relation between the work of Charles Darwin and that of Alfred Russel Wallace, the latter of whom independently formulated the theory of evolution. Indeed, Wallace might have published before Darwin except for a British gentlemanly agreement in which their respective formulations were made public simultaneously. But it is Darwin, rather than Wallace, who is commonly credited with the theory of evolution. This is because Darwin, not Wallace, performed the exhaustive research, developed the theory in detail, and published several elaborate reports. Wallace's work was true and new, as far as he had gone, but he did not develop the theory in detail or base his formulation on many data. Darwin, in great contrast, spent decades developing diverse forms of data and elaborating the theory in terms of the data.[24] Because of this, Darwin's work had a much more solid evidential base and conceptual purchase than Wallace's sketchily formulated speculations. Therefore, Darwin rather than Wallace is viewed as the inventor of the theory of evolution.

The situation is the same in social science research, including analytic ethnography. Indeed, publications displaying several or even all the six foregoing features or tendencies of analytic ethnography, but which are not developed, are not scarce. However, in the absence of empirical and conceptual development, people who see themselves as analytic ethnographers discount these writings as only skillful exercises in speculation (which are not mean achievements, to be sure, just as Wallace's achievement was not).

The meaning of a "developed treatment" differs among strategies of research. In analytic ethnography, the idea of a developed treatment has focused on the three interrelated variables or dimensions of (a) the degree of conceptual elaboration, (b) the balance between conceptual elaboration and data presentation, and (c) the degree of interpenetration of conceptual elaboration and data presentation.[25]

The dimension of conceptual elaboration refers, operationally, to the number of major conceptual or analytic divisions and subdivisions that form the main body of a report. In grounded theory jargon, this is the dimension of conceptual density, specificity, and interlinkage or integration (Strauss and Corbin 1990, 109, 121, 253–54). The central concern is for researchers to provide evidence of having given detailed thought to the one or more propositions used to structure and analyze the data. The prime evidence of such detailed thought is a conceptual scheme of some reasonable complexity that works in tandem with the other two dimensions of development.

Consistent with their qualitative biases, I suppose, ethnographers' attention to elaboration has not, nevertheless, given rise to quantitative formulations of what exact degrees of elaboration ought to be displayed in what circumstance of reporting. In the absence of quantitative materials, I can only report my impression that article-length analyses tend to have on the order of three to five major elements that elaborate a proposition and a similar number of subdivisions within each element. Reports noticeably falling short of or radically exceeding this broad middle course are likely to be labeled *underelaborated* or *overelaborated*.

The possibilities of under- and overelaboration lead into the second dimension of developed treatment, the degree of balance between a conceptual scheme and the presentation of data. Extremely overelaborated conceptual schemes squeeze out, so to speak, the opportunity to present data. In this "analytic excess," authors become so engrossed in the logic of conceptualizing that they fail to report very much of the rich, concrete reality to which the analysis purportedly refers. In the other direction, that of "descriptive excess," there is too much description relative to analysis, to the point of being a simple history or journalistic narrative.

As with the first dimension (the degree of elaboration), I have observed only "order-of-magnitude" guidelines regarding balance among analytic ethnographers. The one I have encountered most frequently suggests that somewhat more than half the pages of an article-length report should consist of qualitative data: accounts of episodes, incidents, events, exchanges, remarks, happenings, conversations, actions, and so forth. Somewhat less than half should be analysis: the major proposition or propositions, abstract categorizing and discussion of the meaning, application, and implications of the data, and so on.

The two dimensions of elaboration and balance come together to display development in the third dimension, that of the interpenetration of data and analysis, which means the continuing and intimate alternation of data and analysis as text. In the analytically ethnographic perspective, analytic passages should not go on very long without reporting empirical materials collected, and vice versa. This alternation is claimed to make the relation between the data and analysis more evident, and to convey ways in which they form a whole.

In the epistemological perspective of grounded theory and analytic ethnography alike, reports are interpenetrated in this fashion because they are based on—have emerged out of—the process of the grounded induction of analysis that I describe above as the fourth main feature of this research strategy. Because of the emergent character of the analysis, interpenetration is not merely an appearance in the report, it is the logical consequence of a thorough working through of the data in analytic terms.

In the analytically ethnographic perspective, the three dimensions and textual practices of elaboration, balance, and interpenetration form a discipline of guiding constraints that result in a developed treatment. Moreover, the discipline entailed in carrying out these three dimensions of development is an additional way in which analytic ethnographers seek to ensure the trueness of their analyses (feature 5, above).

These, then, are the seven tendencies or practices that, construed as an ideal type, make up the strategy of research called analytic ethnography. With this specimen before us, let me now consider some of the issues it raises—its successes and failings—and its future.

❖ FAILINGS AND FUTURES

Analytic ethnography obviously has major virtues and successes that need to be recognized and that provide the context for discussing its failings and futures. Foremost among these has been its role as a disciplined, cutting-edge strategy of empirical and conceptual innovation (or dare I say "discovery"?). A great many of the innovations the method has produced have become classic writings in a wide variety of specific, substantive specialties. One irony is that although these classics are, methodologically speaking, analytic ethnographies, they are commonly not perceived as such because of their substantive encasement. The innovation or discovery fruits it has produced historically, and that it continues to produce, justify its continued practice, although we must be prepared also to pay the significant price of atomized inquiry that I will discuss in a moment.

As commonly practiced, analytic ethnography is labor-intensive but, in relative terms, it is inexpensive and doable in ways that several other strategies of research are not. If we must choose between no research or research not premised on deep familiarity—which may increasingly be our choices—analytic ethnography is, to me, preferable. Better the limitations and liabilities of analytic ethnography than no new knowledge or "knowledge" not rooted in intimate experience with its subject.

On the failings side, the tendency to transform a mere strategy of research into a vehicle for creating social knowledge per se is a central problem. In making a means into an end, I fear that analytic ethnographers have adopted the model we see practiced by some "theory groups" that use experiments or surveys as the only proper method of producing knowledge. Historically, one main criticism of such monomethod research has been that it allowed a research strategy to drive substance. The substance was shaped by what was feasible and practical with the use of the method rather than by the logic of the content. It happens that users of experiments and surveys who have striven to do this are also enamored with testing carefully preformed hypotheses. This kind of guidance has served to mask the extreme degree to which the hypotheses formed and tested are a function of the method. Some at least gloss of advance could thus be maintained. Even with the gloss of hypothesis testing, allowing a method to drive the substance can come to ruin, as it did in the now defunct study of small groups (Mullins 1973).[26]

The same methods-driven mind-set has, to a significant degree, taken hold in the use of analytic ethnography. In that case, it has meant, in contrast, near chaos. With research explicitly not driven by preformed hypotheses, not even a gloss of coherence and advance could arise. Instead, a thousand flowers have bloomed, so to speak, and although this has been a magnificent display of sorts, what all these efforts come to has been exceedingly problematic, save for the classic innovative fruits I mention above, which have been a rather small portion of all analytic ethnographies.

Interestingly, in celebrating unfettered inquiry, deep familiarity, and newness (features 2, 3, and 6), many analytic ethnographers seem not to worry themselves about this scattered and inchoate landscape. Instead, many—along with ethnographers of other stripes—have thought that these features of their work, combined with capturing the perspective of the people studied, were sufficient to justify their efforts.[27]

For this reason, efforts such as those by Prus (1987, 1994) on how attention to generic social processes can address this failing are very noticeable for their rarity. Prus should be strongly commended for calling our attention to scattering and fragmentation and for starting a program of remedy, but his program, although substantive, is still method driven; that is, it is conceived as moving forward by means of analytic ethnography. As I have said just above about allowing experiments or surveys to drive one's research, centerpiecing analytic ethnography presents the same danger.

One might argue, though, that analytic ethnography, properly applied, is different from other methods and that, in this case, allowing the method to drive the substance is allowable. It might be the case that some specific kinds of substance fit quite productively with a particular method. The task is then the more refined problem of identifying proper and precise fits between method and substance. One does not indiscriminately either embrace or reject method-driven inquiry. Thus it is possible that Prus has found a proper match between the method of analytic ethnography and the substance of the generic social processes he identifies. (It is also possible that there is a unique fit between Stanford-centered experimentation and the status theories associated with that experimentation.) This is, however, an empirical rather than a logical question that can be settled a priori. We cannot know in the absence of completed efforts that we examine and evaluate.

The possibility of fit between substance and method brings us to a further aspect of the chaotic scattering of analytic ethnography. Although scattering is evident, it is not an infinite scattering. The several thousands of analytically ethnographic studies produced over the last almost half a century are not entirely unrelated. Instead, there are at least a few major clusters of substantive similarity. What is odd about this—and a failing of analytic ethnographers—is the infrequency with which there have been efforts to consolidate substantive clusters into coherent, overall pictures, even if these are pictures that none of the authors of the individual reports would have had in mind. Lyn Lofland's (1989) consolidation of analytic ethnographies of public place behavior is thus notable not simply for its substantive achievement but for the rarity of such consolidation efforts. (Her consolidation is all the more ironic because it is heavily based on studies published in the *Journal of Contemporary Ethnography*, a place that makes the existence of this body of work quite visible. As Holmes said to Watson about his failure to perceive an "obvious" architectural feature of 221 Baker Street, "You see but you do not observe.")[28]

Putting aside continued virtuoso performances that become classics in substantive areas and the imponderables of consolidations, what might be said of other aspects of the future of analytic ethnography? Two matters seem most pertinent. First, I think we will see the spread of a modified form of analytic ethnography in which its fourth feature—emergent analysis—will be modified and the other six features retained. I use the word "modified" rather than changed to indicate that analysis will continue to be significantly emergent but nevertheless much more attuned to specific research questions or even hypotheses at the outset of the research. This modification is already practiced with some regularity in the network of analytic ethnographers in which David Snow is a key mentor and collaborator.[29] In discussing feature 6 above—new content—I spoke of this development as "new conceptual elaboration," a procedure in which the inquiry derives specifically from existing conceptual development but nevertheless uses new data to elaborate, refine, or revise existing conceptualization. To some, this will seem like a move toward a more "normal science" process and they will decry it for this reason. So long as this does not displace less preformed versions of emergent analysis I think that this is a very positive development.[30]

Second, and in conclusion, at the outset I referred to the fact that vast questionings of a good deal of what has been called ethnography— and of social science itself—have arisen in some quarters over recent years.[31] These questionings are of many kinds and their implications for analytic ethnography therefore vary. Putting the epistemologically nihilistic questionings aside, the more specific of the new concerns will serve to strengthen the craft but not to change its essential nature. I have in mind, specifically, attention given to presentational or "rhetorical" formats (e.g., Atkinson 1990, 1992) and to the power and domination dimensions of the role of the social researcher (e.g., Denzin and Lincoln 1994).

The most challenging and unresolvable of these new questionings, though, are competing conceptions of the nature and role of intellectuals in society, the matter I described above as the struggle over fettered and unfettered inquiry. The future of analytic ethnography, of social research, and of intellectual life in general is bound up with what will be the larger fate of intellectuals as a grouping. To what degrees and in what ways will inquiry be fettered or unfettered? Not being able to predict the contours and outcomes of this struggle, I can only say that the future of analytic ethnography is open, but then, would one expect an analytic ethnographer of symbolic interactionist bent to say anything else?

Although I prefer the side of unfettered inquiry, I understand and sympathize with pressures for intellectuals to prove themselves useful in society. Various other social groupings are often, indeed, quite forceful and effective in enticing, shaming, or even harassing intellectuals into helping them with their projects or causes. Such groupings include, of course, the exploitive powerful, the exploited powerless, and the merely mainstream practical. Lack of confidence in or understanding of the path of unfettered inquiry makes the pleadings or scoldings of these groupings all the more irresistible. Hence intellectuals, including ethnographers, join up (or should I say get converted or brainwashed?). Such fetterings are likely to continue to be the paths taken by many intellectuals, including ethnographers (and because of deep familiarity, perhaps especially by ethnographers, ironically enough). Erving Goffman seems to have recognized this likelihood, and even though he preferred unfettered inquiry, he allowed, in his very last published words, that

> if one *must* have warrant addressed to social needs, let it be for unsponsored analyses of the social arrangements enjoyed by those with institutional authority—priests, psychiatrists, school teachers, police, generals, government leaders, parents, males, whites, nationals, media operators, and all the other well-placed persons who are in a position to give official imprint to versions of reality. (Goffman 1983, 17, emphasis added)

I have supplied the emphasis given the word "must" in this passage to suggest that Goffman is saying, "well, if you *must* . . .," then at least scrutinize the powerful rather than others. I infer him to say that your analysis will be fettered, but in providing information on "well-placed persons," you are at least sowing the seeds of unfettering. One can hope that this is, at the very minimum, a key feature of the future.

❖ NOTES

1. Sharp criticisms of an earlier formulation of this article (titled "Evaluating Qualitative Fieldstudies: Applying the Criteria of Trueness, Newness and Importance") stimulated this revision and reframing. Extremely helpful clarifiers of what I am trying to say were Sheryl Kleinman, Gary Fine, three anonymous referees for this journal, and its coeditors. I thank them all for their detailed attention and patience. In addition, I am much indebted to the constructive counsel of Lyn H. Lofland.

2. Denzin and Lincoln (1994, xi) remark on assembling their *Handbook of Qualitative Research*: "We confronted disciplinary blinders—including our own—and discovered there were separate traditions surrounding each of our topics within distinct interpretive communities." Atkinson and Hammersley (1994, 257, 258) opine: "Across the spectrum of the social sciences, the use and justification of ethnography is marked by diversity rather than consensus ... [and it is a] highly complex and contentious discursive field." Altheide and Johnson (1994, 497) observe: "This is a chaotic ... time for ethnography and all of its newly emergent forms." Richardson (1994, 524) declares, "This is a time of transition, a propitious moment."

3. Denzin and Lincoln (1994, part II, "Major Paradigms and Perspectives") for example, present six charting chapters. Denzin (1994, 502) suggests that "four major paradigms (positivist and postpositivist, constructivist, critical) and three major perspectives (feminist, ethnic models, cultural studies) now structure qualitative writing." Richardson (1994, 521–22) presents an extremely detailed charting, some forms within which are "narrative of the self," "ethnographic fictional representations," "poetic representations," "ethnographic drama," and "mixed genres."

4. See Becker (1963) and Davis (1963, 1972). Oddly, despite quite distinctive features, histories of ethnography have not so far treated this cohort in its own right. Instead, it has been pushed back as simply a continuation of pre-World War II Chicago sociology or classified forward as part of the decades following World War II.

5. Spector and Faulkner (1980) review five such journals that had formed by 1980.

6. For additional compilations of examples of, and citations to, the genre see Prus (1987, 1994), Lofland (1971, 1976), and Lofland and Lofland (1984, 1995).

7. The *Oxford English Dictionary*, which might be accorded more than ordinary authority in this matter, defines ethnography as "the scientific description of nations or races of men, with their customs, habits, and points of difference."

8. As an additional contextual matter, note that my central object of analysis is "an inquiry." This is to be distinguished from thinking in terms of "approaches" to research or to understanding society, which leads one too easily into conceptions of abstract "paradigms" and kindred units, examples of

which are given in notes 2 and 3 above, and instances of which are abundant in Denzin and Lincoln (1994).

9. Waggish readers have of course already asked: Is this an analytic ethnography of analytic ethnography? The answer is no. There are several useful and valid forms of analysis and reflection that are far short of the scale of effort and discipline required by analytic ethnography. Although I can claim some participant familiarity with analytic ethnography (feature 3), I do not here attempt to analyze it in the full breadth of all seven features. Indeed, properly to do so would require a book rather than an article-length report. My treatment here is, instead, an analytic essay—which is a different kind of intellectual work. Further, given that the seven features or tendencies are variables, the most appropriate, larger research strategy is probably quantitative content analysis rather than analytic ethnography.

10. Even though seldom stated so starkly in works of instruction on social research, these eight questions nevertheless make up their underlying agenda. Oddly, I have found elementary textbooks of composition to be clearer than social research manuals on asking basic questions (e.g., Decker and Schwegler 1990). Further, students of inquiry as a generic (i.e., outside social) science mince no words on the question of what are basic questions—as in Adler (1940, 183–84), from whom I borrow. See, in addition, Strauss and Corbin (1990, chaps. 9 and 10) and Hammersley (1990, 41) on "types of claim."

11. Examples of generic propositional analyses are elaborated with numerous examples from analytic ethnographies in chapter 7 of Lofland and Lofland (1984, 1995).

12. Sections of the text in this section are adapted from Lofland (1974, 102–3; Lofland and Lofland 1984, 123–24).

13. Cf. Hammersley's (1992, chap. 1) use of this image in discussing "theoretical description," a discussion that does not, however, distinguish between generic propositional framing (feature 1) and "developed treatment" (feature 7).

14. Consider, for example, Fred Davis's (1973) distinction between the martian and convert views of society. Part of the appeal of Peter Berger's (1963) *Invitation to Sociology* has to do with his vision of unfettered inquiry or a naturalistic mind-set. See also Collins (1993, 311): "Sociology offers something virtually no one else in our society has: a clear sight of the pattern beyond the local viewpoints of the various participants [in society, the] . . . capacity to rise above particular viewpoints." Under the label "importance," Hammersley (1990, 107–13; 1992) has wrestled toward a conception of unfettered inquiry and comes fairly close to achieving it.

15. C. Wright Mills captures the conception of a "larger audience" well when he counsels would-be writers: "It is very important for any writer to have in mind just what kinds of people he is trying to speak to.. . . To write is to raise a claim to be read, but by whom?.. . . One answer [is to] . . . assume that you have been asked to give a lecture on some subject you know well, before an audience of teachers and students from all departments of a leading university, as well as an assortment of interested persons from a near-by city. Assume that such an audience is before you and that they have a right to know; assume that you want to let them know. Now write" (Mills 1959, 221).

16. For an especially clear and recent example of unfettered inquiry, I recommend Hunt and Benford's (1994) analysis of themes of talk heard among activists in several peace groups in which they participated. The content of the

talk they report deals with a wide variety of things that were deeply meaningful to the activists studied: how they came to be in the movement, points of disillusionment, times of witnessing "inhumane and immoral happenings," ways in which they had been guided and inspired by others, and the horrendous effects of violence and injustice, among other topics of talk. Observing other peace groups, a number of independent researchers have reported a concrete empirical reality that is virtually identical to that portrayed by Hunt and Benford (see Lofland 1993 and reports discussed there). The Hunt and Benford report differs from these other studies, however, in that the researchers did not harness themselves to the immediate frames of reference and social agenda of the participants under study. Transcending such fettering bonds, Hunt and Benford instead ask themselves wider, larger, and longer-term questions derived from thinking about social movements *sub specie aeternitatis*, specifically, how do people—movement activists in this case—"construct and align personal and collective identities" (Hunt and Benford 1994, 489)? Their answer is an analysis of the "identity talk" relating to "associational declarations, disillusionment anecdotes, atrocity tales, personal-is-political reports, guide narratives, and war stories" (Hunt and Benford 1994, 486–88). Instead of celebrating and commiserating with activist angst—the more common fettered exercise—Hunt and Benford press forward with the more profound and unfettered task of dispassionately dissecting its dynamics (cf. Lofland 1993).

17. As I read them, the authors of chapters 8, 9, 10, 20, and 33, among others, in the Denzin and Lincoln *Handbook of Qualitative Research* (1994) advocate fettered, descriptive inquiry.

18. The most comprehensive single bibliographic compilation as of the late 1980s was Gravel and Ridinger (1988). Denzin and Lincoln (1994) contains discussion of some material published in the late 1980s and early 1990s. In passing the thirty-item mark in 1993, the Sage Qualitative Research Methods Series provides a miniature library focused on these questions.

19. Strauss and Corbin (1994, 275, 277) state that "grounded theory is a general methodology, a *way of thinking about and conceptualizing data* . . . [that is] applicable to quantitative as well as qualitative studies" (emphasis in original).

20. In addition, it bears remarking that the task of organizing a mass of unstructured data predates "grounded theory" formalization of the process and is effectively carried on quite independently of knowing anything about it. That is, emergent analysis is a ubiquitous and ancient human practice, one for which "grounded theory" threatens to become a tedious and pedantic mystification. Independently of grounded theory, emergent analysis is commonly treated in elementary research textbooks (e.g., Cuba 1988), as well as in more advanced works such as Barzun and Graff (1957 and later editions) (the text that crystallized my consciousness of emergent analysis). Because emergent analysis is basic human thinking and induction, it is not accurate to say that the "core features of the Strauss approach are present [in qualitative studies], even when Strauss and associates are not directly named" unless one equates human thinking and "the Strauss approach" (Denzin 1994, 513).

21. Denzin and Lincoln's *Handbook of Qualitative Research* (1994) is thus remarkable for how little space is devoted to problems of assessing the trueness of space-time specific assertions. This same scantness is likewise apparent in the more than thirty issues of the Sage Qualitative Research Methods papers. Hammersley's (1990) "critical guide" to ethnography is noteworthy as an exception, but even his treatment is quite brief (and appears in portions

of chapter 4). One is forced to look to elementary textbooks of research methods for simply a list of the major problems and pitfalls (e.g., Babbie 1992, 20–27, 305–8).

22. See Hammersley (1990, 113–17) on "contribution."

23. Although otherwise fettered in many ways, this admirable spirit is very strongly displayed in Burawoy and company's collection of early reconnaissance reports, reports that are in this sense "ethnography unbound" (the title of the collection) (Burawoy et al. 1991).

24. This empirical and conceptual development also contributed to the confidence people could have in the trueness of the theory. The theory had to stand the test of the data in the course of elaborating its internal and external implications.

25. Some of this discussion of elaboration, interpenetration, and balance is quoted and adapted from Lofland (Lofland 1971, 128–29; Lofland 1974, 106–9; Lofland and Lofland 1984, 145–47).

26. In sociology, the *Social Psychology Quarterly* continues to provide many examples of how research can be hobbled by slavish adherence to the experimental method. The *Journal of Contemporary Ethnography* exhibits much the same problem, differing only in its method of hobbling (pun intended) (cf. Lofland 1987, 34–39).

27. Enchantment with ethnographic (or, more broadly, qualitative) methods can also induce the expectation that every report of it should be "interesting." Thus, "for 30 years, I have yawned my way through numerous supposedly exemplary qualitative studies. Countless numbers of texts have I abandoned half read, half scanned" because this reader would "find the text boring" (Richardson 1994, 516–17). Why, though, should a text be interesting simply because it uses a specific research method? Instead, unless one is a methodologist, a report is of interest only if one has substantive reasons for wanting to know what it says. Expecting every ethnography to be fascinating simply because it is an ethnography is like expecting every report of an experiment or a survey to be fascinating only by virtue of the respective methods. Clearly, reports using these methods may or may not be fascinating as a function of what one is trying to learn about. Here, again, the means becomes the end in inquiry. (This muddled confusion of ends and means is seen more broadly in the propensity to focus on how a "tale" is told rather than on what it tells, a confusion pioneered by Van Maanen 1988.)

28. Among other consolidations of note is Helen Ebaugh's *Becoming an Ex: The Process of Role Exit* (1988), which is a generalization of her earlier analytic ethnography, *Out of the Cloister* (1977). (Irony on irony, her analytic ethnography and its generalizing consolidation stem from training at Columbia and the influence of Robert Merton.) I must also include myself in this criticism, although I did at one point make a stab at it (in Lofland 1976).

29. See, for example, Snow and Anderson (1993), Benford (1993), and Hunt and Benford (1994).

30. Pun intended.

31. The literature of this questioning is vast. Denzin and Lincoln (1994) provide a large, serviceable compendium of it and references to it. Agger (1991) is a good guide to its broader development in social science. The January 1993 issue of *Contemporary Sociology* carries a review symposium on it with regard to ethnography, within which the remarks of Snow and Morrill (1993) provide appropriate counterpoint to Denzin and Lincoln.

❖ REFERENCES

Adler, M. J. 1940. *How to read a book: The art of getting a liberal education.* New York: Simon & Schuster.

Adler, P. A., and P. Adler. 1987. The past and future of ethnography. *Journal of Contemporary Ethnography* 16:4–24.

Agger, B. 1991. Critical theory, poststructuralism, postmodernism: Their sociological relevance. *Annual Review of Sociology* 17:105–31.

Altheide, D. L., and J. M. Johnson. 1991. Text without context and the problem of authority in ethnographic research. *Studies in Symbolic Interaction* 12: 135–48.

———. 1992. Tacit knowledge: The boundaries of experience. *Studies in Symbolic Interaction* 13:283–98.

———. 1994. Criteria for assessing interpretive validity in qualitative research. In *Handbook of qualitative research*, edited by N. K. Denzin and Y. S. Lincoln, 485–99. Thousand Oaks, CA: Sage.

Athens, L. H. 1984a. Blumer's method of naturalistic inquiry: A critical examination. *Studies in Symbolic Interaction* 5:241–57.

———. 1984b. Scientific criteria for evaluating qualitative studies. *Studies in Symbolic Interaction* 5:259–68.

Atkinson, P. 1990. *The ethnographic imagination: Textual constructions of reality.* London: Routledge.

———. 1992. *Understanding ethnographic texts.* Newbury Park, CA: Sage.

Atkinson, P., and M. Hammersley. 1994. Ethnography and participant observation. In *Handbook of qualitative research*, edited by N. K. Denzin and Y. S. Lincoln, 248–61. Thousand Oaks, CA: Sage.

Babbie, E. 1992. *The practice of social research.* 6th ed. Belmont, CA: Wadsworth.

Barzun, J., and H. F. Graff. 1957. *The modern researcher.* New York: Harcourt, Brace.

Becker, H. S. 1963. *Outsiders: Studies in the sociology of deviance.* New York: Free Press.

Becker, H. S., with P. Richards. 1986. *Writing for social scientists: How to start and finish your thesis, book, or article.* Chicago: University of Chicago Press.

Benford, R. D. 1993. You could be the hundredth monkey: Collective identity and vocabularies of motive in the nuclear disarmament movement. *Sociological Quarterly* 34:195–216.

Berger, P. L. 1963. *Invitation to sociology.* Garden City, NY: Doubleday.

Blumer, H. 1969. *Symbolic interactionism: Perspective and method.* Englewood Cliffs, NJ: Prentice Hall.

Burawoy, M., A. Burton, A. A. Ferguson, K. J. Fox, J. Gamson, N. Gartrell, L. Hurst, C. Kurzman, L. Salzinger, J. Schiffman, and S. Ui, eds. 1991. *Ethnography unbound: Power and resistance in the modern metropolis.* Berkeley: University of California Press.

Burchfield, R. W., ed. 1987. *The compact edition of the Oxford English dictionary complete text reproduced micrographically.* Vol. 3, *A supplement to the Oxford English dictionary, volumes I-IV.* Oxford, UK: Oxford University Press.

Charmaz, K. 1983. The grounded theory method: An explication and interpretation. In *Contemporary field research: A collection of readings*, edited by R. M. Emerson, 109–26. Boston: Little, Brown.

Collins, R. 1993. What does conflict theory predict about America's future? *Sociological Perspectives* 36:289–313.

Cuba, L. J. 1988. *A short guide to writing about social science.* New York: HarperCollins.

Davis, F. 1963. *Passage through crisis*. Indianapolis: Bobbs-Merrill.

———. 1972. *Illness, interaction and the self*. Belmont, CA: Wadsworth.

———. 1973. The Martian and the convert: Ontological polarities in social research. *Urban Life and Culture* 2:333–43.

Decker, R. E., and R. A. Schwegler. 1990. *Decker's patterns of exposition 12*. New York: HarperCollins.

Denzin, N. K. 1994. The art and politics of interpretation. In *Handbook of qualitative research*, edited by N. K. Denzin and Y. S. Lincoln, 500–15. Thousand Oaks, CA: Sage.

Denzin, N. K., and Y. S. Lincoln, eds. 1994. *Handbook of qualitative research*. Thousand Oaks, CA: Sage.

Ebaugh, H. 1977. *Out of the cloister: A study of organizational dilemmas*. Austin: University of Texas Press.

———. 1988. *Becoming an ex: The process of role exit*. Chicago: University of Chicago Press.

Glaser, B., and A. Strauss. 1967. *The discovery of grounded theory*. Chicago: Aldine.

Goffman, E. 1983. The interaction order. *American Sociological Review* 48:1–17.

———. 1989. On fieldwork. Transcribed and edited by L. H. Lofland. *Journal of Contemporary Ethnography* 18:123–32.

Gove, P. B., ed. 1971. *Webster's third new international dictionary of the English language unabridged*. Springfield, MA: G. & C. Merriam.

Gravel, P. B., and R. B. M. Ridinger. 1988. *Anthropological fieldwork*. New York: Garland.

Hammersley, M. 1990. *Reading ethnographic research: A critical guide*. London: Longman.

———. 1992. *What's wrong with ethnography? Methodological explorations*. New York: Routledge.

Heirich, M. 1970. *The beginning: Berkeley, 1964*. New York: Columbia University Press.

———. 1971. *The spiral of conflict: Demonstrations at Berkeley 1964–1965*. New York: Columbia University Press.

Huberman, A. M., and M. B. Miles. 1994. Data management and analysis methods. In *Handbook of qualitative research*, edited by N. K. Denzin and Y. S. Lincoln, 428–44. Thousand Oaks, CA: Sage.

Hunt, S. A., and R. D. Benford. 1994. Identity talk in the peace and justice movement. *Journal of Contemporary Ethnography* 22:488–517.

Johnson, J. M., and D. L. Altheide. 1990. Reflexive accountability in ethnography. *Studies in Symbolic Interaction* 11:25–33.

———. 1993. The ethnographic ethic. *Studies in Symbolic Interaction* 14:95–107.

Kurtz, P. 1983. *In defense of secular humanism*. Buffalo, NY: Prometheus.

———. 1992. *The new skepticism: Inquiry and reliable knowledge*. Buffalo, NY: Prometheus.

Lofland, J. 1971. *Analyzing social settings: A guide to qualitative observation and analysis*. Belmont, CA: Wadsworth.

———. 1972. Editorial introduction. *Urban Life and Culture* 1:3–5.

———. 1974. Styles of reporting qualitative field research. *American Sociologist* 9(3):101–11.

———. 1976. *Doing social life: The qualitative study of human interaction in natural settings*. New York: Wiley.

———, ed. 1978. *Interaction in everyday life: Social strategies*. Beverly Hills, CA: Sage.

Lofland, J. 1987. Reflections on a thrice-named journal. *Journal of Contemporary Ethnography* 16:25–40.

———. 1993. *Polite protesters: The American peace movement of the 1980s.* New York: Syracuse University Press.

Lofland, J., and L. H. Lofland. 1984. *Analyzing social settings: A guide to qualitative observation and analysis.* 2d ed. Belmont, CA: Wadsworth.

———. 1995. *Analyzing social settings: A guide to qualitative observation and analysis.* 3d ed. Belmont, CA: Wadsworth.

Lofland, L. H. 1989. Social life in the public realm: A review. *Journal of Contemporary Ethnography* 17:453–82.

McCall, G. J., and J. L. Simmons. 1969. *Issues in participant observation: A text and reader.* Reading, MA: Addison-Wesley.

Mills, C. W. 1969. *The sociological imagination.* New York: Oxford University Press.

Mullins, N. C. 1973. *Theories and theory groups in contemporary American sociology.* New York: Harper & Row.

Prus, R. 1987. Generic social processes: Maximizing conceptual development in ethnographic research. *Journal of Contemporary Ethnography* 16:250–93.

———. 1994. Generic social processes and the study of human lived experiences: Achieving transcontextuality in ethnographic research. In *Symbolic interaction: An introduction to social psychology,* edited by N. J. Herman and L. T. Reynolds, 436–58. Dix Hills, NY: General Hall.

Rauch, J. 1993. *Kindly inquisitors: The new attacks on free thought.* Chicago: University of Chicago Press.

Richardson, L. 1994. Writing: A method of inquiry. In *Handbook of qualitative research,* edited by N. K. Denzin and Y. S. Lincoln, 516–29. Thousand Oaks, CA: Sage.

Sanjek, R. 1990. On ethnographic validity. In *Fieldnotes: The makings of anthropology,* edited by R. Sanjek, 385–418. Ithaca, NY: Cornell University Press.

Schutz, A [1932] 1967. *The phenomenology of the social world.* Evanston, IL: Northwestern University Press.

Snow, D., and L. Anderson. 1993. *Down on their luck: A study of homeless street people.* Berkeley: University of California Press.

Snow, D., and C. Morrill. 1993. Reflections on anthropology's ethnographic crisis of faith. *Contemporary Sociology* 22:8–11.

Spector, M., and R. Faulkner, 1980. Thoughts on five new journals and some old ones. *Contemporary Sociology* 9:477–82.

Strauss, A. L. 1987. *Qualitative analysis for social scientists.* New York: Cambridge University Press.

Strauss, A. L., and J. Corbin. 1990. *Basics of qualitative research: Grounded theory procedures and techniques.* Newbury Park, CA: Sage.

———. 1994. Grounded theory methodology: An overview. In *Handbook of qualitative research,* edited by N. K. Denzin and Y. S. Lincoln, 273–85. Thousand Oaks, CA: Sage.

Van Maanen, J. 1988. *Tales of the field: On writing ethnography.* Chicago: University of Chicago Press.

Wolcott, H. F. 1990. *Writing up qualitative research.* Newbury Park, CA: Sage.

8

Increasing the Generalizability of Qualitative Research

Janet Ward Schofield

❖ TRADITIONAL VIEWS OF GENERALIZABILITY

Campbell and Stanley (1963) laid the groundwork for much current thinking on the issue of generalizability just over twenty-five years ago in a groundbreaking chapter in the *Handbook of Research on Teaching*. They wrote, "*External validity* asks the question of *generalizability:* To what populations, settings, treatment variables, and

AUTHOR'S NOTE: Much of the research on which this paper is based was funded by the Office of Naval Research, Contract Number N00 14-85-K-0664. Other research utilized in this paper was funded by Grant Number NIE-G-78-0126 from the National Institute of Education. However, all opinions expressed herein are solely those of the author, and no endorsement by ONR or NIE is implied or intended. My sincere thanks go to Bill Firestone and Matthew Miles for their constructive comments on an earlier draft of this paper.

measurement variables can the effect be generalized?" (p. 175; emphasis in original). They then went on to list four specific threats to external validity: the interaction of testing and the experimental treatment, the interaction of selection and treatment, reactive arrangements, and the interference of multiple treatments with one another. Although Campbell and Stanley specifically included populations, settings, treatments, and measurement variables as dimensions relevant to the concept of external validity, the aspect of external validity that has typically received the lion's share of attention in textbook and other treatments of the concept is generalizing to and across populations. This may well be due to the fact that, because of advances in sampling theory in survey research, it is possible to draw samples from even a very large and heterogeneous population and then to generalize to that population using the logic of probability statistics.

Campbell and Stanley (1963), as well as many others in the quantitative tradition, see the attempt to design research so that abstract generalizations can be drawn as a worthy effort, although issues connected with internal validity are typically given even higher priority. Thus researchers in the quantitative tradition have devoted considerable thought to the question of how the generalizability of experimental and quasi-experimental studies can be enhanced. Such efforts are consistent with the fact that many quantitatively oriented researchers would agree with Smith (1975) that "the goal of science is to be able to generalize findings to diverse populations and times" (p. 88).

In contrast to the interest shown in external validity among quantitatively oriented researchers, the methodological literature on qualitative research has paid little attention to this issue, at least until quite recently. For example, Dobbert's (1982) text on qualitative research methods devotes an entire chapter to issues of validity and reliability but does no more than mention the issue of generalizability in passing on one or two pages. Two even more recent books, Kirk and Miller's *Reliability and Validity in Qualitative Research* (1986) and Berg's *Qualitative Research Methods for the Social Sciences* (1989), ignore the issue of external validity completely. The major factor contributing to the disregard of the issue of generalizability in the qualitative methodological literature appears to be a widely shared view that it is unimportant, unachievable, or both.

Many qualitative researchers actively reject generalizability as a goal. For example, Denzin (1983) writes:

> The interpretivist rejects generalization as a goal and never aims to draw randomly selected samples of human experience. For the interpretivist every instance of social interaction, if thickly described (Geertz, 1973), represents a slice from the life world that is the proper subject matter for interpretive inquiry . . . Every topic . . . must be seen as carrying its own logic, sense of order, structure, and meaning. (pp. 133–134)

Although not all researchers in the qualitative tradition reject generalization so strongly, many give it very low priority or see it as essentially irrelevant to their goals. One factor contributing to qualitative researchers' historical tendency to regard the issue of external validity as irrelevant and hence to disregard it is that this research tradition has been closely linked to cultural anthropology, with its emphasis on the study of exotic cultures. This work is often valued for its intrinsic interest, for showing the rich variety and possible range of human behavior, and for serving a historical function by describing traditional cultures before they change in an increasingly interconnected and homogeneous world. For researchers doing work of this sort, the goal is to describe a specific group in fine detail and to explain the patterns that exist, certainly not to discover general laws of human behavior.

Practically speaking, no matter what one's philosophical stance on the importance of generalizability, it is clear that numerous characteristics that typify the qualitative approach are not consistent with achieving external validity as it has generally been conceptualized. For example, the traditional focus on single-case studies in qualitative research is obviously inconsistent with the requirements of statistical sampling procedures, which are usually seen as fundamental to generalizing from the data gathered in a study to some larger population. This fact is often cited as a major weakness of the case study approach (Bolgar, 1965; Shaughnessy & Zechmeister, 1985).

However, the incompatibility between classical conceptions of external validity and fundamental aspects of the qualitative approach goes well beyond this. To give just one example, the experimental tradition emphasizes replicability of results, as is apparent in Krathwohl's (1985) statement: "The heart of external validity is replicability. Would the results be reproducible in those target instances to which one intends to generalize—the population, situation, time, treatment form or format, measures, study designs and procedures?" (p. 123). Yet at the heart of the qualitative approach is the assumption that a piece of qualitative research is very much influenced by the researcher's individual attributes and perspectives. The goal is *not* to produce a standardized set of results that any other careful researcher in the same situation or studying the same issue would have produced. Rather it is to produce a coherent and illuminating description of and perspective on a situation that is based on and consistent with detailed study of that situation. Qualitative researchers have to question seriously the *internal* validity of their work if other researchers reading their field notes feel the evidence does not support the way in which they have depicted the situation. However, they do not expect other researchers in a similar or even the same situation to replicate their findings in the sense of independently coming up with a precisely similar conceptualization. As long as the other researchers' conclusions are not inconsistent with the original account, differences in the reports would not generally raise serious questions related to validity or generalizability.

In fact, I would argue that, except perhaps in multisite qualitative studies, which will be discussed later in this paper, it is impractical to make precise replication a criterion of generalizability in qualitative work. Qualitative research is so arduous that it is unlikely that high-quality researchers could be located to engage in the relatively unexciting task of conducting a study designed specifically to replicate a previous one. Yet studies not designed specifically for replication are unlikely to be conducted in a way that allows good assessment of the replicability issue. Of course it is possible, even likely, that specific ideas or conclusions from a piece of qualitative work can stimulate further research of a qualitative or quantitative nature that provides information on the replicability of that one aspect of a study. However, any piece of qualitative research is likely to contain so many individual descriptive and conceptual components that replicating it on a piece-by-piece basis would be a major undertaking.

❖ THE INCREASING INTEREST IN
   GENERALIZABILITY IN THE QUALITATIVE TRADITION

In the past decade, interest in the issue of generalizability has increased markedly for qualitative researchers involved in the study of education. Books by Patton (1980), Guba and Lincoln (1981), and

Noblit and Hare (1988), as well as papers by Stake (1978), Kennedy (1979), and others, have all dealt with this issue in more than a cursory fashion. Two factors seem to be important in accounting for this increase in attention to the issue of generalizability. First, the uses of qualitative research have shifted quite markedly in the past decade or two. In the area of education, qualitative research is not an approach used primarily to study exotic foreign or deviant local cultures. Rather it has become an approach used widely in both evaluation research and basic research on educational issues in our own society. The issue of generalizability assumes real importance in both kinds of work.

The shift in the uses of qualitative work that occurred during the 1970s was rapid and striking. The most obvious part of this shift was the inclusion of major qualitative components in large-scale evaluation research efforts, which had previously been almost exclusively quantitative in nature (Fetterman, 1982; Firestone & Herriott, 1984). The acceptance of qualitative research as a valid and potentially rich approach to evaluation progressed to the point that Wolcott (1982) wrote, with only some exaggeration, "By the late 1970s the term 'ethnography' . . . had become synonymous with 'evaluation' in the minds of many educators" (p. 82). Evaluations are expensive and time-consuming undertakings. Although formative evaluations are usually site-specific, the worth of a summative evaluation is greatly enhanced to the extent it can inform program and policy decisions relating to other sites. In fact, as Cronbach (1982) points out, when summative evaluations are reported, no more than a fraction of the audience is interested primarily in the specific program and setting that was the object of the study. Even at the study site itself, by the time the evaluation is completed, changes may well have occurred that have important consequences for program functioning and goal achievement. Thus the question of whether an evaluation's findings can usefully be generalized to a later point in time at the site at which the evaluation was conducted is an issue that, although often ignored, requires real consideration.

The issue of generalizability is also salient for more basic qualitative research on educational issues in this country. Funding agencies providing resources for qualitative studies of educational issues are presumably interested in shedding light on these issues generally, not just as they are experienced at one site. For example, I am currently directing a qualitative study of computer usage in an urban high school. It is clear that the impetus for the funding of this study by the Office of Naval Research derived from concerns about the Navy's own computer-based education and training efforts, not from concerns about the public schools. Quite apart from the goals of funding agencies, many qualitative researchers themselves hope to accomplish more than describing the culture of the specific school or classroom that they have chosen to study. For example, Peshkin (1982) writes of his study of school and community in a small town in Illinois, "I hoped . . . to explicate some reality which was not merely confined to other places just like Mansfield" (p. 63), a hope tellingly reflected in the title of his book, *Growing Up American* (1978), as opposed to "Growing Up in Illinois" or "Growing Up in Mansfield." This desire to have one's work be broadly useful is no doubt often stimulated by concern over the state of education in our country today. It is also clearly reinforced by the fact that, unlike most readers of ethnographic reports of exotic cultures, most readers of qualitative reports on American education have had considerable exposure during their own school years to at least one version of the culture described. Thus, unless the researcher chooses a very atypical site or presents an unusually insightful analysis of what is happening, the purely descriptive value of the study may be undercut or discounted.

So far I have argued that qualitative research's shift in both purpose and locale in the last decade or two has contributed to an increased interest in generalizability among qualitative researchers. There is yet one other factor contributing to this trend—the striking rapprochement between qualitative and quantitative methodologies that has occurred in the last decade (Cronbach et al., 1980; Filstead, 1979; Reichardt & Cook, 1979; Spindler, 1982). Exemplifying this trend is the shift in the position of Donald Campbell. Campbell and Stanley (1963) at one point contended that the "one-shot case study," which is one way of describing much qualitative research, has "such a total absence of control as to be of almost no scientific value" (p. 176). However, more recently Campbell (1979) wrote a paper to "correct some of [his] own prior excesses in describing the case study approach" (p. 52) in which he takes the, for many, rather startling position that when qualitative and quantitative results conflict, "the quantitative results should be regarded as suspect until the reasons for the discrepancy are well understood" (p. 52).

One result of the rapprochement that has occurred is that qualitative and quantitative researchers are more in contact with each other's traditions than had typically been the case heretofore. As is often the case when a dominant tradition makes contact with a minority one, the culture and standards of the dominant group make a significant impact on the members of the minority group. This trend has most likely been reinforced by the fact that a great deal of the qualitative research on education conducted in the past fifteen years has been embedded within multimethod evaluation projects undertaken by private research firms that have traditionally specialized in quantitative research. Thus the concept of external validity and the associated issue of generalizability have been made salient for qualitative researchers, whose own tradition has not predisposed them to have given the issue a great deal of thought.

❖ RECONCEPTUALIZING GENERALIZABILITY

Although many qualitative researchers have begun to recognize the importance of dealing with the issue of generalizability, it is clear that the classical view of external validity is of little help to qualitative researchers interested in finding ways of enhancing the likelihood that their work will speak to situations beyond the one immediately studied—that is, that it will be to some extent generalizable. The idea of sampling from a population of sites in order to generalize to the larger population is simply and obviously unworkable in all but the rarest situations for qualitative researchers, who often take several years to produce an intensive case study of one or a very small number of sites. Thus most of the work on generalizability by qualitative researchers in this decade has dealt with developing a *conception* of generalizability that is useful and appropriate for qualitative work.

A second approach to the issue of generalizability in qualitative research has been very different. A number of individuals have worked on ways of gaining generality through the synthesis of preexisting qualitative studies. For example, Noblit and Hare (1988) have recently published a slim volume on meta-ethnography. Substantially earlier, Lucas (1974) and Yin and Heald (1975) had developed what they call the "case survey method." Ragin (1987) has presented yet another way of synthesizing qualitative studies, one that employs Boolean algebra. I will discuss these approaches to generalizing from qualitative case studies briefly at the end of this chapter. At the moment, I would like to focus on issues connected with the first approach—that is, with transforming and adapting the classical conception of external validity such that it is suitable for qualitative work.

Important and frequently cited discussions of conceptions of generalizability appropriate in qualitative work can be found in Guba and Lincoln (1981, 1982), Goetz and LeCompte (1984), and Stake (1978). Guba and Lincoln's stance on the issue of generalizability is aptly summarized in two excerpts of their own words. Guba and Lincoln write:

> It is virtually impossible to imagine any human behavior that is not heavily mediated by the context in which it occurs. One can easily conclude that generalizations that are intended to be context free will have little that is useful to say about human behavior. (1981, p. 62)

They go on to say:

> The aim of (naturalistic) inquiry is to develop an idiographic body of knowledge. This knowledge is best encapsulated in a series of "working hypotheses" that describe the individual case. Generalizations are impossible since phenomena are neither time- nor context-free (although some transferability of these hypotheses may be possible from situation to situation, depending on the degree of temporal and contextual similarity). (1982, p. 238)

Given these views, Guba and Lincoln call for replacing the concept of generalizability with that of "fittingness." Specifically, they argue that the concept of "fittingness," with its emphasis on analyzing the degree to which the situation studied matches other situations in which one is interested, provides a more realistic and workable way of thinking about the generalizability of research results than do more classical approaches. A logical consequence of this approach is an emphasis on supplying a substantial amount of information about the entity studied and the setting in which that entity was found. Without such information, it is impossible to make an informed judgment about whether the conclusions drawn from the study of any particular site are useful in understanding other sites.

Goetz and LeCompte (1984) place a similar emphasis on the importance of clear and detailed description as a means of allowing decisions about the extent to which findings from one study are applicable to other situations. Specifically, they argue that qualitative studies gain their potential for applicability to other situations by providing what they call "comparability" and "translatability." The former term

> refers to the degree to which components of a study—including
> the units of analysis, concepts generated, population characteristics,
> and settings—are sufficiently well described and defined that
> other researchers can use the results of the study as a basis for
> comparison. (p. 228)

Translatability is similar but refers to a clear description of one's theoretical stance and research techniques.

Stake (1978) starts out by agreeing with many critics of qualitative methods that one cannot confidently generalize from a single case to a target population of which that case is a member, since single members often poorly represent whole populations. However, he then goes on to argue that it is possible to use a process he calls "naturalistic generalization" to take the findings from one study and apply them to understanding another *similar* situation. He argues that through experience individuals come to be able to use both explicit comparisons between situations and tacit knowledge of those same situations to form useful naturalistic generalizations.

Several major themes can be found in the work of qualitative researchers who have written recently on the concept of generalizability. Whether it is Guba and Lincoln (1981, 1982) writing of fittingness, Goetz and LeCompte (1984) writing of translatability and comparability, or Stake (1978) discussing naturalistic generalizations, the emerging view shared by many qualitative researchers appears to involve several areas of consensus. First of all, there is broad agreement that generalizability in the sense of producing laws that apply universally is not a useful standard or goal for qualitative research. In fact, most qualitative researchers would join Cronbach (1982) in arguing that this is not a useful or obtainable goal for any kind of research in the social sciences. Second, most researchers writing on generalizability in the qualitative tradition agree that their rejection of generalizability as a search for broadly applicable laws is not a rejection of the idea that studies in one situation can be used to speak to or to help form a judgment about other situations. Third, as should be readily apparent from the preceding discussion, current thinking on generalizability argues that thick descriptions (Ryle, cited in Geertz, 1973) are vital. Such descriptions of both the site in which the studies are conducted and of the site to which one wishes to generalize are crucial in allowing one to search for the similarities and differences between the situations. As Kennedy (1979) points out, analysis of these similarities and differences then makes it possible to make a reasoned judgment about the extent to which we can use the findings from one study as a "working hypothesis," to use Cronbach's (1982) term, about what might occur in the other situation. Of course, the generally unstated assumption underlying this view is that our knowledge of the phenomena under study is sufficient to direct attention to important rather than superficial similarities and differences. To the extent that our understanding is flawed, important similarities or differences may inadvertently be disregarded.

❖ THREE TARGETS OF GENERALIZATION

Given the growing emphasis on generalizability in qualitative research and the emerging consensus about how the concept of generalizability might most usefully be viewed by qualitative researchers, two questions present themselves:

- ◆ To what do we want to generalize?
- ◆ How can we design qualitative studies in a way that maximizes their generalizability?

It is to these two questions that I will devote the majority of the rest of this chapter. Although I will use the term *generalize* here and elsewhere, it is important that the reader recognize that I am not talking about generalization in the classical sense. Rather, I use it to refer to the process as conceptualized by those qualitative researchers to whose work I have just referred.

I believe that it is useful for qualitative researchers interested in the study of educational processes and institutions to try to generalize to three domains: to *what is*, to *what may be*, and to *what could be*. I will deal with these possibilities one at a time, providing the rationale for striving to generalize to each of these kinds of situations and then suggesting some ideas on how studies can actually be designed to do this.

Studying What Is

From one perspective the study of any ongoing social situation, no matter how idiosyncratic or bizarre, is studying *what is*. But when I use the phrase *studying what is,* I mean to refer to studying the typical, the common, or the ordinary. The goal of describing and understanding cultures or institutions as they typically are is an appropriate aim for much current qualitative research on educational institutions and processes. If policy makers need to decide how to change a program or whether to continue it, one very obvious and useful kind of information is information on how the program usually functions, what is usually achieved, and the like. Thus the goal of studying *what is* is one important aim for many kinds of summative evaluations. It is also appropriate outside of the area of evaluation for researchers hoping to provide a picture of the current educational scene that can be used for understanding or reflecting on it and possibly improving it. Classic works of this type that focus primarily on *what is* are Wolcott's *The Man in the Principal's Office* (1973) and Jackson's *Life in Classrooms* (1968). If one accepts the goal of designing research to maximize the fit between the research site and *what is* more broadly in society, an obvious question that arises is how this can be accomplished within the context of the qualitative tradition.

Studying the Typical. One approach sometimes used is to study the typical (Bogdan & Biklen, 1981; Goetz & LeCompte, 1984; Patton, 1980; Whyte, 1984). Specifically, I would argue that choosing sites on the basis of their fit with a typical situation is far preferable to choosing on the basis of convenience, a practice that is still quite common.

The suggestion that typicality be weighed heavily in site selection is an idea that needs to be taken both more and less seriously than it currently is. When I say that it needs to be taken more seriously than it currently is, I am suggesting that researchers contemplating selecting a site on the basis of convenience or ease of access need to think more carefully about that decision and to weigh very carefully the possibility of choosing on the basis of some other criterion, such as typicality. When I say that the strategy of selecting a typical site needs to be taken less seriously than it may sometimes be, I intend to point out that choosing a typical site is not a "quick fix" for the issue of generalizability, because what is typical on one dimension may not be typical on another. For example, Wolcott (1973) chose to focus his ethnographic study of a principal on an individual who was typical of other principals in gender, marital status, age, and so forth. This choice most likely substantially enhanced the range of applicability or generalizability of his study. Yet such a typical principal operating in an atypical school or an atypical system or even an atypical community might well behave very differently from a typical principal in a typical school in a typical system. The solution to this dilemma cannot be found in choosing typicality on every dimension. First of all, not too many typical principals operate in environments that are typical in every way. So this strategy gains less in the realm of generalizability or fittingness than it might appear to at first glance. More important, even if one could achieve typicality in all major dimensions that seem relevant, it is nonetheless clearly true that there would be enough idiosyncrasy in any particular situation studied so that one could not transfer findings in an unthinking way from one typical situation to another.

Carried to extremes or taken too seriously, the idea of choosing on the basis of typicality becomes impossible, even absurd. However, as a guiding principle designed to increase the potential applicability of research, it is, I believe, useful. This is especially true if the search for typicality is combined with, rather than seen as a replacement for, a reliance on the kind of thick description emphasized by Guba and Lincoln (1981, 1982), Goetz and LeCompte (1984), and Stake (1978). Selection on the basis of typicality provides the potential for a good "fit" with many other situations. Thick description provides the information necessary to make informed judgments about the degree and extent of that fit in particular cases of interest.

In arguing that qualitative researchers would do well to seek to study the typical, I am not suggesting that we study the typical defined solely by national norms. Research that followed this prescription would greatly increase our knowledge of typical situations, but in a nation as diverse as the United States, it would provide too restricted, pallid, and homogeneous a view of our educational system. My emphasis on typicality implies that the researcher who has decided on the kind of institution or situation he or she wants to study—an urban ghetto school, a rural consolidated school, or a private Montessori school—should try to select an instance of this kind of situation that is, to the extent possible, typical of its kind. Such an approach suggests, for example, that a researcher interested in studying mathematics teaching choose to observe classrooms that use a popular text and generally accepted modes of instruction, rather than falling for convenience's sake into the study of classrooms that may well do neither of these. Furthermore, to the extent preliminary investigation of possible sites suggests that some or all are atypical in certain regards, careful thought about the possible implications of this atypically for the topic under study may help to aid in site selection.

In sum, the point of my argument here is that choosing a site for research on the basis of typicality is far more likely to enhance the potential generalizability of one's study than choosing on the basis of convenience or ease of access—criteria that often weigh more heavily than they should. However, even if one chooses on the basis of typicality, one is in no way relieved of the necessity for thick description, for it is foolhardy to think that a typical example will be typical in all important regards. Thus thick description is necessary to allow individuals to ask about the degree of fit between the case studied and the case to which they wish to generalize, even when the fit on some of the basic dimensions looks fairly close.

Performing Multisite Studies. An alternate approach to increasing the generalizability of qualitative research was evident in the sudden proliferation in the 1970s of multisite qualitative studies. Such studies were almost always part of federally funded evaluation efforts focusing on the same issue in a number of settings, using similar data collection and analysis procedures in each place. Well-known examples of this approach include the Study of Dissemination Efforts Supporting School Improvement (Crandall et al., 1983; Huberman & Miles, 1984) and the study of Parental Involvement in Federal Educational Programs (Smith & Robbins, 1984). One of the primary purposes of conducting such multisite studies is to escape what Firestone and Herriott (1984) have called the "radical particularism" of many case studies and hence to provide a firmer basis for generalization.

The multisite studies conducted in the 1970s were extremely varied, although they were all quite expensive and tended to take several years to complete. At least two kinds of variation have special implications for the extent to which this approach actually seems likely to produce results that are a good basis for generalization to many other situations. The first of these is the number of sites studied. Firestone and Herriott's (1984) survey of twenty-five multisite case study efforts found major variation on this dimension, with one study including as few as three sites and another covering sixty. All other things being equal, a finding emerging repeatedly in the study of numerous sites would appear to be more likely to be a good working hypothesis about some as yet unstudied site than a finding emerging from just one or two sites.

A second dimension on which multisite studies vary, which is also likely to affect the degree of fit between these studies and situations to which one might want to generalize, concerns the heterogeneity of the sites chosen for study. Generally speaking, a finding emerging from the study of several very heterogeneous sites would be more robust and thus more likely to be useful in understanding various other sites than one emerging from the study of several very similar sites (Kennedy, 1979). Heterogeneity can be obtained by searching out sites that will provide maximal variation or by planned comparisons along certain potentially important dimensions. An example of the second strategy can be found in the parental-involvement study previously mentioned. The sites chosen for study were selected to allow comparison between urban and rural settings, between those with high and low reported degrees of involvement, and so forth (Smith & Robbins, 1984). This comparative strategy is potentially quite powerful, especially if there is heterogeneity among cases within each of the categories of interest. For example, if several rather different rural cases all share certain similarities that are not found in a heterogeneous group of urban cases, one has some reasonable basis for generalizing about likely differences between the two settings. Although the most obvious comparative strategy is to select cases that initially differ on some variable of interest as part of the research design, it is also possible to group cases in an *ex post facto* way on the basis of information gathered during the fieldwork. For example, if one were studying numerous very different classrooms and found that student achievement gains were quite high in some and quite low in others, one could compare these two sets of classrooms as a strategy for trying to suggest factors that contribute to high or low gains.

In sum, the possibility of studying numerous heterogeneous sites makes multisite studies one potentially useful approach to increasing the generalizability of qualitative work to *what is*. Yet I am very hesitant to see this approach as the only or even the best solution to the problem. First, such studies can be quite expensive, and the current lull in their funding highlights the extent to which such research is dependent on federal dollars that may or may not be forthcoming. Second, as Firestone and Herriott (1984) point out, budget constraints make it likely that studies including very large numbers of sites are less likely than studies of a relatively small number of sites to be able to devote intensive and prolonged care to studying the details of each site. Thus there is typically a trade-off to be made between the increased potential for generalizability flowing from studying a large number of sites and the increased depth and breadth of description and understanding made possible by a focus on a small number of sites. In suggesting that an increased number of sites leads to increased generalizability, I am assuming that enough attention is paid to each site to ensure that problems of internal validity do not arise. To the extent such problems do arise, generalizability is obviously threatened, since one cannot speak meaningfully of the generalizability of invalid data. The fact that roughly 40 percent of the multisite studies surveyed by Firestone and Herriott (1984) involved just one or two short visits to the research site raises serious questions about whether such studies can appropriately be categorized as qualitative research in the usual sense of that term. The term *qualitative research,* and more especially the word *ethnography,* usually implies an intensive, ongoing involvement with individuals functioning in their everyday settings that is akin to, if not always identical with, the degree of immersion in a culture attained by anthropologists, who live in the society they study over a period of one or more years (Dobbert, 1982; Spindler, 1982; Wolcott, 1975). Thus it is conceivable, though not logically necessary, that attempts to gain generalizability through studying large numbers of sites undercut the depth of understanding of individual sites, which is the hallmark of the qualitative approach as it has come to be understood.

Studying What May Be

The goal of portraying typical schools—or, for that matter, typical instances of federal educational programs as they now exist—is, I believe, worthwhile. Yet accepting this as our only or even primary goal implies too narrow and limited a vision of what qualitative research can do. I would like to suggest that we want to generalize not only to *what is* but also to *what may be.* Let me explain. Here I am proposing that we think about what current social and educational trends suggest about likely educational issues for the future and design our research to illuminate such issues to the extent possible. Let me use some of my own current research to illustrate this possibility, without implying that it is the best or only example of such an approach.

One very obvious and potentially important trend in education recently has been the increasing utilization of microcomputers in instruction. In fact, microcomputers are being adopted in schools at an almost frantic pace (Becker, 1986) in spite of tight educational budgets and a generally acknowledged tendency on the part of educational institutions to resist rapid change. There is a clear division of opinion about the likely consequences of this trend. At one extreme are those who see computers as having the capability to revolutionize education in absolutely fundamental ways. Proponents of this school of thought make the rather startling claim that "the potential of computers for improving education is greater than that of any prior invention, including books and writing" (Walker, 1984, p. 3). Others take quite a different stance, emphasizing the inherent conservatism of the teaching profession with regard to pedagogical change and the failure of other highly touted educational innovations to bring about far-reaching changes. Thus it seemed important to me to design a research project focused on understanding the impact of computer usage on students and classrooms (Schofield & Evans-Rhodes, 1989; Schofield & Verban, 1988). One could approach this issue with an emphasis on what is. For example, it would be possible to choose a school that is presently typical in terms of the uses it makes of computers in instruction. But this strategy encounters an immediate problem if one's goal is to speak to what may be. Changes in both microcomputer technology and in individuals' level of experience with computers have been so rapid in the past decade that a study of what is today could arguably be a study of primarily historical interest by the time it gets conducted, written, and published. In hopes of not just documenting the present, which is rapidly becoming the past, but of speaking to the future, I have made a number of methodological decisions that, in their abstract form, may be of use to others interested in making their work applicable to what may be.

Studying the "Leading Edge" of Change.   First, since it is hard to know what kinds of computer usage will become most typical or popular in the future, I have made a point of studying a broad array of uses rather than just one particular kind. More important, I have not looked only for heterogeneity of usage but for types of usage that are now in their infancy but that many informed observers see as likely to be common in the future. Thus I consciously chose to study a school that not only uses computers as they are currently employed around the country to teach computer programming and word processing in fairly typical ways but that also was the field test site for the kind of artificially intelligent computer-based tutor that researchers in a number of centers around the country are currently developing for classroom use (Feigenbaum & McCorduck, 1983; Lawler & Yazdani, 1987). I see this choice as a step in the direction of increasing the chances that this work will "fit" or be generalizable to the educational issues important at the time the work is published. But this is only a mere first step.

Probing Factors Likely to Differentiate the Present from the Future.   One of the big problems in trying to make one's work applicable to even the fairly near future is, as Cronbach (1975) has so eloquently argued, that people and institutions change. Thus it is logically impossible to see the future even when studying futuristic uses of artificial intelligence, because one is studying that future technology in the context of a present-day institution peopled with individuals who are shaped by the era in which they live.

There is no completely satisfactory solution to this situation, but a partial one emerged as I grappled with the issue. It is to think through how the present and the future are likely to differ. Then the research can be structured in a way that explicitly probes the impact of things that are likely to change over time. Of course, if the analysis of the likely differences between present and future is wrong, this approach will not be particularly useful. But if the analysis is accurate, this strategy has the potential to enhance greatly the usefulness of the study.

Let me illustrate in concrete terms how I have done this. Given the rapidity with which computers are being adopted for use in widely varying arenas of life, especially in schools, it seems a reasonable expectation that one major difference between now and five to ten years in the future is what might be called the "novelty factor." Specifically, many of today's high school students are having their first real introduction to the computer, or at least to its use for educational purposes, in their high school classrooms. However, in ten years it is rather unlikely that high school students will be having their first exposure to educational computing in the tenth or eleventh grade. I have used this assumption, which is, I think, relatively uncontroversial, to influence the shape of my study in a way that will allow it to speak more adequately to the future. For example, in interviews students were specifically asked about the impact of novelty on their reactions to the computer and its importance in shaping their feelings about computer usage. Similarly, observers in the study carefully looked for reactions that appeared to be influenced by students' unfamiliarity with the computers. Moreover, I have been careful to find out which students have had prior computer experience and what kind of experience this has been in order to see as clearly as possible whether these students differ from those for whom computer use is a completely novel experience. The fact that students were observed during the full course of the school year allowed assessment of whether any initial differences in students' reactions due to prior experience were transitory or relatively long-lasting. To the extent that novelty is crucial in shaping students' reactions, I will be forced to conclude that my study may not help us understand the future as well as it might otherwise. To the extent that students' reactions appear to be more heavily influenced by things that are unlikely to change in the near future, such as adolescents' striving for independence from adult control, the likely applicability of the findings of the study to the near future is clearly increased.

Considering the Life Cycle of a Phenomenon.   The preceding discussion of the possible impact of novelty on students' reactions to educational computing brings up an important point regarding qualitative work and the issue of generalizability. The ethnographic habit of looking at a phenomenon over substantial time periods allows assessment of one aspect of generalizability that quantitative research usually does not— of where a particular phenomenon is in its life cycle and what the implications of this are for what is happening. Qualitative research, when studying a dynamic phenomenon, is like a movie. It starts with one image and then moves on to others that show how things evolve over time. Quantitative research, in contrast, is more typically like a snapshot, often taken and used without great regard for whether that photograph happened to catch one looking one's best or looking unusually disheveled. This point can be illustrated more substantively by briefly discussing a study that I carried out in a desegregated school during its first four years of existence (Schofield, 1982/1989). The study tracked changes in the school by following two different groups of students from the first day they entered the school to graduation from that school three years later. Important changes occurred in race relations over the life of the institution and over the course of students' careers in the school. Such findings suggest that in asking about what happens in desegregated schools and what the impact of such schools is on students, it is important to know where both the students and the institution are in their experience with desegregation. Yet virtually all quantitative studies of desegregation, including, I must admit, some of my own, tend to ignore these issues completely. In fact, as I discovered in reviewing the desegregation literature (Schofield & Sagar, 1983), many do not even supply bare descriptive information on the life-cycle issue. Paying attention to where a phenomenon is in its life cycle does not guarantee that one can confidently predict how it will evolve. However, at a minimum, sensitivity to this issue makes it less likely that conclusions formed on the basis of a study conducted at one point in time will be unthinkingly and perhaps mistakenly generalized to other later points in time to which they may not apply.

Studying What Could Be

As mentioned previously, I would like to argue that qualitative research on education can be used not only to study *what is* and *what may be* but also to explore possible visions of *what could be*. By studying what could be, I mean locating situations that we know or expect to be ideal or exceptional on some *a priori* basis and then studying them to see what is actually going on there.

Selecting a Site that Sheds Light on What Could be.   When studying what could be, site selection is not based on criteria such as typicality or heterogeneity. Rather it is based on information about either the *outcomes* achieved in the particular site studied or the *conditions* obtaining there. Perhaps the best-known example of site selection based on outcomes is choosing to study classrooms or schools in which students show unusual intellectual gains, as has been done in the voluminous literature on effective schools (Bickel, 1983; Dwyer, Lee, Rowan, & Bossert, 1982; Phi Delta Kappan, 1980; Rutter, Maughan, Mortimore, Ouston, & Smith, 1979; Weber, 1971). For an example of site selection based on the conditions obtaining at the site, a less common approach, I will again make reference to my own work on school desegregation.

When thinking about where to locate the extended study of a desegregated school mentioned previously, I decided not to study a typical desegregated school. First, given the tremendous variation in situations characterized as desegregated, it is not clear that such an entity could be found. Second, there is a body of theory and research that gives us some basis for expecting different kinds of social processes and outcomes in different kinds of interracial schools. In fact, in the same year in which the *Brown* v. *Board of Education* decision laid the legal basis for desegregating educational institutions, Gordon Allport (1954) published a classic analysis of racial prejudice in which he argued that interracial contact can either increase or decrease hostility and stereotyping, depending on the kind of conditions under which it occurs. Specifically, he argued that in order to ameliorate relations between groups such as blacks and whites three conditions are especially important: equal status for members of both groups within the contact situation, a cooperative rather than a competitive goal structure, and support for positive relations from those in authority. A substantial amount of empirical and theoretical work stemming from Allport's basic insight has been carried out in the past three and a half decades, most of which supports his emphasis on the crucial importance of the specific conditions under which intergroup contact occurs (Amir, 1969; Aronson & Osherow, 1980; Cook, 1978; Pettigrew, 1967, 1969; Schofield, 1979; Schofield & Sagar, 1977; Slavin, 1980; Stephan, 1985).

It is clear that desegregating school systems often take little if any heed of the available theory and research on how to structure desegregated schools in a way likely to promote positive intergroup relations, perhaps at least partly because much of this work is laboratory based and hence may seem of questionable use in everyday situations. Thus selecting a site for study on the basis of typicality might be expected to yield a site potentially rich in sources of insight about the problems of desegregated education but weak in shedding light on what can be accomplished in a serious and sophisticated effort to structure an environment conducive to fostering positive relations between students. Since both scholars in the area of intergroup relations and the public are well aware of the potential for difficulties in desegregated schools, the task of seeing whether and how such difficulties can be overcome seems potentially more informative and useful than that of documenting the existence of such difficulties. Thus I chose to study a site that at least approximated a theoretical ideal. My goal was not to generalize to desegregated schools as a class. Rather it was to see what happens under conditions that might be expected to foster relatively positive outcomes. If serious problems were encountered at such a site, there would be reason to think that problems would be encountered in most places or, alternatively, to revise or reject the theory that led to the site selection. However, if things went well at such a site, the study would then provide an opportunity to gain some insight into how and why they go well and into what the still-intractable problems are.

Of course, the strategy of choosing a site based on some *a priori* theoretical viewpoint or, for that matter, any seriously held expectation about it raises a difficult problem. If one is unduly committed to that viewpoint, one's analysis of both what happens and why may be heavily influenced by it, and one may not ask whether other more fruitful perspectives might emerge from a more dispassionate approach to studying the situation. This is the very danger that has led to the development of such elaborate safeguards in the quantitative tradition as the double-blind experiment. Although such procedures are rarely used in the qualitative tradition, a substantial literature on the issue of internal validity in qualitative research offers assistance with this problem to the researcher who pays it close heed (Becker, 1958; Bogdan & Biklen, 1981; Glaser & Strauss, 1967; Goetz & LeCompte, 1984; Guba, 1981; Guba & Lincoln, 1981; Kirk & Miller, 1986; Miles & Huberman, 1984a, 1984b; Patton, 1980; Strauss, 1987). Furthermore, if one's purpose is not to support or reject a specific *a priori* theory but to discover, using an approach that is as open as possible, what is actually happening in a site that was chosen with the assistance of a particular theory, problems related to internal validity are somewhat mitigated. For example, the fact that I chose to study a school that theory suggested might be conducive to positive relations did not keep me from exploring in considerable depth problems that occurred there (Sagar & Schofield, 1980; Schofield, 1981, 1982/1989).

One characteristic of the school chosen for the study was especially helpful in assessing the degree to which the theory on which the site was chosen was useful. Specifically, for various reasons, conditions in two of the three grades in this school came much closer than conditions in the remaining grade to meeting those that theory suggests are conducive to producing positive relations. Thus it was possible to assess intergroup relations as the children went from one kind of environment to another within the school (Schofield, 1979, 1982/1989; Schofield & Sagar, 1977). This suggests one very useful strategy for studying what may be—selecting an "ideal" case and a comparative case that contrasts sharply on the relevant dimensions.

Generalizing From an Unusual Site to More Typical Ones.   Although I indicated above that my goal was to learn about the possibilities and problems associated with a *certain kind* of desegregated education, I would like to argue that studying a site chosen for its special characteristics does not necessarily restrict the application of the study's findings to other very similar sites. The degree to which this is the case depends on the degree to which the findings appear to be linked to the special characteristics of the situation. Some of the findings from the study I have been discussing were clearly linked to unusual aspects of the school and hence have very limited generalizability to other situations, although they may nonetheless be important in demonstrating what is possible, even if not what is generally likely. For example, I found very low levels of overt racial conflict in the school studied (Schofield & Francis, 1982). It would obviously be misguided to conclude on the basis of this study that intergroup conflict is unlikely in all desegregated schools, since the school's emphasis on cooperation, equal status, and the like did actually appear to play a marked role in reducing the likelihood of conflict.

However, other findings that emerged from the study and were also related to atypical aspects of the situation may have a greater degree of applicability or generalizability than the finding discussed above. For example, I found the development of a color-blind perspective and of an almost complete taboo against the mention of race in the school studied (Schofield, 1986, 1982/1989). Since the emergence of the color-blind perspective and the accompanying taboo appeared to be linked to special characteristics of the school, I would not posit them as phenomena likely to occur in most desegregated schools. But I feel free to argue that *when* they do develop, certain consequences may well follow because these consequences are the logical outcomes of the phenomena. For example, with regard to the taboo against racial reference, if one cannot mention race, one cannot deal with resegregation in a straightforward way as a policy issue. Similarly, if one cannot mention race, there is likely to be little or no effort to create or utilize multicultural curricular materials. Thus, although the taboo against racial reference may not occur in a high proportion of desegregated schools, when it does occur the study I carried out gives a potentially useful indication of problems that are likely to develop.

I would now like to turn to a third finding of the study, one so unrelated to the atypical aspects of the situation studied that it is a reasonable working hypothesis that this phenomenon is widespread. After I observed extensively in varied areas of the school and interviewed a large number of students, it became apparent that the white children perceived blacks as something of a threat to their physical selves. Specifically, they complained about what they perceived as black roughness or aggressiveness (Schofield, 1981, 1982/1989). In contrast, the black students perceived whites as a threat to their social selves. They complained about being ignored, avoided, and being treated as inferior by whites, whom they perceived to be stuck-up and prejudiced (Schofield, 1982/1989). Such findings appear to me to be linked to the black and white students' situation in the larger society and to powerful historical and economic forces, not to special aspects of the school. The consequences of these rather asymmetrical concerns may well play themselves out differently in different kinds of schools, but the existence of these rather different but deeply held concerns may well be widespread.

I have gone into some detail with these examples because I think they raise a crucial point for judging the applicability or generalizability of qualitative work. One cannot just look at a study and say that it is similar or dissimilar to another situation of concern. A much finer-grained analysis is necessary. One must ask what aspects of the situation are similar or different and to what aspects of the findings these are connected.

❖ GENERALIZING THROUGH AGGREGATION OR COMPARISON OF INDEPENDENT STUDIES

This paper has argued that it is possible to achieve greater generalizability of qualitative research to situations of interest than is often now the case by following some of the design suggestions discussed above. However, there is another approach to increasing the generalizability of qualitative case studies that should not be ignored. This other strategy aims not at increasing the generalizability of one study or a set of studies planned in conjunction with each other but at finding ways to aggregate, compare, or contrast already existing studies. One of these strategies was first laid out some time ago by Yin and Heald (1975). Another promising approach is suggested by Ragin's (1987) recent work on a strategy that he calls the "qualitative comparative method."

A third very different approach has been outlined recently by Noblit and Hare (1988).

The Case Survey Method

Yin and Heald (1975) point out that case studies, whether qualitative or quantitative, are very prevalent in many fields. The nub of the problem from their perspective is that while "each case study may provide rich insights into a specific situation, it is difficult to generalize about the studies as a whole" (p. 371). Their solution to this problem is to propose a method for aggregating the information from separate studies. They call the method they developed the "case survey method." Basically this method consists of several steps. First, the literature relevant to one's interest is located. Then these studies are subjected to close scrutiny, so that those failing to meet certain crucial methodological requirements can be removed from the set to be analyzed. Then coders go through each of the remaining case studies with the goal of using the information contained therein to complete a set of closed-ended questions. These questions pertain to the topic of one's study and constitute the data set ultimately used in the case survey approach. For example, Yin and Heald (1975) discuss a study of the effectiveness of urban decentralization efforts in which the closed-ended questions covered (1) the nature of the case study itself, (2) the context in which the decentralization effort occurred, (3) the characteristics of the specific effort at decentralization, and (4) five possible outcomes of decentralization. One then uses the material in the questionnaires to search for patterns on which generalizations can be based. The strategy for producing these generalizations is the use of statistical tests of association between different variables. For example, Yin and Heald report a statistically significant positive association between their judgments of the quality of specific case studies and the degree to which the study concluded that decentralization succeeded. The case survey procedure is parallel in some respects to the procedures suggested more recently by Miles and Huberman (1984a, 1984b) for aggregating data from multisite studies. However, Miles and Huberman tend not to emphasize statistical significance, perhaps because the number of studies in many multisite qualitative endeavors is so small as to preclude attaining statistical significance unless the effects are of extraordinary strength.

As Yin and Heald (1975) acknowledge, there are clear limitations to the approach they suggest. First, of course, there must be a substantial body of literature available relevant to a particular topic for this procedure to work well. For example, Yin and Yates (1975) aggregated data from more than 250 studies of urban decentralization. When the number of available cases is small, statistical techniques lack power, since each case study must be treated as a single observation. Also, in such cases the number of variables worthy of coding may well be large compared to the number of sampling points (i.e., case studies), which also poses statistical problems. Second, the case survey method, with its emphasis on reducing the rich descriptive material provided in many case studies to uniform quantifiable data, risks ignoring unique factors that may be crucial to understanding specific cases or kinds of cases. Third, as Yin and Heald (1975) note, the case survey method may be more suited to inquiries focusing on outcomes rather than on process. Because of the numerous limitations of the case survey method, Yin (1981) has concluded that the "case-survey method should be used in highly selective situations" (p. 63) and that other methods for comparing across cases may ultimately prove more fruitful.

Unfortunately, the development of other methods for comparing and aggregating across cases, especially cases that have not been planned as part of a unified multisite effort, are not well developed. Although the work of Miles and Huberman (1984a, 1984b) and Yin (1984) provides many useful design and analysis suggestions for investigators planning multisite studies, relatively little methodological guidance is available to researchers who wish to compare studies that were designed and executed independently. A crucial difference between these two cases, of course, is that in the former one can obtain some degree of uniformity in the information gathered. This is crucial for the kinds of pattern-producing techniques suggested by Miles and Huberman and by Yin. There are other important differences as well. For example, in a multisite study with central direction it is at least theoretically possible, if not eminently practical, for one individual to have access to the raw data from all the different sites. However, such is generally not the case when one is trying to conduct comparisons of previously published case studies or ethnographies. Thus, at this point in time, our ability to achieve generalizations through the comparison of independently conducted pieces of qualitative work on a particular topic is quite limited.

The Qualitative Comparative Method

One promising new strategy for aggregating case studies has recently been developed by Ragin (1987). Ragin starts with the premise that two of the distinctive traits of case studies, and of case-oriented comparative research more generally, are their attention to cases as wholes and to the possibility that several different sets of circumstances can lead to the same outcome. He argues that most attempts to aggregate numerous case studies using quantitative approaches tend not to make use of these strengths and thus do not make full use of the databases on which they are built. To remedy this situation, Ragin proposes an approach that he calls the "qualitative comparative method." This approach is based on Boolean algebra, the algebra of sets and logic. Although a full discussion of this technique is beyond the scope of this paper, since it would require introducing readers to the basics of Boolean algebra, it is possible briefly to discuss Ragin's general approach without becoming unduly technical.

First, Ragin's techniques can be used with widely varying numbers of case studies as one's raw data. In this regard it is more flexible than the case survey method, which is suitable only when relatively large numbers of case studies are available because of its dependence on the concept of statistical significance. Second, the techniques can be used either with preexisting case studies or with multisite studies planned with the qualitative comparative strategy in mind. All that is necessary are data that allow one to build truth tables—that is, categorical information on the variables of major interest to the analysis. Ragin argues that his approach allows one to examine complex and multiple patterns of causation, to produce parsimonious explanations, to study cases both as wholes and as parts, and to evaluate competing explanations. Ragin presents several extended and sharply contrasting examples of the varied ways in which the approach he uses can be applied. Although his approach seems better suited in many ways to aggregating qualitative case studies than the case survey method, since a Boolean approach allows one to take better advantage of the characteristic strengths of case studies, it is too early to understand completely either its full potential or the various problems that individuals using this approach will face.

Meta Ethnography

Consideration of the techniques discussed above suggests that both the case survey method and attempts at case comparison are often based on a logic that seeks to generalize by aggregating studies. Noblit and Hare (1988) suggest that such an effort is misdirected, arguing that efforts at aggregation tend to ignore the interpretive nature of qualitative research and to miss much of what is most important in each study. They believe it is possible to systematically compare very diverse cases in order to draw cross-case conclusions. However, they see such an effort as best conceptualized as the *translation* of studies into one another rather than as their aggregation. They call this translation "meta-ethnography."

Noblit and Hare argue that studies of similar topics can be seen as directly comparable, as essentially refutational, or as together suggesting a new line of argument. Once a preliminary look at the material to be synthesized suggests which of the above is the case, a translation and synthesis is attempted. This process may refute the initial assumption about the relation between the cases, but it would generally be expected not to do so.

In order to perform the translation and synthesis, Noblit and Hare suggest a focus on and a listing of the concepts, themes, and metaphors that the author of each study utilizes. The meta-ethnographer lists and organizes these themes and then attempts to relate them to one another. This somewhat abstract process is perhaps best clarified by a brief example. Noblit and Hare exemplify the idea of a reciprocal translation of studies by comparing Collins and Noblit's (1978) research in a desegregated school to Wolcott's study, *The Man in the Principal's Office* (1973). The comparison makes sense and, in fact, is only possible because Collins and Noblit's study laid great emphasis on the role of the principal in the desegregated school they studied. Noblit and Hare list the terms used in both studies to describe the context in which the principal functioned, the principal's behavior, and the like. The meta-ethnography then consists of a discussion of the ways in which the two situations and studies appear to be similar and different and, more important, of the extent to which the themes developed in each are adequate to handle the other ethnography as well. These judgments are based on attributes of the themes, such as their economy, cogency, and scope. For example, Wolcott describes the conduct of the principal he studied as characterized by patience and prudence. Collins and Noblit compare two different principals in a particular school. The first was said to have created negotiated order in the school. His successor, with a far different style, created what Collins and Noblit characterized as a bureaucratic order. After discussing the particulars of the two studies, Noblit and Hare (1988) conclude that a translation between them is possible but that Wolcott's metaphors are more adequate to this task than those of Collins and Noblit. This means that Wolcott's concepts were able to capture what occurred in the Collins and Noblit study in a fuller and more adequate way than the Collins and Noblit themes fit the Wolcott study. Of course, it is possible in a meta-ethnography that none of the studies compared will have characterized its themes in a way that adequately fits all others, even though there are many parallels. In such a case, the hope is that the individual doing the meta-ethnography may be able to produce new, more inclusive concepts that work better than those from any particular study.

❖ SUMMARY AND CONCLUSIONS

Although qualitative researchers have traditionally paid scant attention to the issue of attaining generalizability in research, sometimes even disdaining such a goal, this situation has changed noticeably in the past ten to fifteen years. Several trends, including the growing use of qualitative studies in evaluation and policy-oriented research, have led to an increased awareness of the importance of structuring qualitative studies in a way that enhances their implications for the understanding of other situations.

Much of the attention given to the issue of generalizability in recent years on the part of qualitative researchers has focused on redefining the concept in a way that is useful and meaningful for those engaged in qualitative work. A consensus appears to be emerging that for qualitative researchers generalizability is best thought of as a matter of the "fit" between the situation studied and others to which one might be interested in applying the concepts and conclusions of that study. This conceptualization makes thick descriptions crucial, since without them one does not have the information necessary for an informed judgment about the issue of fit.

This paper argues that three useful targets for generalization are *what is, what may be,* and *what could be* and provides some examples of how qualitative research can be designed in a way that increases its ability to fit with each of these situations. Studying *what is* refers to studying the typical, the common, and the ordinary. Techniques suggested for studying *what is* include choosing study sites on the basis of typicality and conducting multisite studies. Studying *what may be* refers to designing studies so that their fit with future trends and issues is maximized. Techniques suggested for studying *what may be* include seeking out sites in which one can study situations likely to become more common with the passage of time and paying close attention to how such present instances of future practices are likely to differ from their future realizations. Studying *what could be* refers to locating situations that we know or expect to be ideal or exceptional on some *a priori* basis and studying them to see what is actually going on there. Crucial here is an openness to having one's expectations about the phenomena disconfirmed.

A very different approach to increasing the generalizability of qualitative research is evident in the work of some scholars who have focused on how to achieve generalizability through the aggregation or comparison of extant independently designed case studies or ethnographies. The case survey approach suggested by Yin and Heald (1975) is promising in a limited number of cases in which comparable information is available from a relatively large number of studies. Case comparison strategies, such as the qualitative comparative method suggested by Ragin (1987), may be more realistic and fruitful in many areas of research; but these comparative techniques are still in the early stages of development. Noblit and Hare (1988) suggest a kind of comparison they call "meta-ethnography," which focuses on the reciprocal translation rather than the aggregation of studies. Although such an approach may have promise, it is so new that its ultimate fruitfulness is still quite untested.

❖ REFERENCES

Allport, G. W. (1954). *The nature of prejudice.* Cambridge, UK: Cambridge University Press.

Amir, Y. (1969). Contact hypothesis in ethnic relations. *Psychological Bulletin, 71,* 319–342.

Aronson, E., & Osherow, N. (1980). Cooperation, prosocial behavior, and academic performance: Experiments in the desegregated classroom. In L. Brickman (Ed.), *Applied social psychology annual* (Vol. 1, pp. 163–196). Beverly Hills, CA: Sage.

Becker, H. J. (1986). Instructional uses of school computers. *Reports from the 1985 National Survey* (Issue No. 1) (pp. 1–9). Baltimore, MD: Center for Social Organization of Schools, Johns Hopkins University.

Becker, H. S. (1958). Problems of inference and proof in participant observation. *American Sociological Review, 23,* 652–659.

Berg, B. L. (1989). *Qualitative research methods for the social sciences.* Boston: Allyn & Bacon.

Bickel, W. E. (1983). Effective schools: Knowledge, dissemination, inquiry. *Educational Researcher, 12*(4), 3–5.

Bogdan, R. C., & Biklen, S. K. (1981). *Qualitative research for education: An introduction to theory and methods.* Boston: Allyn & Bacon.

Bolgar, H. (1965). The case study method. In B. B. Wolman (Ed.), *Handbook of clinical psychology* (pp. 28–30). New York: McGraw-Hill.

Brown v. Board of Education (1954). 347 U.S. 483.

Campbell, D. T. (1979). Degrees of freedom and the case study. In T. D. Cook & C. S. Reichardt (Eds.), *Qualitative and quantitative methods in evaluation research* (pp. 49–67). Beverly Hills, CA: Sage.

Campbell, D. T., & Stanley, J. (1963). Experimental and quasi-experimental designs for research on teaching. In N. Gage (Ed.), *Handbook of research on teaching* (pp. 171–246). Chicago: Rand McNally.

Collins, T., & Noblit, G. (1978). *Stratification and resegregation: The case of Crossover High School.* Final report of NIE contract #400-76-009.

Cook, S. W. (1978). Interpersonal and attitudinal outcomes in cooperating interracial groups. *Journal of Research and Development in Education, 12,* 97–113.

Crandall, D. P., et al. (1983). *People, policies and practices: Examining the chain of school improvement* (Vols. 1–10). Andover, MA: The Network.

Cronbach, L. J. (1975). Beyond the two disciplines of scientific psychology. *American Psychologist, 30,* 116–127.

Cronbach, L. J. (1982). *Designing evaluations of educational and social programs.* San Francisco: Jossey-Bass.

Cronbach, L. J., Ambron, S. R., Dornbusch, S. M., Hess, R. D., Hornik, R. C., Phillips, D. C., Walker, D. F., & Weiner, S. S. (1980). *Toward reform of program evaluation.* San Francisco: Jossey-Bass.

Denzin, N. K. (1983). Interpretive interactionism. In G. Morgan (Ed.), *Beyond method: Strategies for social research* (pp. 129–146). Beverly Hills, CA: Sage.

Dobbert, M. L. (1982). *Ethnographic research: Theory and application for modern schools and societies.* New York: Praeger.

Dwyer, D. C., Lee, G. V., Rowan, B., & Bossert, S. T. (1982). *The principal's role in instructional management: Five participant observation studies of principals in action.* Unpublished manuscript, Far West Laboratory for Educational Research and Development, San Francisco.

Feigenbaum, E. A., & McCorduck, P. (1983). *The fifth generation: Artificial intelligence and Japan's computer challenge to the world.* Reading, MA: Addison-Wesley.

Fetterman, D. M. (1982). Ethnography in educational research: The dynamics of diffusion. In D. M. Fetterman (Ed.), *Ethnography in educational evaluation* (pp. 21–35). Beverly Hills, CA: Sage.

Filstead, W. J. (1979). Qualitative methods: A needed perspective in evaluation research. In T. D. Cook & C. S. Reichardt (Eds.), *Qualitative and quantitative methods in evaluation research* (pp. 33–48). Beverly Hills, CA: Sage.

Firestone, W. A., & Herriott, R. E. (1984). Multisite qualitative policy research: Some design and implementation issues. In D. M. Fetterman (Ed.), *Ethnography in educational evaluation* (pp. 63–88). Beverly Hills, CA: Sage.

Geertz, C. (1973). Thick description: Toward an interpretive theory of culture. In C. Geertz (Ed.), *The interpretation of cultures* (pp. 3–30). New York: Basic Books.

Glaser, B., & Strauss, A. (1967). *The discovery of grounded theory.* Chicago: Aldine Publishing.

Goetz, J. P., & LeCompte, M. D. (1984). *Ethnography and qualitative design in education research.* Orlando, FL: Academic Press.

Guba, E. G. (1981). Criteria for assessing the trustworthiness of naturalistic inquiry. *Educational Communication and Technology Journal, 29,* 79–92.

Guba, E. G., & Lincoln, Y. S. (1981). *Effective evaluation: Improving the usefulness of evaluation results through responsive and naturalistic approaches.* San Francisco: Jossey-Bass.

Guba, E. G., & Lincoln, Y. S. (1982). Epistemological and methodological bases of naturalistic inquiry. *Educational Communication and Technology Journal, 30,* 233–252.

Huberman, A. M., & Miles, M. B. (1984). *Innovation up close: How school improvement works.* New York: Plenum Press.

Jackson, P. W. (1968). *Life in classrooms.* New York: Holt, Rinehart and Winston.

Kennedy, M. M. (1979). Generalizing from single case studies. *Evaluation Quarterly, 3*(4), 661–678.

Kirk, J., & Miller, M. L. (1986). *Reliability and validity in qualitative research.* Beverly Hills, CA: Sage.

Krathwohl, D. R. (1985). *Social and behavioral science research: A new framework for conceptualizing, implementing, and evaluating research studies.* San Francisco: Jossey-Bass.

Lawler, R. W., & Yazdani, M. (Eds.). (1987). *Artificial intelligence and education: Learning environments and tutoring systems* (Vol. 1). Norwood, NJ: Ablex Publishing.

Lucas, W. (1974). *The case survey method: Aggregating case experience.* Santa Monica, CA: Rand.

Miles, M. B., & Huberman, A. M. (1984a). Drawing valid meaning from qualitative data: Toward a shared craft. *Educational Researcher, 13,* 20–30.

Miles M. B., & Huberman, A. M. (1984b). *Qualitative data analysis: A sourcebook of new methods.* Beverly Hills, CA: Sage.

Noblit, G. W., & Hare, R. D. (1988). *Meta-ethnography: Synthesizing qualitative studies.* Newbury Park, CA: Sage.

Patton, M. Q. (1980). *Qualitative evaluation methods.* Beverly Hills, CA: Sage.

Peshkin, A. (1978). *Growing up American: Schooling and the survival of community.* Chicago: University of Chicago Press.

Peshkin, A. (1982). The researcher and subjectivity: Reflections on an ethnography of school and community. In G. Spindler (Ed.), *Doing the ethnography of schooling: Educational anthropology in action* (pp. 48–67). New York: Holt, Rinehart and Winston.

Pettigrew, T. (1967). Social evaluation theory: Convergences and applications. In D. Levine (Ed.), *Nebraska Symposium on Motivation* (Vol. 5). Lincoln: University of Nebraska Press.

Pettigrew, T. (1969). Racially separate or together. *Journal of Social Issues, 25,* 43–69.

Phi Delta Kappan. (1980). *Why do some urban schools succeed? The Phi Delta Kappa study of exceptional urban elementary schools.* Bloomington: Phi Delta Kappa and Indiana University.

Ragin, C. C. (1987). *The comparative method: Moving beyond qualitative and quantitative strategies.* Berkeley: University of California Press.

Reichardt, C. S., & Cook, T. D. (1979). Beyond qualitative *versus* quantitative methods. In T. D. Cook & C. S. Reichardt (Eds.), *Qualitative and quantitative methods in evaluation research* (pp. 1–33). Beverly Hills, CA: Sage.

Rutter, M., Maughan, B., Mortimore, P., Ouston, J., & Smith, A. (1979). *Fifteen thousand hours: Secondary schools and their effects on children.* Cambridge, MA: Harvard University Press.

Sagar, H. A., & Schofield, J. W. (1980). Racial and behavioral cues in black and white children's perceptions of ambiguously aggressive acts. *Journal of Personality and Social Psychology, 39,* 590–598.

Schofield, J. W. (1979). The impact of positively structured contact on intergroup behavior. Does it last under adverse conditions? *Social Psychology Quarterly, 42,* 280–284.

Schofield, J. W. (1981). Competitive and complementary identities: Images and interaction in an interracial school. In S. Asher & J. Gottman (Eds.), *The development of children's friendship.* New York: Cambridge University Press.

Schofield, J. W. (1986). Causes and consequences of the colorblind perspective. In S. Gaertner & J. Dovidio (Eds.), *Prejudice, discrimination and racism: Theory and practice* (pp. 231–253). New York: Academic Press.

Schofield, J. W. (1989). *Black and white in school: Trust, tension, or tolerance?* New York: Teachers College Press. (Original work published 1982)

Schofield, J. W., & Evans-Rhodes, D. (1989, May). *Artificial intelligence in the classroom: The impact of a computer-based tutor on teachers and students.* Paper presented at the 4th International Conference on Artificial Intelligence in Education, Amsterdam, The Netherlands.

Schofield, J. W., & Francis, W. D. (1982). An observational study of peer interaction in racially-mixed "accelerated" classrooms. *Journal of Educational Psychology, 74,* 722–732.

Schofield, J. W., & Sagar, H. A. (1977). Peer interaction patterns in an integrated middle school. *Sociometry, 40,* 130–138.

Schofield, J. W., & Sagar, H. A. (1983). Desegregation, school practices and student race relations. In C. Rossell & W. Hawley (Eds.), *The consequences of school desegregation* (pp. 58–102). Philadelphia, PA: Temple University Press.

Schofield, J. W., & Verban, D. (1988). Computer usage in the teaching of mathematics: Issues which need answers. In D. Grouws & T. Cooney (Eds.), *Effective mathematics teaching* (pp. 169–193). Hillsdale, NJ: Erlbaum.

Shaughnessy, J. J., & Zechmeister, E. B. (1985). *Research methods in psychology.* New York: Knopf.

Slavin, R. E. (1980). Cooperative learning. *Review of Educational Research, 50,* 315–342.

Smith, A. G., & Robbins, A. E. (1984). Multimethod policy research: A case study of structure and flexibility. In D. M. Fetterman (Ed.), *Ethnography in educational evaluation* (pp. 115–132). Beverly Hills, CA: Sage.

Smith, H. W. (1975). *Strategies of social research: The methodological imagination.* Englewood Cliffs, NJ: Prentice Hall.

Spindler, G. (1982). General introduction. In G. Spindler (Ed.), *Doing the ethnography of schooling: Educational anthropology in action* (pp. 1–13). New York: Holt, Rinehart and Winston.

Stake, R. E. (1978). The case-study method in social inquiry. *Educational Researcher, 7,* 5–8.

Stephan, W. J. (1985). Intergroup relations. In G. Lindzey & E. Aronson (Eds.), *The handbook of social psychology* (Vol. 2, pp. 599–658). New York: Random House.

Strauss, A. L. (1987). *Qualitative analysis for social scientists.* Cambridge, UK: Cambridge University Press.

Walker, D. F. (1984). Promise, potential and pragmatism: Computers in high school. *Institute for Research in Educational Finance and Governance Policy Notes, 5,* 3–4.

Weber, G. (1971). *Inner-city children can be taught to read: Four successful schools.* Washington, DC: Council for Basic Education.

Whyte, W. F. (1984). *Learning from the field: A guide from experience.* Beverly Hills, CA: Sage.

Wolcott, H. F. (1973). *The man in the principal's office: An ethnography.* New York: Holt, Rinehart and Winston.

Wolcott, H. F. (1975). Criteria for an ethnographic approach to research in schools. *Human Organization, 34,* 111–127.

Wolcott, H. F. (1982). Mirrors, models, and monitors: Educator adaptations of the ethnographic innovation. In G. Spindler (Ed.), *Doing the ethnography of schooling: Educational anthropology in action* (pp. 68–95). New York: Holt, Rinehart and Winston.

Yin, R. K. (1981). The case study crisis: Some answers. *Administrative Science Quarterly, 26,* 58–64.

Yin, R. K. (1984). *Case study research: Design and methods.* Beverly Hills, CA: Sage.

Yin, R. K., & Heald, K. A. (1975). Using the case survey method to analyze policy studies. *Administrative Science Quarterly, 20,* 371–381.

Yin, R. K., & Yates, D. (1975). *Street-level governments: Assessing decentralization and urban services.* Lexington, MA: D. C. Heath.

9

Judging the Quality
of Case Study Reports

Yvonna S. Lincoln and Egon G. Guba

❖ INTRODUCTION

The emergence of alternative paradigms to guide inquiry has raised serious questions about how the quality of such inquiry might be judged. In contrast to conventional positivism (or its near cousin, post-positivism), which has had several centuries in which to devise and refine quality criteria, these emergent forms are still in their infancy, with respect to how to judge both the quality of the inquiry *process* and the inquiry *product*. In our earlier writing (Guba, 1981; Lincoln, 1986; Lincoln & Guba, 1985, 1986), we have endeavored to address the process question, proposing one set of criteria under the rubric of *trustworthiness* criteria and a second set under the rubric of *authenticity*

Reprinted from Yvonna S. Lincoln and Egon G. Guba, "Judging the Quality of Case Study Reports," *Qualitative Studies in Education*, 3(1), 53–59. Copyright 1990 by Taylor & Francis Ltd. Reprinted by permission.

criteria. In this paper we shall address the product question, asking what sorts of quality judgments can be brought to bear in order to assess the typical *product* of alternative paradigm inquiry: the case report. Among those most interested in this issue are researchers utilizing the new paradigm (or traditions within the paradigm [Jacob, 1988]); persons chairing dissertation committees; persons and agencies commissioning alternative paradigm research, evaluations, and policy studies; and, more important, editors who find case studies or reports coming across their desks for review and publication.

Judging the quality of process, while critical in understanding the premises under which an inquiry was undertaken and why the case report takes the form that it does, as Smith (1987) suggests, is very different from judging the quality of the product of an inquiry. Process judgments can tell the reader something about the trustworthiness and authenticity of a given study, but they say little about the quality *of the narrative presented*. Since the ability of a given case study to evoke a vicarious response is directly related to its quality as a narrative, criteria for judging the *case report per se* are coequally critical for judging the quality of the process.

Drawing on and extending the work of Zeller (1987) and our own previous work, we will describe and explicate four classes of criteria which address the goodness of alternative inquiry case reports. We have argued elsewhere that case reports, rather than more technical reports, are the logically best form for reporting on alternative paradigm work (see especially Lincoln & Guba, 1985) because they provide an appropriate vehicle for the "thick description" (Geertz, 1973) which is so essential to an understanding of context and situation; they serve as metaphors useful to the reader to stretch and test his or her own knowledge; they provide the information and sophistication needed to challenge the reader's current construction and enable its reconstruction; they serve as "idea catalogs" from which the reader may pick and choose in ways relevant to his or her own situation; and, most important, they provide the vicarious experience from which the reader may learn (as we do from all experience). We discuss four classes of criteria: *resonance, rhetoric, empowerment,* and *applicability*.

❖ RESONANCE CRITERIA

By resonance criteria we mean criteria that assess the degree of fit, overlap, or reinforcement between the case study report as written and the basic belief system undergirding that alternative paradigm which the inquirer has chosen to follow. For example, if the alternative paradigm is what we have chosen to call the naturalistic or constructivist paradigm (Lincoln & Guba, 1985), the case study report must at the very least reflect the multiple realities constructed by the respondents in the inquiry; demonstrate in what ways it has taken account of the mutual shaping of phenomenal elements in that site; rely on "pattern theories" (Kaplan, 1964) rather than on a priori theories, especially such as may assume cause and effect; reject generalizability (Cronbach, 1975) and the drawing of nomothetic conclusions (avoid making recommendations which look like or which can be interpreted as generalizations); display and take account of the value influences (Bahm, 1971) that impinge on the inquiry, including the values which dictated the choice of a problem, the values which impelled the choice of theoretical formulation or framework (if any), the values dictating the choice of paradigm, the values inherent in the research site (including those of all stakeholder groups), and the values of the investigator himself or herself; and, finally, reflect the investigator's involvement in such a way as to make clear that objectivity, being unachievable in any event, is not an aim.

With respect to the last point, a portion of the case study ought to be given over to considerations of conscious reflexivity. That is, some portion of the methodological treatment ought to comprise reflections on the investigator's own personal experience of the fieldwork (Punch, 1985). Any case study is a construction itself, a product of the interaction between respondents, site, and researcher. As such, the construction is rooted in the person, character, experience, context, and philosophy of the constructor. That constructor, the inquirer, has an obligation to be self-examining, self-questioning, self-challenging, self-critical, and self-correcting. Any case study should reflect these intensely personal processes on the part of the researcher.

❖ RHETORICAL CRITERIA

By rhetorical criteria, we mean those relevant to assessing the form, structure, and presentational characteristics of the case study. Zeller (1987) has attempted to develop four such criteria "imposed by the dictates of good writing" (pp. 197–198). First, a case study might be judged on the criterion of *unity*, which suggests that the components of a study are "well-organized" and "should advance some central idea, either initially or eventually discernible to the reader," by means of the narrative structure (Zeller, 1987, p. 198). But the idea of unity goes beyond organization and the advancement of some central ideas. It encompasses structural characteristics such as coherence and corroboration. By coherence, we mean to assert that the case study must exhibit a unique internal consistency, logic, and harmony. By corroboration, we mean that the evidence for assertions that are made, conclusions that are drawn, meanings that are inferred, and metaphoric usage attempted must be internally substantiated and self-evident from the way in which data are displayed. In short, there ought not be loose ends, stories left dangling, or characters who disappear from the cast.

The second rhetorical criterion posed by Zeller (1987, pp. 189–199) is *overall organization*. Here, elements similar to those that mark great fiction assume a greater importance, and the case study might be judged in the same way as the structure of a novel or short story. Is there rising action, climax, falling action? From whose point of view is the story being told, first person, second person, or third person? Who is the narrator, and what are his or her roles?

Zeller's third rhetorical criterion is *simplicity* or *clarity*. It has been argued that a strength of the case study is its accessibility to many persons who could not comprehend a typical scientific technical report. Simplicity and clarity are achieved by the "careful construction of sentences (shunning inappropriate usage of the third person and passive voice), a thorough rigorous editing, and thorough avoidance of jargon or technical language" (p. 201). The use of "natural language," or the language, terms, and meanings of respondents, aids and abets making the case report more accessible, since the natural or local language is often vastly different from the style of scientific prose, which is a "stripped-down, cool style that avoids ornamentation" in the interests of "empty[ing] language of emotion and convinc[ing] the reader of the writer's disengagement from the analysis" (Firestone, 1987, p. 17). The language of the street and community is not the language of the scientific establishment. *Recapturing* the more natural language of respondents is more than mere insertion of appropriate quotations from field notes at modest intervals. It involves the selection and array of arguments framed in ways that engage and "maximize the reader's interest and involvement" (Zeller, 1987, p. 199) and that are "rich with the sense of human encounter" (Stake, 1978).

Finally, Zeller contends that writing a case study that fulfills the requirements of rhetorical criteria demands *craftsmanship*. Writing, rewriting, and writing again and again are probably the only techniques for advancing the art of craftsmanship. But it is evident when we see it. Some of the elements of craftsmanship that are evident in already extant case studies, particularly those which have come to be classics over the years, are clear when a textual analysis is done. We believe that craftsmanship—careful writing—is apparent when a narrative exhibits some or all of the following characteristics.

1. *It has power and elegance.* The case-study-as-construction is characterized by grace, on the one hand, and by precision on the other. The case study should be examined for its level of discourse, for the incisiveness of vocabulary, heuristic and evocative value of the metaphor employed, the degree of insightfulness, and its rhetorical function or persuasiveness.

2. *It is creative.* The case study should go a step beyond present constructions and understanding, proposing novel ideas and/or new grounds for negotiation of reconstruction. This creativity may express itself by providing latent meanings for manifest understandings, by exhibiting playfulness or irony in achieving understanding or communication, or by posing as yet unanswered or answerable questions which, when dealt with, will break new ground.

3. *It is open and problematic.* The case study should be open to negotiation and reconstruction. Its tentative, exploratory, and problematic character should be clear to the reader. The case study itself should propose actions that might lead to its own reconstruction or reinterpretation, including especially ways in which it can be tested against other constructions.

4. *It is independent.* A personal construction is the most examined position to which an individual can come. Therefore, a construction ought not to be a passive acceptance and/or restatement of someone else's construction (a "received view," in the words of feminists). Rather, it should be the product of an active process, a kind of personal hermeneutic which has forced the constructor to shed false or divided consciousness in some form, and which takes into account the world as experienced by the constructor. The writing should demonstrate the intellectual wrestling that the writer went through in coming to his or her conclusions and should

demonstrate the writer's ability to think "outside" that construction
to which he or she may have been socialized. In other instances, it
will mean that the same setting will be presented very differently
by different researchers working at the same time. For example, if
one is male and the other female, he will "experience" the setting
in a masculinist manner, while she may experience the setting in a
feminist manner. The constructions are separate, independent
ways of knowing, and both must be honored for the rhetorical criterion of independence to be met.

5. *It should demonstrate the writer's emotional and intellectual commitment
    to craftsmanship.* It ought not to appear to be "thrown together," as
    if for the sake of an assignment or a contract. It should demonstrate
    the fact that the writer has developed the construction as far as
    present knowledge and sophistication permit. It should display
    passion in advancing the construction.

6. *It should display courage.* The construction should be extended
    beyond "safe" limits. It should display a certain element of
    risk-taking, of putting the writer's ego on the line, of invitation to
    criticism. The writer should be willing to stand behind the con-
    struction and to act in accordance with it, social pressures
    notwithstanding.

7. *It should display egalitarianism.* A given construction should demon-
    strate the assumption of an egalitarian stance with respect to other
    persons (for instance, respondents and informants) with whom
    one may come into contact while discharging the processional
    inquiry role. While all constructions are not equally informed and
    sophisticated, all persons have the moral right to have their con-
    structions respected and presented. Disagreements should be
    negotiated, not overruled by virtue of a superior position of power
    which the writer may hold. The effect of an egalitarian posture is
    to empower all significant others equally.

Clearly, not all case studies will display all these criteria equally
strongly. Nevertheless, elements of all the rhetorical criteria ought to be
explicit or implicit in a reading of the study. Fulfillment of the rhetorical criteria ought to be apparent either in the methodological section of
the case study or in the case study itself.

❖ EMPOWERMENT CRITERIA

By empowerment criteria, we mean those assessing the ability of the case study to evoke and facilitate action on the part of readers. Such criteria include fairness, educativeness, and actionability (Lincoln & Guba, 1986), or the power of such an inquiry to enable those whom it affects directly or indirectly to take action on their circumstances or environments or those environments in which they are significant others. For instance, an inquiry might help a professor whose major responsibility is the teaching of a mathematics methods course to enable his or her student teachers to understand better how students acquire mathematics concepts.

At the least, empowerment implies consciousness-raising. Perhaps it means providing arguments that readers can use in their own situations should they attempt action based on the case report. Empowerment assuredly means that case studies should avoid ending their narratives only with "suggestions for further research." It means making clear what action steps are indicated by the inquiry—not just what we have, but what our findings say about where we should be going.

❖ APPLICABILITY CRITERIA

By applicability criteria, we mean those which assess the extent to which the case study facilitates the drawing of inferences by the reader that may have applicability in his or her own context or situation. (Inferences, however, should not be confused with generalizations, which are context-free and time-free laws regarding human behavior.) Under *transferability*, we have argued earlier (Guba, 1981; Lincoln & Guba, 1985) that transference can take place between contexts A and B if B is sufficiently like A on those elements or factors or circumstances that the A inquiry found to be significant (and those salient factors will vary from inquiry to inquiry). In order to make that judgment possible for a reader, we have said that "thick description" is needed, not in the sense of long and detailed descriptions, although that may be necessary, but in the sense which Geertz (1973) uses the term, as making clear levels of meaning.

But transferability is surely only one frame within which we can discuss applicability. How else could a case study make it possible for a reader to draw out applications that might prove useful for his or her own situation? Might application still be possible even if the situations are essentially *dissimilar*? We would suggest at least three ways in which this might occur.

First, a case might provide a sense of vicarious, *"deja vu"* experience. In this situation, a reader can "learn" from the experience, and, as is the case with all learnings, make application even in situations that do not appear on their faces to be similar. If one is a principal in a school and is reassigned to another school, however different from the first, the first experience "stands one in good stead." So one criterion in this category is whether or not vicarious experience is enabled.

It is important to note that under rhetorical criteria, we argued for many of the elements that make for good style in all forms of narrative writing, particularly essays and novels. In both those forms, the powers of persuasion and vicarious experience are critical in judging the success of the work itself. Thus, elements that may be called rhetorical criteria are the very ones that render the "experience" of a case study vicarious; that is, fulfilling rhetorical criteria can buttress a positive judgment on applicability criteria. Criteria for judging products are interrelated, and strength in one set of criteria may contribute to strength in another set, just as strength and power in some forms of quantitative analyses may be thought of as lending strength to other criteria (e.g., robustness of analytic technique may lend greater certainty to conclusions). The important point to be made here is that criteria may enhance or undermine each other.

Second, a case might be used as a metaphor or used in a metaphoric sense. Guba (1978), citing Burke (1969, p. 503) and Petrie (1976, p. 40), noted that a metaphor is a "device for seeing something in terms of something else," or it may be "conceived of broadly as encompassing visual metaphors and even theories—models as they are often called in the sciences." In metaphors, two terms and the relationships between them are utilized to extend understandings. The first term, the *subject term* (or topic, tenor, or principal subject), is "that term which the metaphor is intended to illuminate. . . . The second term, the *metaphoric term*, is that term which [is] used to illuminate the subject term . . . [and is also called] the vehicle, the referent, or the subsidiary subject" (pp. 7–8). The two relationships between the subject and metaphoric terms that are important for the purposes of this criterion are the *ground* and *tension*. Ground refers to the way in which the subject and metaphoric terms are alike, and the meaning of the metaphor cannot "be comprehended unless the ground is understood by [means of] the subject." On the other hand, the tension "of a metaphor 'is the literal incompatibility of the topic and the vehicle'" (Ortony, Reynolds, & Arter, 1977, p. 6, cited in Guba, 1978, p. 8), or the way in which the subject and the metaphoric terms are dissimilar.

The learning which can take place when the case serves as a metaphor is, therefore, two-fold: on the one hand, the case serves to provide fodder for thinking of the ways in which two situations are similar; on the other hand, the "tension" aspects allow the reader to discover ways in which the contexts of the case and his or her own situations are different. Since the "ground" of the metaphor is usually implicit, rather than explicit, two additional problems are raised. First, the reader must understand the implicit ground, or the way in which two things (the subject and metaphoric terms) are alike. Second, the reader must be able to utilize the tacit learnings that implicit grounds imply, make those tacit learnings more or less propositional (and therefore accessible to others), and act upon them.

Third, and finally, a case could be used as a basis for re-examining and reconstructing one's own construction of a given phenomenon. The case may provide new (or better) information. It may raise the reader's level of sophistication. Or it may provide the interpretation critical to erasing false or divided consciousness. In any case, re-examination of one's personal construction is called for, and such examination may well lead to a reconstruction. Some, if not all, case studies ought explicitly to invite the reader to that task and make it possible to pursue it.

❖ CONCLUSION

We have argued that case studies which are reports of alternative paradigm inquiries (not all case studies will qualify) should meet specific criteria. We have implied strongly that *product* criteria are as important as *process* criteria, and that studies which can be shown to meet these product criteria will fulfill important functions within the emergent paradigm. First, such studies will *resonate* with the belief system of the alternative paradigm. That is, their basic assumptions will be exemplified in every way by the means and manner of the study's methodology or design strategy, and the final product of the inquiry will be composed with the emergent paradigm's world view in mind.

Second, case studies will *rhetorically exemplify* the interpersonal involvement which characterized that form of inquiry, making the reader an interactive partner with the writer in reaching understandings and drawing implications. We have suggested, in the section on rhetorical criteria, that the "stripped-down, cool" style of scientific, conventional technical reports ought to be replaced with the language that demonstrates the passion, commitment, and open political stance of the writer, eschewing the artificial neutrality which permeates most technical research reports. All inquiry supports some political and social agenda; hence, we have tried to describe a rhetoric for products of alternative inquiry that would bring those agendas to the forefront of social action where they may be debated in open forum, as a participatory democracy would demand.

Third, we have argued that case studies which can be shown to meet these criteria will *empower, activate, and stimulate* the reader to a level of responsiveness and use that does not characterize research reports typically.

Finally, we have suggested that studies that meet *applicability* criteria facilitate application of study insights by providing experience or vicarious experience through the use of powerful metaphors and by stimulating re-examination and reconstruction of the reader's existing construction.

We believe strongly (indeed, passionately) that even if only the last idea were all that could be accomplished, we would have begun a revolution in utilizing the products of social science research.

❖ REFERENCES

Bahm, A. J. (1971). Science is not value-free. *Policy Sciences, 2,* 391–396.

Burke, K. (1969). *A grammar of motives.* Berkeley: University of California Press.

Cronbach, L. J. (1975). Beyond the two disciplines of scientific psychology. *American Psychologist, 30,* 116–127.

Firestone, W. A. (1987). Meaning in method: the rhetoric of quantitative and qualitative research. *Educational Researcher, 16,* 16–21.

Geertz, C. (1973). Thick description: toward an interpretive theory of culture. In C. Geertz (Ed.), *The interpretation of cultures* (pp. 3–30). New York: Basic Books.

Geertz, C. (1988). *Works and lives: the anthropologist as author.* Stanford, CA: Stanford University Press.

Guba, E. G. (1978). *The use of metaphors in constructing theory* (Paper and Report Series, No. 3, Research on Evaluation Program). Portland, OR: Northwest Regional Educational Laboratory.

Guba, E. G. (1981). Criteria for assessing the trustworthiness of naturalistic inquiries. *Educational Communications and Technology Journal, 29,* 75–92.

Jacob, E. (1988). Clarifying qualitative research: a focus on traditions. *Educational Researcher, 17,* 16-19, 22–24.

Kaplan, A. (1964). *The conduct of inquiry.* San Francisco: Chandler.

Lincoln, Y. S. (1986). *The development of intrinsic criteria for authenticity: a model for trust in naturalistic researches.* Paper presented at the annual meeting of the American Educational Research Association, San Francisco, CA.

Lincoln, Y. S., & Guba, E. G. (1985). *Naturalistic inquiry.* Beverly Hills, CA: Sage.

Lincoln, Y. S., & Guba, E. G. (1986). But is it rigorous? Trustworthiness and authenticity in naturalistic evaluation. In D. D. Williams (Ed.), *Naturalistic evaluation* (pp. 73–84). New Directions for Program Evaluation, No. 30. San Francisco, CA: Jossey-Bass.

Ortony, A., Reynolds, R. E., & Arter, J. A. (1977). *Metaphor: theoretical and empirical research* (Technical Report No. 27). Urbana, IL: University of Illinois, Center for the Study of Reading.

Petrie, H. G. (1976). Do you see what I see? The epistemology of interdisciplinary inquiry. *Educational Researcher, 5,* 9–15. Also reprinted in *The Journal of Aesthetic Education, 10,* 29–43.

Punch, M. (1985). *The politics and ethics of fieldwork* (Sage University Paper Series on Qualitative Research Methods, Vol. 2). Beverly Hills, CA: Sage.

Smith, D. (1987). The limits of positivism in social work research. *British Journal of Social Work, 17,* 401–416.

Stake, R. (1978). The case study method in social inquiry. *Educational Researcher, 7,* 5–8.

Zeller, N. (1987). *A rhetoric for naturalistic inquiry.* Unpublished doctoral dissertation, Indiana University.

10

Narrative Analysis

Catherine Kohler Riessman

❖ INTRODUCTION: LOCATING NARRATIVE

The study of narrative does not fit neatly within the boundaries of any single scholarly field. Inherently interdisciplinary, it extends the "interpretive turn" in the social sciences (Geertz, 1973, 1983; Rabinow & Sullivan, 1979/1987). As realist assumptions from natural science methods prove limiting for understanding social life, a group of leading U.S. scholars from various disciplines are turning to narrative as the organizing principle for human action (Bruner, 1986, 1990; Cronon, 1992; Rosaldo, 1989; Sarbin, 1986b; Schafer, 1980, 1992). Developments in European theory set the stage for this "narrative turn" (Bakhtin, 1981; Barthes, 1974; Ricoeur, 1981, 1984). Todorov coined the term *narratology* in 1969 in an effort to elevate the form "to the status of an object of knowledge for a new science" (quoted in Godzich, 1989, p. ix).

Storytelling, to put the argument simply, is what we do with our research materials and what informants do with us. The story metaphor emphasizes that we create order, construct texts[1] in particular contexts. The mechanical metaphor adopted from the natural sciences (increasingly questioned there) implies that we provide an objective description of forces in the world, and we position ourselves outside to do so.

Narrative analysis takes as its object of investigation the story itself. I limit discussion here to first-person accounts by respondents of their experience, putting aside other kinds of accounts (e.g., our descriptions of what happened in the field and other researcher narrativizations, including the "master narratives" of theory).[2] The purpose is to see how respondents in interviews impose order on the flow of experience to make sense of events and actions in their lives. The methodological approach examines the informant's story and analyzes how it is put together, the linguistic and cultural resources it draws on, and how it persuades a listener of authenticity. Analysis in narrative studies opens up the forms of telling about experience, not simply the content to which language refers. We ask, Why was the story told *that* way?

Nature and the world do not tell stories, individuals do. Interpretation is inevitable because narratives are representations. There is no hard distinction in postpositivist research between fact and interpretation (Stivers, 1993). Human agency and imagination determine what gets included and excluded in narrativization, how events are plotted, and what they are supposed to mean. Individuals construct past events and actions in personal narratives to claim identities and construct lives.

> How individuals recount their histories—what they emphasize and omit, their stance as protagonists or victims, the relationship the story establishes between teller and audience—all shape what individuals can claim of their own lives. Personal stories are not merely a way of telling someone (or oneself) about one's life; they are the means by which identities may be fashioned. (Rosenwald & Ochberg, 1992, p. 1)

Not merely information storage devices, narratives structure perceptual experience, organize memory, "segment and purpose—build the very events of a life" (Bruner, 1987, p. 15). Individuals become the autobiographical narratives by which they tell about their lives. These private constructions typically mesh with a community of life stories, "deep structures" about the nature of life itself.

Personal Narratives as Data

Locating narratives of personal experience for analysis is not difficult. They are ubiquitous in everyday life. We can all think of a conversation when someone told in exquisite detail what she said, what he said, what happened next—a recapitulation of every nuance of a moment that had special meaning for her. Psychotherapists encounter narratives of personal experience every day and use them to change lives by retelling and constructing new and more fulfilling ones (Schafer, 1992; White & Epston, 1990). Telling stories about past events seems to be a universal human activity, one of the first forms of discourse we learn as children (Nelson, 1989) and used throughout the life course by people of all social backgrounds in a wide array of settings. "So natural is the impulse to narrate," wrote H. White (1989), that the form is almost inevitable for any report of how things happened, a solution to "the problem of how to translate *knowing* into *telling*" (p. 1, emphasis in original).

Research interviews are no exception. Respondents (if not interrupted with standardized questions) will hold the floor for lengthy turns and sometimes organize replies into long stories. Traditional approaches to qualitative analysis often fracture these texts in the service of interpretation and generalization by taking bits and pieces, snippets of a response edited out of context. They eliminate the sequential and structural features that characterize narrative accounts (for a critique of mainstream methods that suppress narrative, see Mishler, 1986).

The precise definition of personal narrative is a subject of debate, to be discussed below. For now, it refers to talk organized around consequential events. A teller in a conversation takes a listener into a past time or "world" and recapitulates what happened then to make a point, often a moral one. In qualitative interviews, typically most of the talk is not narrative but question-and-answer exchanges, arguments, and other forms of discourse.

Respondents narrativize particular experiences in their lives, often where there has been a breach between ideal and real, self and society. Those I studied often told long stories about their marriages to explain their divorces (Riessman, 1990a). Individuals facing the biographic disruption of chronic illness reconstruct a coherent self in narratives (Bury, 1982; Riessman, 1990b; Williams, 1984). Embodying the self in stories can occur in settings where the self is being disembodied, such as medical examinations (Young, 1989).

Despite the seeming universality of the discourse form, some experiences are extremely difficult to speak about (Roth, 1993). Political conditions constrain particular events from being narrated. The ordinary response to atrocities is to banish them from awareness (Herman, 1992). Survivors of political torture, war, and sexual crimes silence themselves and are silenced because it is too difficult to tell and to listen. Rape survivors, for example, may not be able to talk about what they experienced as terrorizing violations because others do not regard them as violations. Under these circumstances, women may have difficulty even naming their experience. If it is spoken about, the experience emerges as a kind of "prenarrative: it does not develop or progress in time, and it does not reveal the storyteller's feelings or interpretations of events" (Herman, 1992, p. 175). Social movements aid individuals to name their injuries, connect with others, and engage in political action. Research interviewers can also bear witness. (For an example involving marital rape, see Riessman, 1992.)

A primary way individuals make sense of experience is by casting it in narrative form (Bruner, 1990; Gee, 1985; Mishler, 1986). This is especially true of difficult life transitions and trauma. As Isak Dinesen said, "All sorrows can be borne if we can put them into a story" (quoted in Arendt, 1958, p. 175). Narrators create plots from disordered experience, give reality "a unity that neither nature nor the past possesses so clearly. In so doing, we move well beyond nature into the intensely human realm of value" (Cronon, 1992, p. 1349). Precisely because they are essential meaning-making structures, narratives must be preserved, not fractured, by investigators, who must respect respondents' ways of constructing meaning and analyze how it is accomplished.

❖ THEORETICAL CONTEXTS

It is perhaps a sign of our times that investigators are questioning how we represent life in scientific work (Lynch & Woolgar, 1990). Qualitative researchers often seek to depict others' experiences but act as if representation is not a problem. Feminists, for example, emphasize "giving voice" to previously silenced groups of women by describing the diversity of their experiences (Fonow & Cook, 1991; Gilligan, 1982; Gluck & Patai, 1991; Reinharz, 1992). I share the goal but am more cautious. We cannot give voice, but we do hear voices that we record and interpret. Representational decisions cannot be avoided; they enter

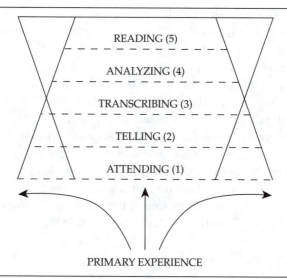

Figure 10.1   Levels of Representation in Research Process

at numerous points in the research process, and qualitative analysts, including feminists, must confront them.

The Representation of Experience

Investigators do not have direct access to another's experience. We deal with ambiguous representations of it—talk, text, interaction, and interpretation. It is not possible to be neutral and objective, to merely represent (as opposed to interpret) the world (Peller, 1987). At the risk of oversimplifying, there are, at a minimum, five levels or kinds of representation in the research process, with porous boundaries between them, depicted in Figure 10.1 (The danger of my representation, of course, is to make the borders more real than semantic.)[3]

To ground what would otherwise be an abstract discussion of the figure, and related interpretive problems, I will make my points inductively and a bit unconventionally. I interweave discussion of the figure with a narrative about an experience on a recent trip to South India.

I went to India to make arrangements for fieldwork I am beginning there on the meaning and management of infertility. For a respite from seemingly endless train rides to meet potential collaborators and locate an appropriate setting for the research, I went to stay for a few days at a tropical resort in Kerala. Early one morning, I took a walk from my hotel, along a deserted beach.

If we adopt the starting point of phenomenology[4] and the lived world of immediate everyday experience, the world of this inhabited beach is "'already there' before reflection begins—as an inalienable presence" (Merleau-Ponty, 1962/1989, p. vii). Walking at dawn, I encounter it at a prelinguistic realm of experience—images, plays of colors and lights, noises, and fleeting sensations—in the stream of consciousness. I am one with the world and make no distinction at this point between my bodily perceptions and the objects I am conscious of that comprise the beach. Like all social actors, I experience this world from the "natural attitude," taking it for granted, not thinking about and analyzing it (Husserl, 1939/1973; Schutz, 1932/1967).

Attending to Experience

Then I attend to and make discrete certain features in the stream of consciousness—reflecting, remembering, recollecting them into observations. I scan the beach (metaphorically speaking) and isolate certain images, which are known in a given language community by certain words—sunlight, sand, waves, fishing. On this particular occasion, the sound of fishermen chanting is the object I attend to, not the smell of the surf, or the feel of the water—yesterday's images. I stop and watch. Men pull in giant nets, their synchronous movements aided by the rhythmic chant between them. The men in patterned lungis eventually sell the fish to women in brightly colored saris who, placing pails filled with fish on their heads, leave for market. By attending, I make certain phenomena meaningful, the first level of representation in Figure 10.1.[5]

There is choice in what I notice, a selection from the totality of the unreflected on, the primary experience. The truth of hearing and vision predominate over touch and smell, for example. The gendered nature of fishing work also strikes me because of theoretical interests and values. I actively construct reality in new ways at this first level of representation, to myself, by thinking.

Telling About Experience

Next comes the telling, the performance of a personal narrative. I come back to the United States from India and subsequently relate to friends at dinner the experience of the walk—coming upon the fishermen, their chant, the women, and my marvel. I re-present the events, already ordered to some degree, to these listeners in conversation, with all the opportunities and constraints the form of discourse entails. Although the walk happened many weeks before in another land, I relate it as one inside the experience, enacting the action in a conversation. My account takes the form of a narrative about what happened: I describe waking up early, taking a walk before breakfast, seeing the fishermen, watching as women arrived with empty pails, my fascination with the division of labor and women's economic self-sufficiency, in India where women are typically depicted as subservient. I describe the setting, characters, unfolding plot, and stitch the story together in a way that makes my interpretation of the events clear. To capture the moment on that particular morning, I describe at great length the sunlight, the colors of the men's lungis and the women's saris, bringing these objects from the real world of the beach to a narrative space in my friends' living room in Cambridge, MA. My rendering draws on resources from my cultural context, notably the gender-based division of labor that all participants in the conversation value as a category of analysis. My friends listen, question, urge me to say more about particular aspects of the exchange between men and women; I, in turn, refashion the events in response to their cues and, to make the importance of the scene real for them, expand on what the moment means in the larger context of my life plans for living and working in India. By talking and listening, we produce a narrative together (Level 2 in Figure 10.1).

In the telling, there is an inevitable gap between the experience as I lived it and any communication about it. Caught in the "prison house of language," in the words of Nietzsche (quoted in Jameson, 1972), there is no way to break through to the ideas to which my words refer because language is "uncommunicative of anything other than itself" (Merleau-Ponty, 1962/1989, p. 188). Yet, without words, the sounds, movements, and images of the beach experience cease to exist. Language makes them real, as it does the gendered practices of fishing because, as Merleau-Ponty suggested,

> our linguistic ability enables us to descend into the realm of our primary perceptual and emotional experience, to find there a reality susceptible to verbal understanding, and to bring forth a meaningful interpretation of this primary level of our existence. . . . By finding meaning in experience and then expressing this meaning in words,

the speaker enables the community to think about experience and not
just live it. (cited in Polkinghorne, 1988, pp. 29–30)

Meaning also shifts in other ways because it is constructed at this
second level of representation in a process of interaction. The story is
being told to particular people; it might have taken a different form if
someone else were the listener. In this case, I am not simply representing the experience on the beach from some neutral place but in a specific conversation with a mentor/friend and his partner, who mean
something to me. In telling about an experience, I am also creating a
self—how I want to be known by them. Beginning the new research
project, my friends have raised questions that have forced me to confront difficult issues, including my position as a privileged, white,
Western woman studying South Asian women's health. My rendering
of the narrative about the beach scene is colored by this context. Like all
social actors, I seek to persuade myself and others that I am a good
person. My narrative is inevitably a self representation (Goffman, 1959).

Transcribing Experience

If either of my friends were acting in their roles as social science investigators, they would have taped the conversation. An audio recording
would be more selective than a video, of course, but in neither case
would the entire conversation be captured. Whatever form of taping
used, they would ultimately have to represent it in some kind of text, a
"fixation" of action, in the words of Ricoeur, into written speech (cited in
Packer & Addison, 1989). Transcribing, the third level of representation
in Figure 10.1, is, like the earlier ones, incomplete, partial, and selective.
     Millett (1971), early in the contemporary feminist movement, com-
mented on the tape recorder:[6]

> Without this device to preserve the very sound of language, we
> should have no idea of how people *really* talk: their pauses, inflec-
> tions, emphases, unfinished sentences, short periods. All attempts to
> mimic spoken language seem terribly mannered, and one comes to
> respect [Gertrude] Stein still more, and to admire how carefully she
> must have listened. (p. 32)

Millett discussed the issue of making a written transcription from an
audiotape of her interviews with women workers in the sex industry
(prostitutes):

> What I have tried to capture here is the character of the English I heard spoken by four women and then recorded on tape. I was struck by the eloquence of what was said, and yet when I transcribed the words onto paper, the result was at first disappointing. Some of the wit of M's black and southern delivery had disappeared, gone with the tang of her voice. . . . J's difficulty in speaking of things so painful that she had repressed them for years required that I speak often on her tapes, hoping to give her support, then later, edit myself out. (p. 31)

Millett's solution, in addition to editing herself out, was to do "a good deal of work to transform spoken to linear-language" (p. 32) or to adopt a loose oral narrative and summarize what the women said. In an effort to display a polyphonic text that respected the different voices of the four women, she ultimately displayed the women's talk in her written text in four columns: a quartet in which voices "were instruments expressing their diverse experiences" (p. 33).

Twenty years later, an investigator wanting to "capture" my beach experience faces similar problems, but in the interim a great deal has been written about transcription practices. Transforming spoken language into a written text is now taken quite seriously because thoughtful investigators no longer assume the transparency of language. Qualitative researchers now ask themselves how detailed transcriptions should be. How, for example, could they best capture the rhythm of my talk about the fisherman's chant? Should they include silences, false starts, emphases, nonlexicals like "uhm," discourse markers like "y'know" or "so," overlapping speech, and other signs of listener participation in the narrative? Should they give clauses separate lines and display rhythmic and poetic structures by grouping lines? Not simply technical questions, these seemingly mundane choices of what to include and how to arrange and display the text have serious implications for how a reader will understand the narrative.

There is no one, true representation of spoken language. Mishler (1991b) makes the analogy to photography, which supposedly "pictures reality." Yet the technology of lenses, films, printing papers, and darkroom practices also have made possible an extraordinary diversity of possible images of the same object. The form of representation reflects the artist's views and conceptions—values about what's important. Photographers, like investigators (transcribers), fix the essence of a figure. By denying viewers (readers) information, they paradoxically provide us room to supply our own. We can invent an entire world analyzing the figures (dialogue), although we know very little about them. But I am getting a little ahead of my story.

Transcribing discourse, like photographing reality, is an interpretive practice. Decisions about how to transcribe, like decisions about telling and listening, are theory driven[7] (Ochs, 1979) and rhetorical; by displaying text in particular ways, we provide grounds for our arguments, just like a photographer guides the viewer's eye with lenses and by cropping images. Different transcription conventions lead to and support different interpretations and ideological positions, and they ultimately create different worlds. Meaning is constituted in very different ways with alternative transcriptions of the same stretch of talk (Mishler, 1991b).

Analyzing Experience

A fourth level of representation in Figure 10.1 enters as the investigator explicitly analyzes the transcript,[8] or typically a number of them. Perhaps the research issue is defining critical moments in the awakening of work identity. Like the moment of my walk along the beach, other social scientists narrativize turning points or epiphanies (Denzin, 1988) in their work lives. The challenge is to identify similarities across the moments into an aggregate, a summation. An investigator sits with pages of tape-recorded stories, snips away at the flow of talk to make it fit between the covers of a book, and tries to create sense and dramatic tension. There are decisions about form, ordering, style of presentation, and how the fragments of lives that have been given in interviews will be housed. The anticipated response to the work inevitably shapes what gets included and excluded.[9] In the end, the analyst creates a metastory about what happened by telling what the interview narratives signify, editing and reshaping what was told, and turning it into a hybrid story, a "false document" (Behar, 1993). Values, politics, and theoretical commitments enter once again. Although a kind of betrayal—the beach story and others like it are born again in an alien tongue—it is also necessary and productive; no matter how talented the original storyteller was, a life story told in conversation certainly does not come ready-made as a book (Behar, 1993), an article, or a dissertation. The stop-and-start style of oral stories of personal experience gets pasted together into something different.

Reading Experience

The fifth and final level of representation in Figure 10.1 comes as the reader encounters the written report. Perhaps an early draft was circulated to colleagues and their comments were incorporated into the so-called final product,[10] or perhaps published work was returned to the people it is about, who may or may not recognize their experience in it or like how they are portrayed. In any case, translations of my original narrative about an experience in India and analytic work on what it means by my social scientist friends in Cambridge inevitably gets into the hands of others, who bring their own meanings to bear. An extract about a beach walk might give some readers a shiver of recognition, whereas others might wonder about my relationship with my subjects— men and women of the fishing village in Kerala. What does my presence as a white English-speaking woman signify, given that Malayalam is the native tongue? How are race and class inscribed in the text?[11] It might be difficult, if not impossible, to get answers to these and similar questions. All a reader has is the analyst's representation.

Every text is "plurivocal, open to several readings and to several constructions" (Rabinow & Sullivan, 1979/1987, p. 12). Even for the same reader, a work can provoke quite different readings in different historical contexts (imagine Flaubert's *Madame Bovary*, for example, before and after the recent feminist movement). Collaboration is inevitable because the reader is an agent of the text (Bruner, 1986). Critical readers include their understandings of the "makings" of a work in their interpretations of it. Because a writer cannot tell all (seemingly irrelevant personal and historical circumstances have been excluded), interpretation may focus on how power and history work through a supposedly objective text. Readers raise historical contingencies and excluded standpoints—of women, people of color, non-Western views—as they dislodge the seemingly secure ground under our representations. Written texts are created within, and against, particular traditions and audiences, and these contexts can be brought to bear by readers. The point is that all texts stand on moving ground; there is no master narrative (Clifford, 1986; Clifford & Marcus, 1986; Sosnoski, 1991).

Ultimately, it is unclear who really authors a text, although Western texts come with individual authors' names penned to them. The meaning of a text is always meaning to someone. The truths we have constructed "are meaningful to specific interpretive communities in limiting historical circumstances" (Clifford, 1988, p. 112). Any finding—a depiction of a culture, psychological process, or social structure—exists in historical time, between subjects in relations of power. Whereas traditional social science has claimed to represent the experiences of populations and cultures, the new criticism states that we cannot speak, finally and with ultimate authority, for others. Our subjects "do not hold still for their portraits" (Clifford, 1986, p. 10; see also Wolf, 1992, regarding how feminists have been making similar postmodern arguments for some time).

The Limits of Representation

Generalizing from my beach walk and its repeated transformations, there are implications for research practices. All forms of representation of experience are limited portraits. Simply stated, we are interpreting and creating texts at every juncture, letting symbols stand for or take the place of the primary experience, to which we have no direct access. Meaning is ambiguous because it arises out of a process of interaction between people: self, teller, listener and recorder, analyst, and reader. Although the goal may be to tell the whole truth, our narratives about others' narratives are our worldly creations. There is no "view from nowhere" (Nagel, 1986), and what might have seemed nowhere in the past is likely to be somewhere in the present or future. Meaning is fluid and contextual, not fixed and universal. All we have is talk and texts that represent reality partially, selectively, and imperfectly.

Each level in Figure 10.1 involves an expansion but also a reduction: Tellers select features from the "whole" experience to narrate but add other interpretive elements. A similar process occurs with transcribing, analyzing, and reading. Framing discussion of the research process in the language of "representation" rather than as "stages" or "perspectives" emphasizes that we actively make choices that can be accomplished in different ways.[12] Obviously, the agency of the teller is central to composing narratives from personal experience, but so are the actions of others—listener, transcriber, analyst, and reader.

The idea of representation brings into view the constructed nature of social scientific work. Said (1979) went even further, and his views have bearing for all researchers:

> [The] real issue is whether indeed there can be a true representation
> of anything, or whether any and all representations, because they are
> representations, are embedded first in the language and then in the
> culture, institutions, and political ambience of the representor. If the
> latter alternative is the correct one (as I believe it is), then we must be
> prepared to accept the fact that a representation is *eo ipso* implicated,
> intertwined, embedded, interwoven with a great many other things
> besides the "truth," which is itself a representation. (pp. 272–273)

Whether we accept ultimate relativism, awareness of levels of representation presses us to be more conscious, reflective, and cautious about the claims we make.

Returning to the issue of giving voice to women's experience, I prefer to think of research as a chorus of voices, with an embedded contrapuntal duet (Gorelick, 1991). There are strains because most researchers are privileged and white and many women we want to include are not. Some voices will have to be restrained to hear voices from below (Rollins, 1985) to create a particular harmony, but a different interpreter might well allow other voices to dominate.[13]

Representing women's experience is limited further because language is often inadequate (DeVault, 1990), and the world as perceived by subjects may be confined and organized by structures of oppression not apparent to participants themselves (Gorelick, 1991; Smith, 1987).[14] Just as gender is not enough in feminist research (Riessman, 1987), giving voice to experience is not either, even as we commit to women's standpoints. Interpreting experience—and this happens at all five levels in Figure 10.1—involves representing reality; we create and re-create voices over and over again during the research process. Nowhere is this more evident than in studies of personal narratives.

Narratives as Representations

I now look more closely at the levels of telling/transcribing/analyzing as they are discussed in narrative theory. The literature is vast, and I enter the field through a path cleared by others, especially Langellier (1989), Martin (1986), and Mishler (1986). There is no binding theory of narrative but instead great conceptual diversity. My limited aim here is to identify key concepts, debates, and interpretive dilemmas that anyone doing research with first-person accounts of experience will have to consider and to provide resources. I make my own position clear below, in discussing examples of narrative studies and the specifics of doing the work.

What Is a Narrative?

There is considerable disagreement about the precise definition of narrative. Among one group the definition is so overly broad to include just about anything. In the clinical literature, for example, there is reference to illness narratives, life stories, and narration in psychotherapy about the past. However compelling narrative may be as a metaphor for telling about lives, systematic methods of analysis and detailed transcriptions are often lacking. The definition of narrative has been quite restrictive among another group. Labov (1972), in particular, assumes all narratives are stories about a specific past event, and they have common properties (described below). Most scholars treat narratives as discrete units, with clear beginnings and endings, as detachable from the surrounding discourse rather than as situated events.

In *Poetics*, Aristotle said that a narrative has a beginning, middle, and end. Ever since, scholars agree that sequence is necessary, if not sufficient, for narrative (on chronicles, see Cronon, 1992; Polanyi, 1985). Labov and Waletzky (1967) argued that stories follow a chronological sequence: The order of events moves in a linear way through time and the "order cannot be changed without changing the inferred sequence of events in the original semantic interpretation" (p. 21). A narrative, according to this definition, is always responding to the question, "And then what happened?" Western assumptions about time marching forward underpin Labov's approach. Young (1987) argued for consequential sequencing: One event causes another in the narrative, although the links may not always be chronological (also see Culler, 1980). Still others argue for thematic sequencing: An episodic narrative is stitched together by theme rather than by time (Michaels, 1981). Western, white, middle-class interviewers seem to expect temporally sequenced plots and have trouble hearing ones that are organized episodically (Riessman, 1987).

In conversation, tellers sometimes let listeners know a story is coming and indicate when it is over, with entrance and exit talk (Jefferson, 1979). "Once upon a time" and "they lived happily ever after" are classic examples in folktales of bracketing devices. But stories told in research interviews are rarely so clearly bounded, and locating them is often a complex interpretive process. Where one chooses to begin and end a narrative can profoundly alter its shape and meaning.[15] Decisions underscore how deeply the listener/interpreter is part of the text.

Not all narratives in interviews are stories in the linguistic sense of the term. Individuals relate experiences using a variety of narrative genres (Riessman, 1991). We recognize a genre by the persistence of certain conventional elements (Mitchell, 1990), which engage us in quite different ways. When we hear stories, for instance, we expect protagonists, inciting conditions, and culminating events. But not all narratives (or all lives) take this form. Some other genres include habitual narratives (when events happen over and over and consequently there is no peak in the action), hypothetical narratives (which depict events that did not happen), and topic-centered narratives (snapshots of past events that are linked thematically). Genres of narrative, with their distinctive styles and structures, are modes of representation that tellers choose (in concert with listeners' expectations, of course), just as filmmakers decide, based on their intentions and the market, what form the script will take and what conventions will be used to represent character and action. Different genres persuade differently; they make us care about a situation to varying degrees as they pull us into the teller's point of view (Riessman, 1991).

Narrative Structures

Like weight-bearing walls, personal narratives depend on certain structures to hold them together. Stories told in conversation share common parameters, although they may be put together in contrasting ways and, as a result, point to different interpretations. Events become meaningful because of their placement in a narrative.

Labov's (1972, 1982; Labov & Waletzky, 1967) structural approach is paradigmatic: Most investigators cite it, apply it, or use it as a point of departure (Langellier, 1989). Narratives, Labov argues, have formal properties and each has a function. A "fully formed" one includes six common elements: an abstract (summary of the substance of the narrative), orientation (time, place, situation, participants), complicating action (sequence of events), evaluation (significance and meaning of the action, attitude of the narrator), resolution (what finally happened), and coda (returns the perspective to the present). With these structures, a teller constructs a story from a primary experience and interprets the significance of events in clauses and embedded evaluation. Using Labov's structural categories to analyze the story of a teacher/parent, Attanucci (1991) shows how multiple interpretations of the moral dilemma he relates are possible. Dichotomous formulations like justice and care (Brown, Tappan, Gilligan, Miller, & Argyris, 1989; Gilligan, 1982) ignore the ambiguities of language that attention to structure brings into view.

Burke's (1945) classic method of analyzing language—dramatism— offers another structural approach that has potential application to a variety of types of narrative, including stories. The grammatical resources that individuals employ to tell persuasive tales are contained in a pentad of terms: act, scene, agent, agency, purpose. "Any complete statement about motives will offer *some kind of* answer to these five questions: What was done (act), when or where it was done (scene), who did it (agent), how he [or she] did it (agency), and why (purpose)" (Burke, 1945, p. xv). Using Burke's grammar to make sense of the contrasting accounts husbands and wives told about a violent incident in marriage, Hydén (1992) shows how male perpetrators favored words that emphasize purpose (*why* he acted as he did), whereas wives emphasize agency (*how* he beat her) and the consequences of the act, both physical and emotional. Hydén relates these language differences to broader themes about the social construction of gender in violent marriages.

Still another approach to structure is represented by Gee (1986), who attends to how a story is said. Drawing on the oral rather than text-based tradition in sociolinguistics, he analyzes changes in pitch, pauses, and other features that punctuate speech that allow interpreters to hear groups of lines together. Using poetic units, stanzas, and strophes to examine the talk of a woman hospitalized for schizophrenia, he shows how organized, coherent, and senseful her speech is (Gee, 1991).[16]

Forms of Telling: Context and Meaning

Narrativization tells not only about past actions but how individuals understand those actions, that is, meaning. Plots vary in type: tragedy, comedy, romance, and satire (H. White, 1973). Tellers pour their ordinary lives into these archetypal forms.

Narrators indicate the terms on which they request to be interpreted by the styles of telling they choose. Something said in a whisper, after a long pause, has a different import than the same words said loudly, without a pause. Tellers use elongated vowels, emphasis, pitch, repetition, and other devices to indicate what is important. Emotion is also carried in these and other audible aspects, although much more research is needed on how affect enters into a narrative. Forms of transcription that neglect features of speech miss important information.

Labov's (1972, 1982; Labov & Waletzky, 1967) structures provide another way into the interpretation of meaning. Narrators say in evaluation clauses (the soul of the narrative) how they want to be understood and what the point is. Every good narrator tries to defend against the implicit accusation of a pointless story, warding off the question: "So what?" In evaluation clauses, which typically permeate the narrative, a teller stands back from the unfolding action and tells how he or she has chosen to interpret it (but see Culler, 1980; Toolan, 1988). Representing a narrative about a moral dilemma with and without the evaluation clauses, Attanucci (1991) displayed how interpretation shifts; "evaluation infuses the account with values and meaning" (p. 323). Access to these and other structures that carry meaning depends on how we, as analysts, create texts from talk: representing speech in continuous lines compared to clauses that allow for structural analysis (Level 3 in Figure 10.1).

Narrative theorists disagree on the importance of the interview context (Level 2) in the analysis of narrative (Level 4). Labov's model leaves out the relationship of teller and listener: "His assumption [is] that narrative is a relation among clauses rather than an interaction among participants" (Langellier, 1989, p. 248). At the other extreme is the Personal Narratives Group (1989b), who examine power relations in the production of personal narratives: Who asks the questions and for what purpose? Some narrative analysts, as detailed below, bring the interviewer into the analysis by including his or her guiding questions, nonlexical utterances, and other signs of puzzlement and understanding (Paget, 1983), showing how meaning is interactionally accomplished. Labov avoided the question of whether a "story is being told primarily in order to report a sequence of events or in order to tell a tellable story" (Culler, 1980, p. 36). Viewing storytelling as a kind of performance (Goffman, 1974; Toolan, 1988), a teller has a fundamental problem: how to convince a listener who was not there that something important happened. In divorce narratives, for example, individuals tell about times in their troubled marriages and persuade through rhetorically effective forms of symbolic expression—how they craft their tales in collaboration with a listener—that the decision to divorce was justified (Riessman, 1990a). Language, as Burke (1950) said, "is not merely descriptive . . . not just trying to tell people how things are. . . . [I]t is trying to *move people*" (p. 41).

Language has three analytically distinct but interdependent functions (Halliday, 1973), and all are essential for the interpretation of meaning. The ideational function expresses the referential meaning of what is said: "content in terms of the speaker's experience and that of the speech community" (p. 37). The interpersonal function concerns the role relationship between speakers, which allows for the expression of social and personal relations through talk. The textual function refers to structure, how parts of a text are connected syntactically and semantically. Meaning is conveyed at all three levels, although the ideational function tends to dominate communication, that is, informational content about people, situations, and ideas that speakers mean their words to convey. But the meaning of what someone says is not simply its content (ideational); how something is said (textual) in the context of the shifting roles of speaker and listener (interpersonal) is critical also. Narrative analysis provides methods for examining, and relating, meaning at all three levels.

The larger social context is important, too, although scholars differ in the extent to which they include it. At one extreme are the conversation analysts (who rarely include anything as long as a narrative in their samples of talk); focus is limited to what participants say and do in a particular interaction. For the Personal Narratives Group (1989b), context is multilayered, involving the historical moment of the telling, the race, class, and gender systems that narrators manipulate to survive and within which their talk has to be interpreted. My preference sides very much with the latter position; the divorce narratives, for example, would have been impossible to interpret without reference to social discourses and politics, specifically, the transformations in marriage and gender relations of the last 150 years. Women and men made sense of their divorces in narratives that contained assumptions about how marital interactions are supposed to occur in late-20th-century America. The text is not autonomous of its context.

Narrative Truths

Finally, I touch on a thorny problem in narrative research: the truth of what a teller says. The earlier discussion of representation and Figure 10.1 suggest how excruciatingly complex the issue is; we cannot rely on the posture of descriptive realism or external criteria, as in positivist methods. Sarbin (1986a) called narrative a root metaphor:

> a way of organizing episodes, actions, and accounts of actions; it is an achievement that brings together mundane facts and fantastic creations; time and place are incorporated. The narrative allows for the inclusion of actors' reasons for their acts, as well as the causes of happening. (p. 9)

Narrative analysts, in practice, approach the issue of truth differently. Some assume that language represents reality: The narrative clauses recapitulate experience in the same order as the original events (Labov & Waletzky, 1967). Others, influenced by phenomenology, take the position that narrative constitutes reality: It is in the telling that we make real phenomena in the stream of consciousness (see Young, 1987, pp. 186–210). Still others, interested in the persuasive aspects of language, argue that narrators inscribe into their tales their ideologies and interests (for a review, see Langellier, 1989). Veroff, Sutherland, Chadiha, and Ortega (in press), for example, interviewed newly married couples and argued that husbands and wives narrate fictions that they present to a listener. These fictions, in turn, "may be the inspirations for acting out a happy or unhappy married life" (p. 9).

The Personal Narratives Group (1989a) wrote of truths in a way that echoes my position:

> When talking about their lives, people lie sometimes, forget a lot, exaggerate, become confused, and get things wrong. Yet they *are* revealing truths. These truths don't reveal the past "as it actually was," aspiring to a standard of objectivity. They give us instead the truths of our experiences. . . . Unlike the Truth of the scientific ideal, the truths of personal narratives are neither open to proof nor self-evident. We come to understand them only through interpretation, paying careful attention to the contexts that shape their creation and to the world views that inform them. Sometimes the truths we see in personal narratives jar us from our complacent security as interpreters "outside" the story and make us aware that our own place in

the world plays a part in our interpretation and shapes the meanings
we derive from them. (p. 261)

Narratives are interpretive and, in turn, require interpretation: They do
not "speak for themselves," or "provide direct access to other times,
places, or cultures" (p. 264). Our analytic interpretations are partial,
alternative truths that aim for "believability, not certitude, for enlarge-
ment of understanding rather than control" (Stivers, 1993, p. 424). I
return to the issue of validation in the conclusion.

The debates in narrative studies just summarized provide important
background for what follows. I draw on relevant facets—definition of a
narrative, attention to structure, meaning and context—at the same
time I adopt an interpretive view.

❖ PRACTICAL MODELS

Poetic Structures and Meaning

The following example is drawn from my own work. *Divorce Talk*
(Riessman, 1990a) examined how a sample of divorcing individuals
make sense of their marriages and themselves and how the process is
accomplished differently by women and men. Divorce brings in its
stead considerable emotional difficulty for both genders and distinctive health problems for each. I wanted to see how emotional difficulties were voiced, and thus constructed, differently by women and men.
I compared the talk about distress of each gender group and looked at
the relationship between these results and a traditional quantitative
analysis of depression for the sample. The two methods yielded very
different findings and showed that women and men have distinctive
vocabularies of emotion that have not been sufficiently acknowledged
in mainstream mental health research.

Narrative Method

I examined in some detail the talk of six members of my sample
(*N*:105), including Cindy (a pseudonym), portions of whose narrative
are represented in Transcript 10.1. A young single parent on welfare,

(Text Continues on Page 239)

Transcript 10.1   Cindy's Narrative

Frame		
03	I've been walking around	
04	in this for the last month or so	
05	feeling that things are very very hard	
06	like I have a cloud over me and I'm very *confused*	

Affect and conflict		
09	I feel like	Stanza 1
10	I am too burdened	
11	and I can't imagine how	
12	to be less burdened	
13	I feel like	Stanza 2
14	I need to be doing everything I'm doing	
15	and so I don't know how to	
16	take some of the burden	
17	off of myself	
19	Well I need to work	Stanza 3
20	in order to earn a living	(money)
21	I need to	Stanza 4
22	go to school	(school)
23	so that I won't always have to work for nothing	
24	I need to	Stanza 5
25	be a good mother	(care of children)
26	'cause that's very important to me	
27	And I'd like to	Stanza 6
28	find a little free time	(time for self)
29	if I can	

Part 1: Money (narrative)	
33	alot of it has to do with the welfare system changing
35	Well I used to be on welfare
37	. . . they cut me a whole lot
38	because I work also
48	but so my choice at that point was
49	either to go off completely
50	and get money from him
51	or quit working
52	and I
53	at that point it sounded like a good idea
54	to quit work
55	so that I could
56	go to school and not feel
57	like I had so many things to do
58	but um financially I just couldn't do it
59	there was no way I could do it.
60	And so with workfare looming ahead
61	I was worried that I'd get
62	forced out of school

(Continued)

Transcript 10.1 (Continued)

63	and I only have like a year to go
64	so because I didn't want to take a chance
65	of being forced out of school
66	I just quit welfare.
75	I don't know how long my job is going to hold out
78	So my financial situation is just
79	completely unstable at this point.

Part 2: School

| 80 | And I ended up taking two incompletes | Stanza 7 |
| 81 | out of three classes I was taking in school. | |

Summary

82	So it's making me think that	Stanza 8
83	trying to go to school	
84	and work and be a good mother is too much	
85	but I don't know how I can not do it.	

Part 3: Care of children

86	And at the same time for some reason	Stanza 9
87	my son's going through a really clingy spell again	
88	And he probably does it right when I can least	
89	afford to deal with it you know.	

Summary

| 90 | So it's just a lot of stuff all at once | Stanza 10 |
| 91 | in the last month or so. | |

Part 4: Self (narrative)

92	and so I've been
93	with all this other stuff I've been
94	actually needy myself
95	you know wanting
96	wanting someone to come home to
97	who would say "Hey sit down
98	I'll fix you a drink
99	let's chit chat about the day"
100	you know someone to nurture me.
101	And so I've been more aware of
	not having that person.

Frame (return to affect and conflict)

102	I feel like	Stanza 11
103	I have to make a decision	
105	I don't know what to decide so	
106	I'm walking around waiting to decide.	

SOURCE: Adapted from Riessman (1990a). Reprinted by permission from Rutgers University Press and the author.

she had a depression score on the quantitative measure that was near the top of the range for women. As she put it, "Things are very very hard." She described four aspects of her life that were causing her difficulty, and these very nearly mirror the four role strains that predict depression for the entire sample of women in the quantitative analysis: children, money, worry about support payments, and lack of help (see Riessman, 1990a).

The form of Cindy's narrative intrigued me. I did not interview her, my coinvestigator did, and she departed from the structured set of questions after administering the depression scale (perhaps because of the many symptoms noted) and asked about "things that had been hard" lately. Cindy spoke at length about the difficulties she was facing and the emotions she was experiencing. The response "felt" like a narrative when I attempted to code it. I found myself not wanting to fragment it into discrete thematic categories but to treat it instead as a unit of discourse; it "sounded" like a narrative when I went to retranscribe it into a form suitable for that kind of analysis. It seemed to be structurally and thematically coherent and tightly sequenced. But it did not meet Labov's (1972, 1982) criteria: There was no plot in the traditional sense, few narrative clauses, and verbs were often in the present tense, not the simple past. These puzzles prompted me to search for other models for representing the discourse, other ways of understanding how Cindy organized her narrative and how she achieved coherence, so as to better grasp its meaning.

Transcript 10.1 displays my structural analysis of Cindy's narrative, informed in part by the work of James Gee (1985, 1986, 1991) on the poetic features of language. This is an ideal realization of the text, because it excludes interactions between teller and listener, false starts, pauses, discourse markers, nonlexical expressions, and other features of spoken language. (For the full narrative, see Riessman, 1990a, pp. 131–134.)

Cindy frames the narrative with a metaphor that binds the beginning of the narrative inextricably to its conclusion. She begins by likening her state of mind to walking, with a cloud over her, unable to see clearly through it. She refers to her unsettled emotions with this same image again, 10 minutes later in the interview, at the end of her long account ("I'm walking around waiting to decide"). The metaphor lends structural coherence to the narrative and suggests how it is bounded, that is, where it begins and ends. Thematically, the metaphor suggests motion and lack of resolution. Cindy has not arrived on some firm emotional ground.

In my representation, Cindy's speech (probably like all speech, linguists argue) has a stanza form, which lends coherence to the narrative. Stanzas are a series of lines on a single topic that have a parallel structure and sound as if they go together by tending to be said at the same rate and with little hesitation between lines. Gee (1985, 1986, 1991) argued that stanzas are a universal unit in planning speech and that poetry, in fact, builds on what we each do all the time. Poetry "fossilizes" and ritualizes what is in everyday speech. In Cindy's case, she gives in stanzas 3–6 a four-part explanation for why she feels so burdened, an explanation that she later expands in the narrative. As she lists the four areas that in her mind are causing her such difficulty— money, school, child care, and no time for herself—she moves from the outside in, from the most macro to the most micro issues. The tight stanza structure articulates a sense of constraint; the roles of provider, student, and mother create conflict because the expectations of each are so discordant, creating insoluble emotional dilemmas. In moving from the social to the personal, the sequence of the stanzas also suggests that Cindy has turned the responsibility for change from the outside inward. She feels the dilemma is hers to resolve, personally and privately, despite the fact that the sources of her distress are social.

Having outlined her four problems in four stanzas, Cindy develops each theme, amplifying in sequential order each of the causes of her distress. In the first part she explores the problem of money. She describes her struggle to support herself and explicitly locates the cause of the problem in the social environment (i.e., "a lot of it has to do with the welfare system changing"). She tells a narrative to explain "what happened," reconstructing and reinterpreting how state budget cuts, changing welfare policies, workfare, and the uncertainties of her job have made her financial situation "completely unstable."

At the time of the interview, Cindy is experiencing the effects of the first of the Reagan budget cuts in welfare expenditures and the beginnings of a new workfare program, which requires that she register for job training as soon as her child turns 6 (he was 5½). Because she is in a 4-year baccalaureate program (not considered "training" by the welfare department in her state), she stands a good chance of being "forced out of school," with only one year to go before graduating and, presumably, becoming more employable. Caught in the irrationality of these policies, Cindy decides to quit welfare. As a consequence, she must rely on child support payments from her former spouse that, she tells us elsewhere in the interview, are irregular and thus a source of worry.

Cindy leaves the narrative mode after summarizing the first part in lines 78–79. She does not tell another formal narrative again until later but instead uses nonnarrative forms in the middle two parts (Parts 2 and 3 of Transcript 10.1) to explain the sources of her distress and the emotional conflicts they create in her. The second part—about the strain associated with school—merely reports in a couplet, succinctly and tersely, how she resolved the dilemma of role overload. Like her earlier statement about financial strain ("I just quit welfare"), the active voice here says how she resolved her dilemmas ("I ended up taking two incompletes"). As if to summarize, she then explicitly restates the theme of being burdened in a 4-line stanza in lines 82–85. The stanza captures the essence of the bind that welfare policies have created for Cindy: Holding a job is necessary because of welfare cuts and work-fare, but going to school is necessary to get a decent job.

In the third part, Cindy elaborates on her problems being a good parent—her 5-year-old son is "going through a really clingy spell again." He's doing this at a time when she can "least afford to deal with it." The irony in her choice of the word "afford" is apparent. Her emotional resources for parenting are as limited as are her financial ones.

In the summarizing couplet of lines 90–91, Cindy makes a statement that ties the three parts together. The recent past has been especially difficult, she says, because of the combination of money, school, and child-care demands ("a lot of stuff all at once"). It is the piling up of role strains that makes her feel burdened, not any single problem.

The fourth part, lines 92–101, picks up on a theme Cindy put forward earlier (no time for herself) but gives it a twist. In the context of "all this other stuff," she's been feeling "actually needy" herself. It is not time alone that she wants as much as somebody to support and nurture her.

The focus of the fourth part is not on events that have happened but events she wishes would happen, and consequently Cindy tells a hypothetical narrative. Through dialogue, she creates a text within a text, a multivoiced narrative (Wolf & Hicks, 1989) with texture and dimensionality that is emotionally affecting because of both what she says and how she says it. To convey the fantasy, she constructs a hypothetical conversation in lines 96–101. Like her son, she wants someone to hold on to.

Cindy concludes the narrative but does not resolve the dilemmas it sets forth. Unlike many narratives about events that have happened in the past, this one, concerning role strains and distress, lacks firm resolution and closure because the narrator is still in the middle of the conflict. She returns in lines 102–106 to the metaphor of walking, the present tense, the phrase ("I feel like") and the stanza structure with which she began the narrative many minutes before. She is preoccupied with making a decision (she mentions this three times in four lines), but exactly what decision is ambiguous. What is clear is that Cindy feels overwhelmed in the face of multiple pressures with no one to help. Although at one level the origins of her problems are distinctly public, her experience of them is personal and private. As she assesses her situation, it will be "resolved" by some decision *she* has yet to make. No political movement is present in Cindy's account, as in Kay's and Sarah's, that could provide alternative understandings and collective solutions.

Figure 10.2 represents a schematic of the essential tension, as I see it, in the structure of the discourse. Lines 3–29 and lines 102–106 speak of enduring conditions that form the context for two narrative segments. Enduring portions of the discourse are not narrative; they last and have an ongoing quality that testifies to the durative, the progressive, and the nonspecific. It is within these enduring states, which begin and end the discourse, that the two narrative segments are embedded, the first a story about a specific past event involving welfare and workfare (lines 33–79) and the second a hypothetical narrative about a dream of being nurtured (lines 92–101). Although there are parts in between, these two narratives are counterposed, which attests to an essential dilemma: the actual and the possible, the real and the wished-for. Just as Cindy's explanation pivots on thematic contrasts (welfare vs. school, child vs. self), so too does its form, juxtaposing the nonnarrative and the narrative, the story and the dream.[17] Like the previous two examples, this is a narrative about discordance: the breach in the ordinary, expected course of a human life, a theme that Cindy realizes through the tight organization of a narrative.

To summarize, my approach offers another model for analyzing extended stretches of talk in research interviews that feel like narratives. It involves reducing a long response, parsing it according to a set of rules into lines, stanzas, and parts, examining its organizing metaphors, and creating a schematic to display the structure—a very

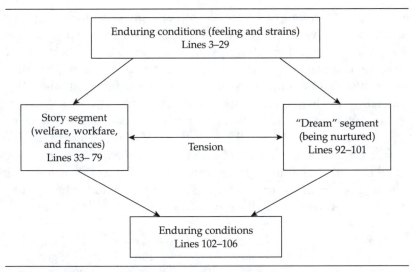

Figure 10.2

different form of analysis than in the previous two examples.[18] (The section below headed "Doing Narrative Analysis" gives more detail on how the reduction was made.)

Questions

Because this is my work, I find it somewhat difficult to examine it critically, but let me try. First, how has talk been transformed into a written text, and how are narrative segments determined? Cindy's long response is reduced, not to a core narrative or skeleton plot—which would leave practically nothing—but with reference to Gee's (1985, 1986, 1991) theory of the units of speech. He draws on oral rather than written, text-based models of language and emphasizes prosodic and paralinguistic aspects, such as changes in pitch and intonation. To discern patterning, I attend to how the narrative is said, that is, the organization of the discourse system into lines, stanzas, and parts. The representation of talk and mode of analysis could be accused of formalism (for a response to this criticism, see Gee, 1991, pp. 15–16), and one potential publisher called my approach "pretentious."

When I began working on Cindy's long response with Gee's theory of discourse units, I was initially skeptical. I wondered whether speech is, in fact, structured as he argues and still prefer to think of poetic structures as a way to represent discourse, not intrinsic to it. Whatever the philosophical differences, repeated listening to tapes sensitized me to subtleties of language that I never was aware of before, and certainly never attended to in previous transcripts—intonation contours, rising and falling pitch, pauses and discourse markers (well, and, so, nonlexical expressions like "uh") that, Gee argues, set off stanzas in a narrative. I found that each of the four parts of Cindy's narrative (see Transcript 10.1) is, in fact, set off with such a marker. As I became more familiar with the transcription conventions, I heard structure: the building blocks of the narrative, groups of lines said together about a single topic, a vignette, in the form of a stanza.

> Each stanza is a particular "take" on a character, action, event, claim, or piece of information, and each involves a shift of focal participants, focal events, or a change in the time or framing of events from the preceding stanza. Each stanza represents a particular perspective, not in the sense of who is doing the seeing, but in terms of what is seen; it represents an image, what the "camera" is focused on, a "scene." (Gee, 1991, pp. 23–24)

The transcript represents a reduction based on my hearing, with the earphones of Gee's theory on my head, of how Cindy said her reply to the question about "things that had been hard" lately. The form of representation draws attention to the transcribing/analyzing interface in Figure 10.1, namely, how decisions about displaying talk are inseparable from the process of interpretation.

Ironically, certain features of speech that are critical to analyzing the structure of the narrative are excluded from the representation of it (e.g., pauses and discourse markers). The interaction between teller and listener that produced the narrative is also not represented. There is no place for an emotional moment between the women as the narrative ends (immediately after the hypothetical narrative in Part 4, there is a long pause, broken by what sounds like sniffling, followed by joint laughing). It could even be argued that Gee's method strips the interview context from the narrative. (Because of this concern, I elected in *Divorce Talk* to present the full response and Transcript 10.1, a strategy that required some persuasion of my editor.)

What is the definition of narrative here? I use the term two ways: first, to describe Cindy's entire response, which meets general criteria (sequence, thematic, and structural coherence); and second, to describe Parts 1 and 4, which meet more limited criteria (temporal order, evaluation). In Figure 10.2, I am departing from Gee's method but make a similar argument for a complex discourse form: embedded narrative segments within an overarching narrative that includes nonnarrative parts. Labov's (1972, 1982; Labov & Waletzky, 1967) theory and the relatively simple stories he analyzes do not provide an adequate model for subjective experiences, events that unfold over time and even extend into the present, as Cindy's narrative does. Hers is as much about affective "actions," things the narrator feels and says to herself, as it is about "what happened" in a more objective sense.[19]

Second, what aspects of the narrative constitute the basis for interpretation? Obviously not interaction; the focus of attention here is on linguistic choices Cindy makes and the patterning of her discourse, or how the text is spoken. Gee (1991) argued that many interpretations are ruled out by the structure of the spoken narrative. My interpretation takes account of structural properties (frames, stanzas, parts), key metaphors (walking), key words ("afford"), verb tense ("I got cut way down" vs. "I just quit welfare"), how substantive themes get developed through these, and other linguistic choices. I go beyond the text and make inferences about context, informed by my politics, notably changing welfare policies and their effect on the situation of single mothers in U.S. society.

By excluding the interaction between teller and listener that produced the narrative, I treat it as sole-authored, as "inside" the designated narrator. The situation of its telling is not part of the interpretation, that is, how the account takes a particular shape and meaning because of the interactional context. It could be argued, for example, that Cindy develops her narrative this way because both speakers agree on a topic, "things that have been hard lately." A different kind of interaction might have produced a different account. (For an extension of Gee's approach to discourse between speakers, see Mishler, 1992.)

Finally, who determines what the narrative means, and are alternative readings possible? Cindy's words and my interpretations are both available, although they are conflated by the way talk is represented (the case in all three examples). The basis for my interpretations, particularly about structure, is not visible in Transcript 10.1, only in the full response (portions of which are reproduced in the following section).

The teller has, if not the final word, at least the first word on which interpretation depends.

When I was analyzing Cindy's long narrative, I was led into my sense of it by its organization. She could have said what she had to say in several different ways. What did the form she chose signify? I claim that we can come close to seeing into her subjective experience—what life "means" to her at the moment of telling—through experiencing the tension in the structure of the narrative (the juxtaposition of the real and the wished for, the story and the dream).[20]

❖ DOING NARRATIVE ANALYSIS

How does an investigator do narrative work? A series of interpretive decisions confront all investigators. Returning to Figure 10.1, investigators must consider how to facilitate narrative telling in interviews (Level 2), transcribe for the purposes at hand (Level 3), and approach narratives analytically (Level 4). My thoughts on these issues are offered, not as a set of prescriptions but as guidelines for getting started. There is no standard set of procedures compared to some forms of qualitative analysis.

Telling

To encourage those we study to attend to and tell about important moments in their lives, it is necessary to provide a facilitating context in the research interview, which implicates the interview schedules we develop. Certain kinds of open-ended questions are more likely than others to encourage narrativization. Compare "When did X happen?" which asks for a discrete piece of information, with "Tell me what happened," which asks for a more extended account of some past time. It is preferable to ask questions that open up topics and allow respondents to construct answers, in collaboration with listeners, in the ways they find meaningful (Mishler, 1986). But even questions that could be answered by a yes or no can generate extended accounts: Studying racism in the everyday lives of black women, Essed (1988) asked, "Have you ever experienced discrimination when you applied for a job?"; many women responded with stories.

To study violence, Labov (1982) asked inner-city youth, "Were you ever in a situation where you thought you were in serious danger of getting killed?" To study moral conflict among teachers/parents, Attanucci (1991) asked, "Would you describe a time when you weren't sure what the right thing to do was and you had to decide?" Because the impulse to narrate is so natural, and apparently universal, it is almost inevitable that these kinds of questions will produce narrative accounts, provided interviewing practices do not get in the way.

Some investigators have developed visual aids to elicit narratives. Veroff et al. (in press) gave the following instructions to the newlywed couples they interviewed:

> Tell me in your own words the story of your relationship. I have no set questions to ask you. . . . I just want you to tell me about your lives together as if it were a story with a beginning, a middle and how things will look in the future. . . there is no right or wrong way to tell your story . . . just tell me in any way that is most comfortable. . . . it's something that couples really enjoy doing . . . each of you can talk, and I hope to hear from both of you. . . . you can agree about the story; you can disagree . . . any way that seems comfortable for you.

To facilitate recall, the interviewer presents a storyboard to the couple and says:

> To help you think of your story, this describes most people's storyline. You see that a storyline for a marriage usually includes each of these parts: how you met; how you got interested in one another; becoming a couple; planning to get married; the wedding itself; what life was like after the wedding; what married life is like right now; and what you think married life will be like in the future. . . . to get you started why don't each of you tell me what your life was like before the two of you met?. . . . now let's hear the story of your relationship. How did it all begin? (pp. 11–12)

Interestingly, couples do not always follow instructions; they do not tell their stories in the linear form Veroff et al. (in press) are looking for.

My preference is for less structure in interview instruments, in the interest of giving greater control to respondents. I advise my students to develop an interview guide (Merton, Fiske, & Kendall, 1956/1990): 5 to 7 broad questions about the topic of inquiry, supplemented by probe questions in case the respondent has trouble getting started ("Can you tell me more about that?" "What was the experience like for you?"). Interviews are conversations in which both participants—teller and listener/questioner—develop meaning together, a stance requiring interview practices that give considerable freedom to both. Listeners can clarify uncertainties with follow-up questions, and "the answers given continually inform the evolving conversation" (Paget, 1983, p. 78).

As someone who has done quantitative and qualitative analysis and attempted to join them in a single study (Riessman, 1990a), I advise students that open-ended questions designed to produce narrative accounts can be combined in the same interview with closed-ended items or self-administered questionnaires. Different data collection methods yield different information, and they have to be interpreted differently. Students typically have to meet academic departmental expectations for quantification, and the approach is better suited to collect certain kinds of data, such as demographic information. Students who combine methods will have to cross borders, risk being defined as illegal aliens, transgress the "hedgerows that define and protect traditional interests and practices" (Mishler, 1991a, p. 102).

Returning to research interviews, narratives often emerge when you least expect them. In studying divorcing women and men, for example, my coinvestigator and I adapted an item originally used by Goode (1956): "Would you state, in your own words, what was the main cause of your divorce" (p. 359). We expected the question to stimulate a list of marital problems, which we could code thematically, as Goode had, and compare the "themes of complaint" in marriages in the 1980s with those in the 1950s. In response to the question, however, many in our sample took the floor and told long stories about their marriages: how they began, what happened during the course, the moment that turned the tide, and so on. In these evolving accounts, an initial complaint often turned out not to be the reason the individual finally decided to leave. (I suspect Goode's sample tried to tell stories too.)

Provided investigators can give up control over the research process and approach interviews as conversations, almost any question can generate a narrative. Sociolinguists argue that events must be "reportable" to warrant a lengthy turn at talk in everyday conversation (Labov, 1982; Polanyi, 1985), but the opposite is also true; tellers can make events reportable in any interaction by making a story out of them. Presumably anything of an experiential nature is worthy of a lengthy account or at least can be made so.

Transcribing

"Crunching text requires text to first be put in crunchable form" (Van Maanen, 1988, p. 131). Taping and transcribing are absolutely essential to narrative analysis. Students invariably struggle with the issue of how to transcribe the tapes of interviews, which in qualitative interviews are often lengthy. Unfortunately, there is no easy answer here because transforming talk into written text, precisely because it is a representation, involves selection and reduction. My general advice is to begin with a rough transcription, a first draft of the entire interview that gets the words and other striking features of the conversation on paper (e.g., crying, laughing, very long pauses). Then go back and retranscribe selected portions for detailed analysis.

In settings where the telling of long stories is not expected, such as medical interviews, patients often have to fight for the floor to tell one. Mishler, Clark, Ingelfinger, and Simon (1989) and Clark and Mishler (1992) selected from rough transcriptions those segments for retranscription that best displayed the subtle process of negotiation between doctor and patient about the relevance of a personal narrative to the medical problem at hand. In one text, the physician fails to attend to the patient's story and she becomes visibly upset, whereas in another case a physician facilitates the development of a story that is essential to the diagnosis. Texts created in retranscription allowed for analysis of interruptions, pauses, and other spoken features of discourse that distinguished attentive patient care.

Investigators often delegate transcription to others, such as graduate students and secretaries. Scholars from a particular theoretical persuasion (e.g., ethnomethodology) often want more detailed transcriptions from the onset, and there are clerical workers who are accustomed to these requests and highly skilled in their ability to represent discourse on a two-dimensional page. Most transcribers, however, will need considerable guidance about how precise to be.

An experience taught me about the issues firsthand. Early in the divorce study, when my coinvestigator went back to check the accuracy of the transcriptions, she discovered utterances on the tape that did not appear in the typescript. In response to our query, the transcriber said she left out asides, talk that "wasn't in answer to the question." Yet these seeming irrelevancies provided context essential to interpretation and, not infrequently, the asides were narratives, the heart of the matter. The edited transcriptions had to be redone.

I spend considerable time scrutinizing the rough drafts of transcriptions, often across a number of interviews, before going to the next level. It is here that analytic induction (Katz, 1983) is most useful. A focus for analysis often emerges, or becomes clearer, as I see what respondents say. Studies, like narrative accounts, are jointly produced; as investigators interact with subjects, analytic ideas change (Mishler, 1992). As I scrutinize transcripts, features of the discourse often "jump out," stimulated by prior theoretical interests and "fore-structures" of interpretation (Heidegger, 1927/1962).

I remember, for example, working with the transcript of an interview with a working-class Puerto Rican woman and noticing places where the middle-class Anglo interviewer misunderstood the sequence of the narrative. Because of a long-standing interest in class and cultural diversity, the interaction caught my attention. To locate more precisely the source of the failure in communication, I needed to relisten to the tape and produce a more detailed rendering of key moments in the conversation. Close textual analysis revealed contrasting assumptions about time between the women—whether a narrative should be organized temporally or topically, not present in interviews between Anglos, which I related to broader cultural themes (Riessman, 1987). Trouble in interaction provided a fruitful beginning point.

I know of no way to avoid the painstaking work of personally retranscribing the sections of text that appear to take a narrative form (which I put brackets around as I'm working with the rough drafts, most of which are nonnarrative, e.g., question-and-answer exchanges, arguments, chronicles, and other forms of discourse). In my experience, the task of identifying narrative segments and their representation cannot be delegated. It is not a technical operation but the stuff of analysis itself, the "unpacking" of structure that is essential to interpretation. By transcribing at this level, interpretive categories emerge, ambiguities in language are heard on the tape, and the oral record—the way the story is told—provides clues about meaning. Insights from these various sources shape the difficult decision about how to represent oral discourse as a written text.

Determining where a narrative begins and ends and the listener/questioner's place in producing it are textual as well as analytic issues. Listening for entrance and exit talk (Jefferson, 1979) often helps define relatively simple narratives. For example, a divorcing man I interviewed complained that his wife put the children before him, then said, "And I'll clarify this with an example," to which I replied, "O.K." We negotiated in this brief exchange an opening in the conversation for a narrative. He then told a long story, which I did not interrupt except to say "uh-huh," about a particular time where his wife refused to accompany him to a dog show (see Riessman, 1990a, pp. 103–104). The word "example" introduced the past-time world of the story, and he made the same word choice many minutes later to signal an exit from the world; the incident was "a classic example of the whole relationship," and he returned from past to present time. Not all narratives are so clearly bounded. Bell (1988) shows how the listener supplies the abstract for several stories.

Once the boundaries of a narrative segment are chosen, I find it useful in retranscribing to parse the narrative into numbered lines. (Jefferson, 1979, presented a widely used system of typescript notation; also see West, 1984, pp. 42–44.) I use Labov's (1972, 1982) framework to see how simple narratives are organized, an essential first step to interpreting them. To review, well-formed stories, according to Labov, are made from a common set of elements and every clause has a function: to provide an abstract for what follows (A), orient the listener (O), carry the complicating action (CA), evaluate its meaning (E), and resolve the action (R). Table 10.1 shows on the left a rough transcription of a portion of a divorce narrative and, on the right, my retranscription of the same stretch of talk into clauses that correspond to Labov's functional elements (noted at the end of each line). Notice how the representation on the left excludes disfluencies and subtle features of the discourse present in the representation on the right, like short pauses (p), utterances of the interviewer (I: uh-huh), verbal emphasis, and word repetitions.

Many narratives do not lend themselves to Labov's framework, although the model often provides a useful starting point. Narratives are not a singular form of discourse, and cross-cultural studies suggest variation in story grammar (McCabe, 1991, in press; Michaels, 1981; Riessman, 1987). Labov makes strong claims from his limited materials for clear beginnings and endings to stories, but there are few rules for partitioning more complex stretches from interviews that feel like narrativizations. Boundaries may depend on the

Table 10.1

Rough Transcription	Retranscription	
This is actually a crucial incident because I finally got up and went into the other room. She was [talking to her lover on the phone] in the laundry room with the door closed. I knocked on the door and said, "When are you going to be done with this?" 'Cause we were going to talk. And she held her hand like this and went "No." And I got absolutely bullshit. I put my fist through the door, which is not the kind of stuff that I do, you know. I'm not a real physically violent person at all.	30	and (p) finally, ah it's, this is actually a crucial incident [A]
	31	because I *finally* got up and (p) [CA]
	32	and (p) went into the other room [CA]
	33	(p) she was in the laundry room with the door closed and [O]
	34	(p) knocked on the door and said [CA]
	35	"When are you going to be done with this?" [CA]
	36	'cause we, we were going to talk. [O]
	37	And she kind of held up her hand like this and went "no." [CA]
	38	And I got absolutely bullshit [E]
	39	I put my *fist* through the door (I:uh-huh) [R]
	40	which is not the kind of stuff that I, that I do, you know [E]
	41	I'm *not* a real physically violent person at *all*. [E]

investigator's overall framework and vice versa: One can locate stories and other narrative segments in a stretch of talk and inductively build a framework. Informants direct interpretation by the way they organize their narratives, including parts and their relation to the whole.

Although parsing helps to closely examine a text, collaborators can differ in parsing the same text. Some variation should be expected "because hearers and readers hear and read differently from each other, and differently from what speakers and writers may intend" (Gee, 1991, p. 27). Figure 10.1 and my earlier discussion suggest how multilayered interpretation is.

Analyzing

Analysis cannot be easily distinguished from transcription. As Mishler (1991b) noted, "How we arrange and rearrange the [interview] text in light of our discoveries is a process of testing, clarifying and deepening our understanding of what is happening in the discourse" (p. 277). Close and repeated listenings, coupled with methodical transcribing, often leads to insights that in turn shape how we choose to represent an interview narrative in our text. As the research report is being prepared, there is also, of course, much more explicit reliance on preferred concepts and theories.

It is not always clear at the beginning of a research project what features of speech will prove to be essential.[21] I discourage students from tightly specifying a question that they will answer with data from narrative accounts because analytic induction, by definition, causes questions to change and new ones to emerge.

Two strategies for data reduction and interpretation are reduction to the core narrative (used by Bell, 1988) and the analysis of poetic structures. Both involve a selection of key aspects of a longer narrative and, for those interested in adapting these approaches, it may help to show more precisely how reductions are made.

The left side of Table 10.2 displays a segment of a narrative, already retranscribed into lines, in which Sarah tells about her DES experience. On the right is Bell's (1988) reduction. The core narrative, which includes all of Labov's elements except evaluation, provides a skeleton plot, a generalizable structure that investigators could use to compare the plots of individuals who share a common life event.

Turning to my reduction of Cindy's account of her emotions and burden, Table 10.3 displays two representations of the first 29 lines. On the left is my retranscription into numbered lines, which are noticeably shorter than Bell's because I was guided by Gee's framework rather than Labov's. I listened for the speaker's changes in pitch to make line breaks rather than attending to the function of a clause in the narrative. Notice how my subsequent reduction of the narrative segment, on the right side of Table 10.3, excludes all the interviewer's utterances, as well as the teller's false starts, breakoffs, and other features that obscure the poetic structures I am interested in. Others are extending Gee's approach to analyze interaction (Mishler, 1992).

Table 10.2

Retranscribed Version of Sarah's Story	Core Narrative of Sarah's Story	
001 L: uh (1) the way I've usually started these is to ask	Abstract	
002 how you found out you were a DES daughter,	002 L:	how you found out you were a DES daughter
003 and what it was like.	003	and what it was like:
004 N: (1) um, it's funny because the, details are fuzzy, in my head	Orientation	
005 what I, think happened, was um (1) (tch)	006 N:	when I was around 19,
006 when I was around 19,	008	I was in college
007 I we-	Complicating action	
008 I was in college	009	and I went, to a, a gyneco-logist to get birth control
009 and I went, to a, a gynecologist to get birth control	011	he was, he knew that I was a DES daughter because I had adenosis (1) um,
010 and, I happened to be lucky with my first exam	012	so he, told y'know he told me (2.5)
011 he was, he knew that I was a DES daughter because I had adenosis (1) um	016	I think shortly after that,
012 so he, told y'know he told me (2.5)	017	[my mother] told me,
013 and I don't remember how it became (laughs) clear between my mother and I,	018	um and I either said "I know already" or, (inhale)
014 that (1.5) that uh 'cause she didn't know I was going to the gynecologist	Resolution/coda	
015 that she (1)	022	and I was so concerned at the time about getting birth control,
016 I think shortly after that,	023	that I think it sort of didn't, um,
017 she told me	024	it never really, became the major part of my life
018 um and I either said "I know already" or, (inhale)	025	(tch) (1.5) it sort of f'flitted in and out
019 um (1) but I didn't learn from her directly first		
020 um I learned it from this doctor (1.5)		
021 L: uhm		
022 N: and I was so concerned at the time about getting birth control,		
023 that I think it sort of didn't, um,		
024 it never really, became the major part of my life		
025 it sort of f'flitted in and out (tch)		

To avoid the tendency to read a narrative simply for content, and the equally dangerous tendency to read it as evidence for a prior theory, I recommend beginning with the structure of the narrative: How is it organized? Why does an informant develop her tale *this* way

Table 10.3

Retranscription	Analysis of Poetic Structures
01 About (p) things that are hard?	FRAME
02 Well um I don't know what's hard (laughs)	03 I've been walking around
	04 in this for the last month or so
03 I've been walking around	05 feeling that things are very
04 in this for the last month or so	very hard
05 feeling that things are very very hard	06 like I have a cloud over me and
06 like I have a cloud over me	I'm very *confused*
07 and I'm very confused	AFFECT AND CONFLICT
08 and I can't (P)	**Stanza 1**
09 I feel like	09 I feel like
10 I am too burdened	10 I am too burdened
11 and I can't imagine how	11 and I can't imagine how
12 to be less burdened	12 to be less burdened
13 I feel like	**Stanza 2**
14 I I need to be doing everything I'm doing	13 I feel like
15 (P) and so I don't know how to	14 I *need* to be doing everything I'm doing
16 take some of the burden	15 and so I don't know how to
17 off of myself (P)	16 take some of the burden
18 *Int.*: Why do you think you need to be doing everything?	17 off of myself
19 Cindy: (P) Well ah I I need to work	ENDURING ROLE STRAINS
20 in order to earn a living.	**Stanza 3 (money)**
21 (p) I need to ah	19 Well I need to work
22 go to school	20 in order to earn a living
23 So that I won't always have to work for nothing.	**Stanza 4 (school)**
24 I need to	21 I need to
25 be a good mother	22 go to school
26 'cause that's very important to me.	23 so that I won't always have to work for nothing
27 (P) And (P) I'd like to	**Stanza 5 (care of children)**
28 find a little free time	24 I need to
29 if I can (laughs).	25 be a good mother
	26 'cause that's very important to me
	Stanza 6 (time for self)
	27 And I'd like to
	28 find a little free time
	29 if I can

in conversation with *this* listener? To the fullest extent possible, I start from the inside, from the meanings encoded in the form of the talk, and expand outward, identifying, for example, underlying propositions that make the talk sensible, including what is taken for granted by speaker and listener. The strategy privileges the teller's experience, but interpretation cannot be avoided. Individuals' narratives are situated in particular interactions but also in social, cultural, and institutional discourses, which must be brought to bear to interpret them. Nor can investigators bypass difficult issues of power: Whose voice is represented in the final product? How open is the text to other readings? How are we situated in the personal narratives we collect and analyze? It is essential, in my view, to open up these interpretive issues for readers to see.

Ultimately, of course, the features of an informant's narrative account an investigator chooses to write about are linked to the evolving research question, theoretical/epistemological positions the investigator values, and, more often than not, her personal biography. If this circularity makes some readers uncomfortable, I can only offer the comfort of a long tradition of interpretive and hermeneutic inquiry. Close analysis of narrative derives legitimation from this tradition and also extends it in new ways.

❖ CONCLUSION

Two large issues remain: validation and the limits of narrative analysis. They represent as-yet unresolved dilemmas for the field. I open up the topics here in the hope that future investigators will carry them forward.

Validation

How are we to evaluate a narrative analysis? Can one tell a better one from a worse one? Prevailing concepts of verification and procedures for establishing validity (from the experimental model) rely on realist assumptions and consequently are largely irrelevant to narrative studies. A personal narrative is not meant to be read as an exact record of what happened, nor is it a mirror of a world "out there." Our readings of data are themselves located in discourses (e.g., scientific, feminist, and therapeutic).

Some might say the criteria of art are sufficient for appraising a "blurred genre" (Geertz, 1983): Does a narrative analysis move us? If narrative work is viewed as literary craft rather than a social scientific activity (Manning, 1987), art is sufficient. Although I welcome artistic representations (too much social science writing is formulaic and technically compulsive), there is need for something more, in my view. What that "more" might be is the topic of this section.

I present a few caveats and distinctions first. The historical truth[22] of an individual's account is not the primary issue. Narrativization assumes point of view. Facts are products of an interpretive process; "facts and interpretations require and shape one another" (Stivers, 1993, p. 421). Individuals construct very different narratives about the same event (Chafe, 1980); there are marked disparities between the ordering of telling and the ordering of occurrences in something as straightforward as a horse race (Goodman, 1980). It is always possible to narrate the same events in radically different ways, depending on the values and interests of the narrator. Telling about complex and troubling events *should* vary because the past is a selective reconstruction. Individuals exclude experiences that undermine the current identities they wish to claim (remember the Anita Hill–Clarence Thomas hearings).

Of course, some individuals lie (I believe Anita Hill) and investigators may apply narrative methods to try to expose lying and uncover what "really happened." But, as Bruner argued (1987), verification criteria turn slippery: Is it adequate that the "story 'covers' the events of a life? But what is coverage? Are not omissions also important? . . . A rousing tale of a life is not necessarily a 'right' account" (p. 14). Plots are not innocent; they have agendas hidden in them that shape what gets excluded and included, as fact and fiction merge. But

> the stories that persons live by are rarely, if ever, "radically constructed"—it is not a matter of them being made-up, "out of the blue," so to speak. Our culturally available and appropriate stories about personhood and about relationships have been historically constructed and negotiated in communities of persons, and within the context of social structures and institutions. (M. White, 1992, p. 124)

Narratives are laced with social discourses and power relations, which do not remain constant over time (e.g., the category of sexual harassment). There is no reason to assume that an individual's narrative will, or should be, entirely consistent from one setting to the next. "Each telling presents one possible version of the action in question. . . . [T]he idea of narration [invokes] the inevitability of alternative descriptions" (Schafer, 1992, p. xvi). In cases of severe trauma, for example, survivors experience significant gaps in memory and stories change as missing pieces are recovered (Herman, 1992). In a word, traditional notions of reliability simply do not apply to narrative studies, and validity must be radically reconceptualized (see Mishler, 1990).

Validation, the process through which we make claims for the trustworthiness of our interpretations, is the critical issue. "Trustworthiness" not "truth" is a key semantic difference: The latter assumes an objective reality, whereas the former moves the process into the social world. There are at least four ways of approaching validation in narrative work. Each has possibilities but also problems.

Persuasiveness

First, there is the criterion of persuasiveness and its cousin, plausibility. Is the interpretation reasonable and convincing? We have all had the experience of reading a piece of research and thinking "but of course," even when the explanation is counterintuitive (my experience reading Ginsburg's *Contested Lives*, 1989). Persuasiveness is greatest when theoretical claims are supported with evidence from informants' accounts and when alternative interpretations of the data are considered. The criterion forces us to document interpretive statements for the benefit of skeptical outsiders.

As Van Maanen (1988) showed so cleverly, however, different rhetorical styles can be equally persuasive. (He is curiously silent about validity.) Success depends on "the analyst's capacity to invite, compel, stimulate or delight the audience . . . not on criteria of veracity" (Gergen, 1985, p. 272). Persuasiveness ultimately rests on the rhetoric of writing—on literary practices—and reader response. What may be the most persuasive interpretation of a narrative text at one historical moment may not be later. Our texts have unstable meanings.

Correspondence

Second, an investigator can take results back to those studied. Lincoln and Guba (1985) described procedures for "the member check, whereby data, analytic categories, interpretations, and conclusions are tested with . . . those . . . groups from whom the data were originally collected" (p. 314). If the investigator's reconstructions are recognizable as adequate representations, Lincoln and Guba maintain that credibility is increased. In anthropology, informants are beginning to be considered as coauthors (see Behar, 1993) and "the ethnographer as scribe and archivist as well as interpreting observer" (Clifford, 1986, p. 17).

It is desirable, as a general rule, to take work back to the individuals and groups who participated in the study. Bell did this with the DES daughters she interviewed, occasionally giving full transcriptions, while finalizing publication to check that any quoted material had been adequately disguised and securing the informant's consent to use a particular narrative (also see Roberts, 1992). It is important that we find out what participants think of our work, and their responses can often be a source of theoretical insight. Returning our interpretations to their home communities is also politically important. When the activists in Fargo, ND, saw Ginsburg's (1989) analysis of their abortion struggle, it generated dialogue between women who previously thought they had nothing in common. The afterlife of a study can be as instructive as the formal research itself (Blackman, 1992).

Whether the validity of an investigator's interpretations can be affirmed by member checks is, however, questionable. Human stories are not static; meanings of experiences shift as consciousness changes. Nor can our theorizing across a number of narratives be evaluated by individual narrators. They may not even agree with our interpretations (so it is important, whenever possible, to clearly distinguish between our views of subjects' lives and their own; see Stivers, 1993). In the final analysis, the work is ours. We have to take responsibility for its truths.

Coherence

Third, there is the coherence criterion. Agar and Hobbs (1982) posited three kinds: global, local, and themal. To show that an interpretation is more than ad hoc, coherence must be as "thick" as possible, ideally relating to all three levels. Global coherence refers to the overall goals a narrator is trying to accomplish by speaking. This could mean, for example, that an interviewee wants to tell a story about past actions. Or the goal could be strategic—impression management—as I argue in the divorce study (Riessman, 1990a): A narrator's (global) goal in developing an account (speaking) is to justify an action (divorce). Local coherence is what a narrator is trying to effect in the narrative itself, such as the use of linguistic devices to relate events to one another. To return to the divorce narratives, individuals used contrasts, juxtaposing events and actions, to make their points (e.g., an utterance about how an interaction is "supposed" to take place in marriage was paired with one that described just the opposite). Themal coherence involves content: Chunks of interview text about particular themes figure importantly and repeatedly. To use the divorce example once again, individuals developed their narratives around a set of common themes (e.g., lack of intimacy and companionship) and within an interview a theme was worked over, again and again.

Agar and Hobbs (1982) showed, based on an interview with a heroin addict, how sometimes the three types of coherence offer different perspectives on the same discourse problem, whereas at other times they reinforce the same perspective. But, "if an utterance is shown to be understandable in terms of the three kinds of coherence, the interpretation is strengthened" (p. 29).

Investigators must continuously modify initial hypotheses about speakers' beliefs and goals (global coherence) in light of the structure of particular narratives (local coherence) and recurrent themes that unify the text (themal coherence). Interpretation of meaning is constrained by the text in important ways, offering a check on ad hoc theorizing. It is difficult to apply Agar and Hobbs's framework to interaction in interviews, and the model assumes a rational speaker with a discourse plan, which will not suit all investigations.

Pragmatic Use

Lastly, there is the extent to which a particular study becomes the basis for others' work. In contrast to other validation criteria, this one is future oriented, collective, and assumes the socially constructed nature of science. Mishler (1990) argued that "knowledge is validated within a community of scientists as they come to share nonproblematic and useful ways of thinking about and solving problems" (p. 422). Given the conservative nature of normal science (Kuhn, 1962/1970), it is not easy to

> rely on the concepts, methods, and inferences of a study, or tradition of inquiry, as the basis for our own theorizing and empirical work. If our overall assessment of a study's trustworthiness is high enough for us to act on it, we are granting the findings a sufficient degree of validity to invest our own time and energy, and to put at risk our reputations as competent investigators. (Mishler, 1990, p. 419)

However compelling a way of thinking about the problem, Mishler's solution does not help an individual investigator argue in a research report for the validity of a narrative analysis. But we can provide information that will make it possible for others to determine the trustworthiness of our work by (a) describing how the interpretations were produced, (b) making visible what we did, (c) specifying how we accomplished successive transformations (see Figure 10.1), and (d) making primary data available to other researchers. Bell (1988) made the full transcriptions of narratives available upon request; I provided a full text alongside the representation in stanzas and parts. We can, in addition, bring our "foundational assumptions [and values] to the surface, not concealing them underneath the methodological artifice of science" (Agger, 1991, p. 120).

No Canon

From this brief review, it is apparent that validation in narrative studies cannot be reduced to a set of formal rules or standardized technical procedures (they are insufficient in quantitative research too; see Messick, 1987). Scholars from a variety of social science disciplines make the same point:

> The sciences have been enchanted by the myth that the assiduous application of rigorous method will yield sound fact—as if empirical methodology were some form of meat grinder from which truth could be turned out like so many sausages. (Gergen, 1985, p. 273)

The stories we tell, like the questions we ask, are all finally about value. (Cronon, 1992, p. 1376)

> Ethnographic truths are . . . inherently partial—committed and incomplete. (Clifford, 1986, p. 7)

There is no canonical approach in interpretive work, no recipes and formulas, and different validation procedures may be better suited to some research problems than to others. For example, it might be useful to determine whether a case study is recognizable to an informant (correspondence), even if the agendas of narrator and analyst are distinct and not always compatible. Plausibility and coherence might be appropriate criteria for comparative case studies. More general theories, developed from narratives, would depend on usefulness to others (pragmatic criteria). Validation in interpretive work is an ongoing, difficult issue that requires attention by narratologists. (For additional ways to think about the topic in qualitative work, see Cronon, 1992; Katz, 1983; Kirk & Miller, 1986; Lather, 1986; Lincoln & Guba, 1985; Packer & Addison, 1989.)

Uses and Limitations of Narrative Analysis

The approach I have outlined here is appropriate for oral, first-person accounts of experience that take a particular form, what Labov and Waletzky (1967) call "natural narrative." Considerable adaptation and/or other methods will be required if data consist of written narratives, such as letters, archival oral histories, autobiographies, researchers' accounts, scientific representations, and theory itself.

Narrative analysis is not useful for studies of large numbers of nameless, faceless subjects. The methods are slow and painstaking. They require attention to subtlety: nuances of speech, organization of a response, local contexts of production, social discourses that shape what is said, and what cannot be spoken. Not suitable for investigators who seek an easy and unobstructed view of subjects' lives, the analytic detail may seem excessive to those who view language as a transparent medium. As outlined at the beginning of this chapter, developments in social theory call for complex treatments of language, including its constitutive aspects. A danger is that narrative analysis can reify linguistic structures, however.

There is tension in narrative studies between generalization, on the one hand, and the "unpacking" of speech and close attention to narrative form, on the other. Our ultimate goals as social scientists are to learn about substance, make theoretical claims through method, and learn about the general from the particular. Individual action and biography must be the starting point of analysis, not the end. Ironically, Ginsburg (1989) can generalize across cases. It is more difficult for others working with personal narratives to make substantive points across interviews. More than one case study is essential if we want to show variation. To reach theoretical levels of abstraction, comparative work is desirable. Yet sample sizes in narrative studies are small, and cases are often drawn from unrepresentative pools. Although a limitation, eloquent and enduring theories have been developed on the basis of close observation of a few individuals (e.g., Breuer's Anna O., Garfinkel's Agnus, Piaget's children). There is a long tradition in science of building inferences from cases.

Narrative methods can be combined with other forms of qualitative analysis, even with quantitative analysis, as argued earlier. This is not an easy task, however. Some fancy epistemological footwork is required because the interpretive perspective that undergirds narrative is very different from the realist assumptions of many forms of qualitative analysis and certainly of quantification. Combining methods forces investigators to confront troublesome philosophical issues and to educate readers about them. Science cannot be spoken in a singular universal voice. Any methodological standpoint is, by definition, partial, incomplete, and historically contingent. Diversity of representations is needed. Narrative analysis is one approach, not a panacea, suitable for some research situations but not others. It is a useful addition to the stockpot of social science methods, bringing critical flavors to the fore that otherwise get lost. Narrative analysis allows for systematic study of personal experience and meaning: how events have been constructed by active subjects.

❖ NOTES

1. *Text* has multiple meanings in contemporary academic discourse. Learning from a lecture Dorothy Smith gave to the Massachusetts Interdisciplinary Discourse Analysis Seminar (MIDAS) in 1992, I use the word very concretely to refer to work that is reproducible (e.g., transcripts of interviews, drafts, publications).

2. For examples of the latter, see Landau (1984) on evolutionary theory, Cronon (1992) on historical narratives, and Schafer (1992) on psychoanalytic theory.

3. Figure 10.1 is a heuristic, a very imperfect visual representation of my argument. At each level, there is both an addition and a reduction. A student suggested a spiral to depict the process, rather than a series of steps. An editor suggested a sixth level to the figure—rereading—which is an interesting idea that I have entertained when discussing *Madame Bovary*. Visual representations are always partial, incomplete, and limited (Lynch & Woolgar, 1990).

4. Phenomenology is not a uniform philosophical discipline. I am drawing primarily on the work of Husserl, Schutz, and Merleau-Ponty and cannot represent here the many distinctions and differences of emphasis within the movement. For a review, see Stewart and Mickunas (1990).

5. Whether there is raw meaning in the primary experience is a point of difference between Schutz and Merleau-Ponty. There is also considerable debate

among scholars about whether language is added after the image (one sees through words to the designated objects) or whether language is inseparable from perceptions, meaning, and social practice. That experience is entirely an artifact of language is an extreme statement of the latter view—a position I am not taking here. For a review of the various positions on language, reality, and meaning in narrative work, see Polkinghorne (1988, pp. 23–31).

6. I thank Susan Bell for bringing to my attention the relevance of Millett's (1971) work for a discussion of transcription practices.

7. *Theory* is not only something academics construct. I am using the term as phenomenologists, such as Schutz (1932/1967), and feminists, such as Smith (1987) and Sosnoski (1991), do: knowledge found in the ordinary thinking of people in everyday life.

8. As noted above, a transcription is already an interpretation. See Mishler (1991a).

9. Restrictions are now placed by indigenous governments on fieldwork, which "condition in new ways what can, and especially cannot, be said about particular peoples" (Clifford, 1986, p. 9).

10. Early readers play crucial roles in the stories about stories that we tell (see Cronon, 1992).

11. For an example involving gender, consider Geertz's (1973) ethnography of Balinese society. The portrait of the cockfight is about men. Balinese women, and Geertz's wife, get marginalized early in his account. When he interprets the society, he may or may not be extending his points to women. We cannot know, but we can ask and question the examples he chooses.

12. I thank Cheryl Hyde for the insight that my language for the problems of research ("representation") emphasizes choice, the investigator's agency.

13. See Behar (1993) for an example of how class and race cleavages between women (investigator and subject) can be brought into the analysis and thicken it. See hooks (1989) for an articulate feminist voice.

14. Yet there is a danger, particularly in comparative research on gender, of imposing categories derived from Western feminist thought onto non-Western women. I am wary of this new form of Western cultural imperialism.

15. For an example from historical research of inclusion and exclusion of Native Americans in narratives about the Great Plains, see Cronon (1992).

16. Other investigators have also attended to poetic devices in ordinary discourse (see Richardson, 1992; Tannen, 1990).

17. I thank Dennie Wolf for her insights about structural tension in Cindy's narrative and for Figure 10.2, which she drafted.

18. In *Divorce Talk*, I combined the approach with a statistical analysis of the entire sample (Riessman, 1990a). Close attention to Cindy's experience provided a context for interpreting a multiple-regression equation, for example. Lack of money became more than a variable that predicted depression: Emotional distress is produced in Cindy's case by social policies that force women to make choices, among job, school, and welfare eligibility, that compromise their efforts to become self-supporting and bring depression in their stead. Similarly, Cindy's experience with a clingy son and her longing for care herself show what other variables in the quantitative model—child care and lack of help—actually mean in context.

19. For more on Cindy's narrative against Labov's criteria, see Riessman (1990a, pp. 253–254).

20. Some might argue for a different interpretation. Although not working with Cindy's narrative but with one Gee (1991) presents, a very experienced student in my doctoral qualitative analysis class said its meaning was self-evident, that Gee's elaborate structural analysis was not needed to make sense of it. The text we were discussing was the long account of a woman suffering from schizophrenia, which Gee represents in lines, stanzas, and strophes that convincingly display coherence. The next week, as an exercise, I presented the class with a different representation of the same stretch of talk, transcribed the normal way, that is, in continuous lines. Most agreed that in this representation the woman's talk was incoherent, and the clinical psychology students were quick to read it as "loose," a "flight of ideas," prima facie evidence of schizophrenic thought process. The text had a different meaning. The exercise moved us all and convinced everyone (except perhaps the skeptical student) that, although texts can be open to several (but not infinite) readings, meaning and textual representation are dependent on one another.

21. So save tapes. I reused some in the early stages of the divorce study, which made retranscription of narratives from them impossible.

22. Spence (1982, pp. 30–33) makes the distinction in psychoanalysis between historical and narrative truth.

❖ REFERENCES

Agar, M., & Hobbs, J. R. (1982). Interpreting discourse: Coherence and the analysis of ethnographic interviews. *Discourse Processes, 5,* 1–32.

Agger, B. (1991). Critical theory, poststructuralism, postmodernism: Their sociological relevance. *Annual Review of Sociology, 17,* 105–131.

Arendt, H. (1958). *The human condition.* Chicago: University of Chicago Press.

Attanucci, J. (1991). Changing subjects: Growing up and growing older. *Journal of Moral Education, 20,* 317–328.

Bakhtin, M. (1981). *The dialogic imagination.* Austin: University of Texas Press.

Barthes, R. (1974). *Introduction to the structural analysis of the narrative* (R. Miller, Trans). New York: Hill & Wang.

Behar, R. (1993). *Translated woman: Crossing the border with Esperanza's story.* Boston: Beacon.

Bell, S. E. (1988). Becoming a political woman: The reconstruction and interpretation of experience through stories. In A. D. Todd & S. Fisher (Eds.), *Gender and discourse: The power of talk* (pp. 97–123). Norwood, NJ: Ablex.

Blackman, M. B. (1992). The afterlife of the life history. *Journal of Narrative and Life History, 2*(1), 1–9.

Brown, L. M., Tappan, M. B., Gilligan, C., Miller, B. A., & Argyris, D. E. (1989). Reading for self and moral voice: A method of interpreting narratives of real-life moral conflict and choice. In M. J. Packer & R. B. Addison (Eds.), *Entering the circle: Hermeneutic investigation in psychology* (pp. 141–164). Albany: State University of New York Press.

Bruner, J. (1986). *Actual minds, possible worlds.* Cambridge, MA: Harvard University Press.

Bruner, J. (1987). Life as narrative. *Social Research, 54*(1), 11–32.

Bruner, J. (1990). *Acts of meaning.* Cambridge, MA: Harvard University Press.

Burke, K. (1945). Introduction: The five key terms of dramatism. In K. Burke, *A grammar of motives* (pp. xv–xxiii). New York: Prentice Hall.

Burke, K. (1950). *A rhetoric of motives*. New York: Prentice Hall.

Bury, M. (1982). Chronic illness as biographical disruption. *Sociology of Health and Illness, 4*(2), 167–182.

Chafe, W. L. (Ed.). (1980). *The pear stories: Cognitive, cultural and linguistic aspects of narrative production*. Norwood, NJ: Ablex.

Clark, J. A., & Mishler, E. G. (1992). Attending to patients' stories: Reframing the clinical task. *Sociology of Health and Illness, 14*(3), 344–372.

Clifford, J. (1986). Partial truths. In J. Clifford & G. E. Marcus (Eds.), *Writing culture: The poetics and politics of ethnography* (pp. 1–26). Berkeley: University of California Press.

Clifford, J. (1988). *The predicament of culture: Twentieth-century ethnography, literature, and art*. Cambridge, MA: Harvard University Press.

Clifford, J., & Marcus, G. E. (Eds.). (1986). *Writing culture: The poetics and politics of ethnography*. Berkeley: University of California Press.

Cronon, W. (1992). A place for stories: Nature, history, and narrative. *Journal of American History, 78*(4), 1347–1376.

Culler, J. (1980). Fabula and sjuzhet in the analysis of narrative: Some American discussions. *Poetics Today, 1*, 27–37.

Denzin, N. (1988). *Interpretive interactionism*. Newbury Park, CA: Sage.

DeVault, M. L. (1990). Talking and listening from women's standpoint: Feminist strategies for interviewing and analysis. *Social Problems, 37*(1), 96–116.

Essed, P. (1988). Understanding verbal accounts of racism: Politics and heuristics of reality constructions. *Text, 8*(1–2), 5–40.

Fonow, M. M., & Cook, J. A. (Eds.). (1991). *Beyond methodology: Feminist scholarship as lived research*. Bloomington: Indiana University Press.

Gee, J. P. (1985). The narrativization of experience in the oral style. *Journal of Education, 167*(1), 9–35.

Gee, J. P. (1986). Units in the production of narrative discourse. *Discourse Processes, 9*, 391–422.

Gee, J. P. (1991). A linguistic approach to narrative. *Journal of Narrative and Life History, 1*(1), 15–39.

Geertz, C. (1973). *The interpretation of cultures*. New York: Basic Books.

Geertz, C. (1983). Blurred genres: The refiguration of social thought. In C. Geertz, *Local knowledge: Further essays in interpretive anthropology* (pp. 19–35). New York: Basic Books.

Gergen, K. J. (1985). The social constructionist movement in modern psychology. *American Psychologist, 40*(3), 266–275.

Gilligan, C. (1982). *In a different voice: Psychological theory and women's development*. Cambridge, MA: Harvard University Press.

Ginsburg, F. D. (1989). *Contested lives: The abortion debate in an American community*. Berkeley: University of California Press.

Gluck, S. B., & Patai, D. (Eds.).(1991). *Women's words: The feminist practice of oral history*. New York: Routledge.

Godzich, W. (1989). The time machine. In W. Godzich & J. Schulte-Sase (Eds.), *Theory and history of literature: Vol. 64. Narrative on communication* (pp. ix–xvii). Minneapolis: University of Minnesota Press.

Goffman, E. (1959). *The presentation of self in everyday life*. New York: Doubleday.

Goffman, E. (1974). *Frame analysis*. New York: Harper & Row.

Goode, W. J. (1956). *Women in divorce*. New York: Free Press.

Goodman, N. (1980). Twisted tales, or, story, study and symphony. In W. J. T. Mitchell (Ed.), *On narrative* (pp. 99–116). Chicago: University of Chicago Press.

Gorelick, S. (1991). Contradictions of feminist methodology. *Gender & Society, 5*, 459–477.

Halliday, M. A. K. (1973). *Explorations in the functions of language*. London: Edward Arnold.

Heidegger, M. (1962). *Being and time* (J. Macquarrie & E. Robinson, Trans.). New York: Harper & Row. (Original work published 1927)

Herman, J. L. (1992). *Trauma and recovery*. New York: Basic Books.

hooks, b. (1989). *Talking back: Thinking feminist, thinking black*. Boston: South End.

Husserl, E. (1973). *Experience and judgement: Investigation in a genealogy of logic* (J. S. Churchill & K. Amerikas, Trans.). Evanston, IL: Northwestern University Press. (Original work published 1939).

Hydén, M. (1992). *Woman battering as marital act: The construction of a violent marriage*. Unpublished doctoral dissertation, Stockholm University, Department of Social Work.

Jameson, F. (1972). *The prison-house of language*. Princeton, NJ: Princeton University Press.

Jefferson, G. (1979). Sequential aspects of storytelling in conversation. In J. Schenkein (Ed.), *Studies in the organization of conversational interaction* (pp. 219–248). New York: Academic Press.

Katz, J. (1983). A theory of qualitative methodology: The social system of analytic fieldwork. In R. M. Emerson (Ed.), *Contemporary field research: A collection of readings* (pp. 127–148). Boston: Little, Brown.

Kirk, J., & Miller, M. L. (1986). *Reliability and validity in qualitative research* (Qualitative Research Methods Series, Vol. 1). Beverly Hills, CA: Sage.

Kuhn, T. S. (1970). *The structure of scientific revolutions* (2nd ed.). Chicago: University of Chicago Press. (Original work published 1962).

Labov, W. (1972). The transformation of experience in narrative syntax. In W. Labov (Ed.), *Language in the inner city: Studies in the Black English vernacular* (pp. 354–396). Philadelphia: University of Pennsylvania Press.

Labov, W. (1982). Speech actions and reactions in personal narrative. In D. Tannen (Ed.), *Analyzing discourse: Text and talk* (pp. 219–247). Washington, DC: Georgetown University Press.

Labov, W., & Waletzky, J. (1967). Narrative analysis: Oral versions of personal experience. In J. Helm (Ed.), *Essays on the verbal and visual arts* (pp. 12–44). Seattle: University of Washington Press.

Landau, M. (1984). Human evolution as narrative. *American Scientist, 72,* 262–268.

Langellier, K. M. (1989). Personal narratives: Perspectives on theory and research. *Text and Performance Quarterly, 9*(4), 243–276.

Lather, P. (1986). Issues of validity in openly ideological research: Between a rock and a soft place. *Interchange, 17*(4), 63–84.

Lincoln, Y. S., & Guba, E. G. (1985). *Naturalistic inquiry*. Beverly Hills, CA: Sage.

Lynch, M., & Woolgar, S. (Eds.). (1990). *Representation in scientific practice*. Cambridge: MIT Press.

Manning, P. K. (1987). *Semiotics and fieldwork* (Qualitative Research Methods Series, Vol. 7). Newbury Park, CA: Sage.

Martin, W. (1986). *Recent theories of narrative.* Ithaca, NY: Cornell University Press.

McCabe, A. (1991). Haiku as a discourse regulation device. *Language and Society, 20*(4), 577–599.

McCabe, A. (in press). *Chameleon readers.* New York: McGraw-Hill.

Merleau-Ponty, M. (1989). *Phenomenology of perception* (C. Smith, Trans.). London: Routledge. (Original work published 1962)

Merton, R. K., Fiske, M., & Kendall, P. (1990). *The focused interview: A manual of problems and procedures.* New York: Free Press. (Original work published 1956)

Messick, S. (1987). *Validity.* Princeton, NJ: Educational Testing Service.

Michaels, S. (1981). "Sharing time": Children's narrative styles and differential access to literacy. *Language and Society, 10,* 423–442.

Millett, K. (1971). *The prostitution papers: A candid dialogue.* New York: Avon.

Mishler, E. G. (1986). *Research interviewing: Context and narrative.* Cambridge, MA: Harvard University Press.

Mishler, E. G. (1990). Validation in inquiry-guided research: The role of exemplars in narrative studies. *Harvard Educational Review, 60*(4), 415–442.

Mishler, E. G. (1991a). Once upon a time. *Journal of Narrative and Life History, 1*(2), 101–108.

Mishler, E. G. (1991b). Representing discourse: The rhetoric of transcription. *Journal of Narrative and Life History, 1*(4), 255–280.

Mishler, E. G. (1992, August). *Narrative accounts in clinical and research interviews.* Paper presented at the conference "Discourse and the Professions," Swedish Association for Applied Linguistics, Uppsala University.

Mishler, E. G., Clark, J. A., Ingelfinger, J., & Simon, M. P. (1989). The language of attentive patient care: A comparison of two medical interviews. *Journal of General Internal Medicine, 4,* 325–335.

Mitchell, W. J. T. (1990). Representation. In F. Lentricchia & T. McLaughlin (Eds.), *Critical terms for literary study* (pp. 11–22). Chicago: University of Chicago Press.

Nagel, T. (1986). *The view from nowhere.* New York: Oxford University Press.

Nelson, K. (1989). *Narratives from the crib.* Cambridge, MA: Harvard University Press.

Ochs, E. (1979). Transcription as theory. In E. Ochs & B. B. Schieffelin (Eds.), *Developmental pragmatics* (pp. 43–72). New York: Academic Press.

Packer, M. J., & Addison, R. B. (Eds.). (1989). *Entering the circle: Hermeneutic investigation in psychology.* Albany: State University of New York Press.

Paget, M. A. (1983). Experience and knowledge. *Human Studies, 6,* 67–90.

Peller, G. (1987). Reason and the mob: The politics of representation. *Tikkun, 2*(3), 28–95.

Personal Narratives Group. (1989a). Truths. In Personal Narratives Group (Ed.), *Interpreting women's lives: Feminist theory and personal narratives* (pp. 261–264). Indianapolis: Indiana University Press.

Personal Narratives Group. (Ed.). (1989b). *Interpreting women's lives: Feminist theory and personal narratives.* Indianapolis: Indiana University Press.

Polanyi, L. (1985). *Telling the American story: A structural and cultural analysis of conversational storytelling.* Norwood, NJ: Ablex.

Polkinghorne, D. E. (1988). *Narrative knowing and the human sciences.* Albany: State University of New York Press.

Rabinow, P., & Sullivan, W. M. (1987). *Interpretive social science: A second look.* Berkeley: University of California Press. (Original work published 1979)

Reinharz, S. (1992). *Feminist methods in social research.* New York: Oxford University Press.

Richardson, L. (1992). The consequences of poetic representation: Writing the other, rewriting the self. In C. Ellis & M. G. Flaherty (Eds.), *Investigating subjectivity: Research on lived experience* (pp. 125–140). Newbury Park, CA: Sage.

Ricoeur, P. (1981). *Hermeneutics and the human sciences: Essays on language, action and interpretation* (J. B. Thompson, Trans.). Cambridge: Cambridge University Press.

Ricoeur, P. (1984). *Time and narrative.* Chicago: University of Chicago Press.

Riessman, C. K. (1987). When gender is not enough: Women interviewing women. *Gender & Society, 1*(2), 172–207.

Riessman, C. K. (1990a). *Divorce talk: Women and men make sense of personal relationships.* New Brunswick, NJ: Rutgers University Press.

Riessman, C. K. (1990b). Strategic uses of narrative in the presentation of self and illness. *Social Science and Medicine, 30*(11), 1195–1200.

Riessman, C. K. (1991). Beyond reductionism: Narrative genres in divorce accounts. *Journal of Narrative and Life History, 1*(1), 41–68.

Riessman, C. K. (1992). Making sense of marital violence: One woman's narrative. In G. C. Rosenwald & R. L. Ochberg (Eds.), *Storied lives: The cultural politics of self-understanding* (pp. 231–249). New Haven, CT: Yale University Press.

Roberts, H. (1992). Answering back: The role of respondents in women's health research. In H. Roberts (Ed.), *Women's health matters* (pp. 176–192). New York: Routledge, Chapman, & Hall.

Rollins, J. (1985). Introduction. In J. Rollins, *Between women: Domestics and their employers* (pp. 5–17). Philadelphia: Temple University Press.

Rosaldo, R. (1989). *Culture and truth: The remaking of social analysis.* Boston: Beacon.

Rosenwald, G. C., & Ochberg, R. L. (1992). Introduction: Life stories, cultural politics, and self-understanding. In G. C. Rosenwald & R. L. Ochberg (Eds.), *Storied lives: The cultural politics of self-understanding* (pp. 1–18). New Haven, CT: Yale University Press.

Roth, S. (1993). Speaking the unspoken: A work-group consultation to reopen dialogue. In E. Imber-Black (Ed.), *Secrets in families and family therapy* (pp. 268–291). New York: Norton.

Said, E. W. (1979). *Orientalism.* New York: Vintage.

Sarbin, T. R. (1986a). The narrative as a root metaphor for psychology. In T. R. Sarbin (Ed.), *Narrative psychology: The storied nature of human conduct* (pp. 3–21). New York: Praeger.

Sarbin, T. R. (Ed.). (1986b). *Narrative psychology: The storied nature of human conduct.* New York: Praeger.

Schafer, R. (1980). Narration in the psychoanalytic dialogue. *Critical Inquiry, 7*(1), 29–54.

Schafer, R. (1992). *Retelling a life: Narration and dialogue in psychoanalysis.* New York: Basic Books.

Schutz, A. (1967). *The phenomenology of the social world* (G. Walsh & F. Lehnert, Trans.). Evanston, IL: Northwestern University Press. (Original work published 1932)

Smith, D. E. (1987). *The everyday world as problematic: A feminist sociology.* Boston: Northeastern University Press.

Sosnoski, J. S. (1991). A mindless man-driven theory machine: Intellectualists, sexualists, and the institution of criticism. In R. R. Warhol & D. P. Herndl (Eds.), *Feminisms: An anthology of literary theory and criticism* (pp. 40–57). New Brunswick, NJ: Rutgers University Press.

Spence, D. P. (1982). *Narrative truth and historical truth: Meaning and interpretation in psychoanalysis.* New York: Norton.

Stewart, D., & Mickunas, A. (1990). *Exploring phenomenology: A guide to the field and its literature.* Athens: Ohio University Press.

Stivers, C. (1993). Reflections on the role of personal narrative in social science. *Signs: Journal of Women in Culture and Society, 18*(2), 408–425.

Tannen, D. (1990). Ordinary conversation and literary discourse: Coherence and the poetics of repetition. In E. H. Benclix (Ed.), *The uses of linguistics* (pp. 15–32). New York: New York Academy of Sciences.

Toolan, M. J. (1988). *Narrative: A critical linguistic introduction.* New York: Routledge.

Van Maanen, J. (1988). *Tales of the field: On writing ethnography.* Chicago: University of Chicago Press.

Veroff, J., Sutherland, L., Chadiha, L., & Ortega, R. M. (in press). Newlyweds tell their stories: A narrative method for assessing marital experiences. *Journal of Personal and Social Relationships.*

West, C. (1984). *Routine complications: Troubles with talk between doctors and patients.* Bloomington: Indiana University Press.

White, H. (1973). *Metahistory.* Baltimore: Johns Hopkins University Press.

White, H. (1989). The rhetoric of interpretation. In P. Hernadi (Ed.), *The rhetoric of interpretation and the interpretation of rhetoric* (pp. 1–22). Durham, NC: Duke University Press.

White, M. (1992). Deconstruction and therapy. In D. Epston & M. White (Eds.), *Experience, contradiction, narrative, and imagination* (pp. 109–147). Adelaide, South Australia: Dulwich Centre.

White, M., & Epston, D. (1990). *Narrative means to therapeutic ends.* New York: Norton.

Williams, G. (1984). The genesis of chronic illness: Narrative re-construction. *Sociology of Health and Illness, 6*(2), 175–200.

Wolf, D., & Hicks, D. (1989). The voices within narrative: The development of intertextuality in young children's stories. *Discourse Processes, 12*, 329–351.

Wolf, M. (1992). *A thrice-told tale: Feminism, postmodernism and ethnographic responsibility.* Stanford, CA: Stanford University Press.

Young, K. G. (1987). *Taleworlds and storyrealms: The phenomenology of narrative.* Boston: Martinus Nijhoff.

Young, K. G. (1989). Narrative embodiments: Enclaves of the self in the realm of medicine. In J. Shotter & K. J. Gergen (Eds.), *Texts of identity* (pp. 152–165). London: Sage.

Part III

Empirical Studies

Predictably, we like these contributions best. They try to answer the question: How do you actually do this stuff well, in one lifetime? We considered a formidable set of criteria in selecting the studies that appear in this section. Here are some of the issues that were foremost in our minds (of course, no study met, or could meet, them all):

♦ *Confirmability:* Are the study's procedures described so explicitly that we can follow the sequence from initial questions to conclusion? Were competing interpretations or conclusions carefully considered?

♦ *Dependability:* Were data collected across a full range of settings, times, and informants? Allowing for the paradoxes and perversities that are part of the stuff of life we work with, do multiple observers' accounts generally converge?

♦ *Authenticity:* Does the account ring true, seem plausible, make for a "vicarious presence" for readers?

♦ *Transferability:* Does the study acknowledge its scope and boundaries? Do descriptions of people, settings, and events allow comparisons with other samples and in other contexts?

♦ *Applicability:* The study may be "dependable," "authentic," and "transferable," but what does it do for evaluators and policy researchers who are interested not only in finding meaning, but in taking concrete action?

♦ *Attention to ethics:* Are value-based or ethical concerns explicitly raised and attended to? (For example, did the researcher provide safeguards for the people studied? Did the researcher report to the people studied if an agreement to do so was made at the start?) Broadly put, the ethical issues are these: Who will benefit from this study? Who could be harmed or betrayed by it?

Fischer and Wertz's 1980 article "Empirical Phenomenological Analyses of Being Criminally Victimized" is one of the rare fully documented analyses of psychological phenomenology. Stemming from the "Duquesne school" under the leadership of Amedeo Giorgi, it combines a variety of highly sensitive data-condensing techniques (illustrated narratives, general condensations, exemplary case synopses) that can be used singly or in combination. In this tour de force, Fischer and Wertz work with more than 50 incidents without recourse to a single algorithm or number. Each method of case condensation is carefully illustrated. The results are compelling.

Next, we cycle back to the relationships among conceptualization, findings, displays, and some "catalytic validity" in the area of social policy and education. In "Qualitative Data Analysis for Applied Policy Research," originally published in 1994, Ritchie and Spencer discuss the peculiarities of applied policy research, then run us through the process of creating provisional frameworks, becoming familiar with settings, gathering information, identifying thematic strands, and choosing among possible interpretations. Each point is well illustrated by three separate studies. These illustrations include a visual mapping of the analytic progression of gathering and sifting information, using a technique that we have a weakness for (see Miles & Huberman, 1994). Illuminating yet astringent displays lead to the framing of workable social policies in fuzzy or controversial areas of policy making.

The authors of the piece that follows clearly describe the adventure of doing qualitative inquiries that begin with a broad framework and then plunge into the field. In their 1995 article "Bounding the Case Within Its Context: A Constructivist Approach to Studying Detracking

Reform," Wells, Hirshberg, Lipton, and Oakes describe their gradual discovery that, although politics and norms within a local school community can make a meaningful frame, issues of school-level change may create a different picture—especially when researchers are on the scene. They show how the research team builds outward from the school site to the local community, in part by "co-constructing" pertinent boundaries with informants—leading to the discovery that the boundaries of cases and the differences in their shapes and sizes are as much a key finding as they are a methodological consideration. This thoughtful methodological pilgrimage taken by arguably "conventional" empiricists is highly instructive for researchers who are looking to combine the logics of qualitative and quantitative research in mindful ways.

Norman Denzin was the first, we believe, to separate the interpretive, or what he calls "the interpretation of a slice of experience," from the descriptive and explanatory facets of qualitative research. In "The Interpretive Process," a chapter first published in 1989 (and that appeared again in 2001 in the revised form it takes here), he illustrates and makes explicit several terms whose meanings have in the past eluded qualitative researchers. He also spells out formerly opaque parts of the interpretive process: deconstructing a phenomenon, bracketing a phenomenon by reducing it to its essential elements, putting a phenomenon into a coherent whole, and (re)contextualizing a phenomenon in an ongoing stream of consciousness. Finally, Denzin provides criteria for assessing the adequacy of interpretive materials.

In her carefully documented 1990 article "Temporality and Identity Loss Due to Alzheimer's Disease," Orona spells out the application of "grounded theory" method to her study of patients with Alzheimer's disease and their families. She shows how the use of line-by-line coding, images, vignettes, diagrams, and memos allows the emergence of working subcategories—four major themes of identity maintenance or loss.

❖ PUBLISHER'S NOTE

Michael Huberman and Matthew Miles had no plan to include a selection from their own work in this book of readings. It seems fitting, however, to round off *The Qualitative Researcher's Companion* with some of their typically straightforward, practical comments on writing about and doing qualitative data analysis. The concluding chapter, "Reflections and Advice," is adapted from the final pages of their classic book *Qualitative Data Analysis: An Expanded Sourcebook* (1994).

❖ REFERENCE

Miles, M. B., & Huberman, A. M. (1994). *Qualitative data analysis: An expanded sourcebook* (2nd ed.). Thousand Oaks, CA: Sage.

11

Empirical Phenomenological Analyses of Being Criminally Victimized

Constance T. Fischer and Fredrick J. Wertz

Within the social sciences, "research" has meant quantitative study—a search for order as revealed through the amount of change in one factor when another is altered (e.g., "self-esteem varies with positive reinforcement"). Social scientists have applied this

AUTHORS' NOTE: This chapter is a revision of a paper prepared as part of a symposium on "Interdisciplinary methods for qualitative description of experience," American Psychological Association, Toronto, 1978. Data collection and public forums were funded by Grant MAY-76-12 from the Public Committee for the Humanities in Pennsylvania (an affiliate of NEH).

Reprinted from Constance T. Fischer and Frederick J. Wertz, "Empirical Phenomenological Analyses of Being Criminally Victimized," in *Duquesne Studies in Phenomenological Psychology*, Vol. 3, edited by Amedeo Giorgi, Richard Knowles, and David L. Smith (pp. 135–158). Copyright 1980 by Duquesne University Press. Reprinted by permission.

method to social phenomena partly because it "was there," already successfully developed by the physical sciences, and partly because it seemed more efficient and objective than the descriptions provided by social philosophers.

Indeed, the quantitative experimental method has served to develop systematic bodies of knowledge so well, that by now their substantial findings also indicate the method's limitations. That is, efficient data production and statistical analysis, even where supportive of hypotheses, can now be seen as incomplete; we also desire an understanding of the particularly human character of social events—their rich, holistic, participative quality. We are becoming ready in many circumstances to forgo mathematical precision for a more complete, if always somewhat ambiguous, comprehension of nonlaboratory life.

Moreover, we are coming to recognize that just as we participate actively in our daily affairs, shaping as well as being shaped by them, so too as scientists we contribute to the shape of what we "discover." Objectivity is best served when we acknowledge our contribution to the form of our findings, encouraging others to approximate our perspective and see for themselves what appears. In this way, a discipline's knowledge, whether developed quantitatively or qualitatively, is recognized as inevitably perspectival, as intersubjective. And qualitative research becomes an appropriate, even necessary, approach to psychological research.

But it is one thing to recognize a need for qualitative research as one of our methods, and it is quite another to develop it in ways that continue to assure consensual validity and replicability. This paper overviews our approach to qualitative research and reports descriptive efforts with a particular topic—being criminally victimized.

Our approach is that of empirical phenomenological psychology, in particular as developed at Duquesne University (see Giorgi, 1970; Giorgi, Fischer, & von Eckartsberg, 1971; Giorgi, Fischer, & Murray, 1975). By "psychology" we refer to the study not only of human behavior, but of situations as they are lived by the individual. By "phenomenological" we refer to our foundations in the European philosophy of that name (see Husserl, 1962/1913; Heidegger, 1962/1927); we have been influenced particularly by the philosopher-psychologist Merleau-Ponty (1962, 1963, 1974). Phenomenology investigates the ways events appear when theories and constructs are for the moment put aside by the researcher. In doing so, phenomenology studies the ways a person's world is inevitably formed in part by the person who lives it. By "empirical" we refer to (a) our reflection upon actual events, and to (b) our making available to colleagues the data and steps of analysis that led to our findings—so they might see for themselves whether and how they could come to similar findings.

We say "similar findings," rather than "the same," because events are necessarily comprehended somewhat differently by different witnesses. Since truth is multiperspectival and revealed by the viewer, description is unfinishable. Nevertheless, in the presence of the same empirical events or reports, researchers do come to agreement about the essential aspects of the phenomenon. A rose may be a different rose to each of us, but we all recognize that it is indeed a rose. The task of our qualitative research is to be explicit about—to make visible—the lived (immediate, unconceptualized) meanings of an event (e.g., perceiving a book, struggling with being criminally victimized) for particular individuals and then across individuals. We may then examine these meanings for what they say of experience in general, or about some particular aspect of experience. In any case, the challenge here, as will be seen throughout this chapter, is that the explicitation must respect the differentiable, yet unitary, and hence ambiguous, character of reality. "Ambiguous" here does not refer to deficient clarity, but rather to the fact that perception and description of reality are dependent upon perspectives (of subjects and researchers), as well as upon which facets are momentarily focal while others remain implied.

Thus far at Duquesne our best developed general research method has been one formalized and developed by Amedeo Giorgi. We ask subjects to describe in detail some particular situation they have experienced, and then document step by step how the researcher culls from the description its essential psychological constituents. All the while we strive to be true to each subject's experience—*not* translating it into any theoretical system. We should stress here that neither we nor Giorgi claims this method to be "the" method of phenomenological psychology; there are other ways of doing it. For instance, some researchers might not emphasize documentation of steps. At Duquesne, some of us have utilized different steps and forms of documentation. We also have made use of other kinds of data, such as researchers' direct observation, and interviews with multiple participants in an event. However, the single-subject report has thus far been the most productive for us. It should be noted that even within this method there is no one right way, since the method not only allows but demands participation of the researcher's unique perspective.

❖ METHODS AND FINDINGS

In keeping with our understanding that researchers inevitably influence the form and content of their findings, we will now specify our multiple interests in this particular research. (a) We hoped to illustrate the usefulness of qualitative research in comparison with the prevailing quantitative work, which is limited to actuarial data (in this case, types, rates, locations, etc., of crime), correlational data (relation of type of crime to criminal personality, relation of fearfulness to kind of victimization, etc.), and outcome data (does the introduction of a foot policeman raise citizens' sense of safety?). Although important, these statistical indicators do not tell us about the *meaning* of being victimized for the victim or for this community. (b) Legislators and government officials and personnel are looking for ways to be responsive to victims; findings pointing to the personal and social implications of criminal victimization could serve as a basis for social action. (c) We wished to develop different forms of findings, ones that would be appropriate for policy-makers, the public, and quantitatively oriented, as well as phenomenological, social scientists. (d) To expedite our work to meet our grant's deadline for presentation of findings at public forums, we tried out a team research method.

Before going on to our research procedures, we should acknowledge that we ran into our share of fieldwork difficulties. The greatest impediment turned out to be the resistant police departments whom we asked for assistance in locating victims. We then used much of our limited time allaying fears of individual policemen who thought we wanted to do an exposé of their investigations. We served as resource persons to frustrated victims, and coped with a suit-threatening father who claimed his daughter's invitation to be interviewed constituted damaging harassment.

Data Collection

Eventually the police department of a township in the Greater Pittsburgh area telephoned a representative sample (by type of crime, time since its occurrence, area of the township, gender of the victim) of persons who reported crimes during the past three years. Eighty percent of the persons reached agreed to participate in either personal or telephone interviews with the Duquesne research team. Together with four doctoral psychology students[1] we conducted 50 interviews, which were taped and transcribed. The interviews tapped a broad range of socioeconomic and education levels, home owners and apartment dwellers, Blacks and Whites. Victims' ages ranged from 18 years to the early nineties. The sample intentionally excluded completed rapes, attempted murders, and corporate crime; it did include assaults, robbery, burglary, theft, attempted rape, vandalism, and harassment.

The two of us and the four other interviewers agreed, as a sensitizing exercise, to jot down notes about our personal experiences of having been the victim of crime. Then we met to discuss, among other issues, what we thought we were likely to find. These recorded anticipations alerted interviewers to possible themes that might require clarification if alluded to by subjects. They also allowed us to become aware of our presuppositions regarding the phenomenon so that we could attempt not to impose them upon our subjects. Later we found that some of our notions had been fulfilled (albeit always in special ways), some modified, and some disconfirmed.

In general, the victims were asked to describe what was going on prior to the crime, what it was like to be victimized, and what happened then. Questions were restricted to requests for clarification or elaboration of what the victim had already said.

Five interviewers each contributed a transcript of a different kind of crime, which each of us then analyzed (in the context of the other interviews each had conducted).

Forms of Results

We will present several forms of results that have been formulated for different purposes. The first two are "Case Synopses"—presentations of the essential constituents of particular case transcriptions. Next we will present excerpts from the "Illustrated Narrative" which was written to provide a jump-off point for citizens' discussion during forums on crime. Then, to provide a more concise general understanding of the phenomenon, a "General Condensation" is presented. Finally, we offer an excerpt from the "General Psychological Structure," which renders the psychology of the experience more explicit. These forms of results are not the only possible ones nor are they all necessary for qualitative research, but they do fulfill the aforementioned purposes of our particular project. (See Table 11.1 for a description of each of the forms of findings.)

Unlike usual practice, in this report we will present the steps of our analyses *after* each particular form of findings. We do this since most readers are unfamiliar with qualitative research, and hence cannot fully understand procedures until they have first seen what they are leading to.

Despite the differences among the forms of results that follow from their various purposes, one will note a pervasive similarity among them. This is due to the powerful unitariness and integrity of the phenomenon addressed, regardless of the form of results. There is no mistaking that they are all descriptions of the same experience.

Case Synopses

The first two forms of our findings to be presented here are synopses of the victimization experience for individual subjects. The Individual Case Synopsis presents what was personally critical to a particular victim's experience. We refer to these "Individual Case Synopses" also as "procedural synopses" since we later draw the General Condensation from what runs in common through them. We did not, however, compose a synopsis for all 50 of our subjects; rather, each researcher used his or her synopses of the five selected transcriptions for comparison with other transcriptions. Herewith is an individual Case Synopsis written by Wertz.

> Upon returning home from a family outing shortly after Christmas, the R family noticed that the bottom panel of the front door was broken, the glass shattered. Mr. R thought that children must have been playing.
>
> When he went inside, he saw the candy dish on the floor rather than on the stereo as usual. He looked around and saw a pair of pants lying on the steps and thought the house might be ransacked. He walked into the living room and when he saw the stereo gone, he was

Table 11.1 Summary of This Study's Forms of Findings[a]
(Question Asked and Type of Description)

Individual Case Synopses

We asked the transcription, "What reveals, is essential to, this person's experience of being criminally victimized?"

We wrote in the person's own words or in very close approximations.

Illustrated Narrative

We asked the Case Synopses and other transcriptions, "What sequences of events and what personal meanings are present across cases?"

We wrote a narrative in terms that characterized across cases but that remained close to experience as directly reported. We mentioned any subgroups for whom the victimization process differed. After each general characterization, we inserted illustrative excerpts from transcriptions.

General Condensation

We asked the Illustrated Narrative and the Individual Case Synopses, as well as the other transcriptions, "What is essential to all these personal meanings? How do they reveal the existential (including social) meaning of being criminally victimized?"

We wrote in general terms that collapsed/gathered the concrete expressions of earlier findings.

Exemplar (post-General) Case Synopses

We asked the Individual Case Synopses, "How does this person's experience exemplify what is true for all victims of crime? That is, what is most evocatively representative of each theme in the General Condensation?"

We wrote in the person's own words or in very close approximations.

General Psychological Structure

We asked of the transcriptions and of the psychological significances discovered in prior case analyses, "What is essential, however implicit, to the psychological organization of any experience of victimization?"

We wrote in general statements that describe the essential constituents of the phenomenon, highlighting their previously implicit horizons and structural interrelations.

---

a. In other empirical-phenomenological studies, researchers (including ourselves) have produced somewhat different forms. For example, the Individual Psychological Structure of particular cases could be included; some researchers prefer to cast their results in first person, present tense for the sake of vividness; and for research purposes (in contrast to public presentations), the Illustrated Narrative has previously not been necessary. We tailored the criteria and names of our forms for this study; these vary from project to project.

The forms of findings are presented in the order in which we developed them. However, the only necessary sequences are that all later analyses are based on the Individual Case Synopses, and that the Exemplar Synopses follow from the General Condensation.

in disbelief. He knew robbing existed but felt "it would never happen to me." He screamed out to his wife, "Don't come in," thinking someone might still be there, but Mrs. R had already gone inside. She was shocked to see the bare wall where their Oriental rug wedding present had hung. Their cedar chest was smashed and broken into. Her shock turned to fear.

Mr. and Mrs. R went next door to call the police and then went back home to figure out just what had happened. By this time, Mr. R was angry, feeling "I'm gonna get somebody for this!" Taking stock, they found the children's Christmas toys gone, including a six-foot teddy bear. The back door was wide open, but the house was not cold, indicating that maybe they scared the thieves away when they got home. The jewelry was gone. It was strange to the Rs, however, that candy was taken although some expensive gifts were left under the Christmas tree. There seemed to be no reason why the thieves took some things that were sentimental but of no monetary value. What hurt most was a bronze Infant of Prague bank which Mr. R's mother had all her life and gave him when she died. It was irreplaceable.

Soon the police arrived. Mr. R thought maybe some of the things could be recovered but the police said, "Tough, forget it," and this broke his confidence. Mrs. R became bitter and thought, "Well, if they're going to let them get away with it, why should I work? I should become a burglar." It seemed like the police accepted crime. The Rs felt ignored by the police, as if they were merely robbery number so and so. Mr. R felt the police investigation was a sham. They dusted for fingerprints but they didn't seem to care. The Rs felt ignored. They had expected the police to sit down and get a list of what was missing, but they said they were too busy. Mrs. R wished they would be more sympathetic but realized that this was just routine for the police, whereas it was anything but routine for her. When one officer explained how missing candy meant the crime could be drug-related, Mr. R was impressed, but on the whole, they were left disappointed by the police.

After the police left, the Rs tried to piece things together themselves. Maybe the thieves thought they'd gotten enough and left, or maybe they heard someone coming. Why were the pants strewn on the stairs? Why did they leave the silver and china and take children's toys? There must have been several of them to carry all that stuff— and they would have needed a truck to haul it. Maybe one was a woman, for they knew which were the expensive women's clothes. They thought the burglars must be callous, pathetic persons. What if they'd come in when the family was home—anything could happen; they could be killed. They could understand taking money, but kids' piggy banks and stuffed animals!

The Rs asked the neighbors if they'd seen anything, but they hadn't. It looked like they were in this all by themselves, with no help. It was a transient neighborhood where no one knew anyone else. Over the next few months, there were a lot of burglaries. It was shocking, unbelievable to the Rs. The neighborhood was becoming a haven for burglars and no one was stopping them. Mrs. R wished there would be more police patrols. Mr. R bought extra locks and made sure the doors were always locked. They had an alarm system put in. One day they came home and the screen door was open, the inside door forced—but the would-be intruders couldn't get in. Another house was robbed that day. These events changed the Rs' outlook. They began talking with neighbors about crime and the neighborhood people became closer. One day Mr. R saw strange men unloading things out of a house down the street and called the police, but the people were only moving. Some neighbors bought dogs, others guns. The Rs felt safer with everybody aware of crime, ready to call the police about anything suspicious.

But the fear had not passed. Mrs. R was afraid to be home alone. She didn't feel safe and it took her a year to get over it. The Rs felt the worst effect was on the children. Whenever they were about to get home after being away, the children became afraid and asked if their toys would still be there. Mr. and Mrs. R replaced the toys, hoping the children would forget the loss, but the new teddy bear became known as "the one we got because we were robbed." Mr. and Mrs. R felt they'd better teach the kids to be safe—not to take candy from a stranger, not to wander far from home, but it was a difficult job because they didn't want to scare the children. They were thankful when the police presented a program in school in which they taught the children safety without scaring them.

However, far from being over, the robbery seemed to mushroom. Mr. and Mrs. R's parents started to put pressure on them to move. They blamed minority groups, which angered the Rs. The parents said, "You've got girls; what's going to happen to them?" The Rs resented the intrusion but looked for another place to live, only to find trouble selling the house due to the crime in the area. They lost $5,000 worth of possessions, and the insurance company only refunded $2,100. Mr. R felt he had been robbed twice. He had to take a second job to cover the loss. Then his friends told him he was stupid for being honest with the insurance company. This made him angry. He thought, "I'm mad because someone robbed me and now you're asking me to be dishonest?" Yet if it happened again, Mr. R thought he might not be so honest, which made him wonder about his own sense of fairness.

A couple of months after the crime, a friend told the Rs of a cache of things found in the woods and given to the police. They went down to the station to see if some of it was theirs but felt like they were treated like dirt. Besides not being allowed to look, Mr. R felt like the officer suspected him of wanting to steal the stuff that wasn't theirs. He could have choked the desk sergeant. It looked as though the police wanted the things themselves to sell and make money on. Now the Rs felt ripped off by the police!

About a year later, the Rs moved and felt better in their new neighborhood. People knew and looked out for each other. They were more conscientious and security-minded, which was why the Rs had decided to live there. One day one of their girls wandered too far from the house and the neighbors called the police. Mrs. R felt "now the girls have not only parents looking out for them but a whole neighborhood." This made them feel secure, protected. One lady regularly patrols with her dog, and they take turns watching each other's houses when someone goes away. Now the Rs lock their doors, tell neighbors when they're leaving, and the kids won't go to sleep until their bikes are locked in the cellar. Mr. R feels his little girls are already like old ladies with their fears and suspicions—always worrying about stealing. Until this day the Rs haven't replaced the stereo out of fear of theft. They bought the heaviest TV made so it couldn't be hauled off. They'll never get an Oriental rug again, seeing it as an invitation to burglars.

The Rs feel the only good that has come out of the experience is that they are more aware. They wish they didn't have to learn this lesson—it makes them sad, but they feel it is necessary to protect themselves. Now in their new secure neighborhood, with all their precautions, they feel it can't happen again.

A later kind of synopsis is what we call an "Exemplar" or "Post-General Synopsis." It is written after the *General* Condensation is completed, as a brief but concrete example of it. This exemplar form is always more succinct than the original synopsis since only those features that illustrate what was true for all the subjects are preserved. The following Exemplar Synopsis was written by Fischer; note that it also serves here as an example of a crime and its aftermath being less disruptive than it was for the R family.

Mrs. K is walking through the shopping center parking lot with her children. She holds her purse lightly, and pays little attention to the sound of kids running. Suddenly these blue-jeaned Black kids grab her purse, which she finds herself releasing for fear of injury. She yells for several minutes for help and for her children to stop chasing the thieves. She grows both increasingly furious and frightened for her children. There is no one to help, only an old lady getting into a car. As the shock wears off, Mrs. K goes to Hornes, and for 10 minutes looks for a policeman to whom to report the details. She doesn't expect much help or recovery of the purse, but they're who you turn to.

She then waits 25 minutes for a police team to arrive. She stands and waits, feeling nervous and frustrated. She figures they went to the parking lot first. The team receives the details, agrees she was right to release the purse, sees her safely back to the car.

That night she finds herself worrying that the thieves now had her address and house keys. But she also figures that they were only after money and would throw away the rest. Her husband says there's no way the police can find the purse.

The next day before she could call in to credit card companies, Mrs. K receives a call from a youngster who knows her and has found her charge plates, and she picks them up. That evening a gentleman calls—he has found the purse in front of his house. She feels good, fortunate, that she got her keys back and had lost only her money and driver's license. She is relieved that the kids hadn't had the keys in their hands at all, and again figures that all they knew to use was the money.

The police report that they have found the culprits, but Mrs. K can't identify them. The police discuss with her how these kids probably have committed other robberies, how when one is opened up he'll rat on another.

Months later Mrs. K feels more jumpy than frustrated or angry and assumes the jumpiness will wear off. Her relatives say they can't believe she still goes to the same shopping center; she does go less often and particularly does not like to go at night. She doesn't like to get close to anybody, and keeps a lookout for stray persons, especially young ones. She holds her purse tightly. She's always been careful, but not to this extent. She feels it's terrible to be so suspiciously protective.

As forms of results, the case synopses provide readers with concrete examples that reverberate with their own lives, thus intimating the full structure of the phenomenon (being criminally victimized). Either form of synopsis provides an instance of the general structure. The briefer Exemplar Synopsis is useful where time or space is limited (as in journal articles), where readers must develop a quick sense of the phenomenon if they are to become interested in reading further (as in reports to legislators or in grant applications), and where the researcher wishes to remind readers of the specific situations from which the more abstract (general) findings arose. The longer Individual (Procedural) Synopsis's richer detail foreshadows the general findings less succinctly but more vividly. We have read this form of findings at community workshops on crime problems, to encourage sensitivity to the individual victim's plight. Perhaps with the assistance of counselors, other victims of crime might find these synopses helpful in exploring and coming to terms with their own experiences.

Now we can describe how we arrived at the above sort of individual (procedural) case synopses. What we want to communicate here is a general sense of ways we approached the transcriptions, rather than instructions on how-to-do-it. Each of us carried out some variation of Giorgi's method of analysis (e.g., 1975, chapter 6). For this study, after reading about 30 of the transcriptions, Fischer's steps toward analyzing each of the five transcriptions were: (a) *familiarization* with the transcriptions by rereadings; (b) *demarcating* transcriptions into numbered units; (c) casting these units into *temporal order*; (d) *organizing* clusters of units into scenes; (e) *condensing* these organized units into nonrepetitive narrative form with nonessential facts dropped. All these steps were accompanied by jotted reflections on emerging themes and psychological significance; these reflections do not appear as such in this synopsis, but they did assist the researcher in recognizing what is essential in a subject's report. The synopsis sticks closely to the subject's language, and shortens the transcription to as much as one-third, depending on the subject's style of reporting. Transcriptions in this study ran 8–30 pages. Information was retained if it was judged to reveal the particular subject's experience of being criminally victimized. Examples of material that did not find its way into synopses are: the name of the bar where the subject waitresses, the ages and number of children shopping with the subject, the occupation of a son-in-law. Aside from being in the third person, the language of the synopsis is more or less the subject's own, with minor changes to facilitate readability. But we were careful here since the "experience" we attempted to synopsize is that of the individual's "lived meanings"—which term implies a context of the person's biography, projects, world.

Here are some details on the analysis steps. The demarcation units most often are single or consecutive sentences. The criterion for a unit was that its phrases require each other to stand as a distinguishable moment in the overall experience. The numbering of the units allows return to the original transcription for context. Examples of units: "So I got all my keys back. I think the only thing I was out was my money and my driver's license" (18), "The police said they did find the boys and they started, had trapped one and the other ratted on the other one (27), but I couldn't identify them so I couldn't help them" (28).

Sometimes the researcher later broke a unit down when he or she realized that part of it belonged better with a different cluster; sometimes such a subunit or a unit was placed with more than one cluster. Some researchers preferred to use smaller, informational units; some preferred larger units that evoke the flow of the situation. The purpose of demarcating is not for technical reliability, but rather for the disciplined thoroughness and accountability it requires of the researcher— disallowing a rush to conceptual closure.

An example of condensation of units:

Unit
"I got everything back, I was very fortunate" (12)
". . . . except my money, yes" (13)
"So I got all my keys back, I think the only thing I was out
  was my money and my driver's license" (18)
"But I was very fortunate" (19)
"So I felt very good that I got anything back" (42)

Synopsis
S felt good, fortunate, that she got her keys back and had lost only
  her money and driver's license.

Again, these steps are not a cut-and-dried technology, but a means of the researcher's becoming and staying in touch with all of a transcription, and of encouraging him or her to struggle with alternate ways of presenting the unitariness of an experience's different aspects. The written work (steps c-e) also is a record for colleagues who wish to see what they can of how the researcher came to these findings, so they may discover implicit assumptions or operations on the part of the researcher, or so they can offer better wordings. The ultimate criterion for success of this phase of the analysis is whether or not the case synopses have been faithful to the reported experiences. The synopses, however, are always provisional; earlier findings are refined as further analyses call for a qualification, an elaboration, a highlighting.

A comment before going on with other forms of our analyses and results: In other studies, we have gone back to our subjects for clarification of the transcription and again later for the subject's impression of whether our synopsis adequately represents his or her experience. Also in other studies we sometimes have returned to earlier subjects with transcriptions or synopses from later subjects, asking if there were any additional features there that had not been made explicit in their own reports. Similarly, we have asked if there were significant differences from other subjects' experience. Sometimes subjects continue into further stages of analyses with us. In this study, under the press of time, we did not return to our original subjects, but instead relied on our 50 transcriptions. Consultation with subjects is usually important since their original description (written or oral) is not the ultimate object of our reflection. Rather, these words are an access to the initial experience to which they refer. The researcher's own experiences (whether of the same phenomenon or related ones) resonate with those reported by subjects, and facilitate reflection upon what had only been implicit for the subject and him/herself.

Illustrated Narrative

Our third form of findings was developed as a handout for panelists and audience at public forums held to explore the human-values aspects of public policy issues, as raised by a panel of township officials, police, citizen representatives, and university humanists, as well as by community members in the audience. The purpose of the handout was to provide all these participants with an immediate sense of the full sweep of the personal meaning of being criminally victimized. We wanted to organize our data according to what we had found was true across subjects, and yet also allow victims to speak for themselves.

The handout was 19 pages, entitled "Being Criminally Victimized: A Qualitative Account." The experience was presented under five captions: (a) Living Routinely, (b) Being Disrupted, (c) Being Violated, (d) Reintegration, and (e) Going On. In each section a general statement was made in bold print; under that within brackets and in lighter print were illustrative quotations from the transcriptions. Some excerpts:

[from Living Routinely:] But unless personal experience has already proven otherwise, he/she nevertheless feels that the

defended against crime could never happen to him/her. ["You think of it; you know nothing like this would have happened to you. That's just the truth"; "I said, 'nah, you've got to be kidding'"; "I always thought it happened to everybody else"; ". . .that it just happened on television"; "In a way you feel that it's never going to happen to you, your house. In one way you think that your house can be robbed any-time but in the back of your mind it's vice versa—my house won't be robbed; it's somebody else's house that's going to be broken into."]

[from Being Disrupted:] Even as the person copes with the threat-ening or discovered crime, he/she scans imaginatively and percep-tually for a still worse outcome. ["I think that night I was more concerned about my house keys. I thought if those kids still had the purse, and my address was in the wallet. . ."; "I told them [her own children] to stop, to come back, cause I didn't know what these kids would do if [my] kids got too close"; "You imagine the worst when it's happening. . . .I just kept thinking my baby's upstairs and I might never see her again"; "By the time I would have got it out, I would have had my head mashed in or shot"; ". . .we had some camera equipment and this type of thing and I looked to see if it was still here"; "I went right for my engagement ring to see if it was still there and my watch."]

[from Being Violated:] Where the victim is subject to recurring crime (the above) indignation or outrage additionally vacillates with despair, hopelessness, resignation. ["Sometimes you wonder, you feel like because there don't seem to be nothing that will solve this nonsense . . . you don't enjoy your homes anymore. . . .. You can only take so much of this stuff. . . . You just feel like putting your house up for sale and getting out of here"; "I'm sorry that I even helped my mother to move here. . . . I really feel bad about it. When I move out I want her to go someplace that's going to be safe too. . . . We've had a nice offer . . . moving out to the borough. . . . I'm scared to death because I don't know how it is."]

[from Re-integrating:] The victim begins to assimilate and over-come the violation by "Doing something" to protect against any future intrusions. ["I've got different locks on my house now but maybe I should really be thinking about a burglar alarm type of thing. Because you don't want that uncertainty, that disruption of what is taking place"; "I had everything in my purse. But I clean out my purse now since then and I leave very little of that kind of stuff in there [pay-check, phone number]."]

. . . At other times, the victim finds him/herself acutely sensitive to the unexpected or unfamiliar. Even while embarrassed about his/her suspiciousness, he/she privately questions strangers'

motives. Similarly, the victim finds him/herself fascinated by, attuned to, diverse news of crime. [". . .I was scared to death when my husband would leave the house. . . . I really am suspicious of every-body . . . even when that police called yesterday and he says this guy's [research interviewer] going to call you. I said, 'well, I don't know . . .' . . . I went to pieces"; ". . .It's funny how in our local news-paper they give all the robberies for the area. I am always reading these and am aware that these robberies are taking place throughout the township and thinking to myself, 'Will we be robbed again?'"]

(for those cases where the victim does recover):

   [from Going On:] As the violation recedes, the person goes on, only upon reflection being aware of the transformation in his/her life. He/she then thinks of the transformation in terms of constricted freedom and of a less trusting but wiser outlook. [". . .more cautious when you walk near people. . . . Not as often, and I don't go at night alone, but I do go up . . . looking out for almost any stray person"; ". . . just something you're going to think about the rest of your life. . . . I'll probably always remember it and watch myself. . . . I don't think it made me stronger. It made me smarter, . . . definitely smarter."]

This form of result was intended to provide temporally ordered sum-maries of the experience while still retaining the concrete particulars for different subjects. Thus it differs from the synopses in its presenta-tion of the general themes of victimization as well as of examples from multiple cases.

   Diverse populations readily understood the handout and reported that it resonated with their personal experiences. Practical implications were easily drawn here on account of the explicitness of the findings for all crime victims. For example, it was apparent from the Illustrated Narrative that unless they were told otherwise, citizens expected police to investigate reported crimes immediately, and then frequently were disappointed and angry. The implication: the caller should be told what to expect (2–5 hours, days, etc.). It also was apparent that victims' first responses were action-oriented: calling insurance companies, arranging for new locks, figuring out how the crime occurred. Only later (days, weeks, months for some) were victims ready to reflect and talk about the social significance of the crime—what it said of society, of their own responsibility, etc. Without such discussion (usually with relatives and close neighbors), victims did not fully recover their sense of agency. Implication: crisis intervention counselors should make themselves available later, not just as at present as part of the initial police response.

Again following our format of presenting procedures after the findings that they led to, we will now describe how we arrived at the above Illustrated Narrative. After the team researchers had completed their case synopses and had compared them against their own other interviews, we again met as a group several times. Fischer presented a temporally ordered list of facts and experiences found in common in her case synopses and in the other transcriptions she had studied (e.g., "Aftermath: . . . trust undermined, vigilance, doubts own perceptions, uncertainty, crime lurks everywhere, restricts hours and radius and openness of earlier routines. . ."). From their own analyses, team members suggested clarifications and modifications, argued, expanded some themes, exchanged examples, and eventually came to agreement on a revised listing.

Fischer then drafted the Illustrated Narrative, organizing it temporally and specifying trends within the narrative (e.g., the differences that occur when persons are repetitively victimized or when persons are subject to physical abuse). She tried to differentiate the constituents of being criminally victimized while still evoking for the reader a sense of their mutuality and flow. In other words, she posed the Narrative in factual/phenomenal form, sticking closely to the experiences as directly reported while generalizing across subjects. Team members suggested more accurate and less technical languaging, and helped to locate excerpts to fill out a range of speech styles and life situations.

At this point we should acknowledge that we also concern ourselves with such issues as sampling, subtypes of a phenomenon, subjects' limitations as reporters, and the function of language. For this paper, we shall make only a few comments. We repeat that our sample is restricted to those persons who reported crimes (nonreporters might, for example, have been less distressed or more fatalistic). As mentioned, we did specify within our findings some distinctions for different kinds of victim circumstances. But although it could be done with our transcriptions, in this study we did not set about to systematically distinguish subtypes. Moreover, in this kind of research, findings are intended to be accurate for every victim; there is no need for probability levels or percentage statements. In this study we found subjects quite adequate as reporters; some were more vivid, explicit, or reflective than others, but each provided a rich access to the phenomenon. It was the researchers', not the subjects', task to do the work of phenomenology: to render the taken-for-granted more explicit.

General Condensation

The next form of our findings to be presented is a general condensation—a compact description of the characteristics common to the transcriptions. In other studies, we have summarized across the individual (case) analyses or condensations to arrive at this general description. In this instance Fischer drafted a condensation using the Illustrated Narrative as a detailed summary of all 50 transcriptions. In either instance the question addressed to the earlier analyses is: "What does this say about human existence as lived through 'being criminally victimized'?" In answering, we try to express the bare essentials of this experience briefly and accurately, encompassing all individual cases. Again, one must stick close to the data, often returning to the transcriptions for a fuller sense of the experience and for a check on the accuracy of one's generalizations. The researcher must choose his or her own balance between vividness and compactness. Here, we wanted something in the one-to-two page range—results that could serve as a handy point of return for a broad range of readers, from citizens to scientists.

Here is the present General Condensation:

> Being criminally victimized is a disruption of daily routine. It is a disruption that compels one, despite personal resistance, to face one's fellow as predator and oneself as prey, even though all the while anticipating consequences, planning, acting, and looking to others for assistance. These efforts to little avail, one experiences vulnerability, separateness, and helplessness in the face of the callous, insensitive, often anonymous enemy. Shock and disbelief give way to puzzlement, strangeness, and then to a sense of the crime as perverse, unfair, undeserved. Whether or not expressed immediately, the victim experiences a general inner protest, anger or rage, and a readiness for retaliation, for revenge against the violator.

> As life goes on, the victim finds him/herself pervasively attuned to the possibility of victimization—through a continued sense of reduced agency, of the other as predatory, and of community as inadequately supportive. More particularly, one continues to live the victimization through recollections of the crime, imagination of even worse outcomes, vigilant suspiciousness of others, sensitivity to news of disorder and crime, criticalness of justice system agents, and desires to make sense of it all.

> But these reminders of vulnerability are simultaneously efforts toward recovery of independence, safety, trust, order, and sense. One

begins to get back on top of the situation through considering or taking precautions against crime, usually by restricting one's range of activities so as not to fall prey again. During this process, the victim tries to understand not only how a criminal could have done and could again do such a thing, but also how he or she (the victim) may have contributed to the criminal's action. Also, one's intermittent readiness for retaliation provides a glimpse of one's own potential for outrageous violence. The victim thus is confronted with the paradoxical and ambiguous character of social existence: the reversible possibilities we all share, such as being agent or object, same or different, disciplined or disruptive, predator or prey. One may move from this encounter to a more circumspect attitude toward personal responsibility.

However, the person's efforts toward such an integration of the victimization are not sufficient. The environment must over time demonstrate that the victim's extreme vigilance is no longer necessary. And other persons must respond with concern and respect for the victim's full plight, including his or her efforts toward sensemaking. All three components are essential for recovery of one's prior life as well as for development of a fuller sense of responsibility, reciprocity, and community. But no component is guaranteed. The absence of any of them eventuates in a deepened victimization of isolation, despair, bitterness, and resignation.

Actually this General Condensation has evolved from half a dozen drafts, each giving up a bit more detail, and varying the way of presenting each constituent so as to evoke its relation to the whole. After the initial analyses, Fischer and Wertz were in agreement about the structure of the phenomenon. Our (productive) disagreements for all the findings were those of writers: what to include for the reader, how to best arrange and language our findings for communication, when to write evocatively and when to write explicitly (given that everything cannot be said at once). As with the Illustrated Narrative, some one person must take primary responsibility for conveying the order of the phenomenon. Indeed, after the Illustrated Narrative, the larger research team had finished its work, since the later analyses each required only one researcher.

The usefulness of the General Condensation is its provision of a succinct sense of the phenomenon, a form of the findings that can be kept in mind by a wide readership. Its "meaning for human existence" form and its compactness afford further practical implications. It is apparent that if the victim is to integrate, i.e., overcome, the experience, he requires something different than such current efforts as financial compensation and child care services while testifying in court. One requires a community that he or she can count on—justice system representatives who do not victimize him further through inconsideration or ineptitude, and community members with whom one can talk through the experience (not just for relief but for sensemaking). It has been known that community ties limit crime; now we notice that they also assist the victim toward recovery.

The General Condensation, because of its succinct brevity, also provides a sharp contrast between the early and later stages of the experience (being victimized and struggling with having been victimized). Recognition of the victim's stage is important for justice system representatives and counselors if they are to properly understand and assist him or her. We might also note that what has been described as the rape victim's experience (cf. Burgess & Holstrom, 1974) seems to be an intense version of what all crime victims undergo (perhaps other victims too?—scapegoats, hostages, flood victims, etc.). We plan to review other implications for social planning and counseling in a separate document.

The limitation of this condensed version of being criminally victimized is that it has not retained the richness of the lengthier versions—their concreteness and the variations within general themes. For some purposes it may also be a limitation that subjects who have not read through other victims' transcriptions do not immediately recognize their own experience in this highly general version.[2]

General Psychological Structure

During each of the above analyses, our approach has been psychological and structural. That is, we have been concerned with out subjects' experience as such (rather than the objective facts of the case, say, as a policeman would report it). We also have attempted throughout to respect the holistic immediacy of the experience rather than isolating any elements of it. In other words, we have regarded description of each culled theme not as separate but as a way of holding the experience still for a moment to reflect upon its diverse simultaneous meanings for the subject. Since in this sense all of our results are at least implicitly psychological and structural, we could include those adjectives in the title of the other forms too. But in this instance we thought it would be more helpful to reserve these terms for the results that provide their most explicit presentation. (Recall that Table 11.1 summarizes the different forms of findings.)

Wertz is the primary researcher/author for this version of criminal victimization. Fischer has been inclined to write an "Elaboration of the General Structure (Condensation)," referring back to Synopses, Condensation, notes, and transcriptions to elaborate the fullness and variations of the phenomenon. In this study, however, while she was working on the Illustrated Narrative for the public forums, Wertz developed the General Psychological Structure directly from his case analyses. Both of these procedures are viable. Before presenting the excerpt from the General Psychological Structure, we will look into some of the analyses that led to it. Once Wertz had organized each transcription into its nonredundant units revelatory of victimization, he systematically studied their psychological significance prior to any explicitly general formulation. His exploratory reflections were often quite lengthy.

Subject: It took me a really long time to get over it. I kept thinking about it. One night I dreamed he was raping me and in the dream he turned into my husband. I woke up hitting my husband. I wouldn't let my husband touch me for weeks. I thought it would ruin my marriage, that I'd have to move back home with my parents.

Wertz: Even after the event of victimization is over, its constituent meanings (e.g., detrimental other, vulnerability, broken social relations) appear in new lived experiences with new objects. Here *S* lives them in relation to her husband, through dreams, perceptions, and thoughts. Why is her husband identified psychologically with the criminal and thus participates in continued victimization rather than being experienced as a helpful other assisting her to safety? There seem to be two ways to understand this psycho-logic. (1) Before the victimization, the horizon of social harmony and safety pervaded the interpretation of all everyday events, including those involving her husband. Now that (through victimization) this is broken and replaced by the horizon of destruction, she is attuned to the dangerous, frightening aspects of others. Still, why her husband? (2) Before she said her husband was "a hard type," "callous," "insensitive," "didn't care about her." These

> meanings are precisely those of the criminal for her, hence the identity via a lived affinity of meaning. Their intrusiveness can no longer be ignored in the new horizon of victimization. S lives her dialog with victimization with her husband. She desires to flee him, thinks of negating him from her world (destroy him in turn by leaving him) and returning to nurturing others (her parents) to re-establish her preferred sociality.

In this reflection we begin to see the psychological structure of an individual's experience—in which the past-present-future and self-world-others interrelations of the transcription unit are becoming explicit. That is, Wertz articulated more fully (a) the implicit, immanent significations of the experience (aspects that have remained hidden from or taken for granted by subjects in their reports), and (b) the structural unity of the experience (the interrelations of its thematized aspects). The purpose of these explorations was not interpretation but explicitation, so that the psycho-logic of the General Psychological Structure would be rendered more deeply and sensitively. It should be mentioned that on the basis of this kind of analysis, for some of the cases Individual Psychological Structures were formulated, pulling these reflections together to disclose the psycho-logic of each of the particular cases. Since for this project we were primarily interested in moving to the General Psychological Structure, this step was for the most part procedural. However, the Individual Structures could well serve as another form of results. Perhaps the full Individual Structures would be especially valuable to counselors of victims. Although we won't present a full example here, the above excerpt shows the kind of thought involved in this level of analysis.

In the movement from the individual case analyses to the General Psychological Structure of victimization, Wertz reflected in the above way on both segments ("nonredundant units") of and the full transcriptions. These could be called preparatory steps toward the General Psychological Structure. In the following example, we see how Wertz's explorations of the structure of a specific case had often already moved toward statements of what is essential to all victimizations. These themes that hold true generally are italicized.

Subject: I used to worry every time I worked—with all those strange men around. I didn't know what to do. Now I take a lot of precautions—I don't talk to strange men or flirt like I used to.

I now wear long skirts. My husband picks me up at work. And now I feel much more secure.

Wertz: Even after the attacker is not present in person, *S* experiences others as potential rapists, and changes her lifestyle, takes precautions to prevent rape from becoming an actuality. *S elaborates the possibilities of victimization well beyond the confines of its original situation, indeed throughout her world—perceptually, imaginatively, and thoughtfully. In direct dialog with these meanings which became elaborated, she comports herself to surpass them, to attempt to exclude them from actuality. These new comportments embody the establishment of agency where it had collapsed ("I did-*n't know what to do") and harmonious relations with others, in short, her preferred order which had been destroyed* by the attacker *and she is attempting to secure a victimization-free future. . ..*

In the next excerpt, we can see how a reflective return to the units of the original transcription can yield general psychological significance essential to understanding the phenomenon.

Transcription Unit

"I went over to Clairton Place. My brother is constable over there. I had gone to the bar where he usually stops in the evening . . . to see him. I had a few drinks and then I left. I came out and a couple of colored men approached me as I was walking to my car. It was right in front of the place. I opened the door to get in, not expecting any trouble."

General Psychological Significance

Before victimization, one acts and interprets the world in terms of social harmony. Victimization thus arises on the ground of one's engagement in a freely chosen project which takes for granted the world's allowance of its unfolding.

In formulating the final General Psychological Structure, Wertz searched back and forth among his Individual Structures, the psychological reflections on each case, and the original transcriptions, with an eye toward how they manifest constituents essential to all victimization. This involved grouping diverse experiences in one transcription and across transcriptions under one general statement, often reformulating that statement to comprehend the diversities of the cases. The constituents finally expressed in the General Psychological Structure not only had to be present in every case analysis but in every instance of victimization that we could imagine. In this most reflective elaboration of the psychological, structural relations among the demarcated units and their thematized meanings, we present most explicitly what was implicit or taken for granted in the subjects' reported experiences.

In its current form the General Psychological Structure runs 18 pages. This version includes transcription quotations illustrating concrete variations of the essential themes. The complex living through of victimization demanded elaboration under several headings to depict its psycho-logical temporality:[3] "Before," "The Emergence," "The Configuration," "The After," "A New Order." In fact we could call these sub-structures since each is an integral whole. Our excerpt will begin at the end of the description of "The Surpassing of Victimization," which is a subheading under "The After," and continue through "A New Order." The reader should bear in mind that for reasons of space, the illustrative quotations have been omitted from this segment, which is intended only to provide an overall sense of how the General Psychological Structure is presented.

> [The General Psychological Structure already has described the three ways in which victimization must be surpassed for complete recovery: the victim's active efforts, the world's repeated reassertion of social harmony, and the active assistance by others.]

> All three aspects of the victim's recovery are mutually implicit and thus each fosters all. For example, in discussion with a caring friend, the victim becomes actively involved (thus overcoming loss of agency), and makes sense of the crime (overcoming shock and confusion), while the friend allows reciprocity and respects the victim's existence in ways that deepen trust (overcoming the predatory relationship). Talking overcomes fear and alienation; speech heals broken community. Perhaps in the light of the possibilities for recovery implicit in the speaking situation, we may understand the unusual willingness of the victims to participate in our interviews. In their longing to be involved in caring community, some seemed to have been waiting for someone to come. One subject exclaimed, "And you're the *first one* to come and talk about this . . . thank you."

> Overcoming victimization is a reversal of victimization's meanings, a reversal that cannot be taken for granted. If the world doesn't change but continues to victimize, or if the victim does nothing about his misfortune, or if others remain indifferent and unavailable, victimization

deepens. The world and others, whose being and precise character are not up to the victim alone, are equal partners in his overcoming the victimization. Insofar as the process of overcoming is fulfilled in its three aspects, there is a mysterious reconstitution of the previously destroyed, taken-for-granted horizon of social harmony, one that allows the person to proceed, undistracted and healed, into a future of his own preference. This process of surpassing is always the surpassing of the particular victimization. For instance, it involved a near rape victim's avoiding strange men, wearing longer dresses, being taken care of and protected by her husband. For a burglary victim, it involved locking the house better, alerting neighbors to be on the lookout, etc. As the person overcomes his past victimization as well as those future possibilities of victimization that he attuned himself to and elaborated upon, the strange and unexpected detrimentality of others fades to a distance and he feels relieved and at home in the renewed horizon of social harmony.

A New Order

Just as victimization testifies to the fragility of the social order, the situation after it has been surpassed asserts its plasticity. We find that what has occurred is a psychological transformation that both conserves and surpasses victimization. The original victimization is present for the person only when spoken about or when something with a similar meaning reminds him of it (like a news show on crime). The event is conserved in its always being available to memory. Yet it is surpassed in the sense that it is not in the present; it is remembered *as past*. It may be recollected with a sigh of relief, which means that it is over.

Nevertheless, victimization is *implicitly* present in the physiognomies of the world and in the person's behavior. However, even though usually lived implicitly, the actualities and possibilities of victimization are powerful. A whole new unexpected realm, whose complex genesis we have described, has been brought close, interrogated, made sense of—in short made a part of the person's world. Crime has become familiar. The sense made is sedimented.

The way a victim recovers and behaviorally maintains safety constitutes a new and abiding style of life (e.g., suspicious, cautious, shy), which implies victimization in its very surpassing of it. Preventive behavior implies victimization by taking precautions against it. The person purposely develops new habits (e.g., locking doors) that reassert his autonomy and safety. Other behavioral manifestations of a new order are the person's unthinking, habitualized avoidance of certain areas or kinds of people, and new lived restrictions (e.g., not going out alone at nights, no buying expensive things for the home). Things (e.g., a dog, floodlights outside the house, an alarm system) also are acquired for protection. They become taken-for-granted reinforcements of the person's preferred order, simultaneously testifying implicitly to the possibility of victimization.

Another transformation is that social relations that form through the struggle with victimization become integrated into the person's ongoing life, be they for better or worse (e.g., closeness to or alienation from police or neighbors). In the new order, some people become more independent, strong, and responsible. Others became more dependent. All these new relations express a person's particular surpassing or not surpassing his victimization. In any case, new behaviors become sedimented and taken for granted as "really me" (e.g., "now I'm shy, I wear long skirts and don't flirt with strange men"), and the world's new presentations become the one and only lived reality (e.g., "you know who you can count on," or "kids have no respect and now they're taking over"). This emergent order is preferred over the victim-world as it was originally experienced and extended, but it is not preferred without reservation. Thus the new behavior (like moving to a new neighborhood, locking the doors) is taken as a necessity in view of the newly threatening profiles of the world (e.g., transient communities are dangerous, people will rip your car off). The process through which these realities and necessities become established is variable, the outcome involving both personal choice and the victim's particular social situation.

There is an interesting ambiguity concerning the presence and absence of victimization in the new order. In one sense it has been made past and put at a distance; it is no longer expected. The behaviors that accomplish this distance attest to the possibility of victimization (e.g., locking the car, not letting children wander from home) and yet have the meaning of securing a certain nonvictimized existence. We can see how, despite the fact that the protective behaviors imply the pervasive possibility of victimization, the person returns existentially to the belief that victimization won't happen to him.

Each person's way of surpassing secures him so that he does not have to continue to live through the meanings of victimization and can instead return to the undaunted establishment of his own life projects. The belief that it won't happen again testifies to the re-established horizon of a harmonious social order, one that has integrated the phenomenon of victimization. Even the person who asserts, "Of course it could happen again," demonstrates the curious ambiguity of victimization's presence and absence in the new order. He pays lip service to or intellectually acknowledges victimization (and does so because it has become established as a reality), but he lives as if social affirmation instead were assured (e.g., he confidently leaves for vacation, trusting in the new burglar-proofing of his home). This existential recession of victimization must occur if the victim is to return to living his own life in an undistracted way. Words like implicit, overcome, receded, distant, and hidden begin to point to the character of victimization in the new order.

To develop the above structure, the question addressed to the transcriptions, to the psychological reflections on them, and to the individual structures was again: "What is essential to this experience, however implicit, across cases?" Within this question, we also asked more thematically, "How does each constituent of the experience relate to, belong with, and permeate each of the others while contributing something unique to the overall structure?" This inquiry of course leads to a specialized form of results not appropriate for all readers.

The advantages of the General Psychological Structure are just this systematic reflection on, and presentation of, the complex structure of the lived experience. It is this level of study that throws most light on the relational nature of human affairs. It is here that comparisons among structures, and of their transformations (restructurations) into other phenomena, can be studied most profitably. For example, this structure shows how victimization modifies or transforms the configuration of everyday lived experience and how through the victim's struggle with the meanings of victimization, a new order of lived experience forms and becomes sedimented. A General Psychological Structure thus contributes to a psychology of change.

Before summarizing this report, we would like to indicate some appropriate comparison and extension studies: (a) the experience of victims who did not report the crime to their police department, (b) the experience of victims in high crime, low protection areas (ghettos in particular), (c) styles of recovery—of relating to community, personal agency, and disruption, and (d) the experience of persons who sustained crimes but did not view themselves as victimized. We may later study the similarities and divergences of other kinds of victimization, such as those of natural disasters (floods, earthquakes) and of technological victimization (e.g., living in a polluted environment).

❖ SUMMARY

This paper has illustrated an alternative to exclusively quantitative research. In the latter tradition human affairs have been divided into "variables" that are then studied in terms of their "effects" on one another. Typically, to determine their separate impacts some of these variables are presumably held constant while others are manipulated. The data representing these manipulated and manipulator variables are frequency of magnitude measurements within categories (e.g., change in number of crimes per category as judges' sentences become stiffer; or number of times senior citizens go out alone correlated with number of lampposts per block).

Quantitative data can provide critical information. But they cannot divulge the various processes through which the amounts came to be. They cannot tell us what it is like to be a senior citizen nor how it is that some find their lives constricted and others do not. Likewise, crime statistics cannot tell us what it is like to go through criminal victimization. Qualitative research can. Ideally research could include both forms of data, each aiding the other's further design of studies. For example, a quantitative attitude survey might be conducted as an efficient means of seeing whether (as suggested by our Illustrated Narrative) changes in a police department's manner of receiving citizens' calls indeed do encourage broader confidence in the justice system. Note that qualitative research suggests which qualitative differences might make a meaningful quantitative difference.

More particularly, this paper has illustrated, albeit in survey fashion, an empirical phenomenological approach to a psychological phenomenon. We have shown some ways in which researchers can take into account the complexity of experience—its essential ambiguity and flow, its already relational, and creative, as well as created, character—and still render its structure visible. The lived world is researchable, and in ways that can be specified and shared with other researchers.

Still more particularly, we have developed and shared what we believe is a rich sense of the experience of being criminally victimized. Through varying forms of analysis we have presented its general structure while preserving individuals' ways of living that structure. Our findings yield both practical implications for public policy and an appreciation for the mutuality of the discerned constituents of this particular experience.

❖ NOTES

1. Robert Bodnar, Mark Johansson, Christopher Mruk, and Michael Schur.

2. A still more compact version of the process of going through criminal victimization is: "Criminal victimization is a violation by one's fellow, an outrageous assault upon one's assumptions about social order as well as upon explicit social covenants. Safety, freedom, sanctity, future are all thrown into question. Existence stands out as uncertain and problematic as one lives the tensions of being simultaneously object and agent, dependent and responsible, same and different, together and separate. Whether the person balances these tensions toward a sense of mutuality with others or falls into alienation depends upon the extent to which he becomes actively involved with what he experiences as responsive community."

3. It should be noted that this does not necessarily correspond to chronological time since in terms of the psychological structure one may return to or continue to live earlier phases while clock time moves forward.

❖ REFERENCES

Burgess, A. W., & Holstrom, L. L. *Rape: Victims of crisis.* Bowie, Md.: R. J. Brady, 1974.

Giorgi, A. *Psychology as a Human Science: A Phenomenological Approach.* New York: Harper & Row, 1970.

Giorgi, A., Fischer, W. F., & von Eckartsberg, R. (Eds.). *Duquesne Studies in Phenomenological Psychology,* Vol. I. Pittsburgh: Duquesne University Press, 1971.

Giorgi, A., Fischer, C. T., & Murray, E. L. (Eds.). *Duquesne Studies in Phenomenological Psychology,* Vol. II. Pittsburgh: Duquesne University Press, 1975.

Heidegger, M. *Being and Time.* New York: Harper & Row, 1962. (originally published in 1927)

Husserl, E. *Ideas: General Introduction to Pure Phenomenology.* London: Collier, 1962. (originally published in 1913).

Merleau-Ponty, M. *Phenomenology of Perception*. New York: Humanities Press, 1962.
———. *The Structure of Behavior*. Boston: Beacon Press, 1963.
———. *The Primacy of Perception*. Evanston: Northwestern University Press, 1964.

12

Qualitative Data Analysis for Applied Policy Research

Jane Ritchie and Liz Spencer

The last two decades have seen a notable growth in the use of qualitative methods for applied social policy research. Qualitative research is now used to explore and understand a diversity of social and public policy issues, either as an independent research strategy or in combination with some form of statistical inquiry. The wider use of qualitative methods has come about for a number of reasons but is underpinned by the persistent requirement in social policy fields to understand complex behaviours, needs, systems and cultures.

'Framework', the analytic approach described in this chapter, was developed in the context of conducting applied qualitative research. It was initiated in a specialist qualitative research unit based within an

Reprinted from Jane Richie and Liz Spencer, "Qualitative Data Analysis for Applied Policy Research," in *Analyzing Qualitative Data*, edited by Alan Bryman and Robert G. Burgess (pp. 173–194). Copyright 1994 by Taylor & Francis Books Ltd. Reprinted by permission.

independent social research institute (Social and Community Planning Research [SCPR]). The work of the institute spans all areas of social and public policy and is undertaken on behalf of central or local government, voluntary organizations, universities, or other public bodies, or it is grant funded by research councils and foundations. All the institute's work can be broadly classified as applied policy research, some of which is initiated by institute members but most of which is generated by the sponsoring bodies.

'Framework' has been refined and developed over the years but the general principles of the approach have proved to be versatile across a wide range of studies. Our aim here is to describe the method in detail; we use examples to show how the approach can be used to move through the various stages of the analytic process. Because the method has been developed for applied policy research, we begin with a brief overview of the kinds of objectives and requirements this sets.

❖ THE NATURE OF APPLIED POLICY RESEARCH

Applied research can be broadly distinguished from 'basic' or 'theoretical' research through its requirements to meet specific information needs and its potential for actionable outcomes. The social policy field makes use of both applied and basic research, but a great deal is of the former kind. However, a very high proportion of applied policy research is quantitative in form, a heritage from the early years of empirical social inquiry and the result of the dominant requirement of policy-makers for facts (Bulmer, 1982: 40-49). Fortunately, this is changing, as is the role played by qualitative methods. At one time, the use of qualitative methods was seen as acceptable if it was confined to a developmental role for statistical investigation. Now it has become recognized that the contributions of qualitative research are much more wide-ranging and that it has an important place in its own right. Most significantly it has a key role to play in providing insights, explanations and theories of social behaviour.

> What qualitative research can offer the policy maker is a theory of social action grounded on the experiences—the world view—of those likely to be affected by a policy decision or thought to be part of the problem. (Walker, 1985: 19)

In applied policy research, qualitative methods are used to meet a variety of different objectives. The questions that need to be addressed will vary from study to study but broadly they can be divided into four categories: contextual, diagnostic, evaluative and strategic:

Contextual: identifying the form and nature of what exists
e.g. What are the dimensions of attitudes or perceptions that are held?
  What is the nature of people's experiences?
  What needs does the population of the study have?
  What elements operate within a system?

Diagnostic: examining the reasons for, or causes of, what exists
e.g. What factors underlie particular attitudes or perceptions?
  Why are decisions or actions taken, or not taken?
  Why do particular needs arise?
  Why are services or programmes not being used?

Evaluative: appraising the effectiveness of what exists
e.g. How are objectives achieved?
  What affects the successful delivery of programmes or services?
  How do experiences affect subsequent behaviours?
  What barriers exist to systems operating?

Strategic: identifying new theories, policies, plans or actions
e.g. What types of services are required to meet needs?
  What actions are needed to make programmes or services more effective?
  How can systems be improved?
  What strategies are required to overcome newly defined problems?

Most research attempts to address more than one of these groups of questions. But in applied policy research, the objectives are usually clearly set and shaped by specific information requirements. Hence any output from the research needs to be appropriately targeted towards providing 'answers', in the form of greater illumination or understanding of the issues being addressed. This in turn has important implications for the form and functions of the analysis undertaken.

In addition to the research objectives, there are other features of applied policy research which may shape the way analysis is undertaken. First, time-scales tend to be shorter rather than longer—usually months rather than years. If government departments and other public agencies are to maximize their use of research, then they need 'answers' in time to influence their policy or planning decisions. Although all public bodies do commission longer-term research, a high proportion has a specified deadline, related to some key activity in the policy process.

Partly as a consequence of limited time-scales, applied research is often carried out by teams of researchers. These may comprise researchers from different disciplines, or be organized to allow individuals to take responsibility for different parts of the research process. Either way, this requires an explicit research methodology which can be viewed, discussed and operated by individuals within the team.

Another common feature is the need for generated data. Although desk research or document analysis usually forms part of a social policy research project (and occasionally is confined to these approaches alone), it is more usual to find that new data are collected. This may be in the form of individual interviews, group discussions or observational work. Certainly, within SCPR, most of the studies have newly generated interview data (either individual or group) and sometimes an observational component.

Qualitative research meets quite different objectives from quantitative research, and provides a distinctive kind of information. For applied policy purposes it may therefore be carried out with some kind of linkage to statistical inquiry (i.e. to help develop, illuminate, explain or qualify statistical research), or it may be entirely independent. Either way, it is important that the particular contributions that qualitative research can make are fully exploited.

Finally, there is an important issue to address in relationship to the visibility of qualitative methods. One of the factors that has almost certainly inhibited the greater use of qualitative methods in social policy fields is the lack of access that commissioners and funders have to the research process. This is particularly so in the conduct of qualitative data analysis. If decisions or actions are to be based on qualitative research, then policy-makers and practitioners need to know how the findings of the research have been obtained. The research community needs to respond to this by making its methods more explicit. This will bring not only greater confidence in the methodology, but also a deeper understanding of what qualitative research can do, and the way in which it can do it.

❖ AIMS OF QUALITATIVE DATA ANALYSIS

Material collected through qualitative methods is invariably unstructured and unwieldy. A high proportion of it is text based, consisting of verbatim transcriptions of interviews or discussions, field notes or other written documents. Moreover, the internal content of the material is usually in detailed and micro form (e.g. accounts of experiences, descriptions of interchanges, observations of interactions, etc.). The qualitative researcher has to provide some coherence and structure to this cumbersome data set while retaining a hold of the original accounts and observations from which it is derived. All of this has implications for the methods of analysis which are developed.

Qualitative data analysis is essentially about detection, and the tasks of defining, categorizing, theorizing, explaining, exploring and mapping are fundamental to the analyst's role. The methods used for qualitative analysis therefore need to facilitate such detection, and to be of a form which allows certain functions to be performed. These functions will vary depending on the research questions being addressed, but, certainly in applied policy research, the following are frequently included:

Defining concepts: understanding internal structures;
Mapping the range, nature and dynamics of phenomena;
Creating typologies: categorizing different types of attitudes, behaviours, motivations, etc.;
Finding associations: between experiences and attitudes, between attitudes and behaviours, between circumstances and motivations, etc.;
Seeking explanations: explicit or implicit;
Developing new ideas, theories or strategies.

'Framework' has been developed to help these aims and outputs to be achieved. It is also designed to facilitate systematic analysis within the demands and constraints of applied policy research previously cited. To both these ends, the method has certain key features, which were central to its development. These are summarized in Figure 12.1.

Grounded or generative: it is heavily based in, and driven by, the original accounts and observations of the people it is about.

Dynamic: it is open to change, addition and amendment throughout the analytic process.

Systematic: it allows methodical treatment of all similar units of analysis.

Comprehensive: it allows a full, and not partial or selective, review of the material collected.

Enables easy retrieval: it allows access to, and retrieval of, the original textual material.

Allows between- and within-case analysis: it enables comparisons between, and associations within, cases to be made.

Accessible to others: the analytic process, and the interpretations derived from it, can be viewed and judged by people other than the primary analyst.

Figure 12.1   Key Features of 'Framework'

❖ 'FRAMEWORK' AS A METHOD OF QUALITATIVE DATA ANALYSIS

'Framework' is an analytical process which involves a number of distinct though highly interconnected stages. Although the process is presented as following a particular order—indeed some stages do logically precede others—there is no implication that 'Framework' is a purely mechanical process, a foolproof recipe with a guaranteed outcome. On the contrary, although systematic and disciplined, it relies on the creative and conceptual ability of the analyst to determine meaning, salience and connections. Real leaps in analytical thinking often involve both jumping ahead and returning to rework earlier ideas. The strength of an approach like 'Framework' is that by following a well-defined procedure, it is possible to reconsider and rework ideas precisely because the analytical process has been documented and is therefore accessible.

The approach involves a systematic process of sifting, charting and sorting material according to key issues and themes. In order to illustrate the method, and to reflect the context and diversity of its applications in applied social policy research, five studies are referenced, one or two for each stage of the analytical process. Table 12.1 outlines the aims, sample, type of data and time-scale for each study.

The five key stages to qualitative data analysis involved in 'Framework' are:

Table 12.1   Summary of Research Studies
Used for Illustrative Purposes

The Study	Type	Aims or Objectives	Sample	Type of Data	Time-Scale
*Talking About Sex**	Contextual	To explore sexual attitudes and behaviours. To study perceived links between sexual practices and health. To develop issues and clarify language for survey.	40 individuals	Depth interviews	10 months
*Thirty Families**	Contextual	To explore the processes that lead to changes in living standards and the impact of these changes on families.	30 families	Depth interviews, 2 interviews per family	2 phases (9 months) with interval of 5 years
*Barriers to the Receipt of Dental Care**	Diagnostic	To identify the range of factors which inhibit people from seeking dental treatment. To generate ideas on ways of overcoming barriers.	108 dental attenders and non-attenders	Depth interviews (40) Group discussions (8)	12 months
*On Volunteering**	Diagnostic and strategic	To identify and explore motivations to volunteer. To examine ways in which volunteers might be attracted and maintained.	70 volunteers and non-volunteers	Group discussions (8)	5 months
*Going on YTS: The Recruitment of Young People With Disabilities**	Evaluative	To evaluate the processes of recruitment in terms of identification of young people with disabilities; their endorsement for special funding; their referral to suitable schemes. To identify good practice.	97 careers officers; government agency staff; managing agents; trainees	Depth interviews (67) Group discussions (4) Observational notes on training schemes provided	12 months

*These publications, based on particular studies, are listed with full details in the references.

familiarization,
identifying a thematic framework,
indexing,
charting,
mapping and interpretation (this being the stage at which the key objectives of qualitative analysis are addressed).

Each of these analytical stages is described and illustrated below.

Familiarization

Before beginning the process of sifting and sorting data, the researcher must become familiar with their range and diversity, must gain an overview of the body of material gathered. Although she or he will have been involved in some, if not all, of the data collection, and will have formed hunches about key issues and emergent themes, it is important at this stage to set these firmly in context by taking stock and gaining a feel for the material as a whole. Where more than one person has been involved in data collection, the analyst can have only a partial or 'second-hand' grasp of colleagues' material. Even where the analyst has been the sole interviewer, it is likely that recollections will be selective and partial.

Essentially, familiarization involves immersion in the data: listening to tapes, reading transcripts, studying observational notes. In some cases it is possible to review all the material at the familiarization stage, for example where only a few interviews have been carried out, or where there is a generous timetable for the research. However, more often than not in applied policy research, the timetable is too pressing or the volume of material too extensive, and a selection must be made for this initial stage.

How the material is selected will depend on a number of features of the data collection process, such as:

the range of methods used,
the number of researchers involved,
the diversity of people and circumstances studied,
the time period over which the material was collected,
the extent to which the research agenda evolved or was modified during that time.

When making a selection, it is important to ensure that a range of different cases, sources, and time periods are reviewed. For example, in the study of barriers to dental care, material was collected by three researchers, through individual and group interviews amongst regular, intermittent and nonattenders. The analyst chose to review both individual and group data for different types of attenders and to include data collected by different researchers. For the study of sexual attitudes and behaviours, five researchers were involved in interviewing, partly to ease the interviewing burden, but also to evaluate the impact of interviewer characteristics, such as age and gender. Consequently, interviews were selected for review to include different interviewers at different stages of the fieldwork period as well as a mix of gender and age of respondents.

During the familiarization stage, the analyst listens to and reads through the material, listing key ideas and recurrent themes. Where a study aims to explore aspects of the research process as well as substantive issues, for example in the study of sexual attitudes and behaviour, notes are also made on the general atmosphere of the interview and the ease or difficulty of exploring particular subjects.

Identifying a Thematic Framework

During the familiarization stage, the analyst is not only gaining an overview of the richness, depth and diversity of the data, but also beginning the process of abstraction and conceptualization. While reviewing the material, the analyst will be making notes, recording the range of responses to questions posed by the researchers themselves, jotting down recurrent themes and issues which emerge as important to respondents themselves.

Once the selected material has been reviewed, the analyst returns to these research notes and attempts to identify the key issues, concepts and themes according to which the data can be examined and referenced. That is, she or he sets up a thematic framework within which the material can be sifted and sorted. When identifying and constructing this framework or index, the researcher will be drawing upon a priori issues (those informed by the original research aims and introduced into the interviews via the topic guide), emergent issues raised by the respondents themselves, and analytical themes arising from the recurrence or patterning of particular views or experiences.

The first version of an index is often largely descriptive and heavily rooted in a priori issues. It is then applied to a few transcripts when categories will be refined and become more responsive to emergent and analytical themes. For these refinements, the researcher looks for conceptualizations which encapsulate and represent diversity of experience, attitude, circumstance, etc.

Devising and refining a thematic framework is not an automatic or mechanical process, but involves both logical and intuitive thinking. It involves making judgements about meaning, about the relevance and importance of issues, and about implicit connections between ideas. In applied social policy research, it also involves making sure that the original research questions are being fully addressed.

The development of a thematic framework can be illustrated from the study of the living standards in unemployment, where one set of issues to be explored concerned patterns of expenditure in unemployment compared with those when last in work. This area of questioning (as outlined in the extract from the topic guide) and the emergent issues noted at the familiarization stage led to index categories as in Figure 12.2.

It will be seen that some of the index categories were virtually identical to specified areas of questioning (e.g. 1.3 Items and activities reduced); others were newly defined from the emergent themes (e.g. 1.5 Changing patterns over time). It should also be noted that the full index contained a total of 59 categories (i.e. 1.1, 2.1, 2.2, etc.), within 8 major subject headings.

Indexes provide a mechanism for labelling data in manageable 'bites' for subsequent retrieval and exploration. They should therefore not be overelaborate in detail at this stage as the analyst needs to retain an overview of all the categories. The more interpretative stages of analysis, which take place later, will produce the refinement of what is contained in each category.

If there is more than one population being studied (as, for example, in the case of the YTS [Youth Training Scheme] study), then it may be necessary to develop separate indexes for each group. Alternatively, it may be possible to keep a common index but deal with additional elements in the material through extra subcategories. Generally it is preferable to keep a common index for the different groups being studied as this helps immediately to identify both common and divergent themes.

TOPIC GUIDE (extract)

Income and expenditure

Current income:
Sources level (in detail)

Income when last employed:
Level, extent of change

Main effects on expenditure:
What has changed; how has
it changed?

Identify items or activities
which have been

Withdrawn:
Why; how important before,
what does the loss mean to
them; what is the effect?

Reduced:
Why; how important before,
what does the reduction mean
to them; what is the effect?

Maintained:
Why; what is their importance,
why not reduced or cut out?

Increased:
Why; what is importance?

Change in patterns of expenditure:
Did changes all happen
immediately or over time?
What caused change in patterns?

INDEX (extract)

Patterns of expenditure

1.1 Expenditure management
1.2 Items and activities
     maintained, increased and
     newly adopted
1.3 Items and activities reduced
1.4 Items and activities
     withdrawn
1.5 Changing patterns over time
1.6 Two weekly patterns

Patterns of management

2.1 Methods of money
     management
2.2 Methods of control
2.3 Changes in lifestyle, financial
     demands
2.4 Critical times, abnormal
     demands
2.5 Previous financial
     commitments
2.6 Other

RESEARCH NOTES AND JOTTINGS

Managing style variable
Critical times when money management,
expenditure hard to control
Control mechanisms
Changing patterns in early and later stages of unemployment.

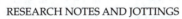

Figure 12.2   Development of a Thematic Framework

Indexing

'Indexing' refers to the process whereby the thematic framework or index is systematically applied to the data in their textual form. Although any textual material can be indexed in this way, the method has mainly been applied to transcriptions of individual and group interviews. All the data, not just those selected for review, are read and annotated according to the thematic framework. Indexing references are recorded on the margins of each transcript by a numerical system which links back to the index, or by a descriptive textual system based directly on the index headings.

Again, applying an index is not a routine exercise as it involves making numerous judgements as to the meaning and significance of the data. For each passage, the analyst must infer and decide on its meaning, both as it stands and in the context of the interview as a whole, and must record the appropriate indexing reference. Single passages often contain a number of different themes each of which needs to be referenced; multiple indexing of this kind can often begin to highlight patterns of association within the data. Of course, this process of making judgements is subjective, and open to differing interpretations. By adopting a system of annotating the textual data, however, the process is made visible and accessible to others; others can see for themselves how the data are being sifted and organized, research colleagues can 'try out' the framework and pool their experiences; the analyst can 'check out' the basis of his or her assumptions.

Figure 12.3 shows a page of an indexed transcript from the living standards study. The first column on the right-hand side replicates the index numbers assigned and any research notes that were made. The far column shows the content of the index categories to which these relate. These would not normally appear on the transcript but have been shown here for the purpose of clarification.

In Figure 12.3, it is possible to see that several different index prefixes appear on one page, even within one speech passage (e.g. 4.1, 1.3, 1.6, 1.4). It is quite common to find that different major topics are connected and interwoven in this way and this is one of the values of indexing. Once these are labelled, the analyst is able to access each reference and, more crucially, to see patterns and the contexts in which they arise. As already suggested, these juxtapositions are often one of the early clues to associations for subsequent stages of analysis.

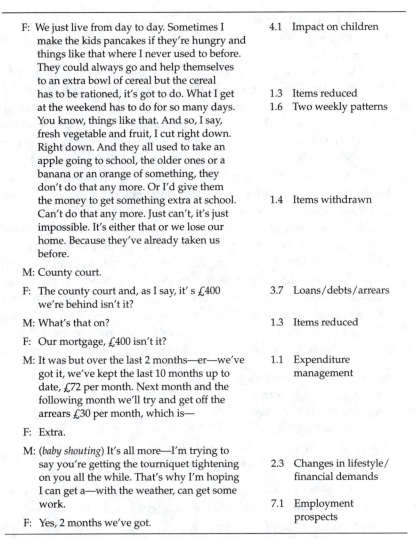

F: We just live from day to day. Sometimes I make the kids pancakes if they're hungry and things like that where I never used to before. They could always go and help themselves to an extra bowl of cereal but the cereal has to be rationed, it's got to do. What I get at the weekend has to do for so many days. You know, things like that. And so, I say, fresh vegetable and fruit, I cut right down. Right down. And they all used to take an apple going to school, the older ones or a banana or an orange of something, they don't do that any more. Or I'd give them the money to get something extra at school. Can't do that any more. Just can't, it's just impossible. It's either that or we lose our home. Because they've already taken us before.	4.1	Impact on children
	1.3	Items reduced
	1.6	Two weekly patterns
	1.4	Items withdrawn
M: County court.		
F: The county court and, as I say, it's £400 we're behind isn't it?	3.7	Loans/debts/arrears
M: What's that on?	1.3	Items reduced
F: Our mortgage, £400 isn't it?		
M: It was but over the last 2 months—er—we've got it, we've kept the last 10 months up to date, £72 per month. Next month and the following month we'll try and get off the arrears £30 per month, which is—	1.1	Expenditure management
F: Extra.		
M: (*baby shouting*) It's all more—I'm trying to say you're getting the tourniquet tightening on you all the while. That's why I'm hoping I can get a—with the weather, can get some work.	2.3	Changes in lifestyle/ financial demands
	7.1	Employment prospects
F: Yes, 2 months we've got.		

Figure 12.3   Example of an Indexed Transcript

Charting

Having applied the thematic framework to individual transcripts, the analyst needs to build up a picture of the data as a whole, by considering the range of attitudes and experience for each issue or theme. Data are 'lifted' from their original context and rearranged according to the appropriate thematic reference. This process, referred to as charting, is described below.

Charts are devised with headings and subheadings which may be drawn from the thematic framework, from a priori research questions, or according to considerations about how best to present and write up the study. How the charts are laid out will depend on whether analysis is to be thematic (for each theme across all respondents) or by case (for each respondent across all themes). Where a thematic approach is adopted, charts are drawn up for each key subject area, and entries made for several respondents on each chart. The ordering and grouping of the individual cases may be linked to characteristics or dimensions that are known or believed to have a significant effect on patterns of experience or behaviour etc. The essential point, however, is that *cases* are always kept in the same order for each subject chart, so that the whole data set for each case can easily be reviewed. Where a case approach is used, one or two charts may be drawn up for each case, with *subjects* recorded in the same order.

In the case of the living standards study, a thematic approach was followed, and six major subject charts were constructed. These covered:

patterns of management,
patterns of expenditure,
personal and social effects,
effects on family life,
standards of living (definition and changes),
employment: activity, attitudes to and job search.

Figure 12.4 shows some of the headings for the chart 'Patterns of expenditure'. Several families were entered on each chart, grouped according to the ratio of their income in unemployment to that when last employed, known as the replacement ratio. By keeping a consistent order for the families on each chart, comparisons could be made between or within cases. It can also be seen that some of the chart headings were identical to index categories (e.g. Items reduced, Two weekly patterns), others reflected newly emergent themes identified while indexing the data (e.g. Periods of new control). For example, this latter heading was introduced to chart data about a period often described in the interviews when families had to introduce new levels of expenditure control.

CHART 3. PATTERNS OF EXPENDITURE FAMILIES WITH REPLACEMENT RATIO 75–90%				
Family	Items maintained	Items reduced	Two weekly patterns	Periods of new control
1				
2				
3 etc.				

Figure 12.4   Example of Subject Chart Headings

Whereas some methods of qualitative analysis rely on a 'cut and paste' approach, whereby 'chunks' of verbatim texts are regrouped according to their index reference, charting involves abstraction and synthesis. Each passage of text, which has been annotated with a particular reference, is studied and a distilled summary of the respondent's views or experiences is entered on the chart. The level of detail recorded varies between projects and between researchers, from lengthy descriptions to cryptic abbreviations for each entry. However, the original text is referenced so that the source can be traced and the process of abstraction can be examined and replicated. Illustrative passages for possible quotation are also referenced by transcript page numbers at this stage.

In the study of recruitment of young people with disabilities to YTS, one of the key subjects to be charted was the way in which different parties defined and interpreted the term 'disability'. Under the overall heading 'definitions of disability', further subheadings were elaborated to include: the 'official definition' (as endorsed by the government agency), the respondents' 'own definition', and 'grey areas' or ambiguities of interpretation or application. Charts were then constructed separately for each group of respondents: careers officers, agency staff and scheme providers. Transcripts were studied according to the appropriate index references, and a summary of each respondent's views entered on the chart. Figure 12.5 shows an example of the chart constructed for careers officers, and illustrates the kind of entries recorded together with the page referencing system.

Respondent	The recruitment of young people with disabilities to YTS CHART 3: DEFINITIONS OF DISABILITY (Careers Officers)		
	3.1 Official definition	3.2 Own definition	3.3 Grey areas
CO1	Includes physical sensory handicaps and learning difficulties. (p. 10) Area officers more flexible than the official guide-lines. (p. 18)	Also add moderate learning difficulties and behavioural problems. (p. 12) 'The naughty boys'. (p. 13)	What about people who are socially disadvantaged? (p. 22) Is inequality a disability? (p. 27) Official view would not accept this. (p. 29)
CO2	Physical/sensory/ mental handicap + behavioural. (p. 15)	Go along with official view. Find it very helpful. (p. 19)	Problem is managing agents take a very narrow view—physical/ sensory only— and the official statistics are based on their returns. (p 27)
CO3			

Figure 12.5   Example of Subject Chart Entries

Mapping and Interpretation

When all the data have been sifted and charted according to core themes, the analyst begins to pull together key characteristics of the data, and to map and interpret the data set as a whole. Although emergent categories, associations and patterns will have been noted and recorded during the indexing and charting phases, the serious and systematic process of detection now begins. It is here that the analyst returns to the key objectives and features of qualitative analysis outlined at the beginning of this chapter, namely:

defining concepts,
mapping range and nature of phenomena,
creating typologies,
finding associations,
providing explanations,
developing strategies, etc.

Which of these the analyst chooses to attempt will be guided by the original research questions to be addressed, and by the themes and associations which have emerged from the data themselves.

Whichever route is followed, the basic processes are the same: the analyst reviews the charts and research notes; compares and contrasts the perceptions, accounts, or experiences; searches for patterns and connections and seeks explanations for these internally within the data. Piecing together the overall picture is not simply a question of aggregating patterns, but of weighing up the salience and dynamics of issues, and searching for a structure rather than a multiplicity of evidence.

This part of the analytical process is the most difficult to describe. Any representation appears to suggest that the analyst works in a mechanical way, making obvious conceptualizations and connections, whereas in reality each step requires leaps of intuition and imagination. The whole process of immersion in the data triggers associations, the origins of which the analyst can scarcely recognize. Because this crucial part of the process is so difficult to encapsulate, a number of different examples are given below, and an attempt made to crystallize and convey the logical and creative pathways followed.

Defining Concepts

In the course of charting references to a particular phenomenon, the analyst may well have begun to identify a number of associated features or descriptions. At this stage, however, she or he systematically examines the charted material, searching for key dimensions and themes.

So, for example, in the living standards study, an analysis was undertaken of how the terms 'living standards' and 'standards of living' were defined by study participants. The case study families, between them, identified nine factors that had a bearing on their judgements of living standards. These were:

the amount of disposable *income* they had,
the items of *expenditure* they could or could not afford,
the level of *choice* or constraint that surrounded their pattern of expenditure,
the level of *financial security* that was felt,
the degree of *struggle* involved in making ends meet,
the material *possessions* they had, or could attain,
the degree to which *expectations* were fulfilled,
the extent to which *self-esteem* could be upheld,
the feelings of *contentment* that surrounded life.

These elements emerged during the course of people describing their present standards of living, or what it had been like before, or how they defined a good or poor standard of living or simply their understanding of the term.

A further example of clarifying definitions is taken from the study of the recruitment to YTS of young people with disabilities, where identifying the range and diversity of concepts of disability was important in order to understand how guide-lines were implemented, and to gain an understanding of the recruitment process. By first listing the characteristics associated with disability, and then ordering them on the dimension of inclusivity-exclusivity, it was possible to devise a scale of definitions, and to identify how different labels were applied. Figure 12.6 illustrates this three-stage process.

Mapping the Range and Nature of Phenomena

A core function of qualitative research is to identify the form and nature of a phenomenon, and where appropriate, to map the polarities. In the study of volunteering, a central objective of the research was to identify key reasons why people might become volunteers. By reviewing the charts for references to attitudes, experiences, images and deterrents, it was possible to draw out key dimensions of motivations to volunteer (see Figure 12.7).

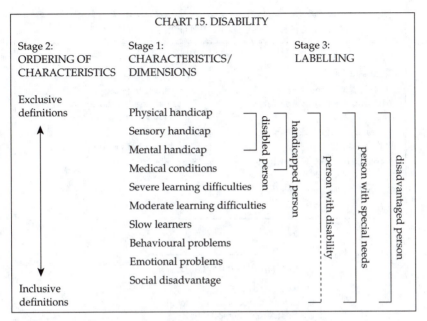

Figure 12.6   Process of Defining Dimensions of a Concept

Creating Typologies

Having identified key dimensions or characteristics of particular social phenomena, the researcher may decide to move on to multidimensional analysis, as in the creation of typologies, where two or more dimensions are linked at different points, giving a range of *types* of cases. In the study of sexual attitudes and behaviours, it was important to establish the nature of people's sexual histories and life-styles in order to understand the context of their views and actions. Key dimensions of sexual life-style were identified as the number of sexual partners over time, and the basis of the relationship(s) or encounter(s). By plotting people's histories and current sexual activity along these two dimensions, a typology of sexual life-styles could be constructed (see Figure 12.8).

Finding Associations

In the course of indexing and charting interview material the analyst may become aware of a patterning of responses; for example it may

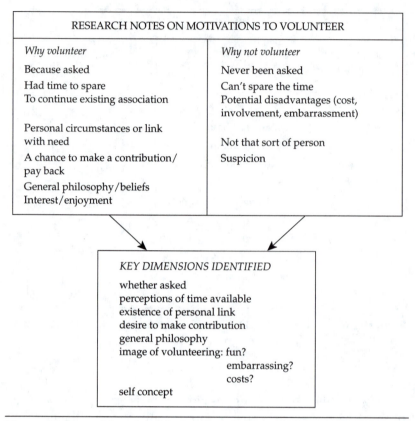

RESEARCH NOTES ON MOTIVATIONS TO VOLUNTEER

Why volunteer	*Why not volunteer*
Because asked	Never been asked
Had time to spare	Can't spare the time
To continue existing association	Potential disadvantages (cost, involvement, embarrassment)
Personal circumstances or link with need	Not that sort of person
A chance to make a contribution/ pay back	Suspicion
General philosophy/beliefs	
Interest/enjoyment	

KEY DIMENSIONS IDENTIFIED

whether asked
perceptions of time available
existence of personal link
desire to make contribution
general philosophy
image of volunteering: fun?
                              embarrassing?
                              costs?

self concept

Figure 12.7   Mapping Motivations

appear that people with certain characteristics or experiences also hold particular views or behave in particular ways. At this stage the analyst will systematically check for associations among attitudes, behaviours, motivations, etc, either those made explicit by respondents themselves or those derived from implicit connections.

In the study of the recruitment of young people with disabilities to YTS, a systematic search among references to disability revealed that particular groups of respondents interpreted 'disability' and applied labels in quite different ways. This association was identified through the process of constructing a central 'labels' chart across all respondent groups. The five different labels associated with disability were chosen to form subheadings, and respondents were plotted according to their

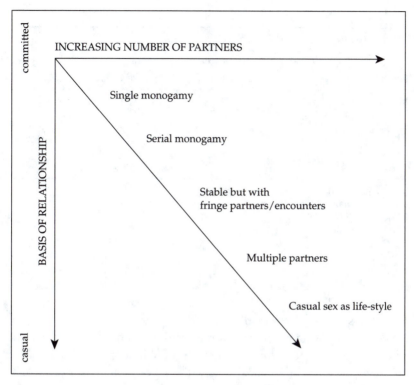

Figure 12.8 Typologies of Sexual Life-Styles

use of particular terms, as shown in Table 12.2. For the sample as a whole, the central chart revealed a clustering of types of respondent under each of the different terms. Whereas careers officers tended to hold the most inclusive definitions and to use labels with the least stigma attached, managing agents of basic schemes held the narrowest definitions, frequently referring to 'the handicapped' and 'the disabled'. This pattern of association is represented diagrammatically in Figure 12.9.

Providing Explanations

A common objective in applied qualitative research is to explain, as well as to illuminate, people's attitudes, experiences and behaviour. Explanations may be sought in order to address the questions that

Table 12.2   Plotting Associations

USE OF LABELS				
Disabled Person	*Handicapped Person*	*Person With a Disability*	*Person With Special Needs*	*Disadvantaged Person*
MA 1 (B)	MA 2 (B)	AS 1	CO 1	CO 3
MA 5 (B)	MA 3 (B)	AS 2	CO 5	CO 4
MA 8 (B)	MA 6 (B)	AS 3	CO 8	CO 6
	AS 6	AS 4	MA 4 (S)	CO 7
		CO 2	MA 7 (S)	
			AS 5	

Key: MA (B) = Managing agent for basic scheme
MA (S) = Managing agent for special scheme
CO = Career officer
AS = Agency staff

triggered the research in the first place, or to account for issues and patterns of behaviour which arise from the research itself.

In the study of sexual attitudes and behaviour, it emerged from the analysis that young heterosexual men and women, whose sexual life-styles suggested they be wise to practise safe sex, were taking no preventative measures at all. They did not consider themselves to be in a high risk group such as people who 'do drugs', or are 'promiscu-ous'. By unpacking how people defined the term promiscuous, it was possible to explain why people did not apply the label to themselves. Key characteristics associated with promiscuity were identified as:

the basis of the relationship (casual),
feelings about sexual partners (absence of),
number of partners over time (compared with own experience),
number of partners co-terminously (more than one).

It became clear that whereas others were described as promiscuous on any one of these counts, people did not label their own behaviour in this way unless all the conditions applied. So, for example, people who had casual sexual encounters or more than one partner at a time did not consider themselves promiscuous if they liked their partners and judged them to be 'nice people'; people who changed partners every few months felt they were exempt because the relationship was 'serious' while it lasted, and so on.

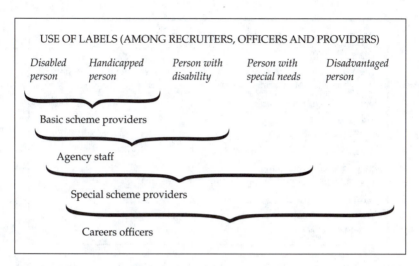

Figure 12.9   Mapping Patterns

Developing Strategies

Much of the research carried out in the policy field has a strategic component; policy-makers commission research into attitudes, behaviours and experiences because they wish to inform their policy decisions. As a result of the process of analyzing qualitative data, and identifying underlying motivations, patterns and explanations, it may be possible to develop strategies for change which arise directly from the qualitative material itself. For example, the volunteering study identified a number of positive and negative conditions which accounted for whether or not people became volunteers. By drawing out the implications of these conditions, it was possible to develop a strategy for attracting and retaining volunteers which directly addressed those issues (see Figure 12.10).

A second example is provided by the dental health study, where a number of barriers to dental care were identified. These in turn led to the formulation of a number of specific strategies that would help people become more regular attenders. Some of these arose out of explicit suggestions made by the respondents themselves, others were derived indirectly from the nature of the problems. So, for example, one key area concerned the cost of dental treatment; specific suggestions made in relation to this were:

ATTRACTING AND RETAINING VOLUNTEERS

change perceptions

need for positive, interesting, caring image, to overcome unprofessional, 'busybody', amateur connotations

practical incentives and help

training
reimbursement for travel expenses

higher profile

provide more information
give a focus for information e.g. identifiable agency

modes of recruitment

personal invitation/overcoming resistance to compulsory schemes

---

Figure 12.10   Developing Strategies

reduce or abolish dental charges,
introduce a clear charging system,
inform patients of the cost of treatment before commitment to carrying it out,
ensure privacy when determining eligibility for free treatment,
(for long-term attenders) provide an incentive of first course of treatment free.

❖ CONCLUSIONS

Because of the nature of SCPR's work, we (and other researchers with us) have had the opportunity to apply 'Framework' on numerous studies. The method, of course, needs to be adapted to suit the aims and coverage of a specific piece of research, but it has proved flexible for a range of different types of studies. It has been applied to in-depth and group interviewing, longitudinal studies, case studies, and projects involving different groups or subpopulations of participants. 'Framework' has also been successfully used jointly by two or more researchers working on a single project, in some cases cross-institutionally.

It will perhaps be apparent that some parts of the process have been relatively easy to display, while others have been much more difficult to capture. Nevertheless, we believe these more elusive stages, particularly those which involve inductive and interpretative thinking, can be made explicit in some form. As already emphasized, we believe this accessibility is important for those who commission and use qualitative research for public policy purposes.

We wish to stress that the analysis method described above is just one approach for synthesizing and interpreting qualitative data. Although it does accommodate all the features we believe to be important, there are certainly other approaches that would equally satisfy these requirements. But, until recently, this has been difficult to know since qualitative researchers have not made their analytic tools accessible. It is important that individual researchers provide documentation of their methods and techniques of analysis, not just in volumes of this kind, but also in research publications and proposals. Only by so doing will the research community widen its pool of analytic knowledge and extend its methodological base.

❖ REFERENCES

Bulmer, M. (1982) *The Uses of Social Research*, London: Allen & Unwin.
Finch, H. (1988) *Barriers to the Receipt of Dental Care*, London: Social and Community Planning Research.
Ritchie, J. (1990) *Thirty Families*, London: HMSO.
Spencer, L. and Whelan, E. (1988) *Going on YTS: The Recruitment of Young People With Disabilities*, Sheffield: Training Agency.
Spencer, L., Faulkner, A., and Keegan, J. (1988) *Talking About Sex*, London: Social and Community Planning Research.
Thomas, A. and Finch, H. (1990) *On Volunteering*, Berkhampsted: The Volunteer Centre, UK.
Walker, R. (1985) *Applied Qualitative Research*, Aldershot: Gower.

13

Bounding the Case Within Its Context

A Constructivist Approach to Studying Detracking Reform

Amy Stuart Wells, Diane Hirshberg,
Martin Lipton, and Jeannie Oakes

S chool reform efforts are perhaps the most studied and least understood phenomena in the field of education. We, like many others,
have tried to understand the complex process of change in schools.

AUTHORS' NOTE: An earlier version of this paper was presented at the American
Educational Research Association Annual Meeting, New Orleans, April 1994. The current version of this article reflects our conversations with other members of our research
team and thoughtful comments by anonymous reviewers.

Specifically, our research team[1] is engaged in a study investigating what happens when someone with power in a racially mixed secondary school decides to reduce ability grouping or tracking—a reform we call "detracking."

Our research question of "what happens when. . ." was informed by our understanding that tracking is an entrenched practice in most American schools and our theoretical framework that recognized that need for not just technical but also normative and political changes in schools before detracking reforms would be feasible (Oakes, 1992; Oakes & Wells, 1995). From the beginning of the study, our research question, guided by our theoretical framework, shaped our "unit of analysis": namely, the phenomenon of detracking reform as a complex and multidimensional school change process.

But the specifics of our research design as a multiple-site, longitudinal case study of secondary schools would take much longer to coalesce—so long, in fact, that we would not have clearly defined and bounded "cases" until the end of our data collection and analysis process, 3 years later. We have learned from our experience and some of the case study methods literature that defining and bounding cases is the catalyst that brings together theory, methodology, and analysis. This activity is not simply a step en route to findings but represents a significant discovery in and of itself. Using this more "constructivist" approach to methodology, we engaged in an iterative process between the theories framing our work and the data we collected in the field. This reflexive process led us to follow the normative and political dimensions of detracking beyond the walls of the schools we studied and into their local communities. In this way, we as researchers were co-constructing our cases with our respondents in the field and thus exploring the local context and interviewing people whom we would not have thought of had we attempted to define and bound our cases before entering the field.

In this article we share with other educational researchers what we see as the benefits and challenges of this more constructivist approach to case study research in education. Our story is especially timely as social science research moves away from positivistic models and toward postmodern paradigms that support a more tentative, inductive, and interpretive form of data collection and analysis (Harper, 1992; McLaren & Giarelli, 1995). Although we realize we are not the first educational researchers to adopt such an approach to qualitative case study research, we felt the need to try to enhance understanding of this approach in a field that is often criticized for being atheoretical and decontextualized (Ozga, 1987).

❖ OUR STUDY AND OUR DILEMMA

Our racially and ethnically diverse team of researchers brought to the detracking study different areas of educational expertise—curriculum, policy, and pedagogy—as well as the perspectives of other disciplines, including sociology, political science, psychology, anthropology, and history. These multicultural, transdisciplinary, and multifaceted inter- pretations enriched our understanding of the complexity of the reform processes and helped each of us be more flexible and creative in think- ing about our research design.

What we did share as a research team was a broad and flexible framework of the multidimensional—normative, technical, and political—aspects of detracking reform in racially mixed schools. Thus, we understood that our study would examine not only changes in school organization, grouping practices, and classroom pedagogy—what we call the "technical" aspects of detracking reform—but also how educa- tors would address well-established school and community norms and political practices that have legitimized and supported tracking as an educational practice. The overarching purpose of our study was to uncover the dynamics of detracking reform in the context of the schools and communities where it is actually occurring and to under- stand what such reform means to those participating in it (Oakes & Wells, 1995).

We chose qualitative case study methodology because we wanted to examine detracking reforms as they affect and are affected by their normative and political milieus. This approach would allow us to examine our unit of analysis—the phenomenon of detracking reform— within its social context (Merriam, 1988; Yin, 1984). We realized that these efforts to "contextualize" detracking reform would lead us to construct cases that reached beyond the walls of the schools and into the surrounding communities, but we were not sure at the outset what that meant.

We also wanted to push theories of school change processes further, and we knew that case study methodology facilitates "theory building," or the process of developing new propositions and generalizations about how and why a phenomenon—such as detracking—unfolds (Eisenhardt, 1989; Yin, 1984). Thus, our theoretical framework informed us that the "situatedness" of detracking reforms in the local community was important and that we therefore needed to collect data outside as well as within the schools to expand or build on this framework. In other words, we knew intuitively and from prior research that reform efforts transcend institutional borders, and thus the boundaries between the schools and their contexts are artificial—constructs of prior ways of thinking about schools as institutions and our habit as researchers to categorize respondents into educators, students, and community members. We understood that community members, in particular parents, sometimes hold as much or more power to control student grouping practices as the educators and that students, as daily "border crossers" between the school and the community, struggle to reconcile the often conflicting norms, values, and belief systems of school and home. These struggles, we knew, would play out in the classrooms, hallways, and lunchrooms of schools in ways that both help and hinder detracking reform. And perhaps most importantly, we recognized, in part because of our familiarity with the "politics of education" literature, that reform efforts, including detracking, vary greatly depending on community characteristics, including racial and socioeconomic composition.

Our multiple-site case study included 10 secondary schools that had taken meaningful steps toward detracking. Our selection of the 10 schools was informed by the case study methodology literature, which argues that case selection in multiple-case or comparative designs is dependent on the theoretical framework that specifies the conditions under which the phenomenon of interest—e.g., detracking reform—is likely to be found (Eisenhardt, 1989). In other words, we were not looking for a random sample of schools from which a particular phenomenon might emerge; rather, we were looking for a select sample of schools in which we knew the phenomenon of detracking was occurring. At the same time, we wanted a sample of schools with different social contexts so that in our cross-case analysis we could draw analytical conclusions about detracking reform that would go beyond the immediate findings in each case and allow us to generalize about the impact of various case contexts—particularly their normative and political dimensions—on the reform efforts (see Oakes & Wells, 1995).

According to Walton (1992, p. 122), the logic of case study research is to demonstrate an argument about how general social forces take shape and produce results in specific settings. "That demonstration, in turn, is intended to provide at least one anchor that steadies the ship of generalization until more anchors can be fixed for eventual boarding."

Thus, we selected our 10 schools based on evidence that real change via detracking reform was taking place as well as our desire for contextual variation in the racial and social class mix of the student body and surrounding community, and among geographic locations and characteristics (e.g., region, urbanicity) of the schools and their districts (Oakes & Wells, 1995). Geographically, the 10 schools we selected are all over the map, with 1 in the Northeast, 3 in the Midwest, 1 in the South, 2 in the Northwest, and 3 in various regions of California. Six are high schools, ranging in size from 1,400 to 3,000 students, and 4 are middle schools with between 550 and 1,300 students. The racial and ethnic composition as well as the socioeconomic status of students within the schools varies widely. Different schools include significant mixes of White, African American, Latino, American Indian/Alaska Native, and/or Asian students.

Once we had selected 10 school sites we immediately began to refer to each of these schools as *cases* without really thinking of what we meant by that term. Because we had not yet visited these schools, we tended to think of our sites institutionally as *schools* and not as larger, interconnected social systems. We planned what was to be the first of three site visits to each of the 10 schools, during which we would conduct in-depth, semistructured interviews; observe the campus, classrooms, and meetings; and collect pertinent documents. Interviews on our first round of site visits were generally with people inside the schools—those who had initiated and were most directly involved with detracking reforms, including school-site administrators, teachers, counselors, and students. We also attempted to collect data on the "district context" during our first round of visits, but we were far less systematic in this endeavor.

Before going to the sites we tried to construct neat categories of people at the school district level—that is, superintendents, district administrators, school board members—and other community members who we thought we would interview at all 10 schools. But on our return from this first round of visits we quickly learned that the school districts and communities surrounding these 10 very different schools did not "fit" our predetermined understanding of what they should be. Furthermore, we became much less certain about exactly what our cases were, how far their boundaries extended, and how to divide our limited time inside and outside the schools.

Thus, while our theoretical framework necessitated that we ascertain the influence of the prevailing politics and norms in the 10 communities on detracking efforts within the schools, we were unclear as to how researchers study both schools and their contexts at the same time.

❖ CONTEXT MATTERS IN SCHOOL REFORM EFFORTS

We revisited the literature on the politics of education at the district level to see how other researchers had dealt with the same dilemma. We found that most of the research on the local politics of education examines the social and political context of schools, especially decision-making processes at the district level, but rarely connects these findings to change efforts within schools. This led us to believe that few researchers before us have tried to examine local context while they are documenting reform efforts within the schools (see Hargreaves, 1985; and Murphy & Hallinger, 1984, for more discussion on this). And yet this politics of education literature clearly demonstrates that the local political contexts of schools vary a great deal in ways that are likely to have a profound impact on the school change process, especially when it comes to contested reforms such as detracking.

Much of this literature examining "local" political contexts and their influence on school-level reforms is outdated, as it was conducted in the 1960s and 1970s; since that time, more educational policymaking and thus policy research shifted to the state level. Still, there are important lessons to be gleaned from this work on the influential role of local context in educational change.

Burlingame (1988) points out that by the early 1960s, research on education policy was heavily focused on local school politics and the power struggles at the school-district level. Community characteristics such as degree of urbanicity, size of city or town, socioeconomic status and race of constituents, heterogeneity of the community, and level of community involvement were all found to have a measurable impact on the way local educational policy decisions were made. In large urban school districts policymakers were generally unresponsive to the needs of their mostly poor and often non-White constituents, whereas studies of suburban districts concluded that the decision-making processes varied greatly depending on the socioeconomic level of the community.

Despite the obvious links between district politics and change within schools, most researchers who studied the politics of education at the local level tended to stay outside of schools. Thus, much of this literature focuses on power struggles between professional educators (mostly at the district level) and lay people and how these struggles are related to several community variables and the current policy issue. But rarely does this research on local, district, and community power struggles (or lack thereof) go the extra step to reveal the interconnectedness of these struggles to the agency of educators—e.g., how community politics affects what happens in faculty meetings and classrooms. And yet, this is the literature that predicts that these political struggles would matter in the day-to-day workings of schools.

There are several reasons why the political scientists and sociologists of education did not take this next step to connect to schools. For one, these researchers were not experts in curriculum or pedagogy, and they avoided studying the relationship between policy decisions at the school board level and what happened in the proverbial black box of the local school site. Also, as statistical methods were refined, and large-scale data analysis became feasible through improved technology, the research conducted by political scientists and sociologists on the politics of education became more quantitative, and therefore even further removed from the school culture (Murphy & Hallinger, 1984, p. 5).

In addition, the sociologists and political scientists who studied the politics of local decision making in education tended to rely on organizational theory or systems analysis—a more rational approach that often underestimates the influence of norms and culture in the political process. For instance, Murphy and Hallinger (1984) point out that policy analysts in education frequently accept the "organizational model" of school systems as loosely coupled entities—that is, seeing the connections between district offices and schools and between school administrators and classrooms as tenuous at best (p. 7). This organizational model, which Murphy and Hallinger see as an overrated explanation for how school districts operate, reduces the importance of the local political context by arguing that district policies have little impact on what takes place in schools and that school administrators' leadership has little impact on classroom practices.

This more rational approach to understanding district-level decision making also underestimates the role that norms and values play in the formation and implementation of educational policies. As Hargreaves and others note, trying to compare and contrast school- and district-level politics through analytic frameworks leads researchers into the realm of ideologies, norms, and belief systems. Mitchell (1974), for instance, argues that one of the primary reasons for studying the context of schools is to develop a solid understanding of the various and often competing ideologies at play throughout the district. He states:

> An adequate understanding of school governance and management must involve a theoretical framework which brings ideological beliefs into proper focus. Only after the ideological belief systems of district citizens, school board members, and professional educators have been effectively mapped can we expect to understand and predict how governance decisions will be made or educational programs enacted in the schools. (p. 43)

This more normative or interpretive understanding of district-level politics and policymaking supports our belief in the need for a more constructivist approach to defining our cases. According to Hawley (1977), researchers studying the politics of education tend to focus on the technical process of decision making at the district level without concerning themselves with the consequences of those decisions for the students these school boards were supposed to serve. He notes that "most political scientists do not approach problem solving by looking back from the point of impact to examine alternative explanations for political outcomes" (p. 328).

Similarly, in Hargreaves's (1985) discussion of the micro-macro problem in sociology of education, he calls upon educational researchers to focus on the middle range between the ethnographic study of classrooms and the large macro- or societal-level research and theory. Without this intermediate or middle-range focus, he writes, there is a tendency to "bolt on observations of what goes on in schools, to speculative understanding and assertions about the very nature of society" (p. 42). He states that what is needed is more research based not just on a single school or classroom, but on the processes in two or more linked settings, drawn from such places as staff meetings, district offices, and teacher union branches. Such middle-range investigation, Hargreaves argues, is interesting not just as an esoteric theoretical project, "but also for the much needed attempt to understand the schooling process in the context of policy changes, economic pressures and so on, and not in isolation from them" (p. 43).

Although the politics of education literature confirmed our belief that context matters when studying school-level reforms, it provided little guidance regarding our methodological quandary of how to bound our cases, how to situate the phenomenon of detracking, given what we know about the influence of community context on school reform.

❖ THE "CONSTRUCTIVIST" APPROACH TO CASE BOUNDING

In thinking about the depth and breadth of our emerging cases, we returned to the methodology literature to find hints about how to study a school and its context at the same time. We looked more specifically at the different perspectives that case study methodologists had brought to bear on the question of "what is a case?" Surprisingly, we found little consistency in the answers to this question. As Ragin notes in the introduction to a book titled *What Is a Case?* (Ragin, 1992, p. 3), the "term 'case' is one of many basic methodological constructs that have become distorted or corrupted over time."

We found that although some case study methodologists stress the importance of following hunches when in the field and defining cases as you go, others presume early identification and bounding of the case and tend to see case definition as a methodological means for coming up with findings rather than a finding in and of itself. Thus, on one end of the spectrum are researchers and methodologists considered "realists" who believe that cases pre-exist as empirical units out there waiting to be studied. Realists argue that there are populations of cases or empirical clusters that researchers need to uncover and analyze. On the other end of the spectrum are "nominalists" who argue that cases are theoretical in nature and that researchers create them through investigation. Thus, from a nominalist perspective, cases do not exist until researchers construct them, or co-construct them with their respondents (Ragin, 1992). We realize that most case study researchers probably fall somewhere in the middle of these two extremes and that the process of bounding a case is generally less systematic and less constructivist than either camp would care to admit.

Perhaps the most "realist" of all the methodologists we read were Goetz and LeCompte (1984), who note that the researcher's task is to determine the groups for which the initial research question is appropriate, the contexts that are potentially associated with the question, and the time periods to which the question may be relevant. "In each case, the researcher sets parameters. Logistical and conceptual constraints affect the choice of groups" (p. 68). Similarly, Bogdan and Biklen (1992) suggest that when proposing a study, researchers should address issues surrounding where the study is to be done, who the subjects are, how the subjects are determined, time for each activity, data that will be included, and how analysis will be conducted. Yet, they also suggest that when determining who the most important subjects are or the boundaries of the cases, researcher "intuition" and the research questions guide what is to be examined.

In the middle of the "realist" vs. "nominalist" spectrum are those methodologists who suggest that researchers use their research question as a guide to deciding whom to interview and what to observe. Miles and Huberman (1994) suggest that the researcher start intuitively; think of the focus, or "heart," of the study and build outward. "Think of what you will not be studying as a way to firm up the boundary. Admit that the boundary is never quite as solid as a rationalist might hope" (p. 27). Although they recommend defining the case as early as possible, they also remind researchers that sampling will further define the case.

But the more nominalist, or what we like to call "constructivist," methodologists suggest that cases are what you make them, and what you make of them depends on the theoretical perspective and framework that grows out of your unit of analysis. This is the "heart" that Miles and Huberman (1994) discuss. But many of the nominalists go further, arguing that cases are socially constructed and co-constructed between the researcher and the respondent. In this way, cases are not really defined or bounded until data collection—and even analysis—is finished.

This "constructivist" view is supported by Howard Becker, who, at a symposium on "What is a case?" argued that to begin research with a confident notion of what this is a case of is counterproductive. Becker noted that such strong preconceptions are likely to hamper conceptual development.

> Researchers will probably not know what their cases are until the research, including the task of writing up the results, is virtually completed. What it is a case of will coalesce gradually, sometimes catalytically, and the final realization of the case's nature may be the most important part of the interaction between ideas and evidence. (cited in Ragin, 1992, p. 6)

Becker argues that researchers should continually ask themselves "What is this a case of?" as they are in the field collecting data. He even goes so far as to suggest that the less sure researchers are of their answers, the better their research may be. Thus, there is no answer to the question "what is a case?" at the beginning of a research project; rather, the question should be asked again and again, and answered only by working through the relation of ideas to evidence (see Ragin, 1992, p. 6).

Ragin notes that researchers who agree with Becker will not claim to know what their research subject is a case of until after most of the empirical part of the project is completed. "Interaction between ideas and evidence results in a progressive refinement of the case conceived as a theoretical construct" (Ragin, 1992, p. 10).

Harper (1992) takes this "inductive" approach to the next level by arguing that researchers are in a sense incapable of making meaning of social phenomena unless they understand the boundaries of these events through the eyes of the people they study. Only through a co-construction of meanings with respondents can researchers truly interpret what it is they have found. He provides a more specific example of this approach to defining and bounding cases in his discussion of research on "communities":

> The boundaries and sociological characteristics of settings are often taken for granted, or defined in an ad hoc manner, meaningful to the researchers but perhaps not to the subjects under study. For example, sociologists often use bureaucratically derived boundaries, such as those defined by census tracts, to define a community. . . . Lining up the sociological definition with bureaucratic definitions makes data accessible and comparable. Yet such definitions may overlook boundaries or characteristics which emerge from an inductive approach grounded in the points of view of community members. (p. 142)

In his research on homeless men, for instance, Harper found that their "community" was not a geographic location but rather a group of people who move together around the country and through various cycles of working, drinking, and migrating. Thus, Harper came to see the "community" of homeless men through their eyes, as "bundles of cultural expectations" that shifted with various cycles and settings, each implying a different set of behaviors. In this way, Harper notes that researchers are entering "moral" or "normative" communities where distinct norms operate and shape meaning. He argues that to interpret these communities, researchers must understand the normative definitions of "objective" concepts such as time and work. Harper adds that most sociologists who studied homeless men traditionally focused only on the institutions found on skid row; thus, these researchers imposed a preconceived and convenient definition of the homeless community on these men, despite the mismatch with their reality and interpretation.

> Defining community one-dimensionally allows us to measure comparable elements, test specific hypotheses, and thus extend or criticize social theories. But doing so confuses a definition reached for expedient reasons with a concept, built from the ground up, which takes into account the points of view of community participants. (1992, p. 146)

Our orientation to defining our cases eventually evolved into this way of thinking about our research sites. Over the course of our three site visits to each school, we began to see our cases more as theoretical constructs that coalesce in the course of the research. Thus, we came to feel more at home with the nominalist or constructivist perspective, arguing that we were co-creating our cases with the help of our respondents in the field. We opted to follow the advice of methodologists in this more open, free-flowing camp because our study was *theoretically* guided by an understanding of school change that transcended school walls. Our initial efforts to prebound our cases had been shaped by our ignorance of what these schools are and what their local social and political contexts meant to their reform efforts.

　　Our own theoretical framework and our multiethnic, multicultural, and transdisciplinary perspectives pushed us to think about how the community contexts of these schools affected and were affected by detracking reforms. But more importantly, we realized that often what mattered more than our "outsider" interpretation of the normative and political dimensions of the communities in which these schools exist was the way in which the educators engaged in detracking reforms interpreted these larger forces. And that while it was logical for us to try to interview the district superintendent at each of our school sites, we had to realize that the title and role of "the superintendent" were vastly different in the various local, normative, and political contexts. As Ramsey (1978) notes, the roles of superintendent, school board member, principal, and so forth are socially constructed by local community norms and politics, with considerable "dissonance exhibited in perception, viewpoint, and mythical representation" (p. 5). These labels or job titles may symbolize different degrees of authority and prestige in different settings, and researchers must not assume they have the same meaning in all schools and communities.

Because the educators who were leading detracking reform within the schools we studied often attributed success, failure, and other elements of the reform to those on the outside, we needed to be familiar with the local politics and social norms that permeate the walls of the schools. We needed this contextual knowledge to interpret the statements, ideologies, and referents of educators within the schools; to understand why educators act as they do; to identify the impetus for particular changes; and to recognize the basis of resistance to change.

Thus, much like Harper (1992), who tried to avoid imposing a predetermined definition of "community" on a group of homeless men, we learned to avoid imposing our predetermined definition of norms and politics on the school communities we studied. We abandoned our static, uniform list of "categories" of respondents from outside the schools and began reaching out to tap the people in the different school communities with the political power to influence detracking reform or the keen insight to help us better understand what the stakes were at each school. At all sites we tried to talk with parents of all races and ethnicities represented at the school; however, other interviews outside schools varied. At most schools we spoke with superintendents and school board members. At several sites we met with members of the business community, when they were involved in the schools, and community leaders (e.g., religious figures, local higher education people) if appropriate or available. In this way, the "category" of people varied widely from site to site, depending on the community's social, political, and economic structure. Thus we tried to move from the school outward, following leads that seemed important from the educators' and students' perspectives. As Walton (1992) explains, "The content and boundaries of cases are reconceived precisely in an effort to forge new generalizations that embrace and supersede earlier understandings" (p. 127).

As we sampled, our cases changed, and as we learned more about the context of each of our schools, we continued to reevaluate who we planned to interview on each consecutive visit and why. Sometimes these decisions became easier, but in many instances, a little knowledge about the politics of the surrounding community piqued our interest and sparked our thinking about the influences of that context on the school change process. And in terms of triangulation, when we heard one thing from the educators in the school and another thing from a group of parents, we became suspicious that we had not heard the whole story from our within-school informants.

Indeed, Maxwell (1992) argues that trying to eliminate threats to "validity" in the initial stages of research design and data collection is not possible in qualitative research. He encourages researchers to address concerns regarding validity only after developing a tentative account of findings. In this way, Maxwell advocates that researchers strive for what he calls "interpretive validity," a concern with what "objects, events, and behaviors mean to the people engaged in and with them" (p. 288). Interpretive validity, therefore, results from researchers' inference from the words and actions of participants in the situations studied—an inference that may be clouded if respondents distort or conceal their views. Still he argues that the meanings and constructions of actors are part of "the reality" that an account must be tested against to be interpretively valid (p. 290). Thus, he argues that researchers must develop their tentative accounts of the phenomenon under study and then return to their sites to seek further evidence that would rule out threats to validity. Maxwell's view complements the more constructivist answer to the question of what is a case, because his conception of validity must be co-constructed with respondents in the field.

In this way, the constructivist method of case definition and bounding was better suited to our flexible and evolving theoretical framework as well as our assumptions that case study research on a school-level reform such as detracking must look at schools as complex organizations within their social and historical contexts (see Oakes, 1987). Our case-by-case exploration of the local school communities pushed us to rethink our framework and to expand what we meant by normative and political dimensions of school change.

Had we not adopted this more constructivist approach to case bounding and theory building we would not have made several important findings that have a strong impact on detracking efforts at our 10 schools. For instance, in virtually all of our schools, our within-school informants tended to minimize the concern and commitment of racial minority parents. Part of our effort in going beyond the school site was to reach less-empowered and less-involved parents as well as members of minority community-based organizations. By listening to their perceptions, we were able to better understand the power relations within each school community that excluded them from meaningful participation at the school site. Had we not learned the "other side of the story," we would not have grasped the significance of the meaning that educators made of these disenfranchised parents' lack of involvement. Although we believed that we were getting at the meanings being made on both sides, and thus we were "interpretively valid," the differences in the interpretations between those respondents inside the school and those in the community caused us to rethink the normative and political dimensions of detracking reform. Because this "meaning" affects the educators' efficacy to carry out detracking reforms, we found that they were overlooking the potential of these disenfranchised parents to act as political allies in their efforts to detrack schools. This finding helps us understand why certain political decisions are made and to unearth norms and ideologies that perpetuate structural inequality (see Yonezawa, Williams, & Hirshberg, 1995).

Similarly, we found that educators were often paralyzed in their efforts to detrack by the threat of White and middle-class flight from the school on the part of parents who had the ability to do so. At some of our school sites this threat was more "real," according to those parents we interviewed, than at others. But without the additional interviews with the parents and community members who have another perspective on this kind of threat, we would have taken the educators' interpretation for granted, assuming in some cases that the threat was more powerful than many of those parents perceived it to be. And yet, the perceived threat of flight, it turns out, is often the mechanism by which the most politically powerful parents make demands on educators and use their political credit to hinder detracking reforms (see Wells & Serna, 1995).

❖ CONCLUSION

Despite our appreciation of the importance of context and the significance of co-constructing cases with our respondents, we were still faced with the very real issue of limited resources, especially time. There can never be enough time to interview and reinterview all those whose information and perspective is important and helpful, especially because the processes we study are fluid. Change continuously occurs—personnel come and go, policies are enacted, respondents' views of reform shift, and political action takes on new and different forms. In this way our study, like all qualitative research, had to be fairly open-ended, but our efforts to venture beyond the walls of the schools made the data collection that much more open. At the same time, we wanted our data from within the schools to be seen as comprehensive and relevant to those who would read our findings and relate the change process within our 10 schools to their detracking efforts.

This struggle to balance the within-school and outside-of-school interviews presented a constant dilemma in the field. On our final round of site visits we took extra researchers or tried to stay an extra day to conduct more community-based interviews; still there was always more—more people to talk to and more perspectives to gather to feel true to our efforts at interpretive validity.

We are now in the process of cross-case analysis of the data we collected, and we have concluded that for our study, the definition of our cases is as much a finding as it is a methodological consideration and that to document the elements that contribute to the social construction of a particular school practice, such as tracking, at and across school sites is a significant research objective.

Thus, in our search for a balance between researching a specific and well-defined "case" and researching its context, we came to understand that they are one and the same. We also learned that these contextualized cases cannot be predetermined as a set of categories of people who need to be interviewed; rather, we must co-construct each case, guided by our theoretical framework and our own personal subjectivities, with the help of our initial respondents in the schools. In this way, we built outward from each school site, identifying those people in the community who had the most influence on or the most distinct insight into the detracking phenomenon that is our unit of analysis.

This meant that in the end, each of our 10 cases was a different shape and size and contained different categories of people; these cross-case differences were in some ways our most interpretive and significant findings about the normative, technical, and political struggles inherent in detracking reform.

❖ NOTE

1. Our 3-year study of 10 racially mixed secondary schools that are detracking is funded by the Lilly Endowment. Jeannie Oakes and Amy Stuart Wells are the coprincipal investigators. Research associates are Robert Cooper, Amanda Datnow, Diane Hirshberg, Martin Lipton, Karen Ray, Irene Serna, Estella Williams, and Susie Yonezawa.

❖ REFERENCES

Bogdan, R. C., & Biklen, S. K. (1992). *Qualitative research for education* (2nd ed.). Boston: Allyn & Bacon.

Burlingame, M. (1988). The politics of education and educational policy: The local level. In N. J. Boyan (Ed.), *Handbook of research on educational administration* (pp. 439–451). New York & London: Longman.

Eisenhardt, K. M. (1989). Building theories from case study research. *Academy of Management Review, 14*(4), 532–550.

Goetz, J. P., & LeCompte, M. D. (1984). *Ethnographic and qualitative design in educational research*. San Diego: Academic Press.

Hargreaves, A. (1985). The micro-macro problem in the sociology of education. In R. Burgess (Ed.), *Issues in educational research* (pp. 21–47). London: Falmer Press.

Harper, D. (1992). Small N's and community case studies. In C. C. Ragin & H. Becker (Eds.), *What is a case? The foundations of social inquiry* (pp. 139–157). Cambridge, UK: Cambridge University Press.

Hawley, W. D. (1977). If schools are for learning, the study of the politics of education is just beginning. In J. D. Scribner (Ed.), *The politics of education: Part 2. The 76th yearbook of the National Society for the Study of Education* (pp. 319–344). Chicago: University of Chicago Press.

Maxwell, J. A. (1992). Understanding and validity in qualitative research. *Harvard Educational Review, 62*(3), 279–300.

McLaren, P. L., & Giarelli, J. M. (1995). Introduction: Critical theory and educational research. In P. L. McLaren & J. M. Giarelli (Eds.), *Critical theory and educational research* (pp. 1–23). Albany: State University of New York Press.

Merriam, S. B. (1988). *Case study research in education: A qualitative approach*. San Francisco: Jossey-Bass Publishers.

Miles, M. B., & Huberman, A. M. (1994). *Qualitative data analysis: An expanded sourcebook* (2nd ed.). Thousand Oaks, CA: Sage Publications.

Mitchell, D. E. (1974). Ideology and public school policy-making. *Urban Education, 7*, 35–59.

Murphy, J. A., & Hallinger, P. (1984). Policy analysis at the local level: A framework for expanded investigation. *Educational Evaluation and Policy Analysis,*
6, 5–13.

Oakes, J. (1987). Tracking in secondary schools: A contextual perspective.
Educational Psychologist, 22(2), 129–153.

Oakes, J. (1992). Can tracking research inform practice? Technical, normative,
and political considerations. *Educational Researcher, 21*(4), 12–21.

Oakes, J., & Wells, A. S. (1995, April). *Beyond sorting and stratification: Creative
alternatives to tracking in racially mixed secondary schools.* Paper presented at
the American Educational Research Association Annual Meeting, San
Francisco.

Ozga, J. (1987). Studying education policy through the lives of the policy-mak-
ers: An attempt to close the macro-micro gap. In S. Walker & L. Barton (Eds.),
Changing policies, changing teachers: New directions for schooling? (pp. 138–150).
Milton Keynes, UK: Open University Press.

Ragin, C. C. (1992). Introduction: Cases of "What is a case?" In C. C. Ragin &
H. Becker (Eds.), *What is a case? The foundations of social inquiry* (pp. 1–17).
Cambridge, UK: Cambridge University Press.

Ramsey, M. A. (1978). Cultures and conflict in local school districts. In F. Lutz &
L. Iannaconne (Eds.), *Public participation in local school districts* (pp. 1–13).
Lexington, MA: Lexington Books.

Walton, J. (1992). Making the theoretical case. In C. C. Ragin & H. Becker (Eds.),
What is a case? The foundations of social inquiry (pp. 121–137). Cambridge, UK:
Cambridge University Press.

Wells, A. S., & Serna, I. (1995, April). *The politics of culture: Politically powerful
parents and detracking in racially mixed schools.* Paper presented at the
American Educational Research Association Annual Meeting, San Francisco.

Yin, R. K. (1984). *Case study research: Design and methods.* Beverly Hills, CA: Sage
Publications.

Yonezawa, S., Williams, E., & Hirshberg, D. (1995, April), *Seeking a new standard:
Minority parent and community involvement in detracking schools.* Paper pre-
sented at the American Educational Research Association Annual Meeting,
San Francisco.

14

The Interpretive Process

Norman K. Denzin

❖ THE STEPS TO INTERPRETATION

There are six phases or steps in the interpretive process. These may be stated as follows:

1. Framing the research question

2. Deconstructing and analyzing critically prior conceptions of the phenomenon

3. Capturing the phenomenon, including locating and situating it in the natural world and obtaining multiple instances of it

4. Bracketing the phenomenon, or reducing it to its essential elements and cutting it loose from the natural world so that its essential structures and features may be uncovered

Adapted from Norman K. Denzin, "The Interpretive Process," in Norman K. Denzin, *Interpretive Interactionism* (2nd ed., pp. 70–84). Copyright 2001 by Sage Publications, Inc.

5. Constructing the phenomenon, or putting the phenomenon back together in terms of its essential parts, pieces, and structures

6. Contextualizing the phenomenon, or relocating the phenomenon back in the natural social world

Discussion of each of these steps is necessary.

Framing the Research Question

The research question is framed by two sources: the researcher and the subject. The researcher with a sociological imagination uses his or her own life experiences as topics of inquiry.

The Sociological Imagination

A person with a sociological imagination thinks critically, historically, and biographically. He or she attempts to identify the varieties of men and women who prevail in given historical periods. Such scholars attempt to examine "the major issues for publics and the key troubles for private individuals in our time" (Mills, 1959, p. 11). Persons with sociological imaginations self-consciously make their own experience part of their research. The sociological imagination is not confined only to sociologists. There are also the "political imagination," the "psychological imagination," the "anthropological imagination," the "historical imagination," and the "journalistic or literary imagination" (see Mills, 1959, p. 19). What matters is the researcher's ability to think reflectively, historically, comparatively, and biographically.

Such a researcher is led to seek out subjects who have experienced the types of experiences the researcher seeks to understand. The subject in the interpretive study elaborates and further defines the problem that organizes the research. Life experiences give greater substance and depth to the problem the researcher wishes to study. Given this interpretation of subjects and their relationship to the research question, the researcher's task of conceptualizing the phenomenon to be studied is easily defined. It is contained within the self-stories and personal experience stories of the subjects. The researcher seeks to uncover how the problematic act or event in question organizes and gives meaning to the persons studied.

The question that the researcher frames must be a *how* and not a *why* question. Interpretive studies examine how problematic, turning-point experiences are organized, perceived, constructed, and given meaning by interacting individuals.

The researcher's framing of the research question involves the following steps:

1. Locating, within his or her own personal history, the problematic biographical experience to be studied

2. Discovering how this problem, as a private trouble, is or is becoming a public issue that affects multiple lives, institutions, and social groups

3. Locating the institutional formations or sites where persons with these troubles do things together (Becker, 1986)

4. Beginning to ask not why but how it is that these experiences occur

5. Attempting to formulate the research question into a single statement

Exemplars: Emotional Experience,
the Alcoholic Self, the Cinematic Racial Order

In *On Understanding Emotion* (Denzin, 1984a), I focused on a single how question: "How is emotion, as a form of consciousness, lived, experienced, articulated, and felt?" This led to an examination of classical and contemporary theories of emotion, an extended analysis of the essence of emotional experience, and two case studies dealing with family violence and emotionally divided selves. I attempted to answer my how question by going to concrete situations where persons interactionally displayed violent emotions.

In *The Alcoholic Self* (Denzin, 1987a) and *The Recovering Alcoholic* (Denzin, 1987b), I asked two how questions: "How do ordinary men and women live and experience the alcoholic self active alcoholism produces?" (1987a, p. 15) and "How is the recovering self of the alcoholic lived into existence?" (1987b, p. 11). These two questions led me to Alcoholics Anonymous, to alcoholic families, and to treatment centers for alcoholism, where I found persons interactionally grappling with the problematics contained in my two how questions.

In my recently completed study of Hollywood's "hood" movies of
the 1990s (e.g., *Boyz N the Hood, Menace II Society*), I examined how a
cinematic racial order that emphasizes violence, drugs, gangs, and the
police is constructed in these films (Denzin, 2001). I compared and
contrasted films made by Anglo, Hispanic, and African American filmmakers. This analysis required a historical treatment of the racial order
and the factors shaping that order in Hollywood film. I moved back and
forth in my analysis from silent film (*The Birth of a Nation*) to the present.

Implementating the How Question

Researchers can implement their how questions in several ways. First,
they may bring persons to a research site. Second, they may go to those
places where persons with the experience of interest naturally interact.
Third, they may study their own interactional experiences. Fourth,
they may examine the scientific, biographical, autobiographical, and
fictional accounts persons have given of their own or others' experiences with the phenomenon in question (Strauss, 1987). It is advisable
for researchers to use as many of these strategies as possible when they
begin to implement their how questions.

Deconstructing Prior Conceptions of the Phenomenon

A deconstructive reading of a phenomenon includes a critical analysis
of how the phenomenon has been studied and how it is presented
and analyzed in the existing research and theoretical literature (see
Denzin, 1984a, p. 11; Derrida, 1981, pp. 35–36; Heidegger, 1982, p. 23).
Deconstructing a phenomenon involves the following steps:

1. Laying bare prior conceptions of the phenomenon, including how
    it has been defined, observed, and analyzed

2. Critically interpreting previous definitions, observations, and
    analyses of the phenomenon

3. Critically examining the underlying theoretical model of human
    action implied and used in prior studies of the phenomenon

4. Presenting the preconceptions and biases that surround existing
    understandings of the phenomenon

Exemplar: Battered Wives

Cho's (1987) social phenomenological analysis of Korean family violence provides an example of how deconstruction works. At the time Cho conducted her study, the major theory operating among researchers examining domestic violence was based on social exchange theory. This theory argues that violence is a normal part of family life and that husbands and wives seek to maximize rewards and minimize costs in their exchange relations. It argues that when the husband perceives an imbalance of exchange he becomes violent and uses physical force as a resource to restore equity in the relationship. This theory has been operationalized with a "severity of violence" scale that measures eight forms of violence: throwing things, pushing and shoving, slapping, kicking and hitting, hitting with something, beating up, threatening with a knife or gun, and using a knife or gun.

Social exchange theory predicts that wives will stay in violent relationships when the rewards are greater than the punishments, and they will leave when the punishments are greater than the rewards. Cho (1987) argues that this framework has the following flaws: (a) It is tautologous—there are no independent measures of rewards and costs, other than leaving and staying; (b) it contains no objective measure of the ratio of rewards and punishments; and (c) it contains no way of measuring a wife's subjective definition of the situation. Hence the theory has no predictive or explanatory power.

Methodologically, this theory rests on the assumptions of positivism. It assumes that family violence has an objective existence in family life that can be measured on a scale. It assumes that observations can be made free of temporal and situational factors. It presumes a linear model of causality. The theory does not address subjective experience or the interpretive process that structures violent interaction (Denzin, 1984b). It views the wife as a passive agent in the violent marriage.

Cho's deconstructive reading of this literature followed the steps outlined above. She developed an interpretive interactionist view of family violence that built from the accounts battered wives gave of their experiences.

The Hermeneutic Circle

"Inquiry itself is the behavior of the questioner" (Heidegger, 1927/1962, p. 24). The basic concepts and questions the investigator brings to a study are part of the research. They "determine the way in which we get an understanding beforehand of the subject-matter . . . every inquiry is guided beforehand by what is sought" (Heidegger, 1927/1962, p. 24). An interpretive circle surrounds the research process. Heidegger (1927/1962) argues:

> This circle of understanding is not an orbit in which any random kind of knowledge may move. . . . it is not to be reduced to the level of a vicious circle or even of a circle which is merely tolerated. . . . What is decisive is not to get out of the circle but to come into it the right way. (p. 195)

Interpretive research enters the hermeneutic circle by placing the researcher and the subject in the center of the research process. A double hermeneutic or interpretive circle is implied. The subject who tells a self-story or personal experience story is, of course, at the center of the life that is told about. The researcher who reads and interprets a self-story is at the center of his or her interpretation of that story. Two interpretive structures thus interact. The two circles overlap to the degree that the researcher is able to live his or her way into the subject's personal experience stories and self-stories. These circles will never overlap completely, for the subject's experiences will never be those of the researcher.

Capturing the Phenomenon

Capturing the phenomenon involves locating and situating what is to be studied in the natural world. Deconstruction deals with what has been done with the phenomenon in the past. Capture deals with what the researcher is doing with the phenomenon in the present, in his or her study. Capture involves the following steps on the part of the researcher:

1. Securing multiple cases and personal histories that embody the phenomenon in question

2. Locating the crises and epiphanies of the lives of the persons being studied

3. Obtaining multiple personal experience stories and self-stories from the subjects in question concerning the topic or topics under investigation (Thompson, 1978).

Exemplars: Battered Wives, the Alcoholic Self

Cho (1987) collected personal experience stories from 64 battered Korean wives. She obtained her stories from women who had called an organization in Seoul, Korea, the Women's Hotline, which received calls from battered wives from 10:00 a.m. to 6:00 p.m. on weekdays and from 10:00 a.m. to 2:00 p.m. on Saturdays. Cho worked as a volunteer in the organization. She took calls from battered wives on the hot line and later held conversations with some of them concerning their battering experiences. From these conversations emerged the personal experience stories that she analyzed in her study.

In my study of the alcoholic self, I went to the places where alcoholics gathered. I presented myself as a person interested in A.A. I have alcoholic family members. I formed friendships with recovering alcoholics and their spouses and children. I also became friends with alcoholism counselors and other treatment personnel in treatment centers. I was able to listen to alcoholics talking in their homes, in public places where they drank, in hospital emergency rooms where they went for medical treatment, in detoxification and treatment centers, and in A.A. meetings.

By capturing the phenomenon being studied, the researcher makes it available to the reader. The researcher presents experiences as they occur or as they have been reconstructed. When the researcher plans to group stories around a common theme, he or she must collect multiple stories. This allows the researcher to compare and contrast the stories of many different individuals located in different phases of the experience under investigation. Multiple stories allow the researcher to identify convergences in experience, although he or she can use any story if it contributes to a general understanding of the phenomenon.

Bracketing the Phenomenon

Bracketing is Husserl's (1913/1962, p. 86) term. In bracketing the phenomenon, the researcher holds the phenomenon up for serious inspection, taking it out of the world where it occurs. The researcher dissects the phenomenon, uncovering, defining, and analyzing its elements and essential structures. The researcher treats the phenomenon as a text or a document; that is, as an instance that is being studied. The researcher does not interpret the phenomenon in terms of the standard meanings given to it by the existing literature. Those preconceptions, which the researcher has isolated in the deconstruction phase, are suspended and put aside during bracketing. In bracketing, the researcher confronts the subject matter, as much as possible, on its own terms.

Bracketing involves the following steps:

1. Locating within the personal experience story or self-story key phrases and statements that speak directly to the phenomenon in question

2. Interpreting the meanings of these phrases, as an informed reader

3. Obtaining the subject's interpretations of these phrases, if possible

4. Inspecting these meanings for what they reveal about the essential, recurring features of the phenomenon being studied

5. Offering a tentative statement about or definition of the phenomenon in terms of the essential recurring features identified in Step 4.

Exemplars: The Balls Story, Battered Wives

Dolby-Stahl (1985) offers a bracketed interpretation of her mother's "balls" story.[1] She took the text of the story apart and interpreted key phrases. She then indicated how those phrases contributed to the essential, interpreted meaning of the story, both for her and for her mother.

Cho's interpretation of the stories of the Korean battered wives she interviewed focused on the importance of resentment (*ressentiment;* see Scheler, 1912/1961) in the Korean family. She based this interpretation on her bracketed reading of the personal experience narratives of the battered wives. This interpretation argued that there are seven stages to resentment once violence enters a marriage: craving for genuine conjugal love, rejection, feelings of hatred, feelings of revenge, repression of revenge, deep resentment, and secret craving for revenge. When a wife reaches the last of these stages, she harbors a desire to kill her husband. A wife speaks:

> Until he comes back at night, I can't sleep. I can't eat, I can't rest. I hate and hate. . . . For 14 years of our marriage, this feeling has built up. My nerve is so weak that I take a pill to rest. . . . I just want to kill him. (quoted in Cho, 1987, p. 250)

Cho's bracketed reading of stories like this led her to develop the interpretation of resentment given above. Cho carefully defines each of the stages listed above (craving, rejection, hatred, and so on) in terms of actual statements made by the Korean wives.

Bracketing and Semiotics

One strategy that is useful in bracketing is semiotics, a technique for reading the meanings of words and signs within narrative and interactional texts (see Barthes, 1957/1972). A semiotic reading directs attention to oppositions and the key words and terms that organize a text. It suggests that these terms (signs) are organized by a code, or a system of larger meanings. These meanings are, in turn, organized in terms of oppositions. The full meaning of a text unfolds as it is told or read. A semiotic reading works from part to whole and from whole to part. It uncovers the codes that organize a text and examines the oppositions that structure its meaning. It draws attention to the multiple meanings of key words and utterances within interactional and narrative texts. It asks the analyst to perform both static and dynamic, or processual, readings of narratives.

A Semiotic Analysis of the Balls Story

Consider again the "balls" story told by Dolby-Stahl's (1985) mother. The larger code that gives the story meaning is the teller's position as a schoolteacher and a mother telling a story about something that happened one day at a country school in Indiana. Within this code are words and phrases (P.E. teacher, coach, basketball) that have specific meanings in the code (e.g., coaches have basketballs). The oppositions that exist in the story deal with (a) men goofing off and women working, (b) men's dirty talk and women's work talk, (c) dumb little things that can embarrass a person to death, and (d) things that aren't funny at the time that are later funny.

The key concept in the story revolves around the word *balls* ("great big basketballs") and the missing word *testicles*. The meaning of the word *balls* is complex. It emerges from within the story and includes balls rolling against the storyteller's door; her statement "What do you mean rolling your balls down the hall!?"; the men bursting out in laughter; and her being embarrassed, realizing that the word *balls* carries a double meaning.

This woman's story, like all personal experience narratives, is doubly complex: First, the experience as it was lived was both funny and embarrassing; second, the experience as told is again funny, but now, in the telling, the teller distances herself from the original experience. Hence the original semiotic meanings of the story are not the same as those contained in its retelling. The first time through, the meanings turned on the storyteller's being embarrassed. Experienced immediately after they occurred and in the retelling, they become funny.

Constructing the Phenomenon

Construction of the phenomenon builds on bracketing. In this stage, the researcher classifies, orders, and reassembles the phenomenon back into a coherent whole. If bracketing is taking something apart, constructing is putting it back together. Construction involves the following:

1. Listing the bracketed elements of the phenomenon

2. Ordering these elements as they occur within the process or experience

3. Indicating how each element affects and is related to every other element in the process being studied

4. Stating concisely how the structures and parts of the phenomenon cohere into a totality

Exemplar: Resentment in Violent Marriages

Cho (1987, p. 249) defined the seven features of resentment (*ressentiment*) in the violent marriage (identified above) and then contextualized them in the following way. She states that in the beginning

> the wife craves . . . love . . . it is rejected by the husband's adultery. . . . the
> incidence of battering happens . . . [and the wife] begins to feel hatred
> toward the husband. . . . the hatred increases as the battering contin-
> ues. She wants revenge. . . . the feelings of revenge are repressed. . . .
> ressentiment arises out of this situation. . . . her craving for revenge
> never stops. . . . the revenge plan . . . [she] has in mind is not to end the
> relationship. . . but to restore it with the punishment. (p. 262)

In this contextualizing statement, Cho creates a processual definition and interpretation of resentment in the violent marriage. She assembles the elements in a sequential manner, indicating how each builds on and influences the others.

The Goal of Construction

The researcher's goal in constructing the phenomenon is to re-create experience in terms of its constituent, analytic elements. In discussing the phenomenological study of emotion, Merleau-Ponty (1964) describes this process in the following words: "One gathers together the lived facts involving emotion and tries to subsume them under one essential meaning in order to find the same conduct in all of them" (p. 62). Replace "emotion" here with the phenomenon in question— battered wives, alcoholism, sexual stories, murders, 12-Step calls, leaving home—and Merleau-Ponty's injunctions still apply. The interpretive interactionist, in the phase of construction, endeavors to gather together the lived experiences that relate to and define the phenomenon under inspection. The goal is to find the same recurring forms of conduct, experience, and meaning in all of them. Construction lays the groundwork for the final step of interpretation, which is contextualization.

Contextualizing the Phenomenon

Contextualizing begins with the essential themes and structures discovered during bracketing and construction. In contextualizing the phenomenon, the researcher attempts to interpret those structures and give them meaning by locating them back in the natural social world. For example, Cho located the resentment Korean wives felt toward their husbands back in their violent marriages. The researcher takes what has been learned about the phenomenon through bracketing and fits that knowledge to the social world where it occurs. This contextualization brings the phenomenon alive in the worlds of interacting individuals. Contextualization locates the phenomenon in the personal biographies and social environments of the persons being studied. It isolates the meanings of the phenomenon for them. It presents the phenomenon in their terms, in their language, and in their emotions. Through contextualization, the researcher reveals how ordinary people experience the phenomenon. The researcher does this by thickly describing occurrences of the phenomenon in the subjects' worlds of interaction. This is often done through performance, as in the poetic-performative works of Anna Deavere Smith.

Contextualizing involves the following steps:

1. Obtaining and presenting personal experience stories and self-stories that embody, in full detail, the essential features of the phenomenon as constituted in the bracketing and construction phases of interpretation

2. Presenting contrasting stories that will illuminate variations on the stages and forms of the process

3. Indicating how lived experiences alter and shape the essential features of the process

4. Comparing and synthesizing the main themes of these stories so that their differences may be brought together into a reformulated statement of the process

The Goal of Contextualization

The researcher's intent in contextualizing the phenomenon being studied is to show how lived experience alters and shapes that phenomenon. The structures of any experience are altered and shaped as they are given meaning by the interacting individuals. Contextualization documents how this occurs.

❖ EVALUATING INTERPRETIVE MATERIALS

By deconstructing, capturing, bracketing, constructing, and contextualizing the phenomenon under investigation, the researcher brings it into sharper focus. The researcher's goal in undertaking these interpretive activities, as indicated earlier, is to create a body of materials that will furnish the foundations for interpretation and understanding. Interpretation clarifies the meaning of an experience. Interpretation lays the groundwork for understanding, which is the process of interpreting, knowing, and comprehending the meaning of an experience. Understanding, through the location of meaning in the experiences of interacting individuals, is the goal of interpretive interactionism.

Ascertaining Meaning

The meaning of an experience or event is established through a triadic interactional process. It involves a person interpreting and acting toward an object, event, or process. This interpretive process brings the event or object into the person's field of experience, where it is acted upon and defined. These interpretations are reflected against the person's ongoing self-definitions. These definitions of self are emotional, cognitive, and interactional, involving feelings and actions taken in the situation. Meaning is biographical, emotional, and felt in the streams of experience of the person. Locating meaning in interaction involves uncovering how a person emotionally and biographically fits an experience into his or her emerging, unfolding definitions of self. It is assumed that this is done through the production of personal experience stories and self-stories. Meaning is anchored in the stories persons tell about themselves. Meaning is always shaped by the effects of particular systems of power and discourse.

The following story is an example. The speaker is an alcoholic who has been sober and free of drugs for nearly 8 months. He is speaking to a group of A.A. members.

> I used to drug and drink with my old friends. We'd picnic and party. One time it went on for 5 days over the 4th of July. Now I don't drink or drug anymore and its like we haven't got anything in common. I mean now that I'm in recovery, my recovery means more than anything else to me. So it's like I don't have these old friends anymore. I've only got friends in recovery now. I've got this customer. He tends bar. He keeps asking me to come by and have a drink. I can't tell him I'm an alcoholic and don't drink anymore. Its like I've lost this friend too. But man, I stand back and look at these people and look at me. It's like they're standin' still, goin' nowhere, and I'm movin' forward. They're back where I used to be. I'm glad I'm a recovering alcoholic and don't have to do that stuff anymore.

The meanings and effects of recovery for this person are given in the above statements. These meanings and effects are shaped by the language and practices of Alcoholics Anonymous. The speaker connects his recovery to the loss of old friends and the gaining of new ones. He connects his recovery as an alcoholic to his statements concerning where he is going and where his friends are. Meaning is given in his experiences.

Interpretive Criteria

Interpretive materials are evaluated in terms of the following criteria:

1. Do they illuminate the phenomenon as lived experience?

2. Are they based on thickly contextualized materials?

3. Are they historically and relationally grounded?

4. Are they processual and interactional?

5. Do they engulf what is known about the phenomenon?

6. Do they incorporate prior understandings of the phenomenon?

7. Do they cohere and produce understanding?

8. Are they unfinished?

Each of these questions requires brief discussion.

Illumination. An interpretation must illuminate or bring alive what is being studied. This can occur only when the interpretation is based on materials that come from the world of lived experience. Unless ordinary people speak, we cannot interpret their experiences.

Thickly Contextualized Materials. Interpretations are built up out of events and experiences that are described in detail. Thickly contextualized materials are dense. They record experience as it occurs. They locate experience in social situations. They record thoughts, meanings, emotions, and actions. They speak from the subject's point of view.

Historical and Relational Grounding. Interpretive materials must also be historical and relational. That is, they must unfold over time and they must record the significant social relationships that exist among the subjects being studied. Historically, or temporally, the materials must be presented as slices of ongoing interaction. They must also be located within lived history.

Process and Interaction. These two dimensions should be clear. An interpretive account must be both processual and interactional. Each example that I have offered here has met this criterion.

Engulfment of What is Known.   Engulfing what is known about the phenomenon in question involves including all that is known to be relevant about it. This means that the interpreter must be an "informed reader" of the phenomenon. Engulfing expands the framework for interpretation. It attempts to exclude nothing that would be relevant for the interpretation and understanding that is being formulated. Because understanding and interpretation are temporal processes, what is regarded as important at one point may at a later time be judged not to be central. Interpretation and understanding are always unfinished and incomplete (see below).

Prior Understandings.   Engulfing merges with the problem of incorporating prior understandings into the interpretation of a segment of experience. Prior understandings include background information and knowledge about the area of interest; concepts, hypotheses, and propositions contained in the research literature; and previously acquired information about subjects and their experiences. Nothing can be excluded, including how the researcher judged the phenomenon at the outset of an investigation. This is the case because the researcher's prior understandings shape what he or she sees, hears, writes about, and interprets. Hence prior understandings are part of what is interpreted. To exclude them is to risk biasing the interpretation in the direction of false objectivity.

Coherence and Understanding.   This criterion concerns whether the interpretation produces an understanding of the experience that coalesces into a coherent, meaningful whole. A coherent interpretation includes all relevant information and prior understandings. It is based on materials that are historical, relational, processual, and interactional. A coherent interpretation is based on thickly described materials. The reader is led through the interpretation in a meaningful way. The grounds for the interpretation are given, and the reader can decide whether to agree or disagree with the interpretation that is offered.

Unfinished Interpretations.   All interpretations are unfinished, provisional, and incomplete (Denzin, 1984a, p. 9). They start anew when the researcher returns to the phenomenon. This means that interpretation is always conducted from within the hermeneutic circle. As a researcher comes back to an experience and interprets it, his or her prior interpretations and understandings shape what he or she now sees and interprets. This does not mean that interpretation is inconclusive, for conclusions are always drawn. It only means that interpretation is never finished. To think otherwise is to foreclose one's interpretations before one begins. That is, an individual should not start a research project thinking that he or she will exhaust all that can be known about the phenomenon by the time the project is completed.

❖ CONCLUSION

In this chapter I have discussed how interpretive researchers formulate their research questions and have shown how researchers conceptualize the phenomena to be studied within the worlds of lived experience. I have also presented the steps taken in interpretive research and the criteria for evaluating such research. Because the subject matter of interpretive studies is always biographical, the lives of ordinary men and women play a central role in the research texts that are created. Their lives and their problems are, after all, the phenomena that interpretive researchers study.

In a certain sense, interpretive researchers hope to understand their subjects better than the subjects understand themselves, to see effects and power where subjects see only emotion and personal meaning (Dilthey, 1900/1976, pp. 259–260). Often researchers form interpretations of their subjects' actions that the subjects themselves would not give. This is so because researchers are often in positions to see things that subjects cannot see. The full range of factors that play on individuals' experiences is seldom apparent to those individuals. Interpretive researchers have access to perspectives on subjects' lives that the subjects often lack. Such researchers also have methods of interpretation available to them that the subjects seldom have (Denzin, 1984a, p. 257). However, the interpretations that researchers develop about their subjects' lives must be understandable to the subjects. If they are not, they are unacceptable.

❖ NOTE

1. This is a reference to the following story, which was told to the folklorist Sandra Dolby-Stahl, her sister, and her sister-in-law by Sandra's mother, Loretta K. Dolby, as the four women were preparing food for a family picnic. The mother had been a fourth-grade teacher at a small rural school for nearly

20 years: "It's just one of those dumb little things that you tell that doesn't amount to a hill of beans. Only, it was the last day of school and everybody was half crazy anyhow, trying to get everything done. And we had our principal and the P.E. instructor, the coach, there; they were goofing off. And I was sitting there trying my darnedest to get everything caught up. And, everything wasn't going so well. And anyhow, I guess everyone was just sort of knowing what they were doing. These men met in the office there, and every once in a while I could hear them laughing. I knew they were telling dirty jokes and everything. And anyhow, we gals—they'd always shut up when we'd get anywhere close. So right at the end there, here the coach came down there, and he had two great big basketballs. And he rolled them clear down there, and they banged up against my door. And I came out of there and said, 'What do you mean rolling your balls down the hall!?' [laughter]

"Those guys—one went that way and one went the other. And pretty soon I heard them burst out laughing, and I went behind my door and slammed the door shut. And I didn't dare show my head out until they'd gone home. . . . Oh, I was embarrassed to death. Crimminee, when he banged those against the door, I came out and said the first thing that came to my mind. I didn't think it was funny til I realized how it sounded. But they vanished" (quoted in Dolby-Stahl, 1985, pp. 55–56).

❖ REFERENCES

Barthes, Roland. (1972). *Mythologies* (A. Lavers, Trans.). New York: Hill & Wang. (Original work published 1957)

Becker, Howard S. (1986). *Doing things together: Selected papers.* Evanston, IL: Northwestern University Press.

Cho, Joo-Hyun. (1987). *A social phenomenological understanding of family violence: The case of Korea.* Unpublished doctoral dissertation, University of Illinois, Urbana, Department of Sociology.

Denzin, Norman K. (1984a). *On understanding emotion.* San Francisco: Jossey-Bass.

Denzin, Norman K. (1984b). Toward a phenomenology of domestic, family violence. *American Journal of Sociology, 90,* 483–513.

Denzin, Norman K. (1987a). *The alcoholic self.* Newbury Park, CA: Sage.

Denzin, Norman K. (1987b). *The recovering alcoholic.* Newbury Park, CA: Sage.

Denzin, Norman K. (2001). *Reading race: Hollywood and the cinema of racial violence.* London: Sage.

Derrida, Jacques. (1981). *Positions* (A. Bass, Trans.). Chicago: University of Chicago Press.

Dilthey, Wilhelm L. (1976). *Selected writings.* Cambridge: Cambridge University Press. (Original work published 1900)

Dolby-Stahl, Sandra K. (1985, January-April). A literary folkloristic methodology for the study of meaning in personal narrative. *Journal of Folklore Research, 22,* 45–70.

Heidegger, Martin. (1962). *Being and time.* New York: Harper & Row. (Original work published 1927)

Heidegger, Martin. (1982). *The basic problems of phenomenology.* Bloomington: Indiana University Press.

Husserl, Edmund. (1962). *Ideas: General introduction to pure phenomenology.* New York: Collier. (Original work published 1913)

Merleau-Ponty, Maurice. (1964). *The primacy of perception.* Evanston, IL: Northwestern University Press.

Mills, C. Wright. (1959). *The sociological imagination.* New York: Oxford University Press.

Scheler, Max. (1961). *Ressentiment* (L. Coser, Ed.; W. H. Holdeim, Trans.). New York: Free Press. (Original work published 1912)

Strauss, Anselm L. (1987). *Qualitative analysis for social scientists.* New York: Cambridge University Press.

Thompson, Paul. (1978). *Voices of the past: Oral history.* Oxford: Oxford University Press.

15

Temporality and Identity Loss
Due to Alzheimer's Disease

Celia J. Orona

❖ IDENTITY CONSTRUCTION IN EVERYDAY LIVING

Defined as an irreversible and degenerative disease of the brain, dementia of the Alzheimer's type (DAT) leads to personality change, loss of memory and cognition, physical disability, and eventual death [1–4]. It is estimated that 80% of those with Alzheimer's disease are cared for in a family setting. Typically, one person in the family

AUTHOR'S NOTE: My thanks to Steve Wallace (University of St. Louis, Missouri) and Eric Juengst (Pennsylvania State University, Medical Center) for taking the time to edit and critique this paper. Special appreciation is also extended to Pat Fox and Barbara Hayes, both of UC, San Francisco. Thanks also to Dr. Todd May for his help on memory and cognition. Portions of the data were collected as resident-in-training at the Alzheimer's and Memory Clinic, University of California, San Francisco.

Reprinted from Celia J. Orona, "Temporality and Identity Loss Due to Alzheimer's Disease," *Social Science and Medicine, 10,* 1247–1256. Copyright 1990 by Elsevier Science Ltd. Reprinted with permission from Elsevier Science.

constellation assumes the moral responsibility of providing care. Indeed, the family as a supportive network for most types of home care has been established [5].

Early studies on the impact of entering the caregiver role focused on the consequences to the caregiver [6–10]. These studies reveal several patterns:

- Over time, providing care for a disabled family member results in a drain on resources;

- Burden of care can be designated as having both a subjective and objective dimension; and

- Subjective burden continues to be experienced by the caregiver long after placement of the Alzheimer's person into a long-term nursing facility.

This paper addresses one specific aspect of the caregiving experience: *temporality* in the context of providing care for a person with Alzheimer's disease as identity loss in that person is experienced. Thus, while the focus is on the subjective experience, the underlying theme is identity loss. In addition, the paper will describe several aspects of a qualitative approach to research as they pertain to the process of grounding the concepts in the data.

Part one of the paper will focus on the process of qualitative research as I experienced it. It is important to note that temporality is but one conceptual "slice" of a larger research project conducted for a doctoral dissertation. Thus, I will describe the early false starts of the research and relate how grounded theory helped me focus on the dissertation topic. Part two is the explication of one dimension of the findings—temporality. As such, the analysis and its conceptualizations focus on temporal aspects of dealing with identity loss in a person with Alzheimer's disease.

❖ THE PROCESS: GROUNDED THEORY

In 1985, at the end of my first year into the doctoral program, I had the opportunity to participate as a team member of an Adult Day Health Center for physically and mentally impaired elderly.[1] The elderly participants attended twice weekly and most were transported in a van. Because I had no idea at that time what my dissertation topic would be (except that it would focus on issues of the elderly), I felt the experience would be helpful.

As the sociologist of the team, my task was to help the staff with activities such as feeding participants, moving those in wheelchairs, leading exercises and games, etc. However, in general, I was free to "hang out," engaging in the participant-observation approach in the tradition of the Chicago School. My plan was simply to observe the interactions between the staff and the participants as well as the inter-actions between the participants. Beyond that, I had no idea what the experience would yield.

Because the program was new to me, I found the first few days somewhat confusing. Besides the participants, there were professional staff members, consulting health professionals, and volunteers. However, it was not long before I was approached by a short, stout woman who introduced herself as "Rose," one of the volunteers. She wondered if I knew where the supplies were kept and if I had met the participants. She took me in hand and assured me that should I have any questions, I need not hesitate in asking for her assistance. After all, it was her job to "know where everything was."

Later, when the director of the program asked if I needed anything, I responded that Rose had already taken me aside to give me informa-tion. I looked toward the far end of the room, where Rose was wiping the tables down. To my surprise, I learned from the director that Rose was no volunteer; she was a participant. In fact, this woman who had so kindly taken me under her wing was a participant suffering from Alzheimer's disease.

What was this disease called Alzheimer's? And who was this woman who looked much as anyone on the street looked, who car-ried on what seemed to be a logical conversation with me? Her name was "Rose M____" and she was in her mid sixties. She lived at home with her adult children. A matronly woman who raised a large fam-ily, she was in the mid stages of Alzheimer's and in the 6 weeks that I worked at the Adult Day Health Center, I witnessed her decline with alarm.

Shortly after that incident, I found that there were other partici-pants who most likely had Alzheimer's disease. They posed for me a most perplexing challenge: to understand what it was like for the families of Alzheimer's victims who cared for them day in, day out, often without respite except for the 2 days at the center.

Each day, I talked to Rose and the others, helped feed them, distracted them, played Bingo with them, watched that they did not hurt one another or themselves, or wander away from the center. Each day, I left the center exhausted. I would ask myself: "What must it be like for the families who know that this situation can only worsen and from which there is but one escape—institutionalization?"

My dreams during this summer were dark. Although I do not recall any of those dreams specifically (never thinking that I might want to use them as "data"), I do recall that they were similar to a dream I had when I was working with wives of stroke victims. In the dream which I recorded at the time, I was in bed and the light from the moon and stars faded until there was blackness. In spite of the blackness, however, I knew there was a large black bird perched at the foot of my bed watching me as I slept. In that dream, I could not tell if the bird was a demon or a friend. Such was the tenor of my summer.

I began to talk to the director about Alzheimer's disease and sought out literature in our library. What I learned was indeed disheartening: progressive degeneration of the brain, loss of memory and cognition, almost certain institutionalization. Each day, I was drawn more and more to those participants who were labeled as having Alzheimer's disease and each day, new questions emerged for me. How did the caregiving relatives cope after working all day to come home and care for their loved ones? Did they spend the evenings "conversing" with the Alzheimer's person? How did they manage to make the decision to institutionalize their loved ones? How did they dress them? Was this an inherited disease?

By the end of the 6 weeks, working on a daily basis with the participants at the center as well as researching the topic in the libraries, I was ready for a vacation. Troubled, fatigued, yet also intrigued, I knew I had a topic for my dissertation. The question was how to narrow it down.

Initially, I had thought that surely one aspect of the caregiving experience would be the pain and anguish when the time came to place the loved one in a long-term care facility. Would there be other such momentous decisions? How did relatives define "profound decisions"? In a small pilot study, I began by examining the process of decision making for those informal caregivers of Alzheimer's persons. I prepared a face sheet and a list of broad questions which included, for example, "What are some of the more difficult decisions you have had to make in the care of _____?" and "Who else takes part in the decision-making process?"

Once having put together a proposal for a pilot project, I was able to locate on my own five relatives who had once cared for (or were caring for at that time) a person with Alzheimer's disease. The interviews lasted from 1.5 to 4 hours. Each interview was conducted in the home of, or a place of convenience for, the respondent.

Interestingly, the following description is representative of the "flavor" of responses I got to what I thought was a critical question. From my notes, I recall that I was sitting in a nicely furnished living room with comfortable furniture, where a stereo system with shelves of long-playing records was evident. "Karla's" home was in a pleasant, upper-middle-class neighborhood. Yet, I could hear in her voice and see in her body the tiredness which had accumulated from the many years of caring for her husband, Michael. When I asked, "What was the process of coming to the decision to place your husband in a nursing home?" she leaned forward:

> Decision? Decision? There was no decision. When it came time, I had no choice. It's like falling in love, no one has to tell you. You know.

For Karla, when the time came, she knew. She described the fatigue, the physical hardship on her; the drain on all her resources, including emotional. She endured the pain of knowing her "partner" of some 40-odd years was gone. During the last stage of the disease, Michael had trouble swallowing. This necessitated emergency trips to the hospital. One trip, however, became significant.

That day as she drove home alone, she looked forward to a house where she could eat a meal while it was still hot, sleep through the night and not have to care for a person who had become a stranger to her; where she did not have to feed and dress a hulking man who fought her every step of the way, who was not even able to stay balanced on the dining room chair. The significance of this drive was that she knew the time had come.

As she described that drive home, I could see in my mind's eye how her home must have looked to her as she reached that realization. However, what I was struck by as I listened to her were my own feelings. I sensed somehow that I had heard another theme. Much as a person working absentmindedly hears an unusual sound in the background and becomes alert, I left her home with that kind of uneasy, perplexed feeling.

I wrote up my notes and listened to the tapes once again. The next two interviews followed quickly with much the same process. All interviews were transcribed and I began my first step: coding.

I began the line-by-line coding as outlined in the grounded theory literature [11–14]. I quickly coded them, writing my notes and impressions on the side margins I had purposely left. Categories emerged. However, the one I had most expected (the profoundness of placement of the Alzheimer's person) was not there with the richness I had anticipated. The issue of decision making was not so very paramount in these particular interviews.

It is the strength of the grounded theory approach, especially as it is informed by the interactionist philosophy, that conceptualizations are grounded in the empirical world. Thus, although I had entered the project with an interest in the decision-making process, I found myself drawn to, and surprised by, categories that had nothing to do with decisions, profound or otherwise. In fact, as I read and reread the interviews, I could literally "see" what the disquietude I had felt in the early interviews was all about.

Each of the first three persons I interviewed made essentially the same exact comment: By the time of the placement, the person they had once known as husband, mother, or wife was "gone." They were institutionalizing "strangers." The person who they had once known had changed to the point of being dead. Karla said it most succinctly, "Michael died a long time ago."

This, then, was the underlying theme I kept hearing in the background. When I asked at what point the other person had changed to be called "different," "gone," each had said: "I don't know but I know he's not the same person!" Identity loss was the central theme in the data.

More interviews followed; however, my focus shifted from decision making to identity loss as perceived by the respondents. Key questions, for example, were "Tell me about your _____ before onset of the disease; what was she/he like?" "What were the first changes you noticed?" Identity loss in a dyadic relationship, within the context of Alzheimer's disease, remained the focus throughout the research project.

In the beginning, I literally sat for days on end with the transcribed interviews spread out before me, absorbing them into my consciousness and letting them "float" about. I wrote memos on whatever struck my fancy or, as one professor called them, my "flights of fancy." These memos included premises about how identity is perceived, what constitutes identity to the average person. I wondered why, if the person was declared "gone," did the relatives hang on to the caregiving experience for so long?

I wrote, sometimes several pages, sometimes only paragraphs, but always following the grounded theory approach. That is, I wrote as the thoughts came to me with no need to be orderly or linear. The only mandate was to write what was emerging from the data [14]. I did not try to make sense of anything yet. Instead, I let the data "talk to me."

Everywhere in my office there were notes of all shapes and sizes until finally, I piled them all in one corner of my desk. Then, there came a point when I felt that a "reading" must take place. For several days, I sat wading through the notes and placing them into what I felt were the major categories, which by then, had been abstracted to a higher level. Thus, "silent partner," "helper," and "neighbors" had been abstracted to the level of *social relations*. "Memory," "clock," and "rituals" were all placed in the category of *temporality*.

Slowly, four major themes emerged around the identity loss process: social relations, reciprocity, moral obligation, and temporality. Identity loss in a member of a dyad as perceived by the other member became the core category, with the four themes constituting the key dimensions of the dissertation. Notations which were not relevant I set aside but did not discard.

I continued with the typical formulation of any research project: reading the literature on Alzheimer's disease and identity, talking to health professionals in the field, and to those professors I had hoped to have on my committee. I continued with more interviews. I continued with the open coding and wrote memos. But most of all, I walked; I sat; I daydreamed.

I found that the slightest imagery could conjure up ruminations about the theme of identity and/or temporality. For example, while driving on a coastal highway, I was struck by the sign cautioning, "Drive carefully, shifting sands." The sign was clear: The sands blew off the dunes onto the highway, making the delineation of the highway and the beach difficult to see. In much the same way, I felt that the delineated identity of the Alzheimer's person was losing its "identifiable edges" or boundaries. Although I wanted to use this metaphor in the analysis, ultimately, I dropped it. What is more important here is that for a while having this imagery helped me understand the process experienced by the caregiving relatives and that I used this imagery to write a memo.

I believe the beauty and strength of the grounded theory approach is that it is *not* linear. Instead, the approach allows for the emergence of concepts out of the data—in a schema that allows for introspection, intuition, ruminating as well as analysis in the "traditional" mode. Indeed, qualitative research, especially in the grounded theory tradition, is not for those who need tight structure with little ambiguity. Strauss says it nicely when he states that "several structural conditions *mitigate against* a neat codification of methodological rules for social research" (emphasis added) [14].

I found the approach more amorphous yet personal in that I was able to use my intuitions and creativity to help me discover and uncover what was conceptually happening in the empirical world. As I have mentioned several times, the process is not a linear one nor did it begin with any clarity. Thus, I cannot say that at step one, I coded and then, step two, I wrote memos and then, I began the analysis. Often, I went from one technique to another and back again. Rather than describe the process of qualitative research, at this point, I will describe how I used some of the techniques to my own advantage.

Coding.   This technique is used with the written interviews or notes in which, line by line, the researcher conceptualizes the data. For those familiar with the grounded theory method, coding each line is the guts of the approach. Though it can sometimes be exciting, especially in the moments of discovery, coding is tedious and takes time. Yet, it is critical.

I did line-by-line coding, first quickly to get impressions and then once again, but this time slowly to test my impressions and to raise each impression to a higher conceptual level. Ideally, coding is done in such a way that the data are raised to a conceptual level immediately. However, I found that if I worked quickly, without too much ruminating, I could come to some "first impressions." This seemed to be an important first step *for me*.

I then went back and more slowly reread the interviews to see if my "impressions" fit and to conceptualize the data. For example, from the early interviews, I made notations in the margins on the following statements from different interviews:

It was the *time of the year* when nobody goes in the yard anyway. . .
At the beginning. . .
It got much worse *later on*.
Who had *ever heard* of Alzheimer's *eleven years ago*.
More and more, he was leaning on me.
Before she would never be like that.
She *used to* love coffee.
Even on *free* days, you're always *up against the clock*.

I found that all my notations on these statements were somehow
related to time and so, when I went back to the second coding, I rela-
beled them all "temporality," writing a memo to myself about the *subjective* and *objective* elements of caregiving for someone. By this time, I
found that color coding was helpful. This was especially true after several runs when I began to see definite conceptual categories emerging
such as "identity" and "temporality."

Memos. Technically, the function of memos is to aid in the formulation
of a grounded theory. However, *how* that end is achieved is left to the
imagination of the researcher, for as Strauss says, "He or she is engaged
in continual internal dialogue" [14]. Thus, I found that memo writing
was used in several ways in various phases of the research.

First, memos were used to free associate, to enter the world of "blue
skying," writing whatever thoughts I became aware of as I read the
interviews or was working on anything at all. I wrote until I felt
depleted on the subject or until I found myself repeating statements or
veering from the topic. I allowed myself the freedom to say whatever I
wanted, in whatever form seemed to flow. I did not attempt to be
grammatically correct or to force myself to find sociological terms to
describe what I was thinking. That, I felt, would come later. Instead, I
went with an idea without monitoring or making judgments about it.

Second, I used memos for the purposes of unblocking. Often, especially during the analysis when I felt I could not quite describe in
words what I felt was occurring in the data, I would begin to "write"
to someone. The "letter" would begin by describing my problem, how
I felt stuck and how I felt sure there was "something" there. I asked
questions of that person (often one of my professors), and had that
person "ask" me questions. The "dialogue" would frequently clarify
and crystallize the concept which seemed to be blocked.

Third, I used memos to document the beginnings of a conceptualization which had emerged from the data, "tracking" its levels from the raw data (words used by the respondents) to my notes in the coding and finally, to the concept. As an example, I recall when I first heard one daughter describe how she gave her mother coffee with her ice cream. The treat was obviously more important to the daughter than to the mother. As I sat in her living room and listened to the ways in which "Nora" took pains to give her mother treats, I felt my eyes tear and the hair on my arms went up.

Later, reading the description of the coffee and ice cream, I kept asking myself why is this so important—other than being touching? For I felt sure that this was important and wrote a memo about what I had heard and then read. I found myself writing about everyday living, idiosyncrasies that make us unique to our loved ones. I thought of the words to the popular song "The way you hold your knife, the way you sip your tea." Here was a relationship between identity and temporality, for as I went back in the data, I found that caregiving relatives used poignant rituals to "hang on to" the loved ones *as they were remembered.*

At this point, let me make note that the use of memos varied. At times, I would use them to unblock; other times, to crystallize a conceptualization. They did not get "better" as time went on; rather, they were used differently for what seemed to be most important at the moment: to unblock, integrate, crystallize, or to "blue sky."

Diagrams.   I used diagrams in several ways. First, I used them *to show process.* Informed by the interactionist philosophy, my study was indeed of a process, that of identity loss. As such, I wanted to "see" the changes that occurred as they were apparent in the data. I also wanted to see the interactions between the players and to graphically document the process as it moved temporally and existentially. These diagrams noted the conditions, strategies, and consequences (or new conditions) of the dyadic relationship as identity of one partner began to slip. For example, it was by way of diagramming that my concept of "existential coordinate" emerged.

Second, I used diagrams *to depict lines of action* with social relations and finally, I used them *to integrate* the relationship between concepts. In this way, I was able to understand the relationship, for example, between the subjective and objective elements of time and how temporality as a dimension impacted the caregiving experience. In much the same way, it was a diagram which "showed" me how objective time and knowledge were related.

I believe diagrams are the least utilized tool in the analytical process yet can yield great understanding of the conceptualizations being developed. If the researcher is unable to graphically depict "what all is going on here," he or she is probably not genuinely clear of the process yet.

What I have tried to depict are several snapshots of one person's experience in the use of grounded theory as a qualitative approach to research. Merely describing the techniques seems insufficient. Intertwined with the utilization of technique—any technique—is how the individual person interprets and makes use of them. In this regard, I have tried to describe, albeit briefly, how I myself used them, and how they fit my own basic style of working. Grounded theory provided the framework for taking observations, intuitions, and understandings to a conceptual level and provided the guidelines for the discovery and formulation of theory.

As I noted previously, four major "themes" or categories emerged from the data: social relations, reciprocity, moral obligation, and temporality. What follows now is a brief discussion of one dimension in the process of identity loss as perceived by the caregiving relative of an Alzheimer's person. More specifically, the following is my conceptualization of the temporally subjective aspects of the caregiving experience.

Each conceptualization is drawn from the empirical world in which a relative encounters the loss of a loved one as "once known" due to Alzheimer's disease. Typically, indicators of identity loss were temporally centered and apparent in activities of everyday living. Three concepts which focus on the temporal aspects of identity loss are: (1) existential coordinates, significant events which alter the person's perspective or worldview; (2) paradoxical meaning in which meaning emerges in a field of mundane tasks of everyday living; and (3) memories of consequence, past experiences which have endured as influential ingredients in the identity maintenance of the respective members of the dyad.

❖ BACKGROUND

The social construction of one's identity is a continual, lifelong process in which maintenance and transformation occur in daily interactions

[15–20]. Many of these interactions take place between members of a family constellation. However, identity is vague, complex, evolving, and often volatile. Thus, a person is never fully "known." Even so, members of a dyad, for example, come to know aspects of one another through countless daily interactions [21]. Indeed, over time, there develop in such relationships myriad gestures, nuances, and idiosyncrasies of everyday living which tell me the other is who I perceive him/her to be, and which, in turn, let me know he/she recognizes me. This pool of knowledge is usually accessible only to the two members of the dyad, and often, is not regarded as "knowledge" by either participant.

Although it is often taken for granted, identity can nevertheless be called into question by a crisis or problematic situation such as the physical and mental deterioration of a loved one who has Alzheimer's disease. Facing personality change, loss of cognition and memory, and physical disability, the person with Alzheimer's disease is typically cared for by a family member [5].

Accounts by family members of Alzheimer's disease patients indicate a common theme: The person with Alzheimer's disease undergoes tremendous change, often to the point of being unrecognizable as the person once known. Moreover, an underlying theme which inextricably informs the process of identity transformation is subjective temporality [22–29]. In the following discussion, I will describe three key ways in which the consequences of identity change are manifested in temporal dimensions.

Three assumptions in a dyadic relationship which are central to my discussion on identity are reciprocity, social structure, and temporality. First, each member *reciprocally* participates in the maintenance and transformation of the other's identity in social interactions. Further, each member, over time, develops an understanding of the boundaries of identity attributes. That is, negotiated boundaries emerge beyond which the person may not venture without the relationship becoming strained; newly formed boundaries are renegotiated. So long as each member continues to relate to the other *as expected*, he or she sustains and maintains the other's identity in taken-for-granted interactions. An understanding of perceived attributes is thus constructed.

Second, there is a *social structure* into which the dyad fits. This web of social relations constitutes the arena for the individual's multiple roles. At work, Jackie is a bus driver providing service to the public as well as a friend to her coworkers. At home, she is a mother, partner, and daughter. In each situation, her role and sense of who she is may be different. Whatever the case, in each situation, the social relations sustain or alter aspects of her identity in daily interactions. Thus, persons confront the conditions of Alzheimer's disease with more than one role as they move, over time, into the respective primary roles of "Alzheimer's victim" and "caregiver."

Finally, the formation and maintenance of relationships includes a *temporal* dimension. Dyadic relationships occur in absolute, clock time, and can usually be located on a specific point on the calendar. Spouses recall their first meeting; parents remember the child's birth. From its beginning point, a history emerges indicating the passage of objective time. Of specific significance to caregivers of the early 1970s is their temporal locations within a historical framework of the disease. This historical location becomes, in itself, yet another temporal dimension. That is, the experience was directly influenced by a lack of knowledge of Alzheimer's disease, both among the lay populace and among health care practitioners at the time. In the terms of Znaniecki [30], a social circle of caregivers was emerging before the authority with expert knowledge had been defined.

However, if identity is formed and maintained in objective, clock time, its formation—and transformation—is experienced in subjective, "lived" time. Indeed, the social construction of reality cannot be "isolated" from time [31]. Participation in relationships is experienced existentially, that is, as experiences in which meaning is created. Memories, good and bad, are socially constructed in the context of the intersecting biographies.

In addition, events are anticipated in a potential future, many of which are taken for granted. In this taken-for-granted world, a person remains "as before," forever performing the little idiosyncrasies that come to make the person as he/she has come to be known. However, as seen in the case of Alzheimer's disease, the person does *not* remain "as before."

This preliminary study draws on in-depth interviews of 10 relatives who assumed the moral responsibility of providing care for a relative with Alzheimer's disease in the early to late 1970s. Open-ended interviews lasted from 2 to 4 hours each and with two exceptions were held in the homes of the caregivers. Interviewees ranged in age from 34 to 74 years and came from varied backgrounds and income groups. In addition, over the past year, data were gathered from weekly case conferences at the Memory Clinic associated with the University, and from participant-observations made at two separate Adult Day Health Care Centers over two 10-week periods. Data collection, coding, and analysis proceeded in the tradition of grounded theory as outlined by Glaser, Strauss, and Schatzman [11–14] and is informed by the interactionist school of thought as well as by Whitehead's theory of time [32].

❖ THE ANALYSIS

Early Indicators

Each respondent described incidents which were examples of his/her relative with Alzheimer's disease symptoms pushing against the negotiated boundaries of identity. That is, their actions in the world of everyday living were uncharacteristic though explainable for a while. Often, the behavior change was subtle and, *in itself*, would not appear problematic to others.

Karla, for example, reported that her husband was a devotee of classical music and proud of his collection of albums. Music was described as "a part of his life." There was not a day when he did not listen to music or record it. "Suddenly," she said, "he was not interested in music anymore. I knew something was wrong." The absence of an identity attribute (his love of music) became an indicator to her that something was amiss.

These types of indicators are often perceived as problematic only to those with intimate knowledge of what the boundaries are.[2] Yet, early signs, both blatant and subtle, were frequently misattributed by friend and relative alike. In the course of trying to normalize the situation, the caregiving relative sought a reason which fit the conditions at that time ("He's just having trouble adjusting to being retired"). In some cases, the relative accepted the reasons given by the person exhibiting the behavior—again because they seemed to fit the situation at the time ("There's a lot going on at work").

These points are elaborated on because they form a critical temporal base of the caregiving trajectory.[3] At point "A" of the trajectory is what I call "irritating indicators": uncharacteristic behavior which caused initial uneasiness in the caregiving relative. The behavior was significant enough to cause attention and concern, but not so grave as to be anxiety-provoking. It is significant to note once again that little was known about Alzheimer's disease in the early 1970s. The "experts" had yet to emerge. The early signs did not portend of disaster to these particular relatives due, in part, to a lack of knowledge of the disease.

Point "B" is the *reciprocal response* to the uncharacteristic behavior, indicated by the relative's attempt to normalize the situation. Thus, "misattributions" emerge in the form of a definition of the situation. Believing he/she had a "real" understanding of what is happening, the caregiving relative relinquished concern, albeit somewhat uneasily. Kate reconstructed the initial months of the disease when neighbors had asked, "What's wrong with Howard? He moves so slowly." She went on to tell me:

> So I said, "Well, he had a Plantar's wart on his foot and he has gone to a doctor and had surgery for it." After the surgery, it was almost every bit as painful. He couldn't exercise and this whole thing slowed him down and I thought that's what was bothering him, and all the overtime at work—because of the plant closing down.

However, there came a point when Kate—like the others—could no longer ignore, deny, or accept any of the prior "normalizing" explanations for the behavior. The person with Alzheimer's symptoms had gone beyond the negotiated boundaries of identity attributes. "I knew something was wrong" is the common theme running through accounts of this time period. Uncertainty prevailed as they "knew" something is wrong—but what? To paraphrase Mead, by virtue of uncharacteristic behavior, the Alzheimer's person has ceased to be the person he/she once was [33].

It is at this juncture (Point C) that the relative mobilized to take action. In most cases, several years elapsed between Points A and B (Irritating Indicators and Misattributions) and Point C (Mobilization) (see Figure 15.1).

Because experts were learning alongside the caregiving relative, the diagnostic process itself took considerable time for these caregivers and often involved several misdiagnoses. Consequently, entering the medical maze frequently added to the pain, uncertainty, and confusion of the caregiver. For example, one doctor responded to Sandra's description of her mother's behavior, "Sounds like syphilis to me," and began appropriate treatment based on that diagnosis.

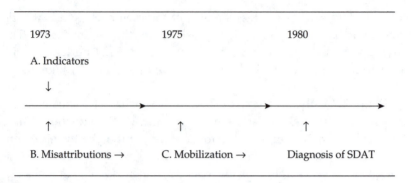

Figure 15.1   Beginning Trajectory of One Caregiver

However, at the point of diagnosis for dementia of the Alzheimer's type, several things happened: uncertainty was diminished and the behavior was legitimized through a name. More critically, *for these particular relatives*—who had no previous knowledge of the disease—the diagnosis with all it implied became a catalyst for what I call an existential coordinate.

❖ EXISTENTIAL COORDINATES

> She was a wonderful driver. . . . As a matter of fact, that was the—that was the one thing when I think I noticed something was wrong. *I knew then and there.* ("Nora": Interview notes)

Existential coordinates are those events which stand out to the person, and *on reflection, reorder the individual's understanding of his/her past and future, and of his/her identity.* In essence, the individual retrospectively reconstructs his/her idea of the past and of the future in terms of current understandings (e.g., the diagnosis). As the person's extant worldview is shattered, what is called for is a different perspective and meaning to life's past events or beliefs as well as new parameters to identity.

These realizations are existential because they are given meaning by the individual and call forth personal values. They are coordinates because they locate the person's sense of identity vis-à-vis a breach in the taken-for-granted construction of a past and future and one moment in time—in this case, the diagnosis. For Nora (who is quoted previously), the moment of time was when she realized her mother could not pass a simple driver's test. Although she did not yet have a diagnosis, she realized the event of that day was fundamentally significant.

Similarly, on hearing the diagnosis, Karla's memories of her husband's neglect of his music, his uncharacteristic quiet moods—all took on new meaning. Her anticipated future (travel in retirement, spending time with grandchildren) was also altered. Moreover, she was faced with the question of who she was in the situation and how she would respond. Said Karla:

> You have to figure out what you're going to do with your life. . . .
> [When] my daughter asked how I was going to cope, I said, "I don't
> know, I may just have to turn things around and find some way I can
> work this out." You can't flounder. You have to do something positive.
> This was my decision.

The events, then, are more than "markers" in a person's life. They are also more than a specific memory, as for example, when we recall where we were when Kennedy was shot. Existential coordinates, then, reorder time and the parameters of identity through the reflection of a single event which crystallizes an ongoing process.

❖ PARADOXICAL MEANING

> I used to do her nails all the time. . . but I'm lucky if I get to cut mine!
> I don't paint hers anymore. I just don't have the time. I'm just so over-
> whelmed that I get to bed so late—and then, it's time to get up!
> ("Jane": Interview notes)

Across the board, caregiving relatives spoke of how their views of time had changed. More than ever, time was experienced as a resource no longer to be taken for granted. In addition, time was also defined in terms of the caregivers' respective realities, that is, "time" became a social construction which emerged in the caregiving experience. One particular aspect which stands out in the social constructions is that of pardoxicality.

Whether it is a child being socialized to specific meal "times" or a tourist fitting into the pace of a different city, we each must respond to a linear time frame superimposed by the social structure. Indeed, in most societies, there is some visible indicator for the most mundane of daily activities, an obdurate reminder in the taken-for-granted world.

In the caregiving experience, relatives faced *paradoxical meaning*, a process in which taken-for-granted activities of everyday living were transformed from a mundane to meaningful level. This juxtaposition of the mundane to the meaningful was paradoxically brought into sharp focus by a ubiquitous element of modern society: the clock.

For the relative caring for an Alzheimer's person, then, the clock became more than an indicator of objective time. It was the symbolic representation of lived or experiential time. Indeed, the clock forced an awareness of the inextricability of lived life and the objective, calendar time.

First, management of taken-for-granted activities was redefined in terms of the clock. Simple tasks like eating and dressing became unremitting challenges. Mundane and routine aspects of day-to-day living were not only problematic for the caregiver, in fact, they came to dominate the day. Other activities, like gardening or reading, dropped away and with them, aspects of the caregiving relative's identity as the most ordinary of chores took more and more time to execute.

As an example, the act of dressing the Alzheimer's person was once a relatively easy task, taking but a few moments. However, dressing progressed to an experience in which each point in the sequence was like a stop frame of a moving film: "Lift this arm, (tapping it) hold it there, let me slip this on, put it down (tapping again). Now let's do the other; lift your arm, hold it there" until the sequence becomes a classic time and motion study. Though *subjectively experienced* as "relatively more" burdensome, in fact, activities of everyday living were also being objectively defined *by the clock* as "taking more time."

Thus the clock became a comparative measure, indicating a "before" and an "after" to activities of everyday living. Today, it took 60 minutes to feed the Alzheimer's person; last month, only 40 minutes. Before that, well, who can remember "before that"? The taken-for-granted aspects of everyday life were no longer experienced as such. When asked what changes had occurred in her life since her mother's illness, Nora sighed, "You know, you never get a whole night's sleep. I don't know what that's like anymore!"

Second, space was existentially redefined by the clock. Sandra, who was in her early forties when she cared for her mother, described how home had evolved into a "prison." For a while, she was able to work and hire a caretaker for her mother; however, the end of her workday had taken on a different meaning for her during the time her mother lived with her:

> So after 5:00, when I would come home, *there was no life after that.* I mean, it was hard for me to go to the store if we were out of milk. You know what I mean? (Interview notes; emphasis added)

However, if taken-for-granted activities became challenges, they were also transformed into "treats," valued for their scarcity in a redefined world. For example, Nora described the bliss of being able to get away for a "lunch where everything is hot and I get waited on for a change"; where the meal is eaten without interruption, a treat made possible by the services of adult day health care. Yet, even here the clock was her constant companion since her "free time" ended at the return of her mother from the day center, as she said.

> You miss being able to—Well, at the drop of a hat, you want to go somewhere. You can't. You always have to stop and think: Now wait a minute; can I go? But you know, you're always up against the time. You're always against the clock. You rearrange your life.

The paradox of the caregiving experience is that in the act of commitment, in the process of transcending the tragedy of loss, the individual comes up against the most mundane, banal, and obdurate fact of life: the clock. The ticking of the clock becomes the tune to which the dance is played. It is the one constant variable around which daily life is organized, and as conceptualized by George Herbert Mead [33], the clock converts a self with a Me and I—to one in which slowly the Me dominates. Spontaneity diminishes and all but disappears. The clock becomes another reminder of a shattered world.

❖ MEMORIES OF CONSEQUENCE

> Anyway, one of the skills which lasted to very near the end was his piano playing. And they found out at [the Adult Day Center]. And he gave a concert and got his picture in the paper . . . brought all this humor into it, like Victor Borge or something. I would love to have been there. I wasn't aware of it. I don't have any of that to remember. (Kate: Interview notes)

It is part of the human condition that identity is inextricably tied to kinship [20]. Like it or not, my name, appearance, and even reputation provide a biographical connectedness to others. One way that this connectedness is socially constructed is through the sharing of memories. However, *memory sharing* requires that I have the ability to be conscious of the temporal aspects of existence. I must have the ability to "recall" past experiences in reminiscing with another. Yet, as the disease progresses, it is this very ability which was being lost to the Alzheimer's person.

No longer able to share family memories—thus providing continuity to the relationship and to the person—relatives nevertheless developed various strategies to use memories in the identity maintenance of the Alzheimer's person.

The third temporal conceptualization, *memories of consequence*, involves the designation and utilization by the caregiving relative of those past experiences which endured as "influential ingredients" in the identity maintenance of the Alzheimer's person. These influential ingredients, in turn, also affected the caregiver's identity by virtue of the reciprocal relationship.

For example, caregiving relatives became aware that they were losing access to a biographical history as reciprocity faded. As the disease progressed, the Alzheimer's person could no longer bear witness to the caregiver. The caregiver was losing a partner who once could validate his/her past existence. Sandra describes the moment her mother no longer recognized her:

> I knew I was losing her. . . . When she did not recognize me, that's what bothered me the most. I'm under the illusion—well, she birthed me. I know she knows me. I've been here, and I *know* she knows me! But she didn't know me. And that was very traumatic for me. (Interview notes)

In turn, the Alzheimer's person was irrevocably losing the opportunity to "render coherent" his/her long life through a shared review of life's memories [31]. Often, a shared life review can help the terminally ill give meaning to life's experiences as well as to provide continuity for those remaining. Yet, most caregiving relatives became painfully aware that this opportunity has been lost. As one wife described:

> However sad it is with cancer patients, it's just worse with Alzheimer's. With Alzheimer's physically they're well, but emotionally and mentally, *he's gone*. With a cancer person, he's still the same person: an Alzheimer's isn't. He has died a long time ago. (Interview notes; emphasis added)

Mitchell, who had decided to keep the truth of the disease from his wife, agonized over his decision long after her death:

> Later, this decision which we managed to keep from her caused me much agony. Too late, I realized I had robbed her of the opportunity to . . . share her emotions and to plan . . . how to use the time we had left to the best advantage.

Memories of consequence were used in a second way as memories of everyday living were recalled and reenacted by the caregiving relatives in order to maintain the symbolic form of social interactions as they once occurred. In the process of *memory keeping*, remnants of the "old" self seemed apparent once again. For example, one young woman told me of the things she did to "hang on to" her mother as she was remembered:

> I would take her out, you know, to movies. I would read to her . . . and she would keep coming in and out, in and out. . . . Oh, she'd kiss me and say, you're so nice—which wasn't different [from before]. She always used to do that. (Interview notes)

The caregiving relative did not assume that the Alzheimer's person understood the significance of the poignant ritual. Instead memory keeping appears to have significance for the relative as an acknowledgment of the person "as before." Said Nora:

> She used to love coffee. Can't stand it now. . . . I give it to her, and of course, I say, "Now it's awful hot." And she lets it get cold, and 'course, cold coffee is terrible. And hot coffee is too hot for her to drink, and she'll taste it and say, "Oh that's bitter. I don't like that." She used to be a great coffee drinker. So now, I spoon a little hot coffee—when we have it—over her ice cream. . . . so she gets a little taste of coffee that way. [imitating her mother] "Ohhh, it tastes good."

These memory-keeping rituals were not moments of ostentatious ceremony, but rather, reenactments of activities of everyday living in which the situation was "normalized" yet simultaneously "made special."

There came a point, however, when even the most durable of memories, memories of the most significant consequence, were not enough. Finally, it became apparent to the caregivers that *even as life was being experienced at the time*, only one participant would have a "memory" of it. Threatened by lack of reciprocal validation, *memory making* became a lonely endeavor for the caregiver, no longer shareable with the Alzheimer's person.

Describing how she had turned her life around in the process of caring for her mother, Debbie sighed wistfully. She told me how unsettled her adolescent years had been and how she had dropped out of high school. She recalled that "toward the end," her mother did not know who or what Debbie had become and how she had changed. Her mother never knew that she had become a grandmother, and although there were "sparks" of recognition, there was no acknowledgment that Debbie had created a good life for herself and for her family:

> I felt sad that she didn't know my girls; she didn't see how I turned out, not that I think I turned out all so great, but I don't think she would have been too unhappy with how I did turn out. (Interview notes)

In the context of caregiving, memories emerged as indicators of events in everyday living that "identified" the Alzheimer's person. More than fleeting images, these enduring memories took on special significance. These memories of consequence endured precisely because they provided value to a number of past experiences which shaped the caregivers' current worldview.

Thus, once designated by the caregiving relative as being "of consequence," the memories were utilized in several ways:

1. Through *reenactment* to preserve the past experiences for continuity;

2. To aid in the *social interaction* with a person as "once known"; and finally,

3. To serve as the basis for *new memories* for another day.

❖ DISCUSSION

Caring for a loved one who suffered from dementia of the Alzheimer's type was a devastating experience in the early seventies when little was known of the disease or its trajectory. Indeed, until Alzheimer's disease became a public issue, the particular caregiving relatives in my study faced the situation alone in a world of "private troubles."

As the Alzheimer's persons changed to the point of being unrecognizable, the caregiving relatives lost remnants of their own identity as the impaired partners were no longer able to reciprocally participate in the relationship.

The caregiving relatives lived with countless daily reminders of the loss that was occurring, progressively apparent as the disease symptoms intensified. While one personal characteristic stood out as significantly lost, the loss was comprised of many subtle actions that were once taken for granted, may have even been endearing or irritating, and were fading.

However, loss of the person "as once known" did not occur without a struggle. These struggles took place in the arena of everyday living. Moreover, caregiving relatives fought to maintain vestiges of the person as known, even when it was not clear if the Alzheimer's person "knew" what was happening, as for example, when Nora gave her mother coffee.

In the accounts of caregiving relatives of Alzheimer's patients, patterns of identity loss emerge. Of special significance to this discussion, attempts at identity maintenance occurred in commonplace activities with little, if any, fanfare. Indeed, the caregiving relatives provided vivid vignettes of identity maintenance where the most profound of commitments is played out in the taken-for-granted world of everyday living. It is as if, once invested in a relationship, the caregiving relative worked to salvage remnants of the other, of their relationship and its history, and of parts of him/herself as well. As reciprocity was lost, the caregiving relative "worked" both sides of the relationship.

With the explosion of information via the popular media, many relatives who face the moment of diagnosis in the late 1980s have greater awareness of the disease and its social, physiological, and emotional consequences. With this understanding come opportunities that the early caregivers did not have, especially as the disease impacts on identity.

First, today's caregiving relatives have the opportunity, if they choose, to participate in the life review process with their loved one before the disease obliterates cognition and memory. This process addresses the issue of continuity vis-à-vis a *past*. In addition, both members of the relationship may face the *future* together while the ability still exists. For example, those with the disease may be adamant about certain aspects of their care (such as heroic measures) and its cost to the family. It is recognized here that Alzheimer's disease is not truly diagnosed as such except by autopsy. Nevertheless, even the remotest chance that such a condition exists may serve as a catalyst for serious dialogue of topics often undisclosed.

Second, those in the support and health services can provide an understanding and acknowledgment of the disease vis-à-vis its existential ramifications. Support must be forthcoming to aid in the loss that is being sustained: that of a person, a relationship, and of a self. If the chronically ill face a loss of self-image as Charmaz [15] suggests, so, too, do those who assume the moral responsibility for providing care.

Identity provides perspective to life's challenges, guides action, and renders coherent a life of change and constancy. This examination of the caregiving experience, then, is presented as a "temporal slice" of a whole, a slice which demonstrates how some relatives faced identity loss and the struggle which took place in the world of everyday living.

❖ NOTES

1. Each team was comprised of one graduate student from the Schools of Dentistry, Medicine, Nursing, Pharmacy, and the Social Sciences.

2. At the other end are those cues which are immediately perceived as problematic by the observer regardless of relationship: erratic driving and the inability to handle simple money transactions, etc. Here, even a stranger would remark on the behavior. Interpretations on the cause of the behavior would vary, of course, and not necessarily be correct, as for example, when erratic driving is attributed to alcohol or drug use.

3. Used in conjunction with "illness trajectory," a term coined by Glaser and Strauss which "refers not only to the physiological unfolding of a patient's disease but to the total organization of work done over that course, plus the impact on those involved with that work and its organization" (Strauss A. et al. *Social Organization of Medical Work*, University of Chicago Press, Chicago, IL, 1985).

❖ REFERENCES

Terry R. D. and Katzman R. Senile dementia of the Alzheimer type. *Ann. Neurol. 14*, 497–506, Nov. 1983.

Cohen G. Historical views and evolution concepts. In *Alzheimer's Disease: The Standard Reference* (Edited by Reisberg B.). Free Press, New York, 1983.

Boyd D. A contribution to the psychopathology of Alzheimer's disease. *Am. J. Psychiat. 93*, 155–175, 1936.

Reisberg B. An overview of current concepts of Alzheimer's disease, senile dementia and age-associated cognitive decline. In *Alzheimer's Disease: The Standard Reference* (Edited by Reisberg B.). Free Press, New York, 1983.

Brody E. M. and Schoonover C. B. Patterns of parent care when adult daughters work and when they do not. *The Gerontologist 25*, 373–381, 1986.

Brody E. M. Patient care as a normative family stress. *The Gerontologist 25*, 19–29, 1985.

Fontana A. and Smith R. W. The shrinking world: Caring for senile dementia patients. Paper presented at *Pacific Sociological Association Conference,* Eugene, Oregon, 1987.

Gilhooly M. L. M. *et al. The Dementias.* Prentice-Hall, Englewood Cliffs, NJ, 1986.

Johnson C. L. and Catalano D. J. A longitudinal study of family supports to impaired elderly. *The Gerontologist 23,* 612–619, 1983.

Zarit S. H. *et al.* Subjective burden of husbands and wives as caregivers: A longitudinal study. *The Gerontologist 26,* 260–266, 1986.

Glaser B. and Strauss A. *The Discovery of Grounded Theory.* Aldine, New York, 1967.

Glaser B. *Theoretical Sensitivity.* Sociology Press, Mill Valley, CA, 1978.

Schatzman L. and Strauss A. *Field Research.* Prentice-Hall, Englewood Cliffs, NJ, 1973.

Strauss A. *Qualitative Analysis for Social Scientists.* Cambridge University Press, New York, 1987.

Charmaz K. Loss of self: A fundamental form of suffering in the chronically ill. *Sociol. Hlth Illn. 5,* 169–195, July 1983.

Gubrium J. *Time, Roles, and Self in Old Age.* Human Sciences Press, New York, 1976.

Hazan H. Continuity and transformation among the aged: A study in the anthropology of time. *Curr. Anthrop. 25,* 567–578, 1984.

Kaufman S. *The Ageless Self: Sources of Meaning in Later Life.* University of Wisconsin Press, Madison, WI, 1986.

Myerhoff B. *Number Our Days.* Simon & Schuster, New York, 1978.

Strauss A. *Mirrors and Masks.* Sociology Press, Mill Valley, CA, 1969.

Simmel G. *The Sociology of Georg Simmel* (Edited by Wolff K. H.). Free Press, New York, 1950.

Mead G. H. *The Philosophy of the Present* (Edited by Murphy A. E.). University of Chicago Press, Chicago, IL, 1932.

Calkins K. Time: Perspectives, markings and styles of usage. *Soc. Probl. 17,* 487–501, 1969.

Denzin N. Under the influence of time: Reading the interactional text. *Sociol. Q. 28,* 327–341, 1987.

Flaherty M. Multiple realities and the experience of duration. *Sociol. Q. 28,* 313–326, 1987.

Lewis J. and Weigert A. The structures and meanings of social time. *Soc. Forces 60,* 432–462, 1981.

Maines D. *et al.* Sociological import of G. H. Mead's theory of the past. *Am. Sociol. Rev. 48,* 161–173, April 1987.

Glaser B. and Strauss A. Temporal aspects of dying as a nonscheduled status passage. *Am. J. Sociol. 71,* 48–59, 1965.

Maines D. The significance of temporality for the development of sociological theory. *Sociol. Q. 28,* 303–311, 1987.

Znaniecki F. *The Social Role of the Man of Knowledge.* Harper & Row, New York, 1940.

Juengst E. Time and value in Whitehead's cosmology. Unpublished paper. Pennsylvania State University, School of Medicine, Hershey, PA, 1981.

Whitehead A. N. *Process and Reality.* Free Press, New York, 1929.

Mead G. H. *On Social Psychology* (Edited by Strauss A.). University of Chicago Press, Chicago, IL, 1956.

16

Reflections and Advice

Matthew B. Miles and A. Michael Huberman

❖ REFLECTIONS

Writing the second edition of *Qualitative Data Analysis* has been a long, sometimes arduous, and always fascinating journey. The experience has reconfirmed the old saw that trying to teach something deepens your understanding of it. The process of clarifying, reformulating, and synthesizing the ideas in this second edition has extended and enriched our thinking about qualitative data analysis methods. We are grateful to the many colleagues who helped us advance.

Throughout the process we have aimed to stay practical, close to the reader's elbow, talking aloud as we went, offering both variations and advice. Some methodological texts tend toward the abstract,

Excerpted and adapted from Matthew B. Miles and A. Michael Huberman, *Qualitative Data Analysis: An Expanded Sourcebook* (2nd ed.). Copyright 1994 Sage Publications Inc.

with brief examples that always seem to work out clearly, even effortlessly. Yet when you actually come to grips with collecting and analyzing real-life data, things seldom work out that way. Research-in-use is almost always more intractable, disjointed, and perverse than research-in-theory, and we have tried to take careful account of that fact. In short, *doing* qualitative analysis is the way you get better at it—and we believe that holds true not just for novices and new entrants to qualitative work, but for wise old dogs as well.

We believe that methodological quagmires, mazes, and dead ends are not necessarily the products of researcher incapacity; rather, they stem from qualitative data themselves. Like the phenomena they mirror, these data are usually complex and ambiguous and sometimes downright contradictory. Doing qualitative analysis means living for as long as possible with that complexity and ambiguity, coming to terms with it, and passing on your conclusions to the reader in a form that clarifies and deepens understanding. It's not surprising that the mechanics of analysis seem formidable or elusive even to experienced analysts—and that researchers have often shied away from making them fully explicit.

It's right to say that qualitative data analysis is a craft—one that carries its own disciplines. There are *many* ways of getting analyses "right"—precise, trustworthy, compelling, credible—and they cannot be wholly predicted in advance.

But we are not alone in experiencing such indeterminacy. The same holds true for experimental and correlational researchers. They use a variety of designs and instruments to study the same problems. They lose subjects from their samples. Their instrumentation behaves strangely. The data from some cases are equivocal, sometimes unfathomable. Researchers make intuitive leaps when looking at data outputs. Quantitative researchers get better at their work by learning how to contend with these normal problems, not by seeking for an ideal design and a fully spelled-out conceptualization. They are not Platonists, but analytic pragmatists, just like qualitative researchers.

We've found that making the steps of analysis explicit makes them less formidable and uncertain, and more manageable. You don't need prolonged socialization or arcane technologies. The core requisites for qualitative analysis seem to be a little creativity, systematic doggedness, some good conceptual sensibilities, and cognitive flexibility—the capacity to rapidly undo your way of construing or transforming the data and to try another, more promising tack. (Those, and a little help from your friends. . . .) None of these qualities is contingent on a battery of advanced "methods courses."

We also don't think that good qualitative analysis necessarily calls for formal prerequisites (e.g., long ethnographic experience, knowledge of scientific logic, deep background in epistemology). Those are all useful tools and can empower the analyses you are interested in doing. But working without them, at least initially, is not fatal—and can help you see what else you need to know to do good analysis.

Qualitative researchers come in many varieties and flavors. The views we have expressed will almost certainly be seen as narrow-minded, even arrogant, by some of our colleagues. We don't want to pretend to be ideology-free or to have the noblest biases—or to be seen as just-plain-folks pragmatists with no understanding of the issues. But our intentions may not always have worked out.

To those colleagues who believe that analysis is an intuitive, nearly incommunicable act, we have insisted that analyses can be workably replicated, and that to be taken seriously you should be fully explicit about what is being done each step of the way.

To those who believe that serious explanation must involve converting words into numbers and manipulating the numbers according to conventional statistical canons, we have said that better, more powerful methods of data analysis are available that illuminate the web of local causality.

To those enamored of long narrative accounts as the sole route to understanding, we have counterposed the idea of focused, organized displays that permit systematic analyses and enhance confidence in findings.

To those who believe that qualitative data analysis requires years of training and apprenticeship, we have offered an expanded set of working methods that can be easily learned, tried on for size, and developed further for particular projects—all in the service of a stronger methodology.

To those colleagues who are pleased with what we have done in the second edition of our book, we express our return pleasure, along with our hope for skeptical testing and revision of our methods, so that we all can advance our craft—or sullen art.

❖ ADVICE

Here we offer some generalized last words of encouragement to our colleagues, of whatever persuasion:

Think display. Given a research question or a puzzling issue in a qualitative database, consider what forms of display (e.g., matrices and networks) are most likely to bring together relevant, transformed data in a way that will permit good conclusion drawing and strengthening of those conclusions.

Be open to invention. The wide range of useful displays we and many others have created reinforces our belief that the universe of useful displays is very large and, like other universes, constantly expanding.

Expect iteration. The mode of analysis we've advocated throughout the book involves shuttling among data reduction, display, and preliminary and verified conclusions. New data enter the picture, new display forms evolve, conclusions get bent and revised. All of these will have back effects on each other, effects that are crucial to the evolving analysis.

Seek formalization, and distrust it. We have steadily emphasized a structured approach to drawing meaning from qualitative data. Becoming more systematic, whatever your epistemological position, strikes us as a priority for those who wish to advance analysis methodology. Of course, increased formalization carries its own risks: narrowness, overconfidence, obsessiveness, blindness to the emergent—and the risk of orthodoxy. When the first edition of *Qualitative Data Analysis* was published in 1984, the field did not need a narrow set of canons to strike fear into the hearts of graduate students and inspire endless casuistry and disputation—and it does not need them now. Patience, trying to do things better, and sharing are more like it.

Entertain mixed models. We have sought to make a virtue of avoiding polarization, polemics, and life at the extremes. Quantitative and qualitative inquiry can support and inform each other. Narratives and variable-driven analyses need to interpenetrate and inform each other. Realists, idealists, and critical theorists can do better by incorporating other ideas than by remaining pure. Think of it as hybrid vigor.

Stay self-aware.   Our own experience has shown us vividly how useful it is to maintain a part of your attention on the processes involved in analysis—from the selection of research questions through coding, the creation of displays, data entry, conclusion drawing, and verification. Only through such sustained awareness can regular self-correction occur—not just during specific analysis episodes, but over time, as the methods themselves iterate and develop. We have suggested supports for self-awareness in the form of documentation logs and—perhaps most essentially—"critical friends" who can supportively counter your taken-for-granted approaches and suggest alternatives.

Share methodological learnings.   The methodological sections of most reports of qualitative studies are still thin. Articles focusing directly on analysis issues and approaches are all too rare. We believe that all researchers who want to advance the craft of qualitative analysis owe it to their colleagues to communicate what they have learned. We advise stronger methodological emphasis in articles and books drawn from qualitative data, and encourage reports of training methods in courses and workshops that have successfully expanded analysis skills. We continue to urge much parallel and divergent effort in order to develop, gradually, a stronger, clearer consensus on how to draw valid conclusions from qualitative data.

In sum, we hope that more and more qualitative researchers will tell each other, concretely and specifically, just how they went about it, and what they learned. Perhaps we can all be as vivid and rich in describing our own work as we are in describing the inner and outer lives of the people we are studying. We owe them, and ourselves, at least that much, and probably a great deal more.

Epilogue

W e have come to the end of our work with a familiar mix of
satisfaction and regret. This is a collection of good stuff, but we
are aware of much good work left out. And we are nagged by a familiar
wish to tie things up—to pull all the strands together—although we
know that this cannot, really should not, be done. These readings are
signposts, not the map itself. No collection can indicate the full range
of qualitative research. Indeed, the future of qualitative inquiry is as
elusive as its past.

But our trade has persisted over time not by ignoring new issues
and procedures but by absorbing them—for example, by stretching the
notion of ethnographic research to include new ways of assessment
and recording. It is true enough that we may no longer have a good
purchase on contemporary conditions of social life, including the "not
yet" of new concepts. But the issue is not whether the work will go on,
but how best to get on with it. We hope that this collection will be a
useful companion in the search.

—A. Michael Huberman
Laconnex, Switzerland

Index

About the Editors

A. Michael Huberman was an internationally recognized theorist, researcher, and consultant on education in the United States, Canada, and Europe. He was Professor of Education at the University of Geneva in Switzerland, where he founded l'Ecole Active, an experimental primary school; a visiting professor at Harvard University; and a senior research associate at The Network, a regional education laboratory of the U.S. Department of Education. His work focused on education policy, school reform, the lives of teachers, and the practical translation of research knowledge into effective school practice. The author of many books, including *Understanding Change in Education* and *The Lives of Teachers*, Huberman was co-author with Matthew B. Miles of *Innovation Up Close* and of the landmark *Qualitative Data Analysis*, the first sourcebook of methods for the systematic analysis of the field notes and case studies that form the basic data of much social science research, a required text in scores of graduate programs worldwide.

Matthew B. Miles, a social psychologist, was Professor of Psychology and Education at Teachers College, Columbia University; Senior Research Associate at the Center for Policy Research; and a consultant to national and international educational research and policy organizations. His work focused on planned change in education, group and organizational studies, the "social architecture" of schools, the dissemination and implementation of research findings in school reform, and advances in qualitative data analysis. Author of fifteen books on educational research and change, he was co-author (with Eben A. Weitzman) of *Computer Programs in Qualitative Data Analysis* and, with his longtime colleague A. Michael Huberman, of the classic *Qualitative Data Analysis*.